13⁵⁰
5R74
41012

An official publication of
THE AMERICAN SOCIOLOGICAL ASSOCIATION
OTTO N. LARSEN, *Executive Officer*

SOCIOLOGICAL METHODOLOGY 1973-1974

Herbert L. Costner
EDITOR

SOCIOLOGICAL METHODOLOGY 1973-1974

 Jossey-Bass Publishers
San Francisco • Washington • London • 1974

SOCIOLOGICAL METHODOLOGY 1973–1974
Herbert L. Costner, Editor

Copyright © 1974 by: Jossey-Bass, Inc., Publishers
615 Montgomery Street
San Francisco, California 94111

&

Jossey-Bass Limited
3 Henrietta Street
London WC2E 8LU

Copyright under International, Pan American, and Universal Copyright Conventions. All rights reserved. No part of this book may be reproduced in any form—except for brief quotation (not to exceed 1,000 words) in a review or professional work—without permission in writing from the publishers.

Library of Congress Catalogue Card Number LC 73-9071

International Standard Book Number ISBN 0-87589-197-7

Manufactured in the United States of America

JACKET DESIGN BY WILLI BAUM

FIRST EDITION

Code 7338

THE JOSSEY-BASS BEHAVIORAL SCIENCE SERIES

SOCIOLOGICAL METHODOLOGY 1973-1974

EDITOR Herbert L. Costner

ADVISORY EDITORS Edgar F. Borgatta*

James Fennessey**

Lowell Hargens***

Herbert Hyman*

Kenneth Land***

Shirley A. Star**

*Term ends with 1973 volume
**Term ends with 1974 volume
***Term ends with 1975 volume

CONSULTANTS

EDITORIAL CONSULTANTS

Robert P. Althauser
Howard M. Bahr
Kenneth D. Bailey
Lewis F. Carter
Kathleen Crittenden
James A. Davis
Otis Dudley Duncan
Bernard M. Finifter
Arthur S. Goldberger
Michael Hannan
David R. Heise
Neil W. Henry
Robert K. Leik

James C. McCann
Howard A. Parker
Samuel Preston
Ronald Pyke
Lynne Roberts
Ronald Schoenberg
Clarence C. Schrag
Karl Schuessler
Seymour Spilerman
Rodney Stark
Judith Tanur
Charles R. Tittle

PROLOGUE

If there is a single dominant feature of sociological methodology today, it is the common feature of a set of methods of analysis variously referred to as causal models, path analysis, and structural equation models. Causal modeling, the most inclusive of the three terms, refers generally to the explicit incorporation of causal reasoning into theoretical formulations and into a corresponding mode of data analysis; the precursors of such models can be found in John Stuart Mill's strategy for social science formulated more than a century ago. Path analysis was developed by Sewell Wright in genetics half a century ago, utilizing regression techniques that originated at the turn of the century. Structural equation models encompass feedback systems as well as the recursive systems of path analysis, and they have been elaborated by economists for more than thirty years. Thus, although they are relatively new to sociology, causal models, path analysis, and structural equation models were flourishing long before sociologists recognized their utility. Their importation into sociology did not introduce causal reasoning to sociologists; such reasoning has always been a prominent feature of our attempts to understand social events. What was largely lacking in sociology until recently was a systematic method of data analysis that corresponded closely to the causal reasoning of sociological theories. Paul Lazarsfeld's "elaboration" techniques were a useful attempt in this direction, as were some early applications of partial correlation; but in retrospect these techniques seem unnecessarily limited and grossly oversimplified. Path analysis and structural equation models necessarily entail a deliberate simplification of reality as well, but they provide a mode of analysis that may better approximate the complexity of our theoretical reasoning and hence have greater utility.

The pervasive influence of causal models, path analysis, and structural equation models in sociological methodology is evidenced not simply by the increasing use of such modes of analysis in empirical sociological studies but also by the ramifications of this mode of thinking in a variety of methodological issues. During the relatively brief period that sociologists have focused attention on these methods, the mode of thinking that they entail has permeated our conceptions of theory construction, measurement problems, and data analysis. Guided by this mode of thinking, we seem to be in the process of redesigning our approaches to multivariate analysis, reconceptualizing earlier notions of reliability and validity, reevaluating the relative merits of standardized and unstandardized coefficients, rethinking the inferences from experimentation, reinterpreting the utility of factor analysis, revising some of our earlier conceptions of macrosociological knowledge, and reassessing the data needs of sociology. This relatively rapid shift in our way of thinking about the methodology of social research has immersed us in a vocabulary that is still relatively new to many sociologists: *identification problems, recursive systems, specification error, correlated errors, structural parameters*, and numerous other terms that all but the relatively recent PhD's (and even some of those) missed in their graduate training.

One is tempted to conclude that we have witnessed in the past decade a true revolution in methodological thinking, one that has brought basically new perspectives embodied in a new terminology. A more tempered assessment leads one to regard these new methods as a formalization of ideas long implicit but only vaguely conceived and sporadically applied. Leaving aside the sometimes formidable technical apparatus, the common feature of these methods of analysis is the explicit recognition of causal assumptions and the explicit incorporation of those assumptions into data analysis and into the qualifications of our conclusions. Thus conceived, these new methods do not appear to be revolutionary but seem instead to be an emerging but major advance toward an adequate methodology of social research. To leave aside the technical apparatus however is to drain these methods of their vitality; it means omitting those aspects of the methods that render them unique and innovative. The technical apparatus, formidable though it might appear, has led to new methodological insights, modified some of our basic perspectives, and spotlighted new ways of conceptualizing problems of social research. Thus conceived, these new methods are a partial break with the cumbersome gropings of the past and open new approaches in research methodology. The felicitous blend of old and new—old purposes and a new technical apparatus for achieving them—seems to be largely responsible for the relatively rapid diffusion (following a tardy start) of these methods among sociologists. As with most other innovations, adoption depends heavily on perceived utility; causal models, path analysis, and structural equation models seem to have struck a responsive chord because they provide a feasible way of dealing empirically with the complex features of a mode of reasoning that we have been trying to use all along.

In this volume, fifth in the continuing series sponsored by the American Sociological Association, the influence of causal models, path analysis, and structural equation models is clearly evident in many of the chapters, although only indirectly relevant to some. Illustrating the varied methodological issues that have been influenced by a causal models approach—from the assessment of validity to the study of social change—these chapters persistently remind us that the assumptions built into the models are crucial to the conclusions we draw in applying them, and that the assumptions themselves are subjected to testing only indirectly if at all. They also remind us that methodologists, even when working within the same general tradition, do not always agree with each other. Two chapters in this volume are commentaries on chapters that follow or precede them; the special purpose of these chapters is to provide alternative perspectives on selected issues that are far from being resolved.

The first chapter, by David Heise, is an introduction to the two chapters that follow; it places the common problem addressed in those two chapters within the larger context of issues in sociological measurement. In his chapter Heise summarizes some salient features of earlier measurement models, discusses the causal models approach to measurement error, and explores how each of these approaches relates to a factor-analytic measurement model. Since the two chapters that follow present different factor-analytic techniques for accomplishing the same general purpose, Heise comments on problems in factor analysis, on the merits of the two approaches outlined in the following chapters, and on the circumstances under which each would seem to be most useful. The second chapter, by David Armor, and the third chapter, by Michael Allen, center around the construction of multiitem scales with maximum reliability and procedures for estimating that reliability.

In Chapter Four Duane Alwin continues the discussion of measurement problems but in a somewhat different vein. The multitrait-multimethod matrix, originally devised by Donald T. Campbell and D. W. Fiske, is his point of departure. Using a path-analytic framework, he compares the Campbell-Fiske criteria for inferring convergent and discriminant validity with three other approaches proposed in the recent literature, including one proposed by Robert P. Althauser and Thomas A. Heberlein in *Sociological Methodology 1970*. Alwin's conclusions do not correspond exactly to those of Althauser and Heberlein, and in the chapter immediately following, Althauser responds to Alwin's chapter and addresses once again some of the general issues involved.

Since covariation is fundamental to most data analysis procedures, including path analysis and related techniques, any distortion or bias in the estimation of covariance or correlation constitutes a serious problem. One potential source of such bias is explored in Chapter Six by Glenn Fuguitt and Stanley Lieberson. There has been for some time a scattered literature on the potentially misleading conclusions that may emerge from correlating ratios with common terms; Fuguitt and Lieberson review that literature and assess the implications of this problem for research conclusions in sociology.

In Chapter Seven Peter Burke and Karl Schuessler examine conceptually different but statistically equivalent ways of doing an analysis of variance. In their discussion Burke and Schuessler show that the analysis of variance may be expressed in fitted constants, regression coefficients, or path coefficients, and they emphasize that the underlying assumptions are similar even when an analysis of variance is done under another name. They point out, however, that the terminology associated with each of these statistically equivalent techniques may be differentially appropriate for studies with different purposes.

In Chapter Eight James Davis writes with a pedagogical purpose. Recognizing that many sociologists may have some difficulty understanding and applying the techniques for analyzing multidimensional contingency tables recently developed by Leo A. Goodman, Davis has designed his chapter to overcome that impediment to the utilization of these potentially valuable tools of analysis. Goodman's techniques are an extension of the general reasoning underlying causal models to data ordinarily analyzed in other and less informative ways. In his exposition Davis attempts to clarify Goodman's concepts for those who may have had difficulty with the original papers, and he illuminates the utility of the techniques with illustrative applications.

Still another illustration of Goodman's procedures is found in Chapter Nine by Howard Schuman and Otis Dudley Duncan. Schuman and Duncan seek not simply to illustrate the application of the Goodman procedures but also to use those procedures in their effort to highlight a persistent problem for survey researchers: the effect of question wording on the conclusions drawn from survey data. Although survey researchers have long recognized that minor differences in question wording may have strong effects on the marginal frequencies, Schuman and Duncan provide examples demonstrating that question wording may also affect the association between responses and respondent characteristics. While they present no final solution, the authors of this chapter remind us that, no matter how sophisticated the analysis, the quality of the conclusions must ultimately rest on the quality of the data analyzed.

In Chapter Ten Douglas Hibbs, Jr., examines problems of statistical estimation and causal inference in time-series regression models. Hibbs notes that cross-sectional studies are more common in social science research than are time-series analyses—a comment no less true of sociology than of Hibbs's own field of political science—but he suggests that the improvement of longitudinal social data will increase the use of time-series models. His chapter is addressed to the solution of some distinctive problems that arise in time-series analysis, among them autoregression, and in the use of dynamic models with feedback effects.

A different mode of time-series analysis is discussed in Chapter Eleven by Thomas Mayer and William Arney. They attempt to make spectral analysis, a technique adopted from communications engineering and new to sociology, intelligible to sociologists because of its potential utility in the analysis of social change.

In the final chapter by Burton Singer and Seymour Spilerman, the authors focus on still another analytical tool in the study of change. Markov process models are familiar to many sociologists, but in the usual application it is assumed that the same transition probabilities apply to all elements in the population. This assumption may be not only intuitively implausible but also suspect on the basis of the lack of fit of the data to the model. Singer and Spilerman discuss mathematical descriptions of the dynamics of transition when this assumption is relaxed, utilizing a distinction between the microscopic and macroscopic process. Whereas traditional Markov analysis has concentrated on building a model that predicts distributions at various points in time, most social analysis has been built on a model that attempts to predict differential distributions for elements with different characteristics, as in regression analysis. Hence the introduction of heterogeneous population assumptions into Markov models, with the potential for establishing a systematic connection between the characteristics of an element and the transition probabilities to which it is subject, may provide the basis for a tie between Markov analysis and other, more widely used modes of analyzing social data.

With the publication of this volume my term as editor of *Sociological Methodology* comes to an end, and I am especially pleased that the Council of the American Sociological Association has selected David Heise to serve as the editor for the next three years. I am happy to take this opportunity to thank the contributors, advisory editors, and consulting editors for their efforts during my period as editor. My major disappointment as editor of *Sociological Methodology* for the past three years has been my inability to attract publishable papers that represent a broad range of methodological issues in current sociology. My major gratification has been the privilege of playing a part in the dissemination of some truly outstanding work on the frontiers of sociological methodology.

HERBERT L. COSTNER

Seattle
January 1974

CONTENTS

Editorial Consultants		viii
Prologue		
	Herbert L. Costner	ix
1. Some Issues in Sociological Measurement		
	David R. Heise	1
2. Theta Reliability and Factor Scaling		
	David J. Armor	17
3. Construction of Composite Measures by the Canonical-Factor-Regression Method		
	Michael Patrick Allen	51
4. Approaches to the Interpretation of Relationships in the Multitrait-Multimethod Matrix		
	Duane F. Alwin	79

5. Inferring Validity from the
   Multitrait-Multimethod Matrix:
   Another Assessment
         Robert P. Althauser   106

6. Correlation of Ratios or
   Difference Scores Having Common Terms
         Glenn V. Fuguitt, Stanley Lieberson   128

7. Alternative Approaches to
   Analysis-of-Variance Tables
         Peter J. Burke, Karl Schuessler   145

8. Hierarchical Models for
   Significance Tests in Multivariate
   Contingency Tables: An Exegesis
   of Goodman's Recent Papers
         James A. Davis   189

9. Questions About Attitude Survey Questions
         Howard Schuman, Otis Dudley Duncan   232

10. Problems of Statistical Estimation
    and Causal Inference in
    Time-Series Regression Models
          Douglas A. Hibbs, Jr.   252

11. Spectral Analysis and the Study
    of Social Change
          Thomas F. Mayer, William Ray Arney   309

12. Social Mobility Models
    for Heterogeneous Populations
          Burton Singer, Seymour Spilerman   356

Name Index   403

Subject Index   408

SOCIOLOGICAL METHODOLOGY 1973-1974

1

SOME ISSUES IN SOCIOLOGICAL MEASUREMENT

David R. Heise
UNIVERSITY OF NORTH CAROLINA

For a discipline that ignored errors of measurement too long, suffering the consequences of low predictive capability and spurious theoretical debate, sociology has recently shown a remarkable turnabout, investing an appreciable proportion of its scholarly pages to analyses of the measurement problem. Of course the concern is not entirely unprecedented: the team that produced the monumental *The American Soldier* showed a keen and sophisticated interest in measurement problems with eventual fruition in Paul Lazarsfeld's latent structure analysis and Louis Guttman's scalogram procedures (Guttman's later work seems less associated with sociometrics than with psychometrics). Yet in the years since World War II the potential impact of latent structure analysis was little realized because only a few passing through Columbia University were exposed to it (a situation remedied recently by Henry and Lazarsfeld, 1968). Guttman scales suffered another fate, becoming for a decade a fetish among American sociologists, applied so often where the underlying model was inappropriate that some metricians turned to discrediting the technique generally (Nunnally, 1967).

The recent resurgence of sociometrics (here the term is used generally rather than specifically for the Moreno technique) is likely to have a significant and beneficial impact on the discipline for several reasons. There is now a solid realization that measurement imprecision is a factor attenuating the relationships we observe and biasing theoretical conclusions. There is a growing realization that variables are related to their indicators in a variety of ways so that different analytic models must be chosen to fit the circumstances rather than applied as matters of taste. And increasingly powerful and sociologically relevant measurement models are being provided as the mathematical analyses of the problems go to a deeper and more general level. A resurgence of metric theory under these conditions is encouraging, even exciting, provided that we simultaneously elaborate metatheory of all kinds, not just metric theory, and that we avoid the development of a statistical subdiscipline maintaining its own arcane paradigm asymptotically insulated from the realities of small-sample research in real situations.

The following two chapters demonstrate the power to be gained by mathematical analysis of measurement problems, and at the same time both illustrate that methodology can be readable and available to the discipline as a whole. Because no translations are needed, this introduction to the two chapters is focused on outlining the broader context of contemporary measurement theory, thereby emphasizing that the techniques discussed in these chapters cannot be separated from substantive theoretical concerns. I shall also compare the two approaches briefly.

MEASUREMENT MODELS

Emotionalization seems to pervade every area of intellectual inquiry, and metric theory is no exception. Factor analysis is a basic tool in the metrician's kit, but until recently this tool was treated almost with disdain by some sociologists. During the same period Guttman scales were the metric workhorse of sociologists, but they received short shrift among some psychometricians. Whatever positive functions emotionalization may serve, it is clear that turning methodological ideas into ideologies impoverishes researchers by restricting their means and thereby restricting the problems they can deal with. As long as a methodological procedure is treated as a fashion, it is not being properly assessed and developed as a specific solution to a specific type of problem. So in hopes of dissipating some affect, let us first consider a few points about metric models that are well known to some but that should be well known to all.

Most metric theory is predicated on the assumption that a concept can be represented in terms of an underlying dimension of variation and that positions on the dimension can be associated with numbers that are subject to at least some kinds of algebraic manipulation. For heuristic purposes let us assume that underlying dimensions have algebraically meaningful intervals even if they do not have an algebraically meaningful zero point. It is further assumed in most metric theory that the position of an entity on an underlying dimension can be assessed in terms of its observed values on a series of indicators because values on indicator variables are determined at least in part by values on underlying dimensions.

The relation between the underlying dimension and its indicator variables may take on three fundamentally different forms as indicated in Figure 1. The first graph shows a dimension with cumulative indicators: were an entity to move from a low to a high position on the underlying dimension, it would show a sequence of changes on the indicator variables—first indicator 1 appears (or increases in magnitude), then indicator 2, then indicator 3, and so on—and once an indicator has changed, it retains its achieved value as the entity moves even further

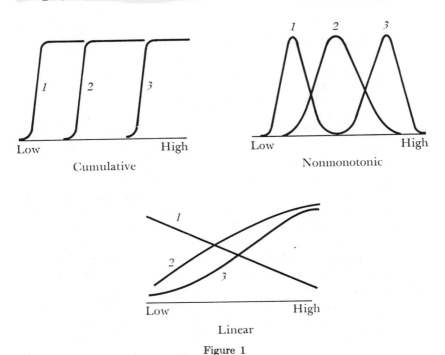

Figure 1

along the scale. This first graph, of course, represents the kind of indicators that are appropriate for Guttman scaling.

In the second graph of Figure 1, indicator values also change sequentially with movement from high to low along the underlying dimension, but now the changes are not cumulative since indicators appear (or increase) and also disappear (or decrease) with movement up the continuum. Such indicators have been the focus in traditional Thurstone scales.

In the third graph we see a set of indicators distinct from the preceding two types in that changes along the underlying dimension do not lead to a special sequence of changes in the indicators; rather movement from high to low continuously increases or decreases the probability that a specific indicator is present or, alternatively, movement increases or decreases the expected value of an indicator. It is convenient to say that such indicators fit a linear measurement model, even though the trace lines may deviate somewhat from straight lines, as long as they increase or decrease monotonically over the full range of the underlying dimension.

At the minimum there are three measurement models—the cumulative, the nonmonotonic, and the linear—that can be applied in a research situation. There are two essential points to be made about these models. First, their applicability in a situation is not a matter of taste but a matter of theoretical and empirical appropriateness. Second, once a model is chosen it dictates the type of analysis that is appropriate—for example, scalogram, unfolding, or factor analysis.

There is little doubt that cumulative scaling has been applied excessively in situations where it is inappropriate, in that some researchers have tried to force nonmonotonic or linear indicators into the cumulative mold; fortunately this overcommitment to the cumulative model seems to be on the decline. Yet one hopes that we shall not now go to the other extreme of neglecting the cumulative model altogether. The cumulative model may be especially appropriate when dealing with problems of growth, development, and evolution, whether the direction of change is toward greater complexity or toward specialization, as long as various features are permanently gained or lost. Traditionally, social-psychological dimensions such as social distance have provided the prime examples of cumulative scales, but there is now evidence that applications are also possible in macrosociology, as, for example, in studying the evolution of societal complexity (Carneiro, 1970). The possibility of cumulation should always be kept in mind when studying dimensions of development; if both theory and data suggest cumulation, then scalogram analysis (or some other dominance scaling procedure—see Shepard and others, 1972) is the most appropriate method to employ.

Especially it is to be noted that factor analysis is not the most meaningful procedure for analyzing cumulative features: factor analysis routinely splits a single cumulative scale into multiple factors of comparatively little substantive interest.

Thurstone scales were originally developed to measure attitudes and values, and no doubt there are still important applications in this area. However, the recent ferment in nonmetric scaling has greatly broadened the applicability of this model as well as its supporting technology. The model is now recognized as applying generally to the definition of social spaces whenever the position of an entity in the space determines its preferences for, or similarities to, other objects in the space. Thus, for example, this model may be particularly appropriate for defining the friendship space of individuals in cliques or for defining the urban space generated by the availability of different services in different kinds of cities. Whenever data can be interpreted in terms of choices or preferences or similarities among objects distributed on a single dimension, a plane, or in a space, then a nonmonotonic model (often referred to as a similarity-preference model) should be considered; when this model applies, data must be "unfolded" using an appropriate scaling procedure (there are many available programs now; see Shepard and others, 1972). Neither scalogram analysis nor factor analysis gives an adequately simple and meaningful set of results for nonmonotonic indicators.

The linear model also received its major development at the psychological level (see Lord and Novick, 1968; Nunnally, 1967), and the general ideas involved in this model are perhaps most familiar to sociologists under the rubric of Likert scales, a specialized adaptation of the model. The model is specifically applicable to the problem of attitude measurement, at least as attitude items are usually constructed, but the model does have wider applicability, possibly at the macrosociological level, wherever some basic force or variable such as population or gross national product continuously affects a series of other variables that may be construed as indicators. Indicators that are linearly dependent on an unmeasured variable are most appropriately analyzed by factor analysis; scalogram or unfolding analyses either waste much available information or yield degenerate solutions suggesting less dimensionality than truly exists.

VARIATIONS OF LINEAR MODEL

So far in describing the various measurement models, it has been presumed that underlying values on dimensions determine values on a set of indicators. Considering the linear model specifically, this situation can be represented in terms of the path diagram shown in Figure 2, where F represents values on the latent dimension, the Xs represent values on the indicators, and the es represent the sources of error treated in aggregate for each indicator. As pointed out elsewhere (as in Heise and Bohrnstedt, 1970) such a diagram corresponds to a factor analysis in which the variable F is not measured directly but is identified indirectly from correlations among the X variables. Conceived in this specialized way—that is, that all correlation among the Xs is due to variation in the unmeasured factor or factors—the linear model reduces to the latent trait model studied at length by psychometricians (see Lord and Novick, 1968).

Recently interest has developed in another formulation involving linear relations between indicators and on latent dimensions in which the unmeasured trait is not a determinant of the indicators but is defined in terms of them—a general variable induced from specifics. An example might be the notion of socioeconomic status defined in terms of the specifics of education, income, occupational prestige, and so forth. Figure 3 shows the basic structure of this model. Note that correlations among the indicators are no longer explained in terms of the unmeasured variable. In fact the indicators need not be correlated at all; but if they are, it is because of their mutual dependence on unspecified variables or because of relations among themselves. When data fit the model illustrated in Figure 3, factor analysis is not the appropriate analytic tool. Indeed a solution is possible only when dependent variables affected by the unmeasured variable F are included in analyses. In this case, canonical analysis is the appropriate analytic device (Hauser and Goldberger, 1971; Van de Geer, 1971; Hauser, 1972), or regression analysis in the simplified case involving a single dependent variable (Sullivan, 1971; Heise, 1972).

The typical goal in using either of these linear models is to define

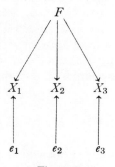

Figure 2

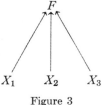

Figure 3

a composite score based on the indicators that can serve as a scale for the unmeasured variable of interest and that can then be applied as a standardized measure in a variety of situations. However, since the introduction of path analysis into sociological research (Duncan, 1966) a different strategy designed to make the most effective use of available information has been developing with some energy (Costner, 1969; Blalock, 1971; Hauser and Goldberger, 1971). The general idea is to treat indicators on an ad hoc basis, specifying their theoretical relationships to unmeasured variables, flexibly treating the indicators in terms of the models in Figures 2 or 3 as the theory demands, and considering the problem of measurement error as just one more aspect of the general problem of model identification, rather than as a separate problem to be dealt with in terms of a separate metric theory. Carried to its most sophisticated level this approach implies that one will rarely carry out such routine statistical procedures as factor analysis or canonical analysis. Rather each sociologist must become adept at specifying elaborate theoretical models and at using general identification programs (Jöreskog and others, 1970). If one adopts this strategy, metric models as such will seem to be oversimplified and mainly of pedagogical value in teaching researchers how to set up models.

Nevertheless it can be said that the preparation of measures apart from their employment in specific theoretical models has at least three benefits. First and perhaps most important is the matter of economy; through item analyses based on an inexpensive pilot study one can usually obtain adequate measurement scales of five or ten indicators, whereas to ensure the same level of measurement without information from prior metric analyses one may have to collect information on two or three times as many variables. In other words, isolated metric analyses allow one to eliminate inefficient indicators prior to the expenses of full-scale data collection. Second, isolated metric analyses have the advantage of focusing attention on the relation between measures and theoretical concepts. The issue here is not that metric analyses involve pure theory whereas model identification approaches constitute dry-bone empiricism; both approaches are empirical and theoretical. Rather the issue is simply that metric analyses focus attention on the conceptualization and operationalization of theoretical concepts whereas this matter is but one step in the model identification approach, a step that may be passed over lightly in the complexity of the analysis. Third, isolated metric analyses encourage the development of standardized scales that can be applied in different studies. Standardization of measures would provide a number of benefits; for instance, there is little to be done about the recurrent complaint against standardized path coefficients (as opposed to unstandardized structural coefficients) as long as we have no standard measures but still want to compare results of different studies of the same population. Finally the model identification procedures typically involve full-information methods of identification, and these techniques may be inappropriate in the early stages of research on a topic since they tend to diffuse the effects of a few erroneous postulates throughout all of one's findings.

Arguments on the side of the model identification approach include, first, that isolated metric analyses practically create an unnecessary methodological phantom—the problem of validity—since isolated scale construction permits the peculiar predicament where we might have an almost perfectly reliable measure that relates to nothing of interest including, perhaps, the variable it was meant to measure. This is largely avoided in the model identification approach by making validity the essential matter of interest and all but ignoring the psychometrician's traditional interest in reliability. A second point is associated with the first: by increasing the theoretical constraints on analysis, the model identification approach decreases the likelihood of developing spurious indicators for a latent variable as is possible when a latent dimension, and the relation of indicators to it, are defined solely in terms of correlations among the indicators. Finally the model identification approach makes far more efficient use of available information in a particular problem by allowing analysis of the specific variance of an indicator as well as of its common variance (that is, the variance shared with other indicators).

PROBLEM OF DEFINING FACTORS

The essential idea involved in factor-analytic scale construction is that both the latent dimension and the optimal scale for measuring it can be defined from the correlations among a set of indicators. That is, factor analysis (used here as a general term covering a variety of similar procedures such as principal-component analysis and canonical factor analysis) defines a latent variable by identifying its correlations with the available indicators. And given such a definition of the latent variable, weights can be assigned to the indicators (as indicated in the chapters by Armor and Allen) to create a composite scale whose values covary with values of the latent variable. Moreover factor-analytic results provide information that can be used to create indices assessing the quality of the resulting scale.

A fact of major importance in the factor-analytic approach to scale construction is that there is no purely mechanical procedure for identifying latent variables with guaranteed theoretical validity. The definition of the latent variables underlying a set of indicators depends on two decisions that must be made in the course of the multivariate analyses—How many relevant latent variables are there? What is the proper pattern of correspondence between different latent variables and key indicators?—and these decisions always involve a subjective element.

Number of Factors

If there are no perfect correlations among indicators, then principal-component analysis yields as many components (or factors) as there are indicators. Other forms of factor analysis (communality solutions) generate fewer factors than there are indicators, but these methods also typically yield extra factors of little substantive interest in that they merely explain correlations that arise out of the idiosyncracies in the sample or that represent uninteresting similarities among indicators. Therefore, whatever the factor-analytic procedure, there remains the question of how many factors should be considered substantively meaningful.

One approach to this problem is to keep extracting factors until the next one to be extracted is not significant when a statistical test is applied. Although this procedure confronts the problem of factors due to sampling variations, the solution can be applied appropriately only in large-sample studies. Furthermore the procedure does not eliminate minor instrument factors (such as a factor corresponding to an attitude item that has been repeated in the same interview), and such factors can lead to distortions when factors must be rotated to improve interpretability.

A second approach is to consider only factors that account for an "interesting" amount of covariation among the indicators; the relevant tests (Rummel, 1970, chap. 15) are generally applied to principal-component analysis and, if one is interested specifically in a communality solution, the principal-component analysis is run first to define the number of factors. One such test rejects any factor with an eigenvalue less than 1.0 (eigenvalues reflect the amount of variance that a component explains). Usually this is too conservative a test in that it draws uninterpretable factors into the analysis. Another approach is to plot the eigenvalues for all principal components in the order of their extraction and to retain only the first few factors that seem large relative to those extracted later. Provided that one retains only factors that are statistically significant the latter test seems to have the advantage of providing some constancy across sample size, although whether this is really so needs to be investigated in greater detail.

The analytic technique advocated in the chapter by Allen seems at first to evade the number-of-factors problem because the procedure extracts factors so that they are simultaneously ordered both in terms of their statistical significance and their explanatory power. Hence it would seem that after the first few factors are extracted it would make relatively little difference whether further factors are retained or discarded since these additional factors are least significant in every sense of the word, and as latent variables they would contribute only minutely to the variance of items to be employed in scales. But, as seen below, this solution to the number-of-factors problem is obtained only by adopting a special solution to the rotation problem.

Rotation Problem

After deciding on the number of factors, one must still decide how to orient the factorial dimensions in order to create interesting correspondences between the factors and the indicator variables. Both principal-component analysis and canonical factor analysis offer solutions to this problem, but it is important to realize that both solutions are numerical, and not substantive, solutions to the rotation problem.

The first principal component is roughly comparable to the variable that would be defined by adding all the available indicators, standardized to equal variance. If all the indicators were uncorrelated, then the composite variable would receive a small, equal contribution from each; if correlations existed among a subset of indicators, then summing across these variables would create a systematic bias in the composite score so that the composite would be influenced more by variables in the subset than by other indicators in the pool being factored. If there were two or more subsets such that the indicators in each subset were correlated only with each other, then each subset would contribute to the first component in much the same way that uncorrelated individual items contribute, except with more impact. Roughly speaking the second component is obtained by regressing all the indicators on the first component variable and then creating a second composite score from the residuals from these regressions. The second composite is uncorrelated with the first because it is based on residuals, and for the same reason it is determined most by the variables that contribute least to the first component. The same procedures are used repeatedly to extract further components. (I have roughly described centroid factor analysis; principal-component analysis is more elegant in that it weights items in the process of making a composite so that the variance of the composite is a maximum at every step. The distinction is important analytically but does not affect the points to be made here.)

In canonical factor analysis the extraction procedure is essentially similar but the indicator variables are modified in two ways before beginning. First, since it is a factor analysis only common variance is analyzed: in effect this means that we do not work with the scores on the original indicators but with the predicted values obtained from the regression of an indicator on all others in the analysis. Second, in canonical factor analysis it is assumed that the unique variances of all indicators are identical (a unique variance is estimated as the variance of the residuals obtained from the regression of an indicator on other indicators). Since the unique variances ordinarily are not equal in the original data, their equality must be generated artificially by changing the scale of each indicator (multiplying by an appropriate constant), thereby creating a set of transformed indicator variables in which the unique variances are all the same. It is these transformed variables that are factored and that determine the definition of the factors, even though the final factor loadings are adjusted to relate to the original scales instead of the transformed scales.

Principal-component analysis defines a set of dimensions with a specific pattern of correspondences to the original indicators, but these dimensions tend to be impure in the sense that each dimension is defined in terms of every indicator, even those that are uncorrelated with others. Factors based only on common variance, as in the canonical solution, are not associated with the specific variance of indicators as is the case in principal-component analysis. But if there are a number of subsets of indicators with high correlations among themselves and low correlations between the subsets, then each subset contributes to each dimension defined in a canonical factor analysis. Moreover, although the canonical dimensions are not twisted in the direction of the unique variances of indicators they do favor indicators that have high correlations with other indicators (since such variables would be defined as having small error variances, so that their scales would be magnified a great deal in the scale adjustment process and they would therefore contribute more to composite scores than would indicators with lower communality). The problem here is that the source of high communality is irrelevant in canonical factor analysis: an indicator has a powerful effect on the definition of latent dimensions if it is heavily influenced by a single latent variable but also if it is influenced by several latent variables or if it simply has high correlations with other indicators as a matter of chance or because the indicators are essentially replications of one another.

Neither principal-component analysis nor canonical factor analysis routinely provides the most sensible definition of latent dimensions. Indeed when several different dimensions are involved in a pool of indicators, both techniques usually define dimensions that are compounds of latent variables rather than pure definitions of them. In other words, despite the mathematical elegance of these "solutions" to the rotation problem they do not necessarily, nor even probably, yield rotations that are substantively meaningful. This is why mechanical rotation procedures (such as varimax) are so commonly employed: they too are solutions to the rotation problem based purely on the numerical considerations, but experience indicates that the required assumptions for these solutions are metatheoretically more realistic than those that define the dimensions in principal-component or canonical factor analyses.

What is too often ignored is that even rotation procedures such as varimax and quartimax operate purely at a statistical level and that statistical considerations alone cannot guarantee a rotation which makes most substantive sense. This is because the meaningfulness of a factor does not depend on the statistical characteristics of its indicators but on their theoretical content, and in ordinary analytic procedures these theoretical considerations are not entered as constraints on the numerical analysis. In short we cannot expect substantive miracles from factor analyses because they operate at a statistical rather than a substantive level, and, without some outside help, correspondences between the two levels are almost coincidental.

On the other hand we do ordinarily provide outside help, and correspondences between statistical outcomes and substantive considerations are then more coincidental. Rather than saying that principal-component analysis and canonical factor analysis do not necessarily provide interesting solutions, it is preferable to state the conditions under which they do provide interesting solutions so that we may design research accordingly.

Generally the first principal component is substantively interesting if one is analyzing a fair number of indicators (say 25 or more) that have been selected carefully at a theoretical level so that only a single latent variable affects all of them. A first canonical factor can be substantively interesting under essentially the same conditions except that one might deal with a smaller pool of indicators (say 15 or more) if the sample size is large (say 200 or more) and if one feels sure that correlations among indicators are purely a function of the latent trait and not of artifactual similarities. Thus the help needed to make these mechanical solutions meaningful occurs before the actual analyses in subjectively deciding what indicators to include in the pool to be factored. Whereas in traditional factor-analytic procedures the subjective element is interjected toward the end in rotating factors to a position that makes the most semantic-theoretical sense, in the procedures being considered here the subjective element must enter at the beginning in terms of defining the item pool.

Conceivably there are instances in which one might not want to make a semantic-theoretical commitment right at the beginning, and certainly there are instances in which what was believed to be a pool dominated by a single latent variable is found to involve several. In these cases interpretative problems unavoidably come at the end in fixing on a final rotation. The great danger then is that one will make sense of anything—indeed this is exactly what Armstrong and Soelberg (1968) demonstrated when they showed that expert judges are able to interpret even random factors—and so in general it is best to avoid this kind of strategy.

Whether they come at the beginning or the end, subjective decisions are always involved in factor analysis; they can never be eliminated by a purely statistical procedure. Perhaps we can hope that as this fact becomes recognized, methodologists will divide their energies more evenly between statistics and metatheory, providing us with other procedures for making theoretical analyses less subjective. If further motivation is needed, it might be noted that a rotation problem arises in all variations of the linear measurement model when more than one unmeasured variable is required to account for the correlations among a set of indicators, and the problem arises also in the interpretation of similarity-preference data. A start in dealing with the subjectivity problem has already been made in the form of facet analysis (Guttman, 1959; Foa, 1965) and in recent advances in confirmatory factor analysis (see Werts and others, 1971). What appears to be an appropriate mathematical apparatus for dealing with concepts is now available in the form of the categorical algebra (see Goguen, 1970; Băianu, 1971).

THETA OR OMEGA CFRM?

The two chapters that follow present alternative ideas concerning the best way to create a composite score and concerning the appropriate statistic for measuring internal-consistency reliability. In one sense the alternatives are not competitive in that each has its appropriate application—one applies when a principal-component analysis has been conducted; the other applies when a canonical factor analysis has been done. In another sense, however, the two approaches are competitive in that one can ask whether their relative advantages indicate that one kind of analysis or the other should be run.

First it can be noted that the two reliability coefficients—theta and omega CFRM—do not seem to differ much in numerical value when applied to empirical scales: this becomes evident in the chapters themselves (and my own analyses, and those of students, further confirm the point). So if one is simply interested in obtaining an estimate of reliability for a scale composed of a pool of indicators, then frequently either coefficient serves equally well.

Armor's discussion provides an extension of theta to situations in which factors have been rotated; presumably a similar extension of omega CFRM could be obtained, but the fact that it is not yet available is a point in favor of theta. On the other hand the original discussion of omega (Heise and Bohrnstedt, 1970) associates this coefficient with a coefficient of invalidity that is useful in constructing short scales with high reliability and low contamination by unwanted factors.

Armor's and Allen's approaches largely parallel one another when viewed from the standpoint of research applicability. Which approach is more theoretically useful in terms of inspiring new insights into the measurement process is another possible basis for evaluation, but one that must be made retrospectively at a later date.

REFERENCES

ARMSTRONG, J. S. AND SOELBERG, P.
    1968 "On the interpretation of factor analysis." *Psychological Bulletin* 70:361–364.

BĂIANU, I.
    1971 "Organismic supercategories and qualitative dynamics of systems." *Bulletin of Mathematical Biophysics* 33:339–354.

BLALOCK, H. M., JR.
    1971 "Causal models involving unmeasured variables in stimulus-response situations." Chap. 19 in H. M. Blalock, Jr. (Ed.), *Causal Models in the Social Sciences*. New York: Aldine-Atherton.

CARNEIRO, R. L.
    1970 "Scale analysis, evolutionary sequences, and the rating of cultures." Chap. 41 in R. Naroll and R. Cohen (Eds.), *A Handbook of Method in Cultural Anthropology*. Garden City, N.Y.: Natural History Press–Doubleday.

COSTNER, H. L.
  1969   "Theory, deduction, and rules of correspondence." *American Journal of Sociology* 75:245–263.
DUNCAN, O. D.
  1966   "Path analysis: Sociological examples." *American Journal of Sociology* 72:1–16.
FOA, U. G.
  1965   "New developments in facet design and analysis." *Psychological Review* 72:262–274.
GOGUEN, J. A.
  1970   "Mathematical representation of hierarchically organized systems." Pp. 112–128 in E. O. Attinger (Ed.), *Global Systems Dynamics*. New York: Wiley-Interscience.
GUTTMAN, L.
  1959   "A structural theory for intergroup beliefs and action." *American Sociological Review* 24:318–328.
HAUSER, R. M.
  1972   "Disaggregating a social-psychological model of educational attainment." *Social Science Research* 1:159–188.
HAUSER, R. M. AND GOLDBERGER, A. S.
  1971   "The treatment of unobservable variables in path analysis." Chap. 4 in H. L. Costner (Ed.), *Sociological Methodology 1971*. San Francisco: Jossey-Bass.
HEISE, D. R.
  1972   "Employing nominal variables, induced variables, and block variables in path analyses." *Sociological Methods & Research* 1:147–173
HEISE, D. R. AND BOHRNSTEDT, G. W.
  1970   "Validity, invalidity, and reliability." Chap. 6 in E. F. Borgatta and G. W. Bohrnstedt (Eds.), *Sociological Methodology 1970*. San Francisco: Jossey-Bass.
HENRY, N. W. AND LAZARSFELD, P. F.
  1968   *Latent Structure Analysis*. Boston: Houghton Mifflin.
JÖRESKOG, K. G., GRUVAEUS, G. T. AND VAN THILLO, M.
  1970   "ACOVS—A general computer program for analysis of covariance structures." *Educational Testing Service Research Bulletin*:70–15.
LORD, F. M. AND NOVICK, M. R.
  1968   *Statistical Theories of Mental Test Scores*. Reading, Mass.: Addison-Wesley.
NUNNALLY, J. C.
  1967   *Psychometric Theory*. New York: McGraw-Hill.
RUMMEL, R. J.
  1970   *Applied Factor Analysis*. Evanston, Ill.: Northwestern University Press.
SHEPARD, R. N., ROMNEY, A. K. AND NERLOVE, S. B.
  1972   *Multidimensional Scaling: Theory and Applications in the Behavioral Sciences*. Vol. 1: Theory. New York: Seminar Press.

SULLIVAN, J. L.
    1971 "Multiple indicators and complex causal models." Chap. 18 in H. M. Blalock, Jr. (Ed.), *Causal Models in the Social Sciences*. New York: Aldine-Atherton.

VAN DE GEER, J. P.
    1971 *Introduction to Multivariate Analysis for the Social Sciences*. San Francisco: Freeman.

WERTS, C. E., LINN, R. L. AND JÖRESKOG, K. G.
    1971 "Estimating the parameters of path models involving unmeasured variables." Chap. 23 in H. M. Blalock, Jr. (Ed.), *Causal Models in the Social Sciences*. New York: Aldine-Atherton.

2

THETA RELIABILITY AND FACTOR SCALING

David J. Armor
THE RAND CORPORATION

The author wishes to express his gratitude to Albert E. Beaton for pointing out the relationship between theta and maximum alpha. David Heise, Donald Olivier, and Fred Mosteller read earlier drafts and provided helpful criticisms and suggestions for the final manuscript.

Reliability measurement of composite variables has attracted a considerable amount of interest among sociologists in the last several years.[1] Although sociologists have always lamented the problem of reliability in sociological measurement, until recently little attention has been paid to techniques of reliability assessment and improvement within the sociological methodology literature itself. While much of the recent

[1] Throughout this chapter the term *reliability* refers to internal-consistancy reliability—as opposed to stability reliability—unless otherwise stated (Heise, 1969).

attention is expository and tutorial in nature, progress has been made in conveying basic principles (Upshaw, 1968; Blalock, 1969), in connecting reliability to path analysis (Siegel and Hodge, 1968; Heise, 1969), and in providing simplified computational procedures (Bohrnstedt, 1969).

In spite of this activity, there are still many technical problems facing the practitioner of reliability assessment and improvement for composite measures. Most procedures for reliability assessment depend on the application of Cronbach's alpha (Cronbach, 1951), and its improvement depends on various steps of item analysis (which I later define as *covariance scaling*; Upshaw, 1968). Unfortunately these methods have several drawbacks for the sociologist and perhaps for other social scientists as well: the mathematical assumptions for alpha reliability are often not met; the usual steps of item analysis—throwing out "bad" items to enhance alpha reliability—may not in fact produce optimum alpha reliability; and item analysis does not include clear and systematic procedures for detecting and taking into account multidimensionality—that is, the presence of mutually independent subclusters of items within the total composite.

This chapter aims to solve some of these problems by describing an approach to reliability based on principal-component factor analysis. This approach rests on a different and, for sociologists, a more realistic definition of composite reliability. Moreover it leads to a little-known measure of reliability I call theta (to distinguish it from alpha reliability) that assesses optimal reliability, and it provides for a method of factor scaling that can take account of multidimensionality in a set of items, thereby enhancing reliability and validity.

Before presenting these methods it is necessary to review current alpha reliability techniques and the associated method of covariance scaling. In this way it will be possible to illustrate more clearly the specific advantages of theta reliability and factor scaling.

ALPHA RELIABILITY

Given an interest in assessing composite reliability, deciding on an appropriate coefficient has been a troublesome step for many investigators. Although the usual definition of reliability is the simple product-moment correlation between two parallel variables that measure "identical" things, there is no single coefficient that has been adopted universally for composite reliability. Guilford (1954) lists ten coefficients, and this is not an exhaustive list. Some of the standard ones he gives are the Spearman-Brown prophecy formula; the split-half and odd-even methods (both of which depend on the Spearman-Brown formula); the Kuder-Richardson formula 20; and Cronbach's alpha. The reason for this multiplicity has to do with the different ways of estimating the error components of a set of items.

Due in part to the conceptual and computational simplicity of the split-half method, it was probably the most commonly used coefficient in sociological research before the middle 1950s. Since that time, however, Cronbach's alpha has become the popular measure of reliability (Cronbach, 1951): it is a general formula that subsumes most of the split-half and Kuder-Richardson coefficients;[2] it has also proved to be a lower bound to the true reliability (Novick and Lewis, 1967). This latter characteristic means that alpha is a conservative estimate of the reliability of a composite. Basically the alpha coefficient treats each item in a composite as a parallel variable. Since moderate departures from the model can be expected, the reliability for each item is estimated by the average inter-item correlation. If we let $\bar{r}$ be the average correlation between items and if we assume that the items are in standard form (or that they have equal variances), then Cronbach's alpha is simply

$$\alpha = p\bar{r}/[1 + \bar{r}(p-1)] \qquad (1)$$

where $\bar{r}$ = mean inter-item correlation; p = number of items. In other words alpha is identical to the Spearman-Brown prophecy formula with the average correlation $\bar{r}$ used to estimate the reliability of each item.

Model

The usual model for the alpha reliability formula given in Equation (1) comes from psychological test theory (Lord and Novick, 1968). This model assumes that the observed score for any item in a composite can be partitioned according to "true" and "error" components. For item i and for any subject j this model is

$$x_{ij} = T_j + e_{ij} \qquad (2)$$

where x_{ij} = the observed score for item i, subject j; T_j = the true score for subject j; e_{ij} = the error score for item i, subject j. That is, all items measure the subject on an underlying property T_j to an equal extent. It is normally further assumed that the error components are uncorrelated with true components (for the same item as well as across different items) and with each other; in other words, all items are parallel forms. It would

---

[2] Cronbach (1951) proved that alpha is the mean of all possible split-half reliabilities.

then be expected that all population (as opposed to sample) inter-item correlations would be equal, as would be all population item variances. Given moderate departures from these assumptions and given that the inter-item correlations and item variances may not be all equal in a sample, Equation (1) provides an estimated reliability by standardizing items and by averaging over observed correlations to obtain an estimate of the true population inter-item correlation.

However adequate this model may be for psychological tests, for many composite measures in sociology these assumptions are not realistic. Since the content of each item in a composite usually differs by a substantial degree, particularly in attitudinal or behavioral composites (such as political efficacy, anomie, social class), we might expect that the true population correlations are not all equal. For example, in a social class index composed of measures of income, education, and occupational status, one usually finds that the correlations are not all equal; the correlations between income and the other two variables are usually lower than the correlation between education and occupation—even for the full U.S. Census (Siegel and Hodge, 1968). A similar case might be made for any number of attitude scales when inter-item correlations are consistently unequal across many different samples.

A more parsimonious and more realistic basis for alpha can be given by utilizing the familiar formula for decomposing the variance of a sum of items. Letting x_{ij} stand for a score on item i for subject j, letting p be the number of items, and letting scale scores $X_j = x_{1j} + x_{2j} + \cdots + x_{pj}$, we have

$$\sigma_X^2 = \sum \sigma_{x_i}^2 + 2 \sum_{i<j} \text{cov}(x_i, x_j) \tag{3}$$

where σ_X^2 = variance of the sum; $\sigma_{x_i}^2$ = variance of item i; $\text{cov}(x_i, x_j)$ = covariance between item i and item j. Or, more compactly,

$$S = I + C \tag{4}$$

That is, the variance of a scale or composite sum S is equal to the sum of the individual item variances I plus the sum of all possible covariances between different items C.

For a set of items in a composite that are measuring the same or similar properties, one would expect the covariances to be large compared to the item variances; therefore we might measure the composite reliability (or scalability) by considering the ratio C/S: this is the proportion of scale variance due to item covariation. Unfortunately this ratio does not have an upper limit of 1, since I is never zero except in the trivial case when all item variances are zero. The maximum value for

C/S is $(p-1)/p$, and this occurs if every item is perfectly correlated with every other item, which means that all $\sigma_{x_i}^2$ are equal and $\text{cov}(x_i, x_j) = \sigma_{x_i}^2$. This suggests an index of composite reliability with the desirable range of 0 to 1 as follows:[3]

$$\text{Composite reliability} = \frac{C/S}{(p-1)/p} = \alpha \qquad (5)$$

That is, alpha can be derived as the proportion of scale variance due to item covariation adjusted to provide an upper limit of 1.

Although this derivation provides the same coefficient, the advantages of the rationale (aside from its simplicity) are that no postulates have to be made about an underlying model of true and error score components and that there is no necessity to make the parallel variable assumptions (such as equality of true scores and equal precision of measurement). It is this latter set of assumptions that may be particularly unrealistic in many sociological applications. On the other hand, if the parallel form assumptions are reasonable for all items in a composite, then alpha as defined in Equations (1) or (5) is an appropriate measure of reliability in the traditional sense. In either case alpha offers a single criterion for estimating the internal consistency and coherency of a set of items making up a scale. The greater the covariation, given a fixed number of items, the greater the value for alpha. A value of zero means that the average covariation is zero; a value of 1 means that all items have intercorrelations equal to 1.

Computational Forms

The formulas for alpha given in Equations (1) and (5) are not particularly useful for computation. It might be helpful to summarize the major computational forms and point out some practical differences between them. It might come as a surprise to some analysts that not all forms produce the same answers, and, given various conditions, that some forms are more appropriate than others.

In the following formulas p is the number of items; r_{ij} is the product-moment correlation between items x_i and x_j; $\sigma_{x_i}^2$ is the variance of item i; X is the sum of the item scores with an associated scale variance σ_X^2; and $\bar{X}$ is the arithmetic mean of the item scores with an associated variance $\sigma_{\bar{X}}^2$. Depending on how the composite scale scores are

---

[3] This formula assumes that all items are scored in the same direction or, if not, that appropriate reversals are made to eliminate negative covariances. With real data it is always possible to make reversals so that C remains positive (and so that alpha is always greater than or equal to zero).

formed, one of the following formulas will be appropriate. If the scale is formed by summing standardized item scores,

$$\alpha = \left(\frac{p}{p-1}\right)\left(\frac{2\sum_{i<j} r_{ij}}{p + 2\sum_{i<j} r_{ij}}\right) \qquad (6)$$

If the scale is formed by summing raw item scores,

$$\alpha = \left(\frac{p}{p-1}\right)\left(1 - \frac{\sum \sigma_{x_i}^2}{\sigma_X^2}\right) \qquad (7)$$

If the scale is formed by averaging raw item scores,

$$\alpha = \left(\frac{p}{p-1}\right)\left(1 - \frac{\Sigma \sigma_{x_i}^2}{p^2 \sigma_X^2}\right) \qquad (8)$$

The choice between these formulas is not just a matter of computational convenience; at least three considerations apply. First, if one is making the traditional parallel-form assumptions, then all item variances should be equal; if they are not (as is usual with most real data), then differences would ordinarily be seen as nonsubstantive and should not be allowed to affect the reliability estimate. In this case standardization of items removes variance differences and Equation (6) can be used. Of course Equation (7) can also be used if the scale variance happens to be known. But Equation (6) is more useful because the scale variance does not have to be known; it depends only on the inter-item correlations and the number of items.

Equations (7) or (8) should be used whenever raw item scores are used to produce the scale scores. Since they employ the actual item variances (which are normally not all equal), these formulas do not produce the same estimate as Equation (6). In effect the alpha coefficient is weighted according to item variances. Whether the reliability according to Equations (7) and (8) is higher or lower than that given by Equation (6) depends on complex relationships between the item variances and the inter-item correlations. Basically scales formed from raw item scores have higher reliability if the items with higher variances have higher correlations; if the opposite holds, then Equation (6) produces a more reliable scale. This relationship should become clearer after theta reliability is derived in the next section.

A third consideration arises when some items have missing observations due to nonresponses. If scales are formed by a straight summation method with no special treatment of nonresponses (that is, if nonresponses are in effect treated as zeros), subjects with many nonresponses will have spuriously low scale scores; the scale variance σ_X^2 will be spuriously large; and the resulting alpha will be spuriously high. In this case it is better to form scale scores by averaging item scores (based on responses present) and to apply Equation (8). Equation (6) is also appropriate in this case, assuming that the r_{ij} are computed without the nonresponses for each pair of items.

Covariance Scaling

Given that real data may depart from the parallel-item assumptions, techniques are necessary to decide on the adequacy of individual items. It is possible that one or more items may not be measuring the property in common to the rest of the items; if so, their elimination might enhance reliability as well as the conceptual clarity of the composite. Under the parallel-item assumptions, the greater the number of items the higher the reliability (this relationship is given by the Spearman-Brown prophecy formula). But in the absence of these assumptions such is not necessarily the case. Specifically items that do not correlate sufficiently with other items in a composite (or correlate in a negative direction after appropriate reversals) may actually reduce the reliability of a composite and should therefore be excluded.[4]

The technique of maximizing the alpha reliability of a composite under various constraints will be called *covariance scaling*. Other terms used to describe this process include *item analysis* (Upshaw, 1968), *test construction* (Cronbach, 1960), *summated ratings* (Edwards, 1957), and *Likert scaling* after the psychologist who invented the agree-disagree item scoring scheme. Sociologists also often use the term *index construction* to denote a similar procedure. The term *covariance scaling* can be applied to all these methods since they are all based on the same basic and self-evident assumption: if a set of items is measuring the same or similar properties and the property comprises a single continuum or dimension, the items should all covary to some extent. For a fixed number of items, the greater and more consistent the inter-item correlations the more reliable the composite.

There is no single, uniform procedure that all researchers follow when constructing a covariance scale. Nonetheless several steps can be identified in the literature; an investigator would normally use at least one of them:

[4] In fact it can be shown that, given an α_p based on p items, the α_{p-1} based on the remaining items after item h has been excluded will be greater than α_p if

$$\sum_{i \neq h}^{p} r_{ih} < p\alpha_p / [p - \alpha_p(p-1)][p - 1 - \alpha_p(p-2)]$$

where r_{ih} is the correlation between item i and item h.

1. Inspection of item face content to ensure clear and consistent meanings
2. Calculation and inspection of item-to-scale correlations to pinpoint items that are not contributing to the scale as a whole[5]
3. Calculation of a T-test for each item between the highest 25 percent and lowest 25 percent of the composite scale scores (usually a substitute for step 2)[6]
4. Examination of all inter-item correlations for patterns of lower or negative correlations
5. Recalculation of alpha reliability after eliminating items according to information obtained in steps 1 to 4

It is unlikely that any but the most careful researchers go through all these steps. Step 4 is probably the one most likely to be left out unless a computer is being used for the analysis. In fact this step is not mentioned in several standard discussions of the method of summed ratings (Edwards, 1957; Upshaw, 1968). As will become clear, however, step 4 contains all the information needed to decide on scalability, and it may be the most important step of all.

The point in describing these familiar techniques is not so much to instruct the reader in covariance scaling; rather I want to be clear about the meaning of my claim that the traditional covariance steps reviewed here do not necessarily result in optimal scales from the standpoint of composite reliability. Although the application of covariance scaling may enhance reliability, the success of the application may depend more on subjective judgments than on analytic criteria. Although subjective judgments can never be eliminated from scaling techniques (nor should they be), the methods of theta reliability and factor scaling offer a substantially more analytic approach that can help to reduce the idiosyncratic variations of individual investigators.

Limitations of Alpha Reliability and Covariance Scaling

It has been pointed out that the method of alpha reliability depends on the assumption that all items in a composite are parallel items, which further implies that all items measure a single underlying scale property equally. Therefore there are two major conditions under which a set of real data clearly violates the assumptions: the items may measure a single property but do so unequally; the items may measure two or

---

[5] The item-to-scale (or item-to-total) correlations should be corrected for item contribution but frequently they are not.

[6] The procedures for this step are described in Edwards (1957).

more independent properties either equally or unequally. Although the techniques of covariance scaling may help some aspects of the first problem they may not do so optimally. As far as the second problem is concerned, covariance scaling offers little or no solution at all. The little help it may offer depends very much on the number of items and the patience of the investigator.

These two problems can be illustrated by simple hypothetical examples. Consider a four-item composite whose intercorrelations are as shown in Table 1. The first three items have intercorrelations that are quite high and consistent, ranging from 0.4 to 0.6. But item 4 has much lower correlations with the other three items (all being 0.1). Assuming that the correlations are based on a sufficiently large sample, it might turn out that the 0.1 correlations are significantly different from zero and an investigator may therefore decide to keep item 4 in the composite. But if item 4 is left in the composite without some kind of weighting, the composite reliability will be lower than if the items are weighted according to their differential contributions. The four-item (unweighted) alpha reliability is 0.63; the composite reliability with weighting is 0.68 (applying the theta technique defined in the next section).

The second problem is generally harder to detect with real data, but the simple hypothetical example in Table 2 offers a clear demonstration. Basically the existence of two or more independent properties in a composite is usually revealed whenever there are two or more sets of items with relatively high within-set correlations and relatively low be-

TABLE 1
Inter-Item Correlations for Hypothetical Four-Item Composite

Item	1	2	3	4
1	1.0			
2	0.6	1.0		
3	0.5	0.4	1.0	
4	0.1	0.1	0.1	1.0

TABLE 2
Inter-Item Correlations Revealing Two Dimensions

Item	1	2	3	4	5	6
1	1.0					
2	0.5	1.0				
3	0.5	0.5	1.0			
4	0.0	0.0	0.0	1.0		
5	0.0	0.0	0.0	0.5	1.0	
6	0.0	0.0	0.0	0.5	0.5	1.0

tween-set correlations. The degree of independence among the properties increases as the between-set correlations approach zero.

Table 2 illustrates a six-item composite whose intercorrelations reveal two independent dimensions, one represented by items 1 to 3 and another by items 4 to 6. Each subset has within-set correlations of 0.5; all the between-set correlations are zero. If all six items are combined into a single scale, the alpha reliability will be 0.60 ($\bar{r} = 0.2$); but if items 1 to 3 and items 4 to 6 are combined into two separate three-item scales, they would each have the substantially higher alpha reliabilities of 0.75. In fact the six-item scale reliability would not surpass the reliabilities of the two three-item scales until the average of all the between-set correlations surpasses 0.2 (holding the within-set correlations constant at 0.5). Quite aside from the question of reliability, of course, is the fact that decomposing the a priori six-item composite into two independent subscales provides new information that may have an important bearing on conceptual and theoretical issues.

Although most investigators could discover the independent dimensions in simple examples whose correlational patterns are as clear as those in Table 2, the situation with real data is generally much more complex. As the number of items increases (say, over ten), as the number of dimensions increases, and as items contribute differentially to each dimension, none but the most patient and diligent analyst would be able to produce optimum scaling with the usual alpha reliability and covariance scaling techniques.

THETA RELIABILITY

With the advent of computer solutions for multivariate methods, many researchers have turned to factor analysis for assistance in identifying the number of properties or dimensions in a set of data and in relating specific items to each dimension. With a few notable exceptions, however, little attempt has been made to relate factor analysis formally to reliability and scaling methods, and almost none of this work is widely known and applied in sociology (Lord, 1958; Bentler, 1968; Heise and Bohrnstedt, 1971). Even factor analysis is not as well understood and applied as it could be. When factor analysis is applied to scaling tasks, the application depends more on the intuition and experience of the investigator than on analytic techniques; it remains more of an art than a technology.

Although the interpretive aspects of factor analysis can never be eliminated, there are a number of procedures that can aid the establishment of optimally reliable scales. The key to these procedures is a formal connection between reliability and scaling provided by principal-component factor analysis.[7] Other factor-analytic methods have been developed, but principal-component analysis offers the most straightforward and precise connection between reliability and scaling. The results of a component analysis enable one to compute an optimal reliability coefficient I call *theta* and to derive optimal scales through a series of steps I call *factor scaling*.

The basic hypothesis of component analysis is that, given a set of p items, the score of a subject on each item can be decomposed into any number of components or factors (up to the total number of items). Generally only a small number of the largest factors in terms of the proportion of the total item variation they represent are given substantive meaning; the remainder are grouped together and considered as an error component or factor. Each nonerror factor, say m of them (with $m < p$), is a hypothetical variable given substantive meaning by individual items according to *factor loadings*—a set of weights determined by the contribution of each item to a given factor. This means that each item can contribute differentially to a given factor (or not at all if the factor loading is zero). Moreover each factor represents a statistically independent source of variation among the set of items, and most component-analysis solutions extract these factors in an order corresponding to the size of their contribution; that is, the first factor accounts for the most variance, the second factor for the second largest amount of variance, and so on. From the standpoint of scaling, principal-component analysis offers a means of detecting the most important independent dimensions among a set of items (if there is more than one) and, for each of these dimensions, provides for differential contributions by individual items.

A principal-component analysis can be used to construct a set of *factor scores*, one set for each factor. A factor score is simply the score of a subject on a given factor: it is in effect a composite scale score based on a weighted sum of the individual items using the factor loadings as the weights. The task of the theta coefficient is to provide a composite reliability estimate for factor scores based on principal-component analysis.

In component analysis the amount of variance accounted for by a factor is called a *root* and is denoted by the symbol λ_k (for the kth factor).[8] Although these quantities are provided by most computer solutions for component analysis, they actually have a simple relationship

---

[7] By principal-component analysis is meant a method of factor analysis whereby unities (1s) are left in the diagonal of a correlation matrix when factoring. See Harman (1967).

[8] The full technical term is *latent root*. Other common terms are *eigenvalue* and *characteristic root*.

to the factor loadings: the kth root is simply the sum of the squared factor loadings for the kth factor. These are the quantities that provide the basis for theta reliability.

Before giving the formula and the derivation for theta reliability, it must be pointed out that there are two general cases in component analysis that need to be distinguished. First, in a single-factor solution the first factor and its root λ_1 suffice for a complete specification of the scale and its reliability. Second, if a multiple-factor solution is adopted meaningful interpretation generally requires a *rotation* of the m factors that are retained. Rotations are dealt with in more detail later; suffice it to say here that after rotation the variance of a factor—which still equals the sum of the squared rotated loadings—no longer equals the mathematical roots derived in the original principal-component solution. Accordingly the symbol λ_k^* is used to denote the variance of the kth rotated factor.

Given a set of p items and a single-factor solution with root λ_1, the reliability of the composite scores based on this factor is given by

$$\theta = [p/(p-1)][1 - (1/\lambda_1)] \tag{9}$$

where λ_1 is the first root of a principal-component solution. Although this formula is not new, it is little known in sociology (Bentler, 1968). It is mathematically equivalent to alpha for a composite scale formed by weighting items according to their principal-component factor loadings; this has been shown by Lord (1958) to be the maximum possible alpha. By taking into account differential item contributions to the central property in common to a set of items, one obtains the maximum composite reliability according to the definition given in Equation (5).

The situation for a multiple-factor solution with rotated factors is somewhat more complicated. Letting ϕ_{hk}^2 stand for the squared correlation between the original unrotated scores for factor h and the new factor k, and given a rotated m-factor solution with original roots $\lambda_1, \lambda_2, \cdots, \lambda_m$, the reliability of the kth set of rotated factor scores is given by

$$\theta_k^* = [p/(p-1)]\left(1 - \sum_{h=1}^{m} \phi_{hk}^2/\lambda_h\right) \tag{10}$$

This formula holds only for orthogonal rotations (such as the varimax solution). The quantity ϕ_{hk} is actually the element in the hth row and kth column of the transformation matrix that maps the original factor loadings into the rotated loadings.

Although theta-star is mathematically similar to theta, it will be clear later that it does not have quite the same utility. Since the number of factors m is by no means a determinate quantity, we cannot say that theta-star offers maximum reliability for each subset of items in a composite. Moreover it turns out that in spite of the weighting, if more than one factor is present optimal reliability is seldom approached if all p items are used to derive the weighted scale scores. Nonetheless theta-star is the proper formula for reliability when one is using the complete set of rotated factor scores from a principal-component analysis.

I now give more precise meaning to the preceding ideas, and I provide a derivation for theta. Given an observed standardized score x_{ij} for subject j on item i, the basic model for component analysis is[9]

$$x_{ij} = a_{i1}f_{1j} + a_{i2}f_{2j} + \cdots + a_{im}f_{mj} + e_{ij} \tag{11}$$

where a_{ik} is a factor loading of item i on factor k; f_{kj} is a factor score for subject j on factor k; e_{ij} is an error component due to random and other specific influences of item i to the observed score. If $m = p$ or if as many factors are extracted as there are items, then $e_{ij} = 0$ for all i, j and the original scores are decomposed perfectly without error. This case is generally uninteresting, however, since one ends up with as many factors as there are items. In most cases an investigator interprets only a small number of factors m; in this event the remaining $p-m$ factors are assumed to represent an error component. The problem of choosing the cutoff for m is taken up in a later section.

It is not necessary to go into the mathematics of exactly how these quantities are obtained; most researchers rely on widely available computer programs for deriving them.[10] For the present it suffices to say that a standard principal-component analysis results in a set of factor loadings a_{ik} that measure the magnitude of the contribution of item i to factor k on a scale ranging from -1.0 to $+1.0$; a set of roots λ_k such that $\lambda_k = \sum_i a_{ik}^2$; and a set of factor scores f_{kj} that provide the score of subject j on factor k. The factor loadings and roots are usually displayed in

---

[9] The assumption of standardized scores does not destroy the generality of the technique. There is usually no a priori reason why items that measure similar properties should be allowed to have differential weights by virtue of arbitrarily different variances; indeed the whole point of factor analysis is to base weights on contributions to underlying factors without regard to initial variances.

[10] It can be noted in passing that the factor loadings are simply the set of latent vectors (eigenvectors, characteristic vectors) which satisfy the characteristic equation $(R - \lambda I)\mathbf{v} = 0$, where R is the correlation matrix with unities in the diagonal, λ is a constant, I is the identity matrix, and $\mathbf{v}$ is a latent vector. The factor loadings in Equation (11) are normalized so that $\mathbf{a}_k'\mathbf{a}_k = \lambda_k$, where $\mathbf{a}_k$ is the vector of factor loadings for factor k; the latent vectors $\mathbf{v}$ are normally assumed to be normalized to 1 ($\mathbf{v}'\mathbf{v} = 1$).

TABLE 3
Factor Loadings and Roots

Item	Factor 1	Factor 2	$\cdots$	Factor m
1	a_{11}	a_{12}	$\cdots$	a_{1m}
2	a_{21}	a_{22}	$\cdots$	a_{2m}
.	.	.		.
.	.	.		.
.	.	.		.
p	a_{p1}	a_{p2}	$\cdots$	a_{pm}
$\sum_{i} a_{ik}^2 =$	λ_1	λ_2		λ_m

matrix form as shown in Table 3. The factor loadings are necessary not only for constructing the factor scores but also for interpreting the factor in terms of the content of the original item. The higher the absolute value of a loading, the greater the contribution of that item to the factor in question.[11]

A root λ_k can be interpreted as the amount of variance in the original set of items accounted for by factor k. Since the total variance in a set of p standardized items is just p, and since the sum of all p roots must also equal p, the ratio λ_k/p is the proportion of total variance due to factor k. These proportions are used to give an idea about the importance of a given factor; moreover the sum of these proportions for m factors tells us how much variation has been explained by the total set of m factors.

Given the factor loadings and roots, it is possible to derive the factor scores from the following simple relationship:

$$f_{kj} = \sum_{i} (a_{ik}/\lambda_k) x_{ij} \qquad (12)$$

In words, the factor scores are just weighted averages of the original standardized scores using the ratio a_{ik}/λ_k as the weight for item i and factor k.

In order to derive theta, consider a single-factor solution with root λ_1, loadings a_{i1}, and scores f_{1j}. We shall use the basic definition of composite reliability provided in Equation (5) as the basis of our derivation; that is, $C(p)/S(p-1)$. Accordingly we need to know the quantities

---

[11] A factor loading can be interpreted as the correlation between an item and the factor scores. A negative loading means that the item has a negative correlation with the factor scores (the higher the item score, the lower the factor score or vice versa).

C and S for the factor scores f_{1j}. We start with the known relationship for S based on a weighted sum of item scores:

$$S = \sum_i w_i^2 \sigma_{x_i^2} + \sum_{i \neq h} w_i w_h \operatorname{cov}(x_i, x_h) = I + C \qquad (13)$$

where w_i are the weights. Since in the case of factor scores the x_i are standardized, we have $\sigma_{x_i^2} = 1$ and $\operatorname{cov}(x_i, x_h) = r_{ih}$. Therefore, since $w_i = a_{i1}/\lambda_1$,

$$\begin{aligned} S = \sigma_{f_1^2} &= \sum_i (a_{i1}/\lambda_1)^2 + \sum_{i \neq h} (a_{i1}/\lambda_1)(a_{h1}/\lambda_1) r_{ih} \\ &= \left(\sum_i a_{i1}^2\right)/\lambda_1^2 + \left(\sum_{i \neq h} a_{i1} a_{h1} r_{ih}\right)/\lambda_1^2 \end{aligned} \qquad (14)$$

And since $\sum_i a_{i1}^2 = \lambda_1$,

$$S = 1/\lambda_1 + \left(\sum_{i \neq h} a_{i1} a_{h1} r_{ih}\right)/\lambda_1^2 \qquad (15)$$

From the basic equations of component analysis we know that $\sum_{i,h} a_{i1} a_{h1} r_{ih} = \lambda_1^2$, so

$$\begin{aligned} \sum_{i \neq h} a_{i1} a_{h1} r_{ih} &= \sum_{i,h} a_{i1} a_{h1} r_{ih} - \sum_i a_i^2 \\ &= \lambda_1^2 - \lambda_1 \end{aligned} \qquad (16)$$

Thus

$$\begin{aligned} S &= 1/\lambda_1 + (\lambda_1^2 - \lambda_1)/\lambda_1^2 \\ &= 1/\lambda_1 + (1 - 1/\lambda_1) \end{aligned} \qquad (17)$$

This means that for the factor scores based on the first principal component, $S = 1$, $I = 1/\lambda_1$, and $C = 1 - 1/\lambda_1$. For the composite reliability from Equation (5) we have

$$\frac{C/S}{(p-1)/p} = [p/(p-1)]C/S = [p/(p-1)](1 - 1/\lambda_1) = \theta \qquad (18)$$

which is the formula for theta given in Equation (9).

That this formula for theta provides the maximum composite reliability (given our definition) follows from a fundamental property of principal components: that the quantity λ_1 is the maximum value for the quadratic form $\sum_{i,h} a_{i1} a_{h1} r_{ih} = \lambda_1^2$. That is, no set of weights a_{i1} other than those provided by the first principal-component factor loadings produce a value larger than the first root.[12] Thus theta gives the maximum value for the ratio $C(p)/S(p-1)$.

[12] In principal-component theory this relationship is generally defined as $\mathbf{v}_1' R \mathbf{v}_1 = \lambda_1$, where the first principal component is that vector $\mathbf{v}_1$ which produces the largest root λ_1 (see footnote 10). With the usual normalization for factor loadings this is equivalent to $\mathbf{a}_1' R \mathbf{a}_1 = \lambda_1^2$.

The derivation for theta-star follows a similar (if more involved) line. Starting with the usual relationship $S = I + C$, for the kth rotated factor scores f_k^* we have

$$S_k = \sigma_{f_k^*}^2 = \sum_{i=1}^{p} w_{ik}^2 \sigma_{x_i}^2 + \sum_{i \neq j=1}^{p} w_{ik} w_{jk} r_{ij} = I_k + C_k \quad (19)$$

Since $S = 1$ for rotated scores as well, all we need to find for our ratio of Equation (5) is the quantity $C_k = \sum_{i \neq j} w_{ik} w_{jk} r_{ij}$. In the case of rotated factor scores, the weight w_{ik} is more complex than for unrotated factor scores:

$$w_{ik} = \sum_{h=1}^{m} (a_{ih} \phi_{hk})/\lambda_h \quad (20)$$

where ϕ_{hk} is the correlation between original factor h scores and the rotated factor k scores, or the (h, k) element in the orthonormal transformation matrix. Using this relationship for C_k we have

$$C_k = \sum_{i \neq j=1}^{p} w_{ik} w_{jk} r_{ij} = \sum_{i \neq j=1}^{p} \left[\sum_{h=1}^{m} (a_{ih} \phi_{hk})/\lambda_h\right]\left[\sum_{h=1}^{m} (a_{jh} \phi_{hk})/\lambda_h\right] r_{ij}$$

$$= \sum_{i \neq j=1}^{p} \left[\sum_{h=1}^{m} (a_{ih} \phi_{hk} a_{jh} \phi_{hk})/\lambda_h^2 r_{ij} + \sum_{h \neq g=1}^{m} (a_{ih} \phi_{hk} a_{jg} \phi_{gk})/\lambda_h \lambda_g r_{ij}\right] \quad (21)$$

$$= \sum_{h=1}^{m} \frac{\phi_{hk}^2}{\lambda_h^2} \sum_{i \neq j=1}^{p} a_{ih} a_{jh} r_{ij} + \sum_{h \neq g=1}^{m} (\phi_{hk} \phi_{gk})/(\lambda_h \lambda_g) \sum_{i \neq j=1}^{p} a_{ih} a_{jg} r_{ij}$$

From the known relationships in principal-component analysis, we have $\sum_{i \neq j} a_{ih} a_{jh} r_{ij} = \lambda_h^2 - \lambda_h$ and $\sum_{i \neq j} a_{ih} a_{jg} r_{ij} = 0$. Therefore

$$C_k = \sum_{h=1}^{m} \frac{\phi_{hk}^2}{\lambda_h^2} (\lambda_h^2 - \lambda_h) = \sum_{h=1}^{m} \phi_{hk}^2 \left(1 - \frac{1}{\lambda_h}\right) = \sum_{h=1}^{m} \phi_{hk}^2 - \sum_{h=1}^{m} \phi_{hk}^2/\lambda_h$$

Since the quantities ϕ_{hk} are from an orthonormal transformation matrix, we know that $\sum_{h=1}^{m} \phi_{hk}^2 = 1$. We have, finally,

$$C_k = 1 - \sum_{h=1}^{m} \phi_{hk}^2/\lambda_h \quad (23)$$

and thus our formula for theta-star

$$\theta_k^* = [p/(p-1)]\left[1 - \sum_{h=1}^{m} \phi_{hk}^2/\lambda_h\right] \quad (24)$$

To sum up there is a fairly simple conceptual basis for the relationship $\alpha \leq \theta$. As we have said, alpha tends to get larger as the amount of covariation in a set of items increases. But alpha assumes that each item is weighted equally and that each inter-item correlation is close to

$\bar{r}$, the average correlation. When this condition is present, theta and alpha are approximately equal. When this is not the case, each item contributes a different amount to the covariance. A factor loading expresses something analogous to the average amount of covariation due to an item: those items with higher correlations with other items have higher factor loadings. Therefore a composite scale that weights items according to the factor loadings expresses a more accurate ratio of covariance to scale variance. Theta and alpha are equal only in the limiting case when all inter-item correlations r_{ij} are equal.

The relationship between α and θ_k^* is more difficult to state since α is appropriate only for a single-factor model. Given an m-factor solution, one can construct m unweighted scales using the highest loading items on each factor. Letting α_k' be the alpha reliability for the subscale corresponding to factor k, empirical results shown later demonstrate that usually $\theta_k^* < \alpha_k'$. Moreover, if each subset of items is refactored as a single-dimension scale and a new theta reliability is computed, say θ_k', then generally α_k' and θ_k' are approximately equal. Given a multiple-factor solution, therefore, optimally reliable scales are derived by applying the usual unweighted covariance techniques to each subset of items rather than by using rotated factor scores. More is said on this issue in the next section.

IMPROVING RELIABILITY BY FACTOR SCALING

There are several ways in which we may use theta reliability and principal-component analysis to enhance the reliability of a composite. First, as we have already seen, if one uses factor scores for composite scale scores instead of the traditional unweighted sum of item scores, the method of theta reliability shows us that we are guaranteed a reliability equal to or greater than that given by alpha reliability. Second, in the case of a single-factor solution we must still raise the question of whether weighting alone takes care of items that do not contribute to a factor (or contribute to only a small extent). That is, will reliability be enhanced—beyond that provided by factor scoring—by factor scales that exclude low-loading an item altogether? By *factor scale* I mean a composite formed to measure a factor by using only the highest-loading items on a factor. Finally, both reliability and conceptual clarity may be improved by adopting a multiple-factor solution (whether or not it was hypothesized). If either of these last two conditions is present, we must again consider the relative benefits of rotated factor scores versus factor scales. In this section I take up some practical considerations that bear on these issues.

Single-Factor Case

Although we know that theta is algebraically larger than alpha, it might be useful to present some simple hypothetical examples that reveal how serious the differences might be and show how we can improve scale reliability. We shall examine an application of factor scaling to real data in a later section.

Table 4 shows four cases, the first three of which involve four items. I have held items 1 to 3 constant so that the difference in reliabilities can be seen as we add different fourth items.

Case 1 reveals the largest discrepancy between theta and alpha (0.05). The reason is that the fourth item has low correlations with the other items and consequently a low factor loading (0.24). A scale score that weights items according to the loadings therefore has a higher reliability than a simple summed score.

In case 2 the fourth item still has somewhat higher correlations and a higher loading (0.44), so that the difference between theta and alpha is diminished to 0.02. In case 3 there is practically no difference between theta and alpha even though the correlations and the loadings do vary considerably. Clearly theta and alpha differ in a substantial way only when some items have consistently lower correlations with all the

TABLE 4
Comparing Theta and Alpha

Case	Item	Correlations				Factor Loading (a_{i1})
		1	2	3	4	
Case 1						
$\lambda_1 = 2.033$	1	1.0				0.86
$\theta = 0.68$	2	0.6	1.0			0.82
$\alpha = 0.63$	3	0.5	0.4	1.0		0.76
	4	0.1	0.1	0.1	1.0	0.24
Case 2		1	2	3	4	
$\lambda_1 = 2.117$	1	1.0				0.87
$\theta = 0.70$	2	0.6	1.0			0.80
$\alpha = 0.68$	3	0.5	0.4	1.0		0.72
	4	0.3	0.2	0.1	1.0	0.44
Case 3		1	2	3	4	
$\lambda_1 = 2.310$	1	1.0				0.81
$\theta = 0.756$	2	0.6	1.0			0.80
$\alpha = 0.754$	3	0.5	0.4	1.0		0.76
	4	0.3	0.4	0.4	1.0	0.66
Case 4		1	2	3		
$\lambda_1 = 2.004$	1	1.0				0.87
$\theta = 0.75$	2	0.6	1.0			0.82
$\alpha = 0.75$	3	0.5	0.4	1.0		0.76

remaining items in a set. Nonetheless we can see that theta is always larger than alpha.

Case 4 shows the statistics for a scale formed by the first three items alone. It is clear that the three-item scale in case 4 is more reliable than the weighted four-item scale in cases 1 and 2 ($\theta = 0.75$ compared to 0.68 and 0.70), and it is almost as reliable as the four-item scale in case 3. In other words, even though factor scores give less weight to the weak items and produce a more reliable scale than a simple unweighted summation, an even higher reliability may be obtained by throwing out weak items altogether.

This fourth case motivates the procedure that I call factor scaling. In some cases the highest reliability is obtained by forming the scale using only items that load highest on a given factor. A scale so formed is called a factor scale to distinguish it from factor scores. Although there is no precise rule to define the highest loadings, experience has shown that items with loadings below 0.3 should be excluded. Items in the 0.3 to 0.4 range are generally borderline; that is, sometimes they increase reliability and sometimes they decrease it, but usually they do not affect it in any appreciable way.

One practical consequence of constructing scales by using only the highest-loading items is that theta and alpha do not often differ by any important degree. This means that one can use the simple, unweighted sum of the item scores for the composite scale without sacrificing reliability. This procedure is only valid, of course, when the items used do not have widely differing factor loadings. Whether one uses the unweighted sums or refactors to get factor scores for the subset of items to be used in the scale is mainly a matter of convenience.

I must issue one important caution at this point. The most reliable scale for one sample of subjects may not correspond to the most reliable scale for another sample. When I suggest that throwing out items may produce a more reliable scale, this holds only in the context of a single sample. If one is building a scale of some type (rather than analyzing data from a particular sample), many samples and many factor analyses must be taken before a final scale can be derived. In this case a "bad" item is one that shows consistently poor factor loadings across different samples. Nonetheless when one is analyzing data from a particular sample and scales are being used, there is no reason not to exclude weak items for that analysis even though they may be maintained when collecting data from other samples.

Multiple-Factor Case

In the event that a set of items measures more than one dimension, the method of factor scaling requires some extension. Although the scaling operations themselves are similar to those for the single-factor case, the mathematical elegance is somewhat diminished if there is more than one factor. The reasons have to do with the nonuniqueness of the rotational methods that are used to interpret a multiple-factor analysis. Given two or more clusters of intercorrelating items, the principal-component solution is not suitable for factor scaling because it maximizes the variance of the first factor, then the second factor after the first factor variance is removed, and so on. Therefore, given two or more independent clusters of items, unless the clusters are perfectly uncorrelated (which is seldom the case) the first factor will pick up more variance than it should.

Figure 1 gives a geometric interpretation of this problem. Without rotation the first factor consists of strong and positive loadings by all items whereas the second factor is bipolar with both positive and negative loadings. The rotated solution associates each factor with one subset of items or the other, facilitating both interpretation and scaling. I want to stress that rotation is not advocated only as a convenience. As we shall see in the real-data example in a later section, rotation can be crucial for identification of those clusters of items that produce the most reliable scales.

Given a set of m principal-component factor loadings $a_{i1}, a_{i2}, \cdots, a_{im}$ and their associated roots $\lambda_1, \lambda_2, \cdots, \lambda_m$ from a set of p items ($1 < m < p$), a new set of rotated loadings $a^*_{i1}, a^*_{i2}, \cdots, a^*_{im}$ and scores $f^*_{1j}, \cdots, f^*_{mj}$ can be found by applying an arbitrary orthogonal transformation to the original loadings and scores. With one exception the rotated loadings and scores have all the properties of the unrotated loadings and scores: they are statistically independent; taken together they explain the same amount of the total variation; and they reproduce the original correlation matrix to the same extent. The exception is that the sum of squares of the loadings $\lambda^*_1, \cdots, \lambda^*_p$ (where $\lambda^*_k = \sum_i a^*_{ik}$) do not equal the original roots. That is, we can say that $\sum_{k=1}^{m} \lambda_k = \sum_{k=1}^{m} \lambda^*_k$ but we also have that $\lambda_k \neq \lambda^*_k$. This means that although the amount of variance accounted for by m factors is invariant under arbitrary orthogonal rotations, the portion of variance attributable to each factor is not. Obviously, then, the scales derived as well as their reliabilities differ depending on the rotational solution. The only way to achieve some standardization at this stage is to specify the rotation method when scales and reliabilities are presented.

Although many different rotational schemes have been devised (Harmon, 1967), the varimax method seems to be the most widely used orthogonal solution at the present time, and it is the one I shall assume throughout. The varimax method rotates all m factors until the factor

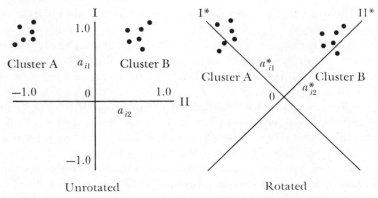

Figure 1. Geometric representation of unrotated and rotated factors.

loadings on all factors attain maximum variance. This means that each factor has items with either very high or very low loadings (in absolute value) within the constraints imposed by the total variance of the loadings. Since this solution tends to give the most satisfactory alignment of factors with clusters of items, given the requirement of factor independence, it seems the most suitable solution for factor scaling.

The most difficult issue by far for most analysts has to do with the number of factors m to extract and rotate. Clearly this number drastically affects the nature and reliability of the scales produced. Unfortunately, however, no single analytic method can solve this problem precisely. About all I can offer here are three rules that may aid the decision.

First, no factor should be used if its root is near to or less than 1. Since factor analysis works on standardized items, the variance of a single item is 1. Therefore a factor whose root is near to 1 explains no more variance than a single item.

Second, after the mth root, if the $m + 1$th and successive roots are fairly equal except for a gradual tapering-off, then m factors should probably be used (or at least rotated for interpretation). A large drop from one root to another followed by slightly decreasing roots usually marks the end of meaningful factors and the beginning of error or specific variance components. There are statistical tests available for testing equality of the remaining roots after m have been extracted, but they depend heavily on sample size and may be of limited use in large sociological studies (Lawley and Maxwell, 1963).

Third, in many sociological studies with inter-item correlations ranging from 0.3 to 0.5, an m that accounts for 40 to 60 percent of the total variance is a good solution. In this context it can be pointed out that, for ten items, single-factor solutions which account for no more than 35 percent of the total variance can produce scale reliabilities on the order of 0.8.[13]

Aside from these rules of thumb, most careful analysts rotate successive numbers of factors until they find a solution that is substantively meaningful and interpretable. Obviously this last criterion is as important as the others.

Given a satisfactory solution of m factors as in the single-factor case, there are two major ways in which to construct scales and compute reliabilities. One method is based on the rotated factor scores; the other uses factor scales based on the highest loading items.

For principal-component factor analysis, factor scores for the rotated factor loadings cannot be computed with a simple formula such as Equation (12). Nevertheless factor scores are usually provided by most computer programs for principal-component analysis. The procedure involves rotating the original factor scores using the same orthogonal transformation matrix that is derived for rotating the factor loadings.

Given rotated factor scores f_{kj}^*, a reliability coefficient can be computed for each factor k by applying the general formula for theta-star given in Equation (10). It must be stressed that these reliabilities are not unique, however, since they depend on a given number of factors and on a given rotational method. I also stress that these reliabilities are generally significantly lower than those obtained by factor scaling.

As illustrated in the single-factor case, even better reliabilities can be obtained by forming scales using only the items that load highly on a given factor. This method is even more important in the multiple-factor case since the existence of two or more rotated factors guarantees that each factor will have many items with loadings close to zero. The set of items that loads highly on each factor (say, above 0.40 or so with no higher loadings on other factors) is taken to form a scale. Since this approach guarantees relatively equal factor loadings (that is, equal item weights), simple unweighted summed scales can be constructed; alpha reliability can then be computed as a close approximation to theta. Alternatively each subset of items can be refactored for a single-factor solution; both factor scores and theta can then be obtained. Items that load high on two or more factors should be excluded if one desires to maintain scale independence.

Although the method of factor scaling generally produces the most reliable scales, there is a disadvantage in that the scales will not

---

[13] The relationship between theta and the proportion of variance explained by the first factor (say, P_1) is given by $P_1 = 1/[p - \theta(p - 1)]$. This can be used in conjunction with differing numbers of items to see what proportion of variance should be explained by the first factor to attain a given theta reliability.

necessarily be orthogonal (uncorrelated). If the cluster of items that defines a factor is somewhat related to another cluster, however, this correlation is probably meaningful. If the correlation becomes too large, of course, it may mean that a smaller number of factors will be a better solution from the perspective of scalability that we have developed.

Rather than giving hypothetical examples to illustrate the multiple-factor case, I shall turn immediately to an example using real data. The issues we have been discussing should be made clear by way of this complete illustration.

EXAMPLE OF FACTOR SCALING

To this point my comparison of factor and covariance scaling has been primarily theoretical rather than empirical. In order to show how to apply these ideas and how to see differences between the two methods, this section presents a full example using real data.

The data are drawn from a survey of college professors' views and behavior regarding the Vietnam War (Armor and others, 1967). A set of 13 attitude items was designed to measure political ideology along a general conservative-liberal dimension. The intention was to construct an attitude scale to measure political liberalism so that political ideology could be related to feelings about the Vietnam War. Although it was known that political ideology is not a unidimensional construct in national cross-sections, the special nature of the sample led to an expectation that there would be a single liberal-conservative dimension in this case. Since the original intention was to create a single scale, it is a particularly appropriate example for comparing unidimensional covariance scaling with multidimensional factor scaling.

Covariance Scaling

Table 5 shows the item wordings along with a number of statistics used in the construction of a covariance scale. All items were scored originally on a 1 to 5 agree-disagree continuum with 5 indicating "strongly agree"; items marked with a minus sign have been reverse-scored so that all items are scored in the same direction (that is, agreeing means more liberal). In addition only respondents who had no missing observations on any of the 13 items were included in the analysis.

If an analyst considered item face content alone, without consideration of the quantitative item-analysis information shown in Table 5, and developed a 13-item scale by a straight summation of item score, the alpha reliability would be 0.72 using Equation (7). The alpha reliability based on $\bar{r}$ (standardized items) is slightly higher in this case (0.73).

TABLE 5
Covariance Scaling for Political Ideology Scale[a]

(a) Item-Scale Correlations

	Item[b]	Uncorrected[c]	Corrected[d]	Reliabilities
1	War is not justifiable under any circumstances	0.608	0.483	$\alpha = 0.72$ for 13-item summed scale [Equation (7); $\sigma_s^2 = 64.95$]
2	Labor unions in large corporations should be given a major part in deciding company policy	0.557	0.428	$\alpha = 0.73$ for 13-item standardized scale [Equation (6); $\bar{r} = 0.163$]
(−)3	A democratic form of government is a superior system to any other yet devised	0.073	−0.062	$\alpha = 0.72$ for 12-item summed scale eliminating item 3 [Equation (7); $\sigma_s^2 = 64.85$]
4	Socialized medicine would be a better way to provide health services than our present system	0.503	0.384	
5	It is up to the government to make sure that everyone has a secure job and a good standard of living	0.434	0.289	
(−)6	It is never wise to introduce changes rapidly, in government or in the economic system	0.367	0.213	
(−)7	In taking part in any form of world organization, this country should make certain that none of its independence and power is lost	0.397	0.255	
(−)8	Unfortunate as it may be, war is sometimes necessary	0.535	0.411	
9	An occupation by a foreign power is better than a nuclear war	0.604	0.481	

(−)10 In general, complete economic security is bad; most men wouldn't work if they didn't need money for eating and living
 11 War could always be avoided
(−)12 Nationalization of the basic industries would lead to an intolerable degree of governmental control
 13 Nationalization of the basic industries would lead to a more equitable distribution of wealth

(b) Correlations[d], Means, and Variance

	1	2	3	4	5	6	7	8	9	10	11	12	13	Means	Variances
1	1.000													2.385	1.889
2	0.223	1.000												2.808	1.749
3	0.014	−0.048	1.000											1.798	1.172
4	0.103	0.334	−0.028	1.000										3.779	1.339
5	0.018	0.315	−0.261	0.324	1.000									3.144	1.697
6	−0.027	0.197	0.088	0.115	0.118	1.000								3.529	1.766
7	0.261	0.207	−0.121	0.005	0.010	0.193	1.000							3.817	1.568
8	0.771	0.197	−0.011	0.059	−0.028	−0.149	0.226	1.000						2.115	1.540
9	0.439	0.115	−0.039	0.325	0.119	0.187	0.260	0.322	1.000					3.250	1.782
10	0.036	0.305	0.005	0.156	0.388	0.244	0.106	0.024	0.065	1.000				3.654	1.821
11	0.622	0.062	−0.043	0.112	0.023	−0.159	0.045	0.579	0.354	−0.020	1.000			2.587	1.934
12	0.588	0.228	0.033	0.329	0.392	0.266	0.177	0.049	0.197	0.387	−0.067	1.000		3.048	1.833
13	0.200	0.314	0.023	0.356	0.227	0.202	0.077	0.249	0.370	0.266	0.147	0.458	1.000	2.865	1.555

[a] $N = 104$ for all statistics.
[b] All items scored on a 1 to 5 agree-disagree scale; reversed items indicated by a minus sign.
[c] Item contribution included.
[d] Significance levels: $r \geq 0.19$ significant at 0.05 level; $r \geq 0.25$ significant at 0.01 level.

A consideration of item-to-scale correlations reveals a substantially lower (and nonsignificant) correlation for item 3. Even if this item is eliminated, however, the alpha reliability of the summed scale based on the remaining 12 items would be unchanged. The remaining items all have significant and fairly consistent item-to-scale correlations; it is unlikely, based on these statistics, that an investigator would change the scale beyond dropping item 3.

The inter-item correlations give more detail about the item relationships and show the problem with item 3: it has a large (and significant) negative correlation with item 4 and generally negligible correlations with the remaining variables. This clearly lowers the average correlation, although in this case not enough to affect alpha reliability significantly. In spite of the item-to-scale correlations, it is apparent from the correlation matrix that a number of the items have low correlations and that some even have slightly negative correlations. A careful inspection of the pairwise correlations might reveal other items that should be eliminated or combined separately to form subscales. Rather than undertaking this tedious job, however, we turn to factor scaling for a more precise and compact method of examining the pattern of relations among the items.

Factor Scaling

The relevant statistics for factor scaling are presented in Table 6. I shall discuss only the first two factors, which account for about 43 percent of the total variance. Because the third root was close to 1 ($\lambda_3 = 1.236$), it was decided to consider at most the first two factors.

If we adopt a single-factor solution, we should focus on the principal-component loadings for the first unrotated factor. The first root is 3.29, accounting for about 25 percent of the total variance. As we can see from the first column of Table 6, there is considerable variation in the item contributions to the first factor. The loadings range from -0.08 for item 3 to 0.65 for item 1. These differences result in a higher reliability for a 13-item scale based on the factor I scores, which take item weighting into account. Theta is 0.75 for the factor I scores, compared to an alpha of 0.72 for the 13-item summed scale. Since in this example only one item is truly weak, the difference between alpha and theta is not great. Obviously the difference between alpha and theta depends on how many "bad" items occur in a set of items being used for a scale.

Rather than exploring other combinations of first-factor items to discover the best single scale, we must consider rejecting the single-factor hypothesis. The second root is fairly large ($\lambda_2 = 2.32$, 18 percent

TABLE 6
Factor Scaling for Political Ideology Scale[a]

Item[b]	Unrotated Principal-Component Loadings		Rotated Loadings	
	I	II	I*	II*
1	0.650	−0.615	0.032	−0.895
2	0.553	0.247	0.567	−0.212
3	−0.082	−0.030	−0.080	0.036
4	0.523	0.283	0.571	−0.165
5	0.438	0.477	0.647	0.033
6	0.262	0.450	0.502	0.137
7	0.377	−0.058	0.228	−0.306
8	0.593	−0.636	−0.023	−0.869
9	0.637	−0.184	0.325	−0.578
10	0.425	0.472	0.634	0.038
11	0.483	−0.637	−0.103	−0.793
12	0.535	0.504	0.735	−0.016
13	0.648	0.217	0.613	−0.300
Roots	$\lambda_1 = 3.289$	$\lambda_2 = 2.322$	$\lambda_1^* = 2.813$	$\lambda_2^* = 2.798$
Percent of total variance	25.3%	17.9%	21.7%	21.5%

Reliabilities

Factor Scores
θ = 0.75   for factor scores based on unrotated factor I
θ_1^* = 0.70   for factor scores based on rotated factor I*
θ_2^* = 0.70   for factor scores based on rotated factor II*

Factor Scales
θ_1' = 0.74   for socialism scale based on items 2, 4–6, 10, 12, and 13 [α_1' = 0.73 using Equation (6)]
θ_2' = 0.85   for pacifism scale based on items 1, 8, and 11 [α_2' = 0.85 using Equation (6)]

[a] N = 104 for all statistics.
[b] See Table 5 for item wording.

of the total variance), and a number of items have higher loadings on factor II than on factor I (namely, items 5, 6, 8, 10, and 11). Therefore we must examine the two-factor solution. For the two-factor hypothesis the rotated loadings must be inspected in order to obtain a more accurate interpretation. These are shown in columns I* and II* in Table 6.

The rotated loadings clearly reveal two relatively orthogonal clusters of items (see Figure 2 for a geometric representation). The cluster of items (2, 4–6, 10, 12, 13) that largely determines factor I* has content concerned mainly with economic issues (the sole exception being item 6); the items that determine factor II* (1, 8, 11) deal with the issue

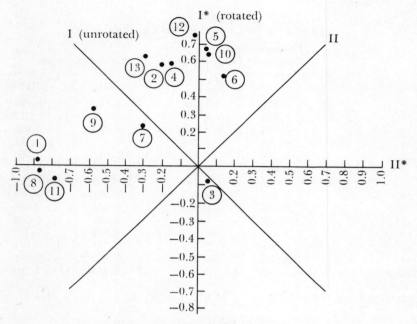

Figure 2. Factor plot for the political ideology items.

of war. Item 3 (attitude toward democracy) and item 7 (maintenance of U.S. power) do not load substantially on either factor. Item 9 ("better red than dead") falls between the two clusters. Accordingly we shall say that factor I* represents a socialism dimension and that factor II* represents a pacifism dimension. This distinction certainly makes sense conceptually, although in the original study this two-factor prediction was not made in advance of seeing the factor analysis.

Aside from the conceptual advantages of the two-factor solution, there are some important quantitative advantages as well. First, the two-factor solution accounts for substantially more variance than the single-factor solution, with each factor accounting for a little more than 21 percent of the total variance. Second, scale reliabilities can be increased substantially. The θ^* reliabilities for the scales based on the full 13-item factor scores are somewhat lower than the unrotated factor I, with theta-star 0.70 for both. If we are guided by the highest rotated loadings in Table 6 and clusters shown in Figure 2, however, and if we refactor items 2, 4–6, 10, 12, and 13 for the socialism scale and items 1, 8, and 11 for the pacifism scale, we then have θ' reliabilities of 0.74 and 0.85. The reliability of the socialism scale is slightly higher than the original 13-item alpha reliability; the pacifism scale reliability is considerably larger. Moreover the alpha reliabilities for these two subscales are 0.73 and 0.85, so that weighted scoring is unnecessary and either alpha or theta can be used to estimate reliability.

In effect the factor analysis enables us to find two relatively homogeneous clusters of items that can be used to construct two independent subscales which closely approximate the basic assumptions behind the alpha coefficient.

A slightly more reliable scale ($\theta = 0.75$) can be obtained by adding items 7 and 9 to the factor I* scale, but this does not seem justifiable in view of the large loading that item 9 has on factor II*. Moreover this raises the correlation between the two subscales from 0.09 (indicating practically independent scales) to 0.20. Adding item 9 to the factor II* scale substantially reduces the latter's reliability. Basically Figure 2 shows that items 7 and 9 fall between the two major clusters and that their inclusion in one scale or the other either decreases reliability or does not sufficiently increase reliability to justify the resultant loss of scale independence.

This example makes it clear that factor scaling can substantially improve scale reliability, particularly when multiple dimensions are present. Reliability can be improved in a single-factor case by identification of items that do not contribute to the central dimension. But whenever multiple dimensions are present, factor scaling is even more important. In the multiple-factor case the reliability of factor scores is often considerably lower than the reliability of factor scales (other things being equal). In the present example the rotated factor score reliabilities were 0.70 each; they were improved to 0.74 and to 0.85 when factor scales were constructed. These factor scales had one further advantage: it made little difference whether alpha (unweighted) or theta (weighted) coefficients were used to estimate reliability.

Validity

I have stated that the ultimate test of the importance of a scale is not simply its internal consistency. The acid test of a sociological measure is its validity; that is, whether it is related to other, external sociological variables within the framework of a model. If scale reliability is important and if we believe that we have enhanced the conceptual clarity and reliability of our measure of political ideology, we should be able to show improved relationships with other variables.

I mentioned that the purpose of building a political ideology scale was to relate it to support for or opposition to the Vietnam War. Using a scale to measure attitudes on Vietnam, we can test the relative validity of the covariance and factor approaches by comparing the predictive power of the original 13-item summed scale with the socialism and pacifism scales derived by the method of factor scaling.

The Vietnam War scale is scored so that a high score indicates strong support for the war and a low score denotes strong opposition. The regression results can be summarized as follows:

		R^2 with Vietnam War Scale
1.	Covariance scaling: 13-item summed scale	0.26
2.	Factor scaling: pacifism scale alone	0.25
	pacifism plus socialism scale	0.30

In other words the model that uses the two more reliable scales raises the explained variance from 26 to 30 percent for our external variable. This is direct evidence that the use of factor scaling to develop more reliable scales can have a substantial impact on the test of a model, even when a covariance scale has an acceptable level of reliability.

COMPARISON OF THETA AND OMEGA

Before concluding it is necessary to make a few comments about the relationship between theta and *omega*, a new reliability coefficient proposed by Heise and Bohrnstedt (1971). Their work represents an important contribution to understanding the relationship between factor analysis and reliability. They take a unique approach by using the technique of path analysis together with traditional factor analysis to derive measures of reliability and validity. At the moment we are most interested in their omega, which like theta is based on factor analysis.

Assuming standardized items for convenience, the formula for omega reliability is

$$\Omega = \left(\sum_{i \neq j} r_{ij} + \sum_i h_i^2\right) \Big/ \left(\sum_{i \neq j} r_{ij} + p\right) \tag{25}$$

where h_i^2 is the communality of item i. The major difficulty in relating omega and theta stems from the reliance of omega on the concept of communality h_i^2. In the classic theory of factor analysis, communality is defined as that component of an item's variance shared in common with the remaining set of items being factor-analyzed. It is to be distinguished from unique variance—that part of an item's variation due to the item alone (including error components). Unfortunately, since the communality depends on the number of factors extracted there is no analytic method for computing a unique, invariant communality for each item. That is, since the communality for item i is defined as

$$h_i^2 = a_{i1}^2 + a_{i2}^2 + \cdots + a_{im}^2 \tag{26}$$

(where the a_{ik} are derived from a common-factor solution and not a principal-component solution) or the sum of squares of the factor loadings of an item on the m factors extracted, we do not have an invariant h_i^2 unless the number of factors m is also invariant. But as I have pointed out, the number of meaningful factors cannot be determined analytically; it depends on the type of factor analysis used and, most of all, on interpretive judgments made by the analyst. Thus for the same set of items omega differs from one analysis to another depending on the method and investigator. In general the greater the number of factors extracted, the greater the omega coefficient.

Since experienced social scientists have acquired a high tolerance for ambiguity, the variant properties of omega may not be viewed as serious ones. There is, however, a second and more serious difference between omega and theta. We have seen that there is no restriction on the hypothesized number of factors for omega. But if an analyst decides there are really two or more independent factors in a set of items, each factor should result in a separate scale. That is the whole point of applying factor analysis in the first place. From the standpoint of reliability theory and covariance scaling, there is no more justification in combining uncorrelated clusters of items into a single scale than there is in combining a set of uncorrelated individual items into a single scale. Thus omega does not assess the reliability of separate scales in the event of multiple dimensions.

The comparison of omega and theta can be done meaningfully only if we consider the single-factor case. In addition it is important to stress that the h_i^2 for omega depends on a common-factor solution, such as the maximum-likelihood method (Lawley and Maxwell, 1963). The a_i^2 obtained from a principal-component solution should not be used in Equation (26) to estimate the h_i^2. If this is done the omega formula results in a reliability estimate that is spuriously high.[14]

Assuming that these conditions are met, what can we say about the difference between omega and theta? First, practical experience with common-factor and principal-component solutions reveals few differences between the relative magnitudes of the factor loadings. That is, although the loadings differ in absolute value both methods generally rank the items in the same order with respect to their contribution to the first factor. Thus if a scale is formed by taking the items with the highest loadings, both methods should result in similar scales. Second, experience also indicates that the values of omega and theta are generally comparable, with variations usually under 0.01. The main point to

---

[14] If all intercorrelations equal r, then α, θ, and Ω should be equal. But using principal-component loadings gives $\Omega = \alpha + (1-r)/\rho\lambda_1$, making $\Omega > \alpha$ or θ unless $r = 1$.

remember is that the theta formula should be used with principal-component analysis and that omega should be used with common-factor solutions assuming a single-factor hypothesis.

SUMMARY

We have reviewed the classic method of covariance scaling, outlining the steps that investigators should take to develop a composite measure of some sociological construct. Although the basic idea of covariance scaling is sound, since it is more appropriate for many sociological concepts than other scaling methods, it has several weaknesses in the traditional ways it is applied to sociological variables. Such steps as item-to-scale correlations and alpha reliability do not take proper account of varying item contributions to a construct, and they cannot uncover the existence of multiple, independent constructs that might be present in a set of items. Theta reliability and factor scaling, based on traditional principal-component factor analysis, is offered as a method of improving scale reliability and conceptual clarity. It presents a means of discovering multidimensionality and allows items to relate differentially to these dimensions. These methods have the advantage of connecting multidimensional scaling closely to the traditional concepts of measurement reliability and scalability.

Perhaps the best way to summarize the technique of factor scaling is to list the steps an investigator can follow when applying the technique for improving scale reliability.

First, select a set of variables that represents a domain within which one or more scales or indices is predicted.

Second, omit any subjects (or other units of analysis) with missing observations for the purpose of factor scaling and reliability computation (factor analysis with mean substitution for missing data gives a good approximation).

Third, apply a principal-component factor analysis, extracting factors until either the roots approach 1 or the roots begin to taper off by approximately equal decrements. Only rarely will it be necessary to take more than four or five factors; even fewer is the norm.

Fourth, if a single-factor hypothesis is supported by the factors, the unrotated first-factor loadings can be used for interpreting the scale. If regular factor scores are used to create the scale, the theta formula of Equation (9) should be used for reliability.

Fifth, if the factor reveals items with small loadings (say, under 0.3 or 0.4) higher reliabilities can be obtained by eliminating the weak items altogether. In this case a simple summed scale can be created (assuming approximately equal item variances; if not, items should be standardized) and alpha reliability can be computed for a reliability estimate. Alternatively the subset can be refactored in order to obtain factor scores and the corresponding theta coefficients.

Sixth, if a multiple-factor solution is suggested on either conceptual or empirical grounds, rotations of two or more factors should be done (using the varimax or some similar method) until an interpretable solution is obtained. Although the rotated factor scores can be used for scales with reliabilities computed according to Equation (10), reliabilities may be substantially higher if only the highest-loaded items on each factor are used for scales. In this case, as with single-factor solutions, scales can be constructed by simple summation and reliability estimates can be made using alpha; alternatively each subset can be refactored for factor scores and theta.

I close with several cautions. First, reliability as we have discussed it pertains only to the internal consistency of a scale. High reliability is no guarantee, in and of itself, of a useful and meaningful construct. Second, there are several other rationales for multidimensional scaling and the covariance model may not be the best one for all sociological applications. In particular, although nonmetric multidimensional scaling is not tied closely to reliability theory there may be applications where reliability (as defined) is not of primary concern and where the nonmetric methods are more appropriately tailored to the problem at hand.

Finally, even if an analyst finds the assumptions of factor scaling suited to his problem he cannot be certain that factor scaling will improve his scaling problem. On the one hand the experienced sociologist who is especially sensitive to the substantive measurement issues in his field of interest may be able to construct highly reliable scales with little or no quantitative assistance (although he may want to have a check on his intuition!). On the other hand factor scaling cannot produce reliable constructs out of a hodge-podge of items assembled without regard to conceptual domain and content. The view presented here is that factor scaling is a quantitative adjunct to scientific intuition and judgment that makes it possible for all analysts—not just the particularly sensitive ones—to produce comparable results.

REFERENCES

ARMOR, D. J. AND OTHERS
    1967   "Professors' attitudes toward the Vietnam war." *Public Opinion Quarterly* (Summer):159–175.

BUTLER, P. M.
    1968   "Alpha-maximized factor analysis and its relation to alpha and cannonical factor analysis." *Psychometrika* 33 (March):335–346.

BLALOCK, H. M., JR.
    1969 "Multiple indicators and the causal approach to measurement error." *American Journal of Sociology* 75 (September):264–272.

BOHRNSTEDT, G. W.
    1969 "A quick method for determining the reliability and validity of multiple-item scales." *American Sociological Review* 34 (August):542–548.

CRONBACH, L. J.
    1951 "Coefficient alpha and the internal structure of tests." *Psychometrika* 16 (September):297–334.
    1960 *Essentials of Psychological Testing.* (2nd ed.) New York: Harper & Row.

EDWARDS, A. L.
    1957 *Techniques of Attitude Scale Construction.* New York: Appleton Century Crofts.

GUILFORD, J. P.
    1954 *Psychometric Methods.* New York: McGraw-Hill.

HARMAN, H. H.
    1967 *Modern Factor Analysis.* (2nd ed.) Chicago: University of Chicago Press.

HEISE, D. R.
    1969 "Separating reliability and stability in test-retest correlations." *American Sociological Review* 34 (February):93–101.

HEISE, D. R. AND BOHRNSTEDT, G. W.
    1971 "Validity, invalidity, and reliability." Pp. 104–129 in E. F. Borgatta (Ed.), *Sociological Methodology.* San Francisco: Jossey-Bass.

LAWLEY, D. N. AND MAXWELL, A. E.
    1963 *Factor Analysis as a Statistical Method.* London: Butterworth.

LORD, F. M.
    1958 "Some relations between Guttman's principal components of scale analysis and other psychometric theory." *Psychometrika* (December):291–296.

LORD, F. M. AND NOVICK, M. R.
    1968 *Statistical Theories of Mental Test Scores.* Reading, Mass.: Addison-Wesley.

NOVICK, M. R. AND LEWIS, C.
    1967 "Coefficient alpha and the reliability of composite measurements." *Psychometrika* 32 (March):1–13.

SIEGEL, P. M. AND HODGE, R. W.
    1968 "A causal approach to the study of measurement error." In H. M. Blalock, Jr. and A. B. Blalock (Eds.), *Methodology in Social Research.* New York: McGraw-Hill.

UPSHAW, H. S.
    1968 "Attitude measurement." In H. M. Blalock, Jr. and A. B. Blalock (Eds.), *Methodology in Social Research.* New York: McGraw-Hill.

3

CONSTRUCTION OF COMPOSITE MEASURES BY THE CANONICAL-FACTOR-REGRESSION METHOD

Michael Patrick Allen
WASHINGTON STATE UNIVERSITY

This is an extended version of a paper presented to the Methodology Section of the American Sociological Association at the 1973 annual meeting in New York. The author is indebted to David R. Heise, Herbert L. Costner, Arthur S. Goldberger, Hubert M. Blalock, and Lois MacGillivray for their critical and constructive comments on earlier versions of this paper. Any errors, of course, are the sole responsibility of the author.

One of the persistent problems in the construction of causal models in the social sciences involves the inevitable gap between empirical measures and theoretical constructs (Blalock, 1968). This problem is often complicated by the presence of significant measurement error. In order to assess the epistemic relationship between particular observed variables and given unobserved constructs, sociologists have formulated explicit measurement models (Siegel and Hodge, 1968; Costner, 1969; Blalock, 1969). These models typically proceed from the assumption that there exist a number of observed variables which can be considered indicators of any particular theoretical construct. One common methodological strategy in such a situation involves the construction of a composite measure or scale comprised of a linear combination of the scores on the observed variables. Composite measures are especially useful in the presence of multicollinearity when the observed indicator variables are highly correlated with one another. Once such a composite measure has been constructed it is possible to include it as a variable in the regression equations of a causal model. Although this strategy is fairly common in practice, the methodological implications of this approach are largely unexplored. In particular, procedures for constructing composite measures that are optimal in terms of reliability and validity have not been employed extensively in sociological research.

Two strategies are available for constructing composite measures that are optimal in the sense of being both maximally reliable and maximally valid. The first strategy is to construct an unweighted linear composite comprised of only the most reliable and valid observed indicator variables. This is by far the most common strategy for constructing composite measures in sociological research. It presupposes the existence of some objective criteria for assessing the reliability and validity of each observed variable. The second strategy is to construct a weighted linear composite in which each observed variable is weighted in accordance with its reliability and validity. This strategy is employed primarily in psychometric research. It requires not only some criteria for assessing the reliability and validity of each observed variable but also a mathematical function for assigning differential linear weights to those variables. Actually it is apparent that the first strategy is simply a special case of the second in the sense that the selected variables are assigned unit weights and the eliminated variables are assigned zero weights. Moreover both strategies typically resort to the same set of criteria for assessing the reliability and validity of each observed indicator variable. The most common criteria are those that involve the application of factor analysis (Nunnally, 1967).

Factor analysis can be characterized as a set of procedures by which the correlations among a set of observed variables are accounted for in terms of a fewer number of unobserved variables or common factors (Harman, 1967, pp. 11-28). The first common factor for a set of observed variables is generally defined to be that unobserved variable which accounts for a greater proportion of the correlation among the observed variables than any subsequent factor. This definition implies that the first factor has higher correlations with the observed variables than any subsequent factor, when the common factors are uncorrelated with one another. When the observed variables are explicitly chosen to be indicators of the same theoretical construct, it is reasonable to conclude that the first common factor corresponds in some sense to the theoretical construct of interest. This interpretation of the first common factor is based on the assumption that the theoretical construct of interest is the primary source of the correlation among the observed indicator variables. Given this interpretation of the first common factor, one obvious criterion to be maximized through the use of a set of differential linear weights for the observed variable scores is the correlation between the resultant composite score and the unobserved score on the first common factor. This is precisely the rationale for the various methods of factor-score estimation (Harman, 1967, pp. 345–374).

In the course of this discussion a method is presented for constructing factor-analytic composite measures. In particular, equations are presented for a set of linear weights which are optimal in the sense that they yield a composite measure which is optimally reliable subject to the condition that it is maximally valid with respect to the first common factor. These optimal weights correspond directly to the linear weights associated with the regression method of factor-score estimation (Thurstone, 1935; Thomson, 1939). The application of the proposed method presupposes, however, that the factors have been obtained from a canonical factor analysis model (Rao, 1955; Harris, 1962). It is well known that canonical factor analysis yields common factors that are maximally related to the observed variables, subject to the condition that subsequent factors are uncorrelated with one another. Canonical factors also possess properties that are optimal for the purposes of constructing factor score estimates (Harris, 1967; McDonald and Burr, 1967). Furthermore this method yields relatively simple equations for the reliability coefficient and the validity coefficient for a composite measure based on these optimal weights. This reliability coefficient is interpretable as the proportion of first-factor variance in the composite score; the validity coefficient is interpretable as the correlation between the composite score and the unobserved first factor score. Consequently the validity coefficient is defined as the square root of the reliability coefficient, which is the relationship between validity and reliability often adopted by classical test theory (Lord and Novick, 1968). Finally, the proposed method provides simplified equations for estimating directly the correlation between the composite measure and any external variable without the computations involved in constructing the composite measure score.

METHOD

It has been suggested that one basis for assigning differential linear weights to the observed variable scores in the construction of a composite measure is to choose weights that yield a composite score which is highly correlated with the first common factor score for that set of observed variables. This is one criterion considered in factor score estimation. This section presents a brief discussion of the regression method of factor score estimation as it pertains to the results of a canonical factor analysis. The justification for this method in terms of the effects these linear weights have on the reliability and validity of a composite measure is reserved for a subsequent section.

The estimation of factor scores can be viewed as an indirect procedure involving two distinct stages. In the first stage the correlations among the observed variables are used to estimate the factor pattern. This pattern consists of the matrix of factor loadings between each observed variable and each unobserved factor. These loadings can be considered as correlation coefficients between the unobserved common factors and the observed variables when the factors are orthogonal or mutually uncorrelated. In the second stage the factor pattern is used to estimate the factor scores for each member of the sample on the basis of the scores for that member on the observed variables. A path diagram of the relationship between the unobserved factor score, the observed variable scores, and the estimated factor score in the case of a single common factor is presented in Figure 1. The absence of direct paths between the observed variables indicates that they are presumed to be independent except for their mutual dependence on the common factor. Residual variance in each observed variable is attributed to a uniqueness component specific to that variable (Lawley and Maxwell, 1971, pp. 1–5).

Several methods have been developed in psychometrics for estimating factor scores. There are certain advantages and disadvantages associated with each method and no single method is universally superior (Harris, 1967). The most common procedure is the regression method (Thurstone, 1935; Thomson, 1939). This method is derived from regression theory and minimizes the discrepancy in a least-squares sense between the unobserved common factor score and the estimated factor score (Lawley and Maxwell, 1971, pp. 106–113; Harman, 1967, pp. 345–374; Rummel, 1970, pp. 433–445). The main advantage of the re-

CONSTRUCTION OF COMPOSITE MEASURES

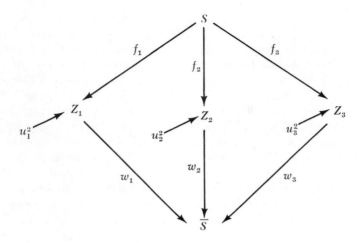

S = unobserved factor score f_i = factor loading
Z_i = observed variable score u_i^2 = residual uniqueness
$\bar{S}$ = estimated factor score w_i = linear weight

Figure 1. Path diagram of unobserved common factor score, observed variable scores, and estimated common factor score.

gression method is that the estimated factor score has a comparatively high correlation with the unobserved common factor score (McDonald and Burr, 1967). Another important property of the regression method is the relative efficiency of the resultant factor score estimates; regression method estimates have smaller variances than the estimates associated with alternative methods of factor score estimation (Maxwell, 1971). Nevertheless there are several disadvantages associated with the regression method: the factor-score estimates are not conditionally unbiased, the estimated factor scores for successive orthogonal factors are not uncorrelated, and the estimated factor scores are not uncorrelated with the successive orthogonal unobserved-factor scores (Harris, 1967; McDonald and Burr, 1967).

The main disadvantages associated with the regression method can be eliminated, however, if the initial factor pattern is obtained from a canonical factor analysis model (Rao, 1955; Harris, 1962). A maximum-likelihood factor analysis model may also be employed since it yields results similar to those obtained from a canonical factor analysis model (Jöreskog and Lawley, 1968; Lawley and Maxwell, 1971). The canonical factor analysis model defines the common factors as unobserved variables that are maximally correlated with the observed variables, subject to the condition that the factors are uncorrelated with one another (Rao, 1955). Moreover both the maximum-likelihood factor analysis model and the canonical factor analysis model impose on the factor pattern a unique restriction that has important consequences for estimated factor scores obtained from the regression method: the estimated factor scores for successive orthogonal factors are uncorrelated and the estimated factor scores are uncorrelated with the successive orthogonal unobserved-factor scores (Harris, 1967; McDonald and Burr, 1967). A path diagram of the relationship between two unobserved common factor scores, four observed variable scores, and two estimated factor scores is presented in Figure 2. The absence of certain direct paths indicates that the two unobserved factor scores are uncorrelated, the two associated factor score estimates are also uncorrelated, and the estimated factor score for each

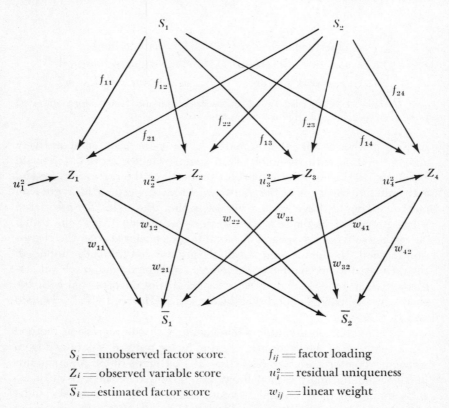

S_i = unobserved factor score f_{ij} = factor loading
Z_i = observed variable score u_i^2 = residual uniqueness
$\overline{S}_i$ = estimated factor score w_{ij} = linear weight

Figure 2. Path diagram of relationship between two uncorrelated unobserved factor scores, four observed variable scores, and two uncorrelated estimated factor scores

common factor is uncorrelated with the unobserved score on the other common factor. These properties simplify the equations for the linear weights associated with the regression method.

The equation for the linear weights derived from the canonical factor regression method (CFRM) is given by (Lawley and Maxwell, 1971, p. 107; Maxwell, 1971, p. 201; Harman, 1967, p. 363):

$$w_i = \frac{f_i/u_i^2}{1 + \Sigma(f_i^2/u_i^2)} \qquad (1)$$

where w_i is the linear weight for observed variable i, f_i is the factor loading between variable i and the first common factor, u_i^2 is the uniqueness of variable i, and the summation is over the i observed variables in the composite. Although the equations are discussed in terms of a factor score estimate for the first common factor, the unobserved score on any common factor can be estimated by employing the factor loadings between that factor and the observed variables. The uniqueness of each observed variable is defined to be equal to one minus the communality of that variable. Although the communalities are unknown initially, the communality of each observed variable is defined as the sum of its squared factor loadings on the common factors. It is important to note that each linear weight is proportional to the quantity in the numerator of Equation (1). The quantity in the denominator of Equation (1) standardizes approximately the resultant composite score. Equation (1) immediately yields the following equation for the composite measure score or factor score estimate:

$$\hat{S} = \Sigma(w_i Z_i) \qquad (2)$$

where $\hat{S}$ is the composite score or estimated score on the unobserved first common factor, w_i is the linear weight for observed variable i from Equation (1), and Z_i is the standard score on observed variable i for each member of the sample. The observed variables must be in standard form with zero means and unit variances before they can be employed to construct the CFRM composite measure. Consequently the resultant composite score has a mean of zero but a variance that is less than one (Harman, 1967, p. 358).

In addition to the advantages that the canonical factor analysis model possesses for purposes of factor score estimation, the model has important statistical properties. In particular when the observed variables are assumed to be normally distributed, the canonical factor analysis model yields maximum-likelihood estimates of the factor loadings (Rao, 1955). It has been noted that the first canonical factor is maximally related to the observed variables in the sense that it has the maximum canonical correlation with the observed variables. In this respect canonical factor analysis also provides a nonarbitrary solution to the rotation problem. The factors obtained from most factor analysis models are not unique in that the factors can be rotated by an unlimited number of orthogonal or nonorthogonal transformations (Harman, 1967, pp. 249–272). Canonical factors are unique, however, because the canonical correlation interpretation of the factors imposes an identification restriction which ensures that the canonical factors are maximally related to the observed variables (Browne, 1969). Moreover it has been suggested that the canonical factor analysis model is superior to alternative models in the usual case where the first common factor is not sufficient to account for the correlations among the observed variables, because the canonical factor analysis model minimizes a function of the residual correlations between the observed variables (Browne, 1969).

In the course of this discussion it has been shown that the canonical factor regression method of constructing composite measures possesses several important properties. First, the first canonical factor is defined as that unobserved variable which is maximally correlated with the observed variables. Second, the regression method of estimating that unobserved factor score yields a composite measure or factor score estimate which is highly correlated with the unobserved factor score and is uncorrelated with subsequent unobserved factor scores or their associated factor score estimates. Third, when the regression method of factor score estimation is employed in conjunction with the results of a canonical factor analysis model, the equation for the linear weights for constructing such a composite measure is greatly simplified. The effects that these weights have on the reliability and validity of a composite measure are discussed in the next section.

OPTIMAL RELIABILITY AND VALIDITY

It has been shown that the canonical factor regression method has several important properties for the construction of composite measures. Specifically the composite score is highly correlated with the first canonical factor and is uncorrelated with subsequent canonical factors and their associated composite scores. Moreover the first canonical factor is defined as that unobserved variable which is maximally correlated with the observed variables. This section demonstrates that the CFRM weights are optimal with respect to the reliability and validity of the resultant composite score. An empirical demonstration of the effects that the CFRM weights have on the reliability and validity of a composite measure is reserved for a subsequent section.

Any discussion of reliability and validity is immediately confronted with the fact that these concepts are defined differently within the contexts of different measurement models. Generally reliability refers to the extent to which a measure is free from measurement error; validity refers to the extent to which a measure is related to the theoretical construct of interest. The traditional measurement model in the social sciences is true score theory as it has been developed in classical test theory (Lord and Novick, 1968). In true score theory the reliability coefficient for a composite measure is defined as the ratio of true score variance to observed score variance in the composite score (Lord and Novick, 1968, pp. 203–204). The primary coefficient of reliability in true score theory is coefficient alpha (Cronbach, 1951), which is a measure of the degree of internal consistency among a set of observed variables. It has been demonstrated that coefficient alpha is only a lower bound to the actual reliability coefficient for a composite measure (Novick and Lewis, 1967). Equality between coefficient alpha and the actual reliability coefficient for a composite measure obtains only when the observed variables are assumed to be essentially tau-equivalent or when the true scores on the observed variables differ by no more than an additive constant. The validity coefficient for a composite measure is defined in true score theory as the correlation between the composite score and some observed criterion variable that corresponds to the theoretical construct of interest (Lord and Novick, 1968, pp. 261–262). In the absence of an observed criterion variable, the validity coefficient is often defined as the square root of the reliability coefficient. This interpretation implies that, since the reliability coefficient is a measure of the proportion of true score variance in a composite score, the validity coefficient is equal to the square root of the reliability coefficient or to the correlation of a composite score with itself (Lord and Novick, 1968, pp. 60–63).

True score theory is of only limited applicability to the problem of constructing composite measures in sociological research. Typically the application of true score theory requires either a relatively large number of observed indicator variables or repeated measurements on a relatively smaller number of observed indicator variables for each theoretical construct. Unfortunately neither condition is characteristic of most sociological research. Moreover true score theory does not provide a systematic solution to the problem of assigning differential linear weights to the observed variables in the construction of a composite measure; it is typically assumed that the composite measure is unweighted (McDonald, 1970).

The major alternative to true score theory is common factor theory. Instead of postulating the existence of a single true score for each observed variable score, common-factor theory implies the existence of a series of common factor scores for each observed variable score. In common factor theory the reliability coefficient is defined as the ratio of common factor variance to observed score variance in the composite measure (Cattell and Radcliffe, 1962). The primary reliability coefficient in common factor theory is coefficient omega (Heise and Bohrnstedt, 1970), which measures the proportion of common factor variance in the composite score. Similarly the validity coefficient in common factor theory is defined as the correlation between the unobserved first factor score and the composite score (Heise and Bohrnstedt, 1970). The validity coefficient does not generally equal the square root of the reliability coefficient because of invalid but reliable variance in the composite score attributable to the other common factors.

Although common factor theory provides exact equations for both the reliability coefficient and the validity coefficient for a composite measure (Heise and Bohrnstedt, 1970), these equations do not immediately yield an equation for differential linear weights that are optimal with respect to the reliability and validity of the resultant composite measure. Nevertheless it is possible to derive equations for the reliability coefficient and the validity coefficient for a composite measure constructed on the basis of the CFRM weights. The complete derivation of these equations involves matrix algebra and for that reason is presented in the appendix to this chapter. Specifically the reliability coefficient for a composite measure in which the observed variable scores are weighted in accordance with the canonical factor regression method is given by

$$\Omega_{\text{CFRM}} = \Sigma(f_i w_i) = \frac{\Sigma(f_i^2/u_i^2)}{1 + \Sigma(f_i^2/u_i^2)} \tag{3}$$

where Ω_{CFRM} is the CFRM coefficient omega, w_i is the linear weight for observed variable i, f_i is the factor loading between variable i and the first common factor, u_i^2 is the uniqueness of variable i, and the summation is over the i observed variables in the composite. Similarly the validity coefficient for a composite measure in which the observed variable scores are weighted in accordance with the canonical factor regression method is given by

$$\rho_{\text{CFRM}} = \sqrt{\Omega_{\text{CFRM}}} \tag{4}$$

where ρ_{CFRM} is the CFRM validity coefficient rho and Ω_{CFRM} is the CFRM reliability coefficient omega. In short the validity coefficient is exactly equal to the square root of the reliability coefficient when the CFRM weights are employed to construct the composite measure. This relationship between the reliability coefficient and the validity coefficient follows from the fact that the canonical factor regression method yields factor score estimates that are uncorrelated with the subsequent unobserved common factor scores and their associated factor score estimates. Although no proof is supplied it is readily verifiable that the CFRM weights yield composite scores that are maximally valid (McDonald, 1968). This means that the composite score contains no invalid but reliable variance that is attributable to other common factors.

Several important and useful interpretations can be made of the equations associated with the canonical factor regression method of constructing composite measures. First the reliability coefficient measures the proportion of the variance in the composite score that is attributable to the unobserved first common factor. Similarly the validity coefficient measures the correlation between the composite score and the unobserved score on the first common factor. Second the validity coefficient is equal to the multiple correlation coefficient between the unobserved first common factor score and the observed variable scores (Harman, 1967, p. 352). This implies that the reliability coefficient indicates the proportion of the variance in the unobserved score for the first common factor which is attributable to the observed variable scores. Third the squared linear weight for each observed variable indicates the direct contribution of that variable to the variance in the unobserved first common factor score (Harman, 1967, p. 353). Similarly the product of the linear weight and the corresponding factor loading for each observed variable indicates the total or direct and indirect contribution of that variable to the variance in the unobserved score for the first common factor. Consequently the reliability coefficient represents the sum of the direct and indirect contributions of each observed variable to the variance in the unobserved first common factor score (Harman, 1967, p. 353). Fourth the variance in the composite score is equal to the reliability coefficient since the composite score is an exact linear function of the observed-variable scores (Harman, 1967, p. 358).

The equations for composite measures constructed in accordance with the canonical factor regression method suggest several criteria for maximizing the reliability and validity of the resultant composite measure. Basically a composite measure becomes more reliable both with increases in the proportion of the variance in the observed variables that are attributable to common factors and with increases in the proportion of that common variance or communality that are directly attributable to the first common factor. Therefore the reliability of a CFRM composite measure approaches unity as all the factor loadings on the first common factor approach unity. In other words a composite measure is absolutely reliable when one common factor accounts for all the variance among a set of observed variables. Furthermore a composite measure becomes more reliable with increases in the number of observed variables that are included in the composite measure. Of course for any nonzero average factor loading, the reliability of a composite measure approaches unity as the number of observed variables in the composite measure increases to infinity. Reliability, then, is a function both of the number of observed variables included in the composite measure and of the magnitude of the factor loadings between the first common factor and those observed variables. As the number of observed variables in a composite measure increases, however, there is an increase in the number of reliable common factors. In composite measures comprised of a large number of observed variables with several reliable common factors, it is difficult to determine which common factor is to be associated with the theoretical construct of primary interest.

The relationship between the average factor loading and the number of observed variables in determining the reliability of a composite measure is presented in Table 1 for the case of a single common factor. The table gives the expected reliability coefficient of a CFRM composite measure for successively larger average factor loadings and for successively greater numbers of observed variables. Moreover the average inter-item correlation coefficient presented in Table 1 is based on the squared average factor loading since the observed variables are assumed to be uncorrelated except through their mutual dependence on

TABLE 1
Estimated Reliability Coefficients for Composite Measures by Average Factor Loading and Number of Variables for the Case of a Single Common Factor

Average Factor Loading	Number of Variables							Average Inter-Item Correlation
	4	8	12	16	20	30	40	
0.30	0.28	0.44	0.54	0.61	0.66	0.75	0.80	0.09
0.35	0.36	0.53	0.63	0.69	0.74	0.81	0.85	0.12
0.40	0.43	0.60	0.70	0.75	0.79	0.85	0.88	0.16
0.45	0.50	0.67	0.75	0.80	0.84	0.88	0.91	0.20
0.50	0.57	0.73	0.80	0.84	0.87	0.91	0.93	0.25
0.55	0.63	0.78	0.84	0.87	0.90	0.93	0.95	0.30
0.60	0.69	0.82	0.87	0.90	0.92	0.94	0.96	0.36
0.65	0.75	0.85	0.90	0.92	0.94	0.96	0.97	0.42
0.70	0.79	0.89	0.92	0.94	0.95	0.97	0.98	0.49
0.75	0.84	0.91	0.94	0.95	0.96	0.98	0.98	0.56
0.80	0.88	0.93	0.96	0.97	0.97	0.98	0.99	0.64
0.85	0.91	0.95	0.97	0.98	0.98	0.99	0.99	0.72
0.90	0.95	0.98	0.98	0.99	0.99	0.99	0.99	0.81

CONSTRUCTION OF COMPOSITE MEASURES

the single common factor. These reliability estimates are derived from a simplified form of Equation (3) given by

$$\hat{\Omega}_{\text{CFRM}} = \frac{n[\bar{f}^2/(1-\bar{f}^2)]}{1 + n[\bar{f}^2/(1-\bar{f}^2)]} \tag{5}$$

where $\hat{\Omega}_{\text{CFRM}}$ is the estimated coefficient omega, $\bar{f}^2$ is the squared average factor loading between the single common factor and the observed variables, and n is the number of observed variables in the composite measure. This same general relationship is presented graphically in Figure 3, where each curve represents the reliability function of a CFRM composite measure with a given average factor loading for successively greater numbers of observed variables. In general, composite measures comprised of a relatively small number of variables with high loadings on the first common factor are more reliable than composite measures comprised of a relatively greater number of variables with low loadings on the first common factor. This is an important property because only

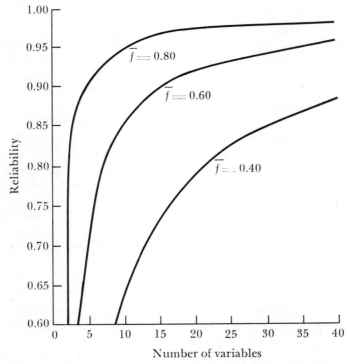

Figure 3. Estimated reliability of composite measures by average factor loading and number of variables for the case of a single common factor.

a single reliable common factor is likely to emerge from a composite measure comprised of a relatively small number of observed variables. Consequently it is somewhat easier to assign a substantive interpretation to a CFRM composite measure when it is comprised of a few observed indicator variables that are highly correlated with the first canonical factor.

It is of interest to note that, when the average inter-item correlation coefficient is substituted for the squared average factor loading, Equation (5) reduces to

$$\hat{\Omega}_{\text{CFRM}} = \alpha_1 = n\bar{r}_{ij}/[1 + (n-1)\bar{r}_{ij}] \tag{6}$$

where $\hat{\Omega}_{\text{CFRM}}$ is the estimated CFRM coefficient omega, α_1 is the coefficient alpha in the case of a single common factor, $\bar{r}_{ij}$ is the average inter-item correlation coefficient, and n is the number of observed variables included in the composite measure. This equation is known in psychometrics as the average inter-item correlation form of coefficient alpha (Nunnally, 1967, pp. 192–196). This identity between the CFRM reliability coefficient and coefficient alpha places this component of common factor theory within the mainstream of true score theory. These two coefficients are equal, however, only when two conditions obtain: first, one common factor must be sufficient to account for the correlations among the observed variables; second, the factor loadings between these variables and the single common factor must be equal. Since true score theory typically employs unweighted composite measures, coefficient alpha generally yields a lower-bound estimate to coefficient omega, the common factor theory reliability coefficient, when more than one common factor is necessary to account for the correlations among the observed variables.

The interpretation of the CFRM reliability coefficient as the squared multiple correlation coefficient between the first common factor and the observed variables yields yet another important interpretation of the reliability coefficient. This interpretation involves the problem of factor score indeterminancy (Guttman, 1955). Since factor score estimation procedures are indirect inasmuch as the scores are inferred from the correlations among the observed variables, there exist an infinite number of factor score estimates for the set of observed variables, even given the same factor pattern (Guttman, 1955, pp. 66–77). However, the degree of indeterminancy in a set of factor score estimates is inversely related to the reliability of those estimates. As the multiple correlation coefficient between the unobserved common factor and the observed variables increases, the minimal possible correlation between any two alternative factor score estimates for the same common factor also increases. Thus when a common factor is absolutely reliable, the alternative factor score estimates are perfectly correlated. Specifically the minimal possible correlation coefficient between any two alternative factor score estimates for the same common factor is given by (Guttman, 1955, pp. 73–74):

$$r_{\hat{s}\hat{s}'} = 2(\Omega_{\text{CFRM}}) - 1 \qquad (7)$$

where $r_{\hat{s}\hat{s}'}$ is the minimal possible correlation coefficient between any two alternative factor score estimates for the same common factor and Ω_{CFRM} is the CFRM reliability coefficient. This relationship between the reliability coefficient and the minimal possible correlation between alternative factor score estimates, which is presented in Table 2, suggests that the choice of a particular method of factor score estimation is immaterial when the unobserved factor score to be estimated is highly reliable. It also demonstrates the necessity for constructing composite measures that are maximally reliable.

This discussion has focused on the effect of the canonical factor regression method on the reliability and validity of the resultant composite measure. It has been shown that this method of constructing composite measures possesses certain important properties in terms of interpreting the associated reliability and validity coefficients. Moreover under certain restrictive conditions there is a direct correspondence between the common factor theory reliability coefficient (coefficient omega) and the true score theory reliability coefficient (coefficient alpha). Finally it has been demonstrated that the reliability and validity of a

TABLE 2
Relationship between Reliability Coefficient for Factor Score and Minimal Correlation between Any Two Alternative Factor Scores for Same Factor

Ω_{CFRM}	$r_{\hat{s}\hat{s}'}$	Ω_{CFRM}	$r_{\hat{s}\hat{s}'}$
1.00	1.00	0.50	0.00
0.95	0.90	0.45	−0.10
0.90	0.80	0.40	−0.20
0.85	0.70	0.35	−0.30
0.80	0.60	0.30	−0.40
0.75	0.50	0.25	−0.50
0.70	0.40	0.20	−0.60
0.65	0.30	0.15	−0.70
0.60	0.20	0.10	−0.80
0.55	0.10	0.05	−0.90

CFRM composite measure are a function both of the degree to which the observed indicator variables are correlated with the unobserved common factor and of the number of observed indicator variables included in the composite measure.

DIRECT ESTIMATION OF EXTERNAL CORRELATIONS

One important advantage of the canonical factor regression method is the simplified equation for estimating directly the correlation between the CFRM composite measure and any external variable. This equation effectively circumvents the burdensome computations involved in constructing composite measure scores from the CFRM linear weights. The only additional information required by this equation is the correlations between the observed variables in the CFRM composite measure and the external variable. The equation for the correlation between the CFRM composite measure and any external variable is (Khan, 1973; Tucker, 1971):

$$r_{\hat{S}Y} = \Sigma(r_{iY}w_i)/\sqrt{\Omega_{\text{CFRM}}} \tag{8}$$

where $r_{\hat{S}Y}$ is the correlation between the CFRM composite measure and the external variable Y, r_{iY} is the correlation between the composite measure observed variable i and the external variable Y, w_i is the CFRM linear weight for observed variable i, and the summation is over the i observed variables in the composite measure. The quantity in the denominator of Equation (8) is simply the square root of the CFRM reliability coefficient (omega). This quantity is equal to the standard deviation of the composite measure since the reliability coefficient is equal to the variance of the CFRM composite measure.

Given the correlation between the CFRM composite measure and an external variable, we can estimate directly the correlation between the external variable and the unobserved common factor score associated with the CFRM composite measure. This correlation is simply the product of the correlation between the unobserved common factor score and the CFRM composite measure score, given by Equation (4), and the correlation between the CFRM composite measure and the external variable, given by Equation (8). The correlation between an external variable and the unobserved common factor score associated with the CFRM composite measure reduces to

$$r_{SY} = \rho_{\text{CFRM}} \, r_{\hat{S}Y} = \Sigma(r_{iY}w_i) \tag{9}$$

where r_{SY} is the correlation between the external variable and the unobserved common factor score, r_{iY} is the correlation between the composite measure observed variable i and the external variable Y, w_i is the CFRM linear weight for observed variable i, and the summation is over the i observed variables in the composite measure. These equations permit the direct estimation of the correlation of a CFRM composite measure and its associated unobserved common factor score with any external variable without the computations involved in constructing the CFRM composite measure scores.

APPLICATION

The equations for the linear weights and the reliability and validity coefficients associated with the canonical factor regression method are easy to compute. Both the factor loadings between each observed variable and each unobserved factor and the communalities for each observed variable are ordinarily obtained as a matter of course in any factor analysis solution. An example of the computational procedures for obtaining the reliability coefficient is presented in Table 3. This example is based on a canonical factor analysis solution for the correlations among six attitudinal items measuring support for the war in Vietnam among a sample of 185 university students. Respondents were asked to indicate the extent of their agreement with each item by selecting one of five ordinal categories ranging from "strongly agree" to "strongly disagree." These response categories were assigned equal interval values ranging from one to five. This procedure for assigning interval values to ordinal categories entails the implicit assumption that these arbitrary equal interval values are randomly distributed about the true interval values for these response categories and that the resultant measurement error is at most random in its effects. The original correlation matrix for these six variables and their specific content are presented in Table 4.

TABLE 3
Example of Computations for CFRM Coefficient Omega

Item	f_i	f_i^2	h_i^2	u_i^2	f_i^2/u_i^2
1	0.767	0.588	0.777	0.223	2.637
2	0.727	0.529	0.697	0.303	1.746
3	0.680	0.462	0.611	0.389	1.188
4	0.724	0.524	0.692	0.308	1.701
5	0.671	0.450	0.596	0.404	1.114
6	0.688	0.473	0.624	0.376	1.258

$$\Sigma(f_i^2/u_i^2) = 9.644$$

$$\Omega_{\text{CFRM}} = \frac{\Sigma(f_i^2/u_i^2)}{1 + \Sigma(f_i^2/u_i^2)} = \frac{9.644}{10.644} = 0.906$$

TABLE 4
Correlations among Six Attitudinal Items Measuring Support of Vietnam War

	Item 1	Item 2	Item 3	Item 4	Item 5	Item 6
Item 1	1.000	0.730	0.671	0.748	0.670	0.713
Item 2	0.730	1.000	0.676	0.724	0.611	0.642
Item 3	0.671	0.676	1.000	0.627	0.607	0.645
Item 4	0.748	0.724	0.627	1.000	0.656	0.601
Item 5	0.670	0.611	0.607	0.656	1.000	0.652
Item 6	0.713	0.642	0.645	0.601	0.652	1.000

Item 1 As long as the Communists persist in their aggression against South Vietnam, America must resist that aggression.
Item 2 We must defeat the Communists in Vietnam to ensure world peace.
Item 3 The U.S. must be willing to run any risk of war which may be necessary to prevent the spread of Communism.
Item 4 War is sometimes necessary and Vietnam is such a case.
Item 5 If peace negotiations fail, we should concentrate on a complete military victory in Vietnam.
Item 6 We can and must save South Vietnam from Communism.

On the basis of this example it is possible to compare the reliability and validity coefficients. An initial estimate of the reliability of an unweighted composite measure comprised of these six variables is provided by the average inter-item correlation form of coefficient alpha (Nunnally, 1967, pp. 192–196; Cronbach, 1951). The average inter-item correlation is 0.665, which yields a coefficient alpha of 0.922. This result suggests that the common factor theory reliability coefficient for an unweighted composite measure based on these six variables is equal to or greater than 0.922. Indeed on the basis of the communalities obtained by extracting six common factors the common factor reliability coefficient (Cattell and Radcliffe, 1962) or coefficient omega (Heise and Bohrnstedt, 1970) for an unweighted composite measure comprised of these six variables is 0.923. Similarly the associated common factor theory validity coefficient for the same unweighted composite measure is 0.836. It is instructive to compare these coefficients with those derived from the canonical factor regression method. On the basis of the same canonical factor analysis solution the CFRM reliability coefficient (coefficient omega) is 0.906. However, the CFRM validity coefficient (coefficient rho) is 0.952. It is evident that the use of the linear weights associated with the canonical factor regression method produces a slight decrease in the reliability of the composite measure. Nevertheless this attenuation in reliability is accompanied by a significant increase in the validity of the composite measure.

One distinct advantage to the CFRM is that the associated reliability and validity coefficients can be computed without actually applying the associated linear weights to the observed variables. This is particularly useful for determining whether or not it is necessary or appropriate to employ the CFRM weights. Furthermore it is of interest to note that the equations for the CFRM reliability and validity coefficients are typically easier to compute than the equations for the common factor theory reliability and validity coefficients for an unweighted composite measure. The canonical factor regression method also provides for the decomposition of the total contribution of an observed variable to a common factor into direct and indirect effects (Harman, 1967, p. 353). This property can be utilized to determine which observed variables contribute the least to the reliability of a particular common factor and its associated composite measure.

An example of the computational procedures for obtaining the optimal CFRM linear weights is presented in Table 5. These linear weights are used in conjunction with the corresponding factor loadings to determine the total, direct, and indirect effects of each observed variable on the first canonical factor. An example of the computational procedures for decomposing the direct and indirect effects of each observed variable on the first common factor is presented in Table 6. These coefficients indicate that the third and fifth variables contribute less to the reliability of the first common factor than the remaining four variables. Since variables that contribute relatively little to the variance of the first common factor can often be deleted from a composite measure without an undue reduction in the resultant reliability of the composite measure, it seems reasonable to construct an abbreviated composite measure of support for the Vietnam War using only those four variables that contributed the most to the variance of the first common factor. Indeed the coefficient alpha for these four variables is 0.900 based on an

TABLE 5
Example of Computations for CFRM Linear Weights

Item	f_i	u_i^2	f_i/u_i^2	w_i
1	0.767	0.223	3.439	0.323
2	0.727	0.303	2.399	0.225
3	0.680	0.389	1.748	0.164
4	0.724	0.308	2.350	0.221
5	0.671	0.404	1.660	0.156
6	0.688	0.376	1.829	0.172

$$w_i = \frac{f_i/u_i^2}{1 + \Sigma(f_i^2/u_i^2)}$$

$$1 + \Sigma(f_i^2/u_i^2) = 10.644$$

TABLE 6
Example of Computations for Total, Direct, and Indirect
Contributions of Observed Variables to First Factor

Item	$f_i w_i$	w_i^2	$f_i w_i - w_i^2$
1	0.248	0.104	0.144
2	0.164	0.050	0.114
3	0.111	0.026	0.085
4	0.160	0.049	0.111
5	0.105	0.024	0.081
6	0.172	0.118	0.088

$\Sigma(w_i^2) = 0.283$ (sum of direct effects)
$\Sigma(f_i w_i - w_i^2) = 0.623$ (sum of indirect effects)
$\Sigma(w_i^2) + \Sigma(f_i w_i - w_i^2) = 0.906$ (sum of direct and indirect effects)
$\Sigma(f_i w_i) = 0.906$ (sum of total effects)
$\Omega_{\text{CFRM}} = 0.906$ (reliability of first factor)

average inter-item correlation of 0.693. A separate canonical factor analysis solution for these four variables yields a coefficient omega for an unweighted composite measure of 0.901. Similarly the validity coefficient for the same unweighted composite measure is 0.853. When the observed variables are weighted in accordance with the canonical factor regression method, however, the reliability coefficient omega is 0.890 and the associated validity coefficient rho is 0.943. Once again the use of the CFRM linear weights produces a slight decrease in the reliability of the composite measure but a substantial increase in its validity. The reduction in reliability results from the elimination of reliable but invalid variance in the composite score attributable to common factors other than the first common factor.

Once the CFRM linear weights for the observed variables in the composite measure have been computed, it is possible to estimate directly the correlation between the CFRM composite measure and any external variable. The only additional information required is the correlations between the observed variables in the CFRM composite measure and the external variable. An example of the computational procedures for estimating directly the correlation between the composite measure and an external variable is presented in Table 7. The external variable in this example is a measure of military experience ranging from no military experience through reserve training to regular enlistment in the military. The correlation between the CFRM composite measure of support for the Vietnam War and the measure of military experience is -0.247. This weak negative correlation is attributable to the weak negative correlations between the measure of military experience and the six attitudinal variables constituting the composite measure of support for

TABLE 7
Example of Computations for Correlation of CFRM Composite
Measure with External Variable

Item	r_{iY}	w_i	$r_{iY}w_i$
1	−0.159	0.323	−0.051
2	−0.147	0.225	−0.033
3	−0.259	0.164	−0.042
4	−0.194	0.221	−0.042
5	−0.220	0.156	−0.034
6	−0.209	0.172	−0.035

$$r_{sY} = \frac{\Sigma(r_{iY}w_i)}{\sqrt{\Omega_{\text{CFRM}}}} = \frac{-0.237}{0.952} = -0.247$$

the Vietnam War. Moreover, the correlation between the measure of military experience and the unobserved common factor score associated with support for the Vietnam War is −0.237. This correlation is weaker than the correlation between the measure of military experience and the CFRM composite measure because of the unreliability and invalidity in the composite measure.

One possible barrier to the application of the CFRM is the limited availability of computer programs for obtaining canonical factor analysis or maximum-likelihood factor analysis solutions. These factor analysis models are relatively new and are computationally more complicated than the ordinary principal factor analysis model. Nevertheless it is possible to obtain approximate canonical factor analysis results from a principal components analysis model when the observed correlations have been appropriately scaled and the resultant principal components loadings have been appropriately rescaled (Rummel, 1970, pp. 121–129). This approximate method begins with the standard matrix of correlations among the observed variables with ones in the principal diagonal. First each correlation coefficient is divided by the product of the standard deviations of the uniqueness of the two corresponding observed variables and each element of the principal diagonal is set to one. Second each principal components loading is multiplied by the standard deviation of the uniqueness of the corresponding observed variable. These rescaled principal components of the scaled matrix of observed correlations are equivalent to the canonical factors associated with an initial canonical factor analysis solution prior to iteration for convergence. The canonical factors are approximate in the sense that they are based on an initial estimate of the uniqueness of each observed variable.

As noted, the uniqueness of each observed variable and therefore its communality are initially unknown. In the course of a canonical factor analysis or a maximum-likelihood factor-analysis solution, the communality of each observed variable can be estimated by the sum of the squared factor loadings between each observed variable and the unobserved common factors. Moreover the number of common factors necessary and sufficient to account for the correlations among the observed variables can be determined through successive applications of the likelihood ratio criterion (Anderson and Rubin, 1956). In the case of an approximate canonical factor analysis solution, the best initial estimate of the communality of an observed variable is the squared multiple correlation coefficient between that variable and the other observed variables in the factor analysis solution. This estimate of communality has the property of being a lower bound to the actual communality of an observed variable (Guttman, 1956). Consequently the uniqueness estimate based on one minus the squared multiple correlation coefficient is an upper bound to the actual uniqueness of an observed variable. Moreover this estimate of the uniqueness of each variable approaches equality with the true uniqueness of that variable as the number of observed variables increases and the number of common factors decreases (Darroch, 1965). It is readily verifiable that the use of the squared multiple correlation coefficient as an estimate of communality yields CFRM reliability and validity coefficients which are lower bounds to the true reliability and validity coefficients. Furthermore as the reliability and validity of a composite measure increase, the discrepancy between the true and estimated reliability and validity coefficients decreases.

CONCLUSION

The canonical factor regression method of constructing composite measures entails an explicit rationale or measurement model. It proceeds from the assumption that there exist a number of observed variables which are considered to be indicators of a particular theoretical construct. Specifically this method assumes that the theoretical construct of interest is the primary source of the correlation among the observed indicator variables. Given this initial assumption it is reasonable to conclude that the unobserved first canonical factor corresponds in some sense to that theoretical construct. This interpretation follows from the definition of the first canonical factor as that unobserved variable which is maximally correlated with the observed variables. The regression method of factor score estimation provides a set of linear weights for the observed variable scores such that the resultant composite measure or factor score estimate is maximally correlated with the unobserved score on the first canonical factor. Moreover this composite measure or factor score estimate is also uncorrelated with subsequent unobserved canonical factor scores and their associated factor-score estimates. These considerations suggest that CFRM weights are optimal with respect to the reliability and validity of the resultant composite measure.

It is possible to assess the reliability and validity of a CFRM composite measure through the equations for the common factor theory reliability and validity coefficients. It has been demonstrated that when the CFRM linear weights are employed the equations for the common factor theory reliability and validity coefficients are greatly simplified. Furthermore the use of the CFRM weights ensures that the validity coefficient for a composite measure is exactly equal to the square root of the reliability coefficient for that composite measure. The CFRM weights eliminate reliable but invalid variance in the composite measure due to subsequent common factors. Indeed the reliability coefficient omega obtained from the canonical factor regression method measures the proportion of the variance in the composite measure that is attributable to the first canonical factor. Similarly the validity coefficient obtained from the canonical factor regression method measures the correlation between the composite score and the unobserved score on the first canonical factor. It can be shown that the CFRM linear weights maximize the validity of a composite measure or the correlation between the composite score and the unobserved score on the first canonical factor.

It has been shown that there is a direct correspondence between the CFRM coefficient omega and the true score theory coefficient alpha. Equality between these two coefficients obtains when one common factor is sufficient to account for the correlations among the observed variables. In terms of true score theory equality between these two coefficients occurs under conditions of essential tau-equivalence or when the true scores on the observed variables differ by no more than an additive constant. Typically coefficient alpha is a lower bound estimate of coefficient omega. Moreover this correspondence demonstrates that the reliability of a composite measure is a function of both the number of observed variables included in the composite and the strength of their correlations with the unobserved common factors. When a composite measure is comprised of a large number of observed variables, however, there is likely to be more than one reliable factor. When more than one factor contributes significantly to the correlation among the observed variables, it is difficult to assign an unambiguous substantive interpretation to the composite measure associated with the first common factor.

In general, composite measures constructed from the CFRM weights possess definite advantages over simple unweighted composite measures. Nevertheless under certain conditions the CFRM yields only marginal improvements in the reliability and validity of a composite measure. This is typically the case when all the CFRM weights are approximately equal. Since any improvements in the reliability and validity of a composite measure are achieved through the differential weighting of the observed variables, only marginal improvements can be obtained when the CFRM weights are almost equal (Rozeboom, 1966, pp. 463–496). Moreover the linear weights are commonly equal when the observed variables are approximately equally correlated with the unobserved first common factor. In other words if the observed indicator variables have been selected such that they are uniformly and highly correlated with the first common factor, an unweighted composite measure comprised of these variables is likely to be so reliable that the use of a set of optimal linear weights cannot produce a significant increase in the reliability and validity of the composite measure. There are many situations, however, in which it is impossible to select only the most reliable and valid observed indicator variables from a larger set of observed indicator variables.

Finally it must be noted that factor score estimation methods do not circumvent all the problems inherent in measuring unobserved variables from the correlations between the observed variables, particularly in the presence of significant measurement error. On the one hand random measurement error reduces the reliability of a composite measure but it does not produce a systematic bias in the factor score estimate. Nonrandom measurement error, on the other hand, contributes to the reliability of a composite measure, but it may well create a bias in the factor score estimate. However, nonrandom measurement error which is uncorrelated with the unobserved first common factor does not produce a bias in the corresponding factor score estimate or composite measure. For example, the presence of a methods factor which is not independent of the trait factor associated with the theoretical construct of interest contributes to the reliability of the composite measure but creates a bias in the composite score (Werts and Linn, 1970). Nevertheless, the equation for the direct estimation of the correlation between the CFRM composite measure and an external variable permits the immediate validation of the composite measure in terms of convergent and discriminant validity.

APPENDIX: DERIVATION OF CFRM COEFFICIENT OMEGA

The matrix algebra equation for coefficient omega (Heise and Bohrnstedt, 1970) can be readily generalized by expanding the single weight vector into a matrix of weight vectors. This generalization transforms the scalar coefficient into a matrix of coefficients corresponding to the different weight vectors given by

$$\Omega = W'(FF')W[W'(R)W]^{-1} \tag{10}$$

where W is the matrix of weight vectors for the observed variable scores, F is the pattern matrix of factor loadings, and R is the observed correlation matrix. The proposed method adopts the matrix of weight vectors associated with the regression method of factor score estimation (Harman, 1967, pp. 350–354) such that

$$W' = F'R^{-1} \tag{11}$$

where F' is the transpose of the factor-pattern matrix and R^{-1} is the inverse of the observed correlation matrix.

The inversion of the correlation matrix in Equation (11) can be circumvented through the use of the fundamental identity of the factor analysis model such that

$$R = FF' + U^2 \tag{12}$$

where U^2 is the diagonal matrix of uniquenesses. Premultiplying Equation (12) by $F'U^{-2}$ yields

$$F'U^{-2}R = (F'U^{-2}F + I)F' \tag{13}$$

where I is the diagonal identity matrix and U^{-2} is the inverse of the diagonal uniqueness matrix. Premultiplying Equation (13) by $(F'U^{-2}F + I)^{-1}$ and postmultiplying the result by R^{-1} yields

$$F'R^{-1} = (F'U^{-2}F + I)^{-1}F'U^{-2} \tag{14}$$

This result can be substituted directly into Equation (11) to yield

$$W' = (F'U^{-2}F + I)^{-1}F'U^{-2} \tag{15}$$

This equation is simplified further by the identification restriction imposed by the canonical-factor-analysis and the maximum-likelihood factor-analysis models that $F'U^{-2}F$ is diagonal. For convenience let $J = F'U^{-2}F$, where J is diagonal. This reduces Equation (15) to

$$W' = (J + I)^{-1}F'U^{-2} \tag{16}$$

Using the identity in Equation (12) the quantity in brackets in Equation (10) can be reduced to

$$W'(R)W = W'(FF' + U^2)W = W'(FF')W + W'(U^2)W \tag{17}$$

Premultiplying FF' by W' and postmultiplying the result by W yields

$$W'(FF')W = (I+J)^{-1}F'U^{-2}(FF')U^{-2}F(I+J)^{-1} \qquad (18)$$

$$W'(FF')W = (I+J)^{-1}JJ(I+J)^{-1} \qquad (19)$$

Similarly, premultiplying U^2 by W' and postmultiplying the result by W yields

$$W'(U^2)W = (I+J)^{-1}F'U^{-2}(U^2)U^{-2}F(I+J)^{-1} \qquad (20)$$

$$W'(U^2)W = (I+J)^{-1}J(I+J)^{-1} \qquad (21)$$

Premultiplying Equations (19) and (21) by $J^{-1}(I+J)$ and postmultiplying both results by $(I+J)$ yields

$$\Omega = W'(FF')W[W'(R)W]^{-1} = J(J+I)^{-1} \qquad (22)$$

The derivation of the CFRM validity coefficient is omitted since it is essentially identical to the derivation of the CFRM reliability coefficient.

REFERENCES

ANDERSON, T. W. AND RUBIN, H.
    1956   "Statistical inference in factor analysis." Pp. 111–150 in J. Neyman (Ed.), *Proceedings of the Third Berkeley Symposium on Mathematical Statistics and Probability*. Vol. 5. Berkeley: University of California Press.

BENTLER, P. M.
    1968   "Alpha-maximized factor analysis (alphamax): Its relation to alpha and canonical factor analysis." *Psychometrika* 33:335–345.

BLALOCK, H. M.
    1968   "The measurement problem: A gap between the languages of theory and research." Pp. 5–27 in H. M. Blalock and A. B. Blalock (Eds.), *Methodology in Social Research*. New York: McGraw-Hill.
    1969   "Multiple indicators and the causal approach to measurement error." *American Journal of Sociology* 75:264–272.

BROWNE, M. W.
    1969   "Fitting the factor analysis model." *Psychometrika* 34:375–394.

CATTELL, R. B. AND RADCLIFFE, J. A.
    1962   "Reliabilities and validities of simple and extended weighted and buffered unifactor scales." *British Journal of Statistical Psychology* 15:113–128.

COSTNER, H. L.
    1969   "Theory, deduction, and rules of correspondence." *American Journal of Sociology* 75:245–263.

CRONBACH, L. J.
    1951   "Coefficient alpha and the internal structure of tests." *Psychometrika* 16:297–334.

DARROCH, J. N.
  1965 "A set of inequalities in factor analysis." *Psychometrika* 30:449–453.
GUTTMAN, L.
  1955 "The determinancy of factor score matrices with implications for five other basic problems of common factor theory." *British Journal of Statistical Psychology* 8:65–81.
  1956 "'Best possible' systematic estimates of communalities." *Psychometrika* 21:273–285.
HARMAN, H. H.
  1967 *Modern Factor Analysis.* (rev. ed.). Chicago: University of Chicago Press.
HARRIS, C. W.
  1962 "Some Rao-Guttman relationships." *Psychometrika* 27:247–263.
  1967 "On factors and factor scores." *Psychometrika* 32:363–379.
HEISE, D. R. AND BOHRNSTEDT, G. W.
  1970 "Validity, invalidity, and reliability." Pp. 104–129 in E. F. Borgatta and G. W. Bohrnstedt (Eds.), *Sociological Methodology 1970.* San Francisco: Jossey-Bass.
JÖRESKOG, K. G. AND LAWLEY, D. N.
  1968 "New methods in maximum likelihood factor analysis." *British Journal of Mathematical and Statistical Psychology* 21:85–96.
KHAN, S. B.
  1973 "Relating factor scores to external variables." *Educational and Psychological Measurement* 33:103–105.
LAWLEY, D. N. AND MAXWELL, A. E.
  1971 *Factor Analysis as a Statistical Method.* (2nd ed.) London: Butterworth.
LORD, F. M. AND NOVICK, M. R.
  1968 *Statistical Theories of Mental Test Scores.* Reading, Mass.: Addison-Wesley.
MAXWELL, A. E.
  1971 "Estimating true scores and their reliabilities in the case of composite psychological tests." *British Journal of Mathematical and Statistical Psychology* 24:195–204.
MCDONALD, R. P.
  1968 "A unified treatment of the weighting problem." *Psychometrika* 33:351–381.
  1970 "The theoretical foundations of principal factor analysis, canonical factor analysis, and alpha factor analysis." *British Journal of Mathematical and Statistical Psychology* 23:1–21.
MCDONALD, R. P. AND BURR, E. J.
  1967 "A comparison of four methods of constructing factor scores." *Psychometrika* 32:381–401.
NOVICK, M. R. AND LEWIS, C.
  1967 "Coefficient alpha and the reliability of composite measurements." *Psychometrika* 32:1–13.

NUNNALLY, J. C.
   1967   *Psychometric Theory*. New York: McGraw-Hill.
RAO, C. R.
   1955   "Estimation and tests of significance in factor analysis." *Psychometrika* 20:93–112.
ROZEBOOM, W. W.
   1966   *Foundations of the Theory of Prediction*. Homewood, Ill.: Dorsey Press.
RUMMEL, R. J.
   1970   *Applied Factor Analysis*. Evanston, Ill.: Northwestern University Press.
SIEGEL, P. M. AND HODGE, R. W.
   1968   "A causal approach to the study of measurement error." Pp. 28–59 in H. M. Blalock and A. B. Blalock (Eds.), *Methodology in Social Research*. New York: McGraw-Hill.
THOMSON, G. H.
   1939   *The Factorial Analysis of Human Ability*. New York: Houghton Mifflin.
THURSTONE, L. L.
   1935   *The Vectors of Mind*. Chicago: University of Chicago Press.
TUCKER, L. R.
   1971   "Relations of factor score estimates to their use." *Psychometrika* 36:427–436.
WERTS, C. E. AND LINN, R. L.
   1970   "Cautions in applying various procedures for determining the reliability and validity of multiple item scales." *American Sociological Review* 35:757–759.

4

APPROACHES TO THE INTERPRETATION OF RELATIONSHIPS IN THE MULTI-TRAIT-MULTIMETHOD MATRIX

Duane F. Alwin
WASHINGTON STATE UNIVERSITY

The author was supported by a National Institute of General Medical Sciences Training Program in Methodology and Statistics (GMO-1526) and by postdoctoral support from Professors William H. Sewell and Robert M. Hauser during the writing of this chapter. Computer analyses were supported by a grant to Professor Sewell from the National Institute of Mental Health (M-6275). Computer facilities were provided by the Madison Academic Computing Center. The author wishes to thank Robert M. Hauser, Arthur S. Goldberger, and Robert P. Althauser for making invaluable comments on an earlier version of this chapter. The responsibility for the contents rests entirely with the author.

Social scientists are increasingly being made aware of the problems associated with inferring relationships among "true" variables on the basis of observed relationships among indicators or scores representing those variables. There is little doubt that considerable error can occur in the measurement of social phenomena, and recent attention has been given to the various ways in which different types of error can affect estimates of the relationships among variables.

Perhaps the major type of measurement error that has been studied is random error (Blalock, 1964, 1969; Siegel and Hodge, 1968; Bohrnstedt, 1969; Heise, 1969; Wiley and Wiley, 1970; Blalock, 1970; Werts and Linn, 1970a; Blalock, Wells, and Carter, 1970; Bohrnstedt and Carter, 1971). These treatments of random error have been primarily concerned with the problem of estimating relationships and effects in simple two- and three-variable systems in which some information is available regarding the amount of random error in the measurement of the variables.

In addition recent attention has been given to a second class of measurement error: nonrandom error. Using multiple indicators Costner (1969) develops a set of procedures for detecting the presence of "differential bias" in bivariate situations. Blalock extends the use of Costner's approach to recursive systems of equations (1969) and the one-variable–two-wave and one-variable–three-wave panel situations (1970).

The use of multiple measures is of course not new to social science. In 1959 Campbell and Fiske proposed the use of the now well-known multitrait-multimethod (MTMM) matrix as a way of assessing the construct validity of social science concepts. Campbell and Fiske argue that the closer two measurements are in time, space, and structure, the more highly they may be expected to correlate as a result. They refer to this systematic or nonrandom contribution to the correlation of two measures generically as *method variance*. A central problem that their approach addresses is the extent to which it is possible to make inferences about basic trait or variable relationships on the basis of intercorrelations among measures of those variables. The MTMM approach is presented as a way of assessing evidence for common variation among variables over and above that due to common method variation or covariation (1959, p. 84).

Recent literature has critically evaluated the suggestions of Campbell and Fiske, and several alternative approaches have been set forth: multimethod factor analysis (Jackson, 1969); the use of consistency criteria (Althauser and Heberlein, 1970; Althauser, Heberlein, and Scott, 1971); and the use of confirmatory factor analysis (Werts and Linn, 1970b; Werts, Linn, and Jöreskog, 1971). This chapter presents a rudimentary comparison of the four approaches, including that of Campbell and Fiske, in terms of the assumptions each makes about the nature of method variance and the implications these different assumptions about error have for the types of procedures used to evaluate the presence and extent of method variance in a given set of measures. It will become apparent that the four approaches are quite dependent on the assumptions, both explicit and implicit, made about nonrandom error, and that the interpretations arising from the application of any one of them rest on the appropriateness of the assumptions involved. This chapter suggests a set of criteria for choosing between the various models of nonrandom error in specific MTMM situations. As an initial step I shall present a review of Campbell and Fiske (1959).

CAMPBELL-FISKE CRITERIA

The general MTMM situation involves the measurement of $p(p \geq 2)$ variables by each of $m(m \geq 2)$ methods of measurement. The correlation matrix in Table 1 presents the general form of the MTMM matrix. The correlations among variables all of which are measured by the same method are included in a monomethod block. In Table 1 there are three methods ($m = 3$) so that there are three monomethod blocks.

TABLE 1
MTMM Matrix for Three Traits and Three Methods

		Method I			Method II			Method III	
Trait	X	Y	Z	X	Y	Z	X	Y	Z
I X	$r_{X_1X_1}$								
I Y	$r_{X_1Y_1}$	$r_{Y_1Y_1}$							
I Z	$r_{X_1Z_1}$	$r_{Y_1Z_1}$	$r_{Z_1Z_1}$						
II X	$\mathbf{r_{X_1X_2}}$	$r_{X_2Y_1}$	$r_{X_2Z_1}$						
II Y	$r_{X_1Y_2}$	$\mathbf{r_{Y_1Y_2}}$	$r_{Y_2Z_1}$						
II Z	$r_{X_1Z_2}$	$r_{Y_1Z_2}$	$\mathbf{r_{Z_1Z_2}}$						
III X				$\mathbf{r_{X_3X_2}}$	$r_{X_3Y_2}$	$r_{X_3Z_2}$	$r_{X_3X_3}$		
III Y				$r_{X_2Y_3}$	$\mathbf{r_{Y_2Y_3}}$	$r_{Y_3Z_2}$	$r_{X_3Y_3}$	$r_{Y_3Y_3}$	
III Z				$r_{X_2Z_3}$	$r_{Y_2Z_3}$	$\mathbf{r_{Z_2Z_3}}$	$r_{X_3Z_3}$	$r_{Y_3Z_3}$	$r_{Z_3Z_3}$

(Monomethod Blocks indicated by boxes on the diagonal; Heteromethod Blocks off-diagonal.)

Note: Values in validity diagonals (MTHM) are in boldface type.

There are two types of entries in a monomethod block: the monotrait-monomethod (MTMM) values and the heterotrait-monomethod (HTMM) values. The monotrait values here are simply the reliabilities of the measured variables; the heterotrait values are the correlations among the different variables within a given method of measurement. In Table 1 $p = 3$; thus there are three $[p(p-1)/2]$ HTMM values in the lower triangle of each monomethod block.

Correlations among variables measured by different methods comprise the heteromethod blocks, which also contain two types of entries: the monotrait-heteromethod (MTHM) values and the heterotrait-heteromethod (HTHM) values. The MTHM values are also referred to as *validity values* since each is a correlation between two presumably different attempts to measure a given variable. The HTHM values are correlations between different methods of measuring different variables. In Table 1 $m = 3$; thus there are three $[m(m-1)/2]$ heteromethod blocks. These blocks are asymmetric submatrices, each containing p MTHM values in the diagonal.

Given the matrix in Table 1 and the terminology outlined above, Campbell and Fiske (1959, pp. 82–83) advance the following criteria for convergent and discriminant validity:

> The entries in the validity diagonal should be significantly different from zero and sufficiently large to encourage further examination of validity. This requirement is evidence of convergent validity. Second, a validity diagonal value should be higher than the values lying in its column and row in the heterotrait-heteromethod triangles. That is, a validity value for a variable should be higher than the correlations obtained between that variable and any other variable having neither trait nor method in common. . . . A third common-sense desideratum is that a variable correlate higher with an independent effort to measure the same trait than with measures designed to get at different traits which happen to employ the same method. For a given variable, this involves comparing its values in the validity diagonals with its values in the heterotrait-monomethod triangles. . . . A fourth desideratum is that the same pattern of trait interrelationship be shown in all of the heterotrait triangles of both the monomethod and heteromethod blocks.

ISSUE OF UNRELIABILITY

In whatever way one conceptualizes method variance it is essentially nonrandom error and as such is conceptually independent of the issue of random measurement error or unreliability. Still Campbell and Fiske (1959, p. 102) point out that "the evaluation of the correlation matrix formed by intercorrelating several trait-method units must take into consideration the many factors which are known to affect the magnitude of correlations. A value in the validity diagonal must be assessed in light of the reliabilities of the two measures involved: e.g., a low reliability for Test A_2 might exaggerate the apparent method variance in Test A_1."

Although Campbell and Fiske propose no systematic way of taking unreliability into account, several writers have considered the possibility of correcting the MTMM matrix for attenuation due to unreliability (see Jackson, 1969, p. 32). Indeed it has been proposed (Heberlein, 1969; Althauser and Heberlein, 1970) that under certain circumstances the MTMM matrix can be corrected for attenuation using conventional correction formulas (see Lord and Novick, 1968, pp. 69–73).

Using the approach elaborated below, such corrections are in general unnecessary. Even so the point initially suggested by Campbell and Fiske (1959) and later recognized by Jackson (1969), Heberlein (1969), Althauser and Heberlein (1970), and others—that the issues of random and nonrandom error should be kept separate—is well taken. The following discussion is designed to shed some light on the question of how these components of error can be estimated.

GENERAL CAUSAL MODEL

Werts and Linn (1970b, p. 209) present the most general form of the MTMM matrix using path-analytic notation. Path-analytic conventions, used also by Althauser and Heberlein (1970), Althauser, Heberlein, and Scott (1971), and Werts, Linn, and Jöreskog (1971), are useful because they allow the assumptions in linear structural models to be made explicit. Of particular interest here of course are assumptions about nonrandom error, and the use of a path-analytic framework allows the comparison of the different conceptualizations of nonrandom method error in the MTMM matrix.

The path diagram for the MTMM matrix in Table 1 is presented in Figure 1. The general model employs $p + m$ unobserved exogenous variables (where p = the number of variables or traits and m = the number of measurement methods), one for each separate trait and one for each separate method; and pm observed endogenous variables, one for each trait-method combination. The model states that nonrandom variation in each measured variable is due to two exogenous sources of variation, one involving trait content and the other involving method content, and further that each exogenous variable is responsible for covariation among specific endogenous variables. Also there is a unique

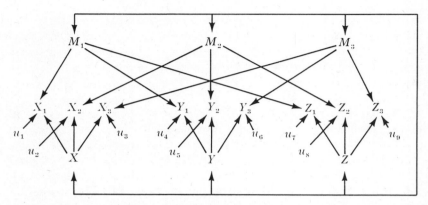

Figure 1. Path diagram for the multitrait-multimethod matrix ($p = 3$, $m = 3$).

random source of variation (a disturbance) in each endogenous variable. This random variation includes specific variation unique to a particular measured variable and variation due to unreliability. This model clearly separates the issues of random and nonrandom error, and since random error is included in the unique source of variation the underlying model is the "true" model and needs no correction. In other words the correction for attenuation is implicit in the model.

The structural equations for the MTMM model in Figure 1 are as follows:

$$X_1 = \beta_1 X + \alpha_1 M_1 + u_1$$
$$X_2 = \beta_4 X + \alpha_4 M_2 + u_2$$
$$X_3 = \beta_7 X + \alpha_7 M_3 + u_3$$
$$Y_1 = \beta_2 Y + \alpha_2 M_1 + u_4$$
$$Y_2 = \beta_5 Y + \alpha_5 M_2 + u_5$$
$$Y_3 = \beta_8 Y + \alpha_8 M_3 + u_6$$
$$Z_1 = \beta_3 Z + \alpha_3 M_1 + u_7$$
$$Z_2 = \beta_6 Z + \alpha_6 M_2 + u_8$$
$$Z_3 = \beta_9 Z + \alpha_9 M_3 + u_9$$

Consistent with the diagram in Figure 1, the disturbance terms (u) are specified to be uncorrelated with the terms X, Y, Z, M_1, M_2, and M_3 and with each other. As Werts and Linn (1970b) point out, this model clearly falls in the class of factor-analytic models. We have specified a model in which each measured variable has nonzero loadings on one trait factor (β) and one method factor (α) but zero loadings on all other trait and method factors. Also the factors, both trait and method, are allowed to be correlated. Thus we have specified a six-factor oblique solution for the MTMM matrix in Table 1. Generally one can posit a $p + m$ oblique factor solution for any MTMM matrix having p variables measured by m methods. Such a model has $2pm + (p + m)(p + m - 1)/2$ independent parameters to estimate from $pm(pm - 1)/2$ entries in the matrix.

The preceding equations can be summarized in matrix notation by $X = BF + U$, where

$$X = \begin{bmatrix} X_1 \\ X_2 \\ X_3 \\ Y_1 \\ Y_2 \\ Y_3 \\ Z_1 \\ Z_2 \\ Z_3 \end{bmatrix} \quad B = \begin{bmatrix} \beta_1 & 0 & 0 & \alpha_1 & 0 & 0 \\ \beta_4 & 0 & 0 & 0 & \alpha_4 & 0 \\ \beta_7 & 0 & 0 & 0 & 0 & \alpha_7 \\ 0 & \beta_2 & 0 & \alpha_2 & 0 & 0 \\ 0 & \beta_5 & 0 & 0 & \alpha_5 & 0 \\ 0 & \beta_8 & 0 & 0 & 0 & \alpha_8 \\ 0 & 0 & \beta_3 & \alpha_3 & 0 & 0 \\ 0 & 0 & \beta_6 & 0 & \alpha_6 & 0 \\ 0 & 0 & \beta_9 & 0 & 0 & \alpha_9 \end{bmatrix}$$

$$F = \begin{bmatrix} X \\ Y \\ Z \\ M_1 \\ M_2 \\ M_3 \end{bmatrix} \quad U = \begin{bmatrix} u_1 \\ u_2 \\ u_3 \\ u_4 \\ u_5 \\ u_6 \\ u_7 \\ u_8 \\ u_9 \end{bmatrix}$$

Note that, as specified above, $E[FU'] = E[UF'] = 0$, and $E[UU'] = U^2$, a diagonal matrix of residual variances. The variance-covariance matrix for the underlying trait and method factors in standard score form is

$$E[FF'] = \begin{bmatrix} 1 & & & & & \\ \rho_{XY} & 1 & & & & \\ \rho_{XZ} & \rho_{YZ} & 1 & & & \\ \rho_{XM_1} & \rho_{YM_1} & \rho_{ZM_1} & 1 & & \\ \rho_{XM_2} & \rho_{YM_2} & \rho_{ZM_2} & \rho_{M_1M_2} & 1 & \\ \rho_{XM_3} & \rho_{YM_3} & \rho_{ZM_3} & \rho_{M_1M_3} & \rho_{M_2M_3} & 1 \end{bmatrix}$$

When $p = 3$ and $m = 3$ there are 33 unknown parameters to estimate from 36 observed correlations, and the preceding set of equations is overidentified.[1] For identification purposes three traits each

---

[1] The use of counting rules to determine identifiability is not necessarily decisive in the general case. There is no substitute for attempting to solve for the unknown coefficients in terms of the correlations, at least in such simple models. In the models presented here, however, the counting rule of thumb is consistent with the identifiability of the models. For an elementary introduction to the identification issue in factor-analytic models see Duncan (1972).

measured by three methods is the minimal situation with regard to the full model. The minimal MTMM situation ($p = 2$, $m = 2$) is therefore underidentified since there are 14 independent parameters and only six observed correlations—too few observed correlations to estimate uniquely the unknown parameters. The $p = 3$, $m = 2$ situation is underidentified as well, with only 15 observed correlations to estimate 22 parameters. Whenever $p \geq 3$ and $m \geq 3$ the general path model set forth by Werts and Linn (1970b, p. 209) can be estimated. Estimation can be carried out by confirmatory factor analysis (Jöreskog, 1969, 1970), for which general computer programs are available (Jöreskog, Gruvaeus, and Van Thillo, 1970). The basic approach allows one to constrain some parameters of a factor-analytic model to zero or to set some unknown parameters equal to each other, estimating the unknown parameters under these constraints. The only restriction is that the model must be identifiable.

CONSISTENCY CRITERION APPROACH

Althauser and Heberlein (1970) consider the $p = 3$, $m = 2$ MTMM situation, which is underidentified in terms of the general model set forth in the preceding discussion, and critically evaluate the Campbell-Fiske criteria for convergent and discriminant validity within this framework. The path diagram that represents the model they posit for their MTMM situation is presented in Figure 2. Besides involving fewer methods this model differs in one other important respect from the one in Figure 1: Althauser and Heberlein posit zero correlations between trait factors on the one hand and method factors on the other.

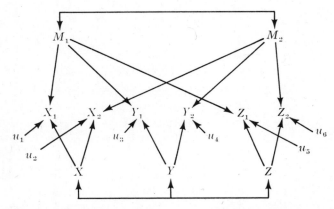

Figure 2. Path diagram for the Althauser-Heberlein MTMM matrix ($p = 3$, $m = 2$).

Thus the variance-covariance matrix among the factors of their model reduces to

$$\begin{bmatrix} 1 & & & & & \\ \rho_{XY} & 1 & & & & \\ \rho_{YZ} & \rho_{YZ} & 1 & & & \\ 0 & 0 & 0 & 1 & & \\ 0 & 0 & 0 & \rho_{M_1 M_2} & 1 \end{bmatrix}$$

Positing these parameters to be zero in the population model underlying the $p = 3$, $m = 2$ MTMM matrix nearly circumvents a grossly underidentified situation. However, knowing these parameters to be zero still leaves 16 unknown parameters to estimate from 15 observed correlations—an impossible task.

Since the model in Figure 2 cannot be estimated without further assumptions on reality, Althauser and Heberlein (1970, p. 161) phrase their problem as one of detecting "the presence of methods effects," which involves only the question of whether one should posit underlying sources of variation due to methods. Following Costner's (1969) consistency criterion approach they suggest the test of an overidentified path model shown in Figure 3. This model differs from the other models presented thus far in that correlations with or paths leading from method sources are absent.

Costner's approach states that the following equality must hold, within limits of sampling error, if the specification of the model in Figure 3 is correct in the population:

$$(r_{X_1 Y_2})(r_{X_2 Y_1}) = (r_{X_1 Y_1})(r_{X_2 Y_2})$$

For an MTMM matrix involving p traits and m methods it is necessary to satisfy $pm(p - 1)(m - 1)/4$ such consistency criteria. For models of this type where $p = 3$, $m = 3$, and where $p = 3$, $m = 2$, for example, one would have nine and three such consistency criteria to meet, respec-

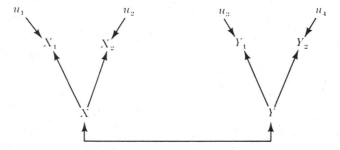

Figure 3. Path diagram for consistency criterion ($p = 2$, $m = 2$).

tively. Similarly for five traits measured by three methods one would have 30 comparisons to make.

It is important to keep the distinction between sample and population clear when making such comparisons. One would rarely expect the preceding equality for sample correlations to hold exactly even when the model is correct in the population (Hauser and Goldberger, 1971, p. 82). The use of the consistency criteria is formally equivalent to the examination of Spearman's (1927) "tetrad differences" one at a time, and Costner notes (1969, p. 262) that standard error formulas for tetrad differences have been worked out.

Althauser and Heberlein (1970, p. 161) apply the consistency criterion approach in order to test the overidentified counterpart of Figure 2 "against various alternative models" but confine their discussion to only one alternative—the one presented in Figure 2. They point out that if the consistency criteria hold, models for which they would not have held, such as Figure 2, can be eliminated from consideration; but if the criteria do not hold, one is in no position to decide which among several potential models is correct for the particular situation.[2] The utility of this approach is quite restricted, given that one's interest often goes beyond the issue of whether there is method variance in his measures.

If one believes that the overidentified version of the model in Figure 2 (see Costner, 1969) represents the structure of content underlying his measured variables, he should convince himself that it corresponds to a classic factor-analytic model in the class of models discussed above (under the section "The General Causal Model"), for which estimation procedures are well developed (Jöreskog, 1969, 1970; see also Hauser and Goldberger, 1971). If the concern is with testing the appropriateness of one's belief, that is, the correctness of the overidentified model, one need only estimate the model and compare the observed correlation matrix and the reproduced matrix generated by the factor-analytic estimation procedure (Hauser and Goldberger, 1971, pp. 91–95). There are goodness-of-fit tests available as well (Jöreskog, 1970, pp. 240–241). Following this procedure obviates the necessity of examining each tetrad difference (consistency criterion) separately. Of course if the

[2] Costner (1969) and Althauser and Heberlein (1970) note that for $m = 2$ there is at least one other model that satisfies the consistency criterion—one in which an underlying variable has an effect on a measure of the other variable. As Costner points out, the consistency criterion is therefore necessary but not sufficient for the fit of the model. There are other cases in which the consistency criteria might hold when the model in Figure 3 is the wrong model. If we consider the general case of the MTMM matrix in Figure 1 and allow for the possibility of negative correlations between traits and methods (such as floor and ceiling effects), satisfaction of a particular consistency criterion has uncertain meaning.

model does not fit the data this procedure leaves one in no better situation than the examination of several consistency criteria in terms of deciding what the correct model should be. If the model does provide a reasonable fit to the data, however, one has estimated (as opposed to tested) his model and he has some efficient estimates of the theoretical parameters of the model (Hauser and Goldberger, 1971).

If on the other hand one does not believe the overidentified version of Figure 2 to be the correct model for the problem and feels that another model might be better (such as in Figure 1), neither approach assists in underidentified situations. But even for identifiable situations the consistency criterion approach is not an approach to estimation and is therefore not a solution to the problem of making inferences regarding basic trait interrelationships. Its primary utility according to Costner (1969) and Althauser and Heberlein (1970) is to provide a test of the overidentified model against specific underidentified alternatives for which the consistency criteria would not hold. The point offered by Hauser and Goldberger (1971) and underscored here is that the estimation of this overidentified model using confirmatory factor analysis can provide an idea as to the fit of the model to the data (a test if you will) without bothering with several consistency criteria. Moreover it provides estimates of the theoretical parameters of the model, including estimates of basic trait interrelationships. Perhaps the most useful strategy is to concentrate on the estimation of the models that one takes to be reasonable for his variables. This method encourages an emphasis on gathering the type of data which would allow such estimation.

Althauser, Heberlein, and Scott (1971) consider some variations on the model in Figure 2 which also make the assumption that underlying traits do not correlate with underlying method sources of variation. These modifications add a new dimension to the problem—the time-order of measurements and the potential effect of initial measurement on subsequent measurements. The full MTMM matrix with which they deal (1971, p. 395) includes two levels or orders of measurement (initial and subsequent) within each monomethod (MM) and heteromethod (HM) block. Each MM and HM block is therefore a sub-MTMM matrix where the time-order of measurement is the method or submethod. Rather than apply their original model (see Figure 2) to each such submatrix they allow the initial measurement of a concept within a block to affect the subsequent measure within the block. They refer to this effect as *reactivity*. Further there is only one method within each MM block so they specify a single general method factor; in the HM blocks they specify one for each separate method as in Figure 2. Within the framework of the model in Figure 2 their modification of the model for the MM submatrices would imply the following: $\rho_{M_1M_2} = 1.0$, $\rho_{u_1u_3}$, $\rho_{u_1u_5}$, $\rho_{u_3u_5}$, $\rho_{u_2u_4}$, $\rho_{u_2u_6}$, $\rho_{u_4u_6} \neq 0$.[3] Such a model has 11 unknown parameters when $p = 2$ and $m = 2$; 18 unknown parameters when $p = 3$ and $m = 2$; and when $p = 3$ and $m = 3$ there are 30 unknowns.[4] So unless p and m are at least equal to 3, there is no hope of estimating such a model without other restrictions. Although Althauser, Heberlein, and Scott place equality restrictions on the model to get estimates of the reactivity parameters, their ultimate suggestion is to test this model against the overidentified model suggested by Costner (1969).

Within the HM blocks Althauser, Heberlein, and Scott maintain the model in Figure 2 with the exception that X_1 has an effect on X_2, Y_1 has an effect on Y_2, and Z_1 has an effect on Z_2 (where the subscript denotes the submethod, that is, the time-order of measurement within a block). These specifications imply the following: $\rho_{u_1u_3}$, $\rho_{u_1u_5}$, $\rho_{u_3u_5}$, $\rho_{u_2u_4}$, $\rho_{u_2u_6}$, $\rho_{u_4u_6} \neq 0$.[5] Such a model has 12 unknown parameters when $p = 2$ and $m = 2$; 19 unknown parameters when $p = 3$ and $m = 2$; and 33 when $p = 3$ and $m = 3$.[6] Unless p and $m = 3$, such a model cannot be identified for purposes of estimation. Again Althauser, Heberlein, and Scott suggest the use of consistency criteria to test the overidentified model (Costner, 1969) against this alternative. The preceding arguments regarding the use of consistency criteria apply here as well. The point is that there is essentially no way of choosing among alternative models when the consistency criteria do not hold, within the limits of sampling error, in such MTMM situations. If one wishes to reduce the potential reactivity of the sort discussed by Althauser, Heberlein, and Scott (1971), he has simply to randomize the order of presentation of the measuring instruments to the respondents in the sample. If this is impossible or if one believes the model including the reactivity parameters to be appropriate for his problem, he should perhaps focus on the problem of collecting the type of data that would allow him to estimate the model of interest.

One final point should be made regarding the consistency criterion approach. Costner originally phrased his "differential bias" problem in

---

[3] Note that the subscripts here refer to the submethods. If the reactive effects posited by this model are zero (nonzero) the correlations among the residual terms noted here are also zero (nonzero). This is simply an alternative way of phrasing the problem of reactivity, although it obviously does not estimate the effects involved.

[4] In general the number of unknown parameters for such a model is $2pm + p(p-1)/2 + p[m(m-1)/2]$.

[5] See footnote 3.

[6] In general the number of unknown parameters for such a model is $2pm + p(p-1)/2 + (p+1)[m(m-1)/2]$.

terms of a model in which sources of nonrandom error (differential bias) were uncorrelated with underlying sources of trait variation (1969, pp. 252, 257). The Althauser-Heberlein statement of the MTMM problem is consistent with this model. This view of method error can be distinguished from a view that incorporates the concept of *correlated error*, sources of error that are correlated with magnitudes of the underlying trait, such as floor and ceiling effects (Lord and Novick, 1968, p. 493; Siegel and Hodge, 1968, pp. 35–36). The latter view is represented by the general model proposed by Werts and Linn (1970b), depicted in Figure 1.

CAMPBELL-FISKE CRITERIA REVISITED

It is pehaps instructive to review the Campbell-Fiske criteria for convergent and discriminant validity in terms of the inferences being made in their application. Campbell and Fiske suggest four possible types of inference from the MTMM matrix, which were reviewed earlier and which are summarized in Table 2. First, if they observe a validity value, for example $r_{X_1 X_2}$, to be "significantly different from zero and sufficiently large to encourage further examination of validity" (1959, p. 82), they essentially wish to infer that the correlation between the two measures of X, free of nonrandom error, is different from zero and of sufficient magnitude, that is, $\beta_1 \beta_4 > 0$. This pure correlation between two attempts to measure the same variable is a refinement of their definition of validity (1959, p. 83).[7] Clearly their discussion of this criterion for convergent validity recognizes that such an inference could be wrong in the sense that the correlation between X_1 and X_2 is also likely to contain covariation due to method covariation. They note that "high correlations between tests might be explained as due either to basic trait similarity or to shared method variance" (1959, p. 85).

Indeed it was the failure of conventional approaches to validation in the psychometric literature that emphasized primarily convergence notions (see Cronbach and Meehl, 1955) which stimulated the efforts of Campbell and Fiske to propose a broader set of criteria. They viewed

[7] It is important to clarify the logic of the approach taken here to deciding the inferences intended by Campbell and Fiske (1959). This is important because it differs somewhat from the approach taken by Althauser and Heberlein (1970) to evaluate the Cambell-Fiske approach. The fundamental questions addressed are the following: What inferences would be made from the intercorrelations in the MTMM matrix if no method effects were present? Under what conditions involving method variance and covariance would these inferences be essentially correct? The first question is answered in Table 2. The second question is considered later in the text.

TABLE 2
Inferences from MTMM Matrix Using the Campbell-Fiske Approach
($p = 3$, $m = 3$)

Observation	Inference
Convergent validity:	
$r_{X_1X_2} > 0$	$\beta_1\beta_4 > 0$
$r_{X_1X_3} > 0$	$\beta_1\beta_7 > 0$
$r_{X_2X_3} > 0$	$\beta_4\beta_7 > 0$
and so on for Y and Z	
Discriminant validity:	
(1)	
$r_{X_1X_2} > r_{X_2Y_1}$	$\beta_1\beta_4 > \beta_4\beta_2\rho_{XY}$
$r_{X_1X_2} > r_{X_2Z_1}$	$\beta_1\beta_4 > \beta_4\beta_3\rho_{XZ}$
$r_{X_1X_2} > r_{X_1Y_2}$	$\beta_1\beta_4 > \beta_1\beta_5\rho_{XY}$
$r_{X_1X_2} > r_{X_1Z_2}$	$\beta_1\beta_4 > \beta_1\beta_6\rho_{XZ}$
and so on for $r_{X_1X_3}$, $r_{X_2X_3}$, and Y and Z	
(2)	
$r_{X_1X_2} > r_{X_1Y_1}$	$\beta_1\beta_4 > \beta_1\beta_2\rho_{XY}$
$r_{X_1X_2} > r_{X_1Z_1}$	$\beta_1\beta_4 > \beta_1\beta_3\rho_{XZ}$
$r_{X_1X_2} > r_{X_2Y_2}$	$\beta_1\beta_4 > \beta_4\beta_5\rho_{XY}$
$r_{X_1X_2} > r_{X_2Z_2}$	$\beta_1\beta_4 > \beta_4\beta_6\rho_{XY}$
and so on for $r_{X_1X_3}$, $r_{X_2X_3}$, and Y and Z	
(3)	
$r_{X_1Y_1} > r_{X_1Z_1} > r_{Y_1Z_1}$	$\beta_1\beta_2\rho_{XY} > \beta_1\beta_3\rho_{XZ} > \beta_2\beta_3\rho_{YZ}$
same pattern must be observed in all heterotrait triangles	

the traditional form of validity assessment—convergent validity—as only preliminary and insufficient evidence that two measures were indeed measuring the same trait. Of course the inferential problem with the criterion for convergent validity involves the possibility of method covariation in the correlation between two attempts to measure a given trait. They indicate that "the clear-cut demonstration of the presence of method variance [and covariance] requires both several traits and several methods" (1959, p. 85). Hence the inception of the MTMM matrix and the criteria for discriminant validity.

The first two criteria for discriminant validity require that the MTHM (validity) values be greater than the relevant HTHM and HTMM values. These criteria suggest that if, for example, $r_{X_1X_2} > r_{X_1Y_2}$ is observed in a sample this is sufficient for the inference that $\beta_1\beta_4 > \beta_1\beta_5\rho_{XY}$; and likewise if, for example, $r_{X_1X_2} > r_{X_1Y_1}$ is observed this is sufficient for the inference that $\beta_1\beta_4 > \beta_1\beta_2\rho_{XY}$. The reverse of these observed inequalities would imply the reverse inference as well. The final criterion that Campbell and Fiske set forth for the evaluation of discriminant validity involves the patterns of relationships in the heterotrait triangles of both monomethod and heteromethod blocks. If one infers, for example, that $\beta_1\beta_2\rho_{XY} > \beta_1\beta_3\rho_{XZ} > \beta_2\beta_3\rho_{YZ}$ from the observation that $r_{X_1Y_1} > r_{X_1Z_1} > r_{X_1Z_1}$, the inferences should be consistent for all heterotrait triangles; that is, one should observe as well that $r_{X_2Y_1} > r_{X_2Z_1} > r_{Y_2Z_1}$ and so forth.

In their critique of the Campbell-Fiske criteria Althauser and Heberlein (1970, p. 161) conclude: "In sum, we find that the criteria for convergent validity can be met, when in fact the measures do not converge since the [validity values] can be inflated by correlated methods. Discriminant validity does not fare much better since we find that only one of three criteria can be interpreted as Campbell and Fiske suggest. An alternative approach is obviously needed to detect the presence of method effects."

Given the path model expressed in Figure 2, Althauser and Heberlein note that the observation that $r_{X_1X_2} > 0$ does not necessarily reflect that $\beta_1\beta_4 > 0$ since in the model for the population $\rho_{X_1X_2} = \beta_1\beta_4 + \alpha_1\alpha_4\rho_{M_1M_2}$, indicating that "even this most appealing criterion for validity may lead to incorrect inference about the validity of measures" (1970, p. 157). As I have noted, to fault the convergent validation criterion is to recognize the need for a multitrait-multimethod approach. Clearly the indeterminancy at this level provided a stimulus for the development of the discriminant criteria. In a strict sense Althauser and Heberlein's criticism of the convergent criterion is no more than a restatement of Campbell and Fiske's rationale for proposing the additional criteria (see Campbell and Fiske, 1959, pp. 81–85).

Althauser and Heberlein also indicate that given the model in Figure 2 only one of the three criteria for discriminant validity is valid— the one comparing the validity diagonals with the values in the heterotrait-monomethod triangles. Their arguments are not reviewed here: they are cogently presented elsewhere (Althauser and Heberlein, 1970, pp. 157–161).[8]

---

[8] I have one minor point of disagreement with their arguments regarding the criterion for discriminant validity involving the comparison of the validity values with the values in the HTMM triangles. Althauser and Heberlein (1970, p. 159) and Althauser, Heberlein, and Scott (1971, p. 379) note that correct inferences from this criterion are possible only when "the epistemic paths are equal and of like sign" and "the method effects are of like sign." The unnecessary condition here is the one regarding the equality of "epistemic paths," that is, the effects of an underlying trait on the trait measures. If in the population, for example, $\rho_{X_1X_2} > \rho_{X_1Y_1} = \beta_1\beta_4 + \alpha_1\alpha_4\rho_{M_1M_2} > \beta_1\rho_{XY}\beta_2 + \alpha_1\alpha_2$, and the method effects α_1, α_2, and α_4 are of like sign, the term $\alpha_1\alpha_2$ is in general greater than the term $\alpha_1\alpha_4\rho_{M_1M_2}$ except as $\rho_{M_1M_2}$ tends to unity. Therefore if $r_{X_1X_2} > r_{X_1Y_1}$ is ob-

A point that is ignored, and perhaps misunderstood, by Althauser and Heberlein's criticism is that there are situations in which the Campbell-Fiske criteria for discriminant validity are generally valid. We need only assume—in addition to the assumptions already made by Althauser and Heberlein (that method and trait factors are uncorrelated, as in Figure 2)—that the effects of methods on measured variables are constant across all such effects of a given method. The structural equations for this situation in the $p = 3$, $m = 2$ case are as follows:

$$X_1 = \beta_1 X + \alpha_1 M_1 + u_1$$
$$X_2 = \beta_4 X + \alpha_2 M_2 + u_2$$
$$Y_1 = \beta_2 Y + \alpha_1 M_1 + u_3$$
$$Y_2 = \beta_5 Y + \alpha_2 M_2 + u_4$$
$$Z_1 = \beta_3 Z + \alpha_1 M_1 + u_5$$
$$Z_2 = \beta_6 Z + \alpha_2 M_2 + u_6$$

Under these assumptions the Campbell-Fiske criteria for discriminant validity are generally valid for all the inferences outlined in Table 2. There appears to be some disagreement with this point in the Althauser-Heberlein discussion. Under their discussion of "Discriminant Validity, First Comparison" (1970, pp. 157–158), they note that the equality of method paths, as we have posited here to make sense of the Campbell-Fiske criteria, "obscure the effects of methods on measures, while we infer that there are no method effects." The validity of this assertion rests on the correctness of the observation that one would infer the absence of method effects merely by positing some to be equal to others. Furthermore Campbell and Fiske did not intend this comparison to be used for inferences about the presence or absence of method variance. They are quite clear on this point (1959, p. 85) stating that "in the multitrait-multimethod matrix, the presence of method variance is indicated by the difference in level of correlation between the parallel values of the monomethod block and the heteromethod block, assuming comparable reliabilities among the tests. Thus the contribution of method variance in Test $[X_1]$ of [Table 1] is indicated by the elevation of $[r_{X_1Y_1}]$ above $[r_{X_1Y_2}]$."

This statement suggests a comparison not considered by Althauser and Heberlein (1970): that the observation $r_{X_iY_i} > r_{X_iY_j}$ suggests the presence of method variance. For example in terms of the model in Figure 2:

$$\rho_{X_1Y_1} > \rho_{X_1Y_2} = \beta_1\rho_{XY}\beta_2 + \alpha_1\alpha_2 > \beta_1\beta_5\rho_{XY} + \alpha_1\rho_{M_1M_2}\alpha_5$$

---

served in a sample the inference that $\beta_1\beta_4 > \beta_1\rho_{XY}\beta_2$ is probably safe, given that $\beta_1, \beta_2,$ and β_4 are of like sign and that $\alpha_1, \alpha_2,$ and α_4 are of like sign. No equality restrictions are necessary for this inference.

Evaluating the inequality to the right of the equal sign, only if $\beta_2 = \beta_5$ would this observation reflect α_1, α_2, or $\alpha_5 \neq 0$, that is, method variance, assuming all positive effects. Thus the inference proposed by Campbell and Fiske regarding the detection of method variance is questionable, and the assumption of the equality of certain method effects does not assist in making the proper inferences in this case.

In contrast, under the conditions of the equality of the method effects emanating from a given method, the inferences drawn from the criteria for discriminant validity are generally valid. Nothing can be done to improve the criterion for convergent validity, but of course it was originally intended only as a prerequisite for discriminant validity. Clearly if the correlation between two presumably different attempts to measure the same concept is only trivially different from zero, further examination of validity with respect to the value of that correlation would be absurd. Under the conditions of the equality of certain method effects, the method effects are no less present in the correlations among trait measures. It is simply that they do not create problems in making inferences regarding the relative magnitudes of the true correlations. For example, in the comparisons of the validity values with the heterotrait-heteromethod values under such assumptions, the inference that

$$\rho_{X_1 X_2} > \rho_{X_2 Y_1} = \beta_1 \beta_4 + \alpha_1 \rho_{M_1 M_2} \alpha_2 > \beta_4 \beta_2 \rho_{XY} + \alpha_1 \rho_{M_1 M_2} \alpha_2$$

is consistent with the inference indicated in Table 2 since the term $\alpha_1 \rho_{M_1 M_2} \alpha_2$ drops out of both sides of the inequality.

In the comparison of validity values with heterotrait-monomethod values, the terms representing method variance and covariance do not drop out as easily but the inferences are in general likely to be valid. For example the inference

$$\rho_{X_1 X_2} > \rho_{X_1 Y_1} = \beta_1 \beta_4 + \alpha_1 \alpha_2 \rho_{M_1 M_2} > \beta_1 \beta_2 \rho_{XY} + \alpha_1^2$$

is only valid under such assumptions when α_1 is greater than $\alpha_2 \rho_{M_1 M_2}$. In the case of minimally correlated methods there is little problem with this inference under these assumptions, but as the correlation between methods tends to unity this inference becomes problematic. Clearly if all method effects are equal there is no problem with this inference, but this stringent assumption is probably unnecessary since α_1 will probably be greater than $\alpha_2 \rho_{M_1 M_2}$, assuming that β_1, β_2, and β_4 are of like sign and that α_1, α_2, and α_4 are of like sign.

The reader should convince himself that the other inferences in Table 2 regarding the discriminant criteria are also valid under these conditions. In summary the viability of the original MTMM matrix approach depends entirely on the assumptions one is willing to make about nonrandom method error. Althauser and Heberlein (1970) are willing to make certain assumptions so that the consistency criteria can be used. Their assumptions, as shown by their critique of Campbell and Fiske, limit the validity of the criteria for discriminant validity proposed by Campbell and Fiske.[9]

It is shown in the preceding paragraphs that another set of assumptions, perhaps no less realistic in the abstract than those which Althauser and Heberlein are willing to make, allow the correct inferences to be drawn from the application of the Campbell-Fiske criteria. It is apparent that some systematic way of choosing among the sets of assumptions is needed.

It should be made clear that Campbell and Fiske make no mention of the equality of certain method effects—this is simply a set of assumptions I have imposed to place their validation criteria in the proper perspective. Since this set of assumptions does allow valid inferences from the use of their criteria for discriminant validity, I shall refer to the model involving these assumptions as the "implicit" Campbell-Fiske model. I trust I am not misrepresenting the original Campbell-Fiske analytic scheme.

Any technique must be evaluated not only with respect to the assumptions it makes but also in terms of the goals it sets for itself. As indicated earlier the Althauser-Heberlein application of Costner's consistency criteria sets forth only the modest goal of detecting the presence of method variance or covariance or both. It might be argued that the application of Costner's technique in the present case would never lead one to accept the overidentified model when it is wrong. Such an argument would make the implicit assumption that traits and methods are not negatively correlated in the population. No way is provided by Althauser and Heberlein or anyone else for deciding when Costner's technique gives valid results and when it does not.

Similarly Campbell and Fiske are also interested in detecting the presence of method variance and covariance, but in addition they seek "evidence for relative validity, that is, for common variance specific to a trait, above and beyond shared method variance" (1959, p. 84). This goal appears to be different from that posed by Althauser and Heberlein and is somewhat more ambitious. The difference lies in the distinction between the presence of method variance and the presence of what we might call "invalidating" method variance. In the implicit Campbell-Fiske model the presence of method variance is not in question—its

---

[9] The assumption of the equality of certain method effects is not palatable to Althauser and Heberlein for purposes of evaluating the Campbell-Fiske criteria, but ironically Althauser, Heberlein, and Scott (1971, p. 385) are willing to make this type of assumption for other purposes.

presence is assumed. Rather the question involves whether the method variance or covariance (shared method variance) appears in such a configuration as to invalidate the inferences one might draw from the relationships among the variable measures. In summary Althauser and Heberlein appear to be looking for method effects; Campbell and Fiske appear to be looking for evidence of trait interrelationships in the presence of method effects. As with the consistency criterion technique for detecting the presence of method variance, the Campbell-Fiske criteria for accomplishing their goals are assumption-dependent. Moreover they provide no way of evaluating the veracity of the assumptions. As Althauser and Heberlein point out, given one set of assumptions the Campbell-Fiske procedures are of little utility; and as I have suggested, under a different set of assumptions their approach makes sense. But how does one judge the appropriateness of a given set of assumptions? This chapter suggests a set of procedures for choosing between the various models of nonrandom error in several multitrait-multimethod situations. Before doing this, however, one more approach, multimethod factor analysis, must be discussed.

MULTIMETHOD FACTOR ANALYSIS

As an alternative to the Campbell-Fiske criteria Jackson (1969) suggests a principal-component decomposition of a modified MTMM matrix. The modification is accomplished by substituting an identity matrix for each monomethod block. This is an attempt to delete method variance from the matrix; the component analysis is intended to reveal an assessment of convergent and discriminant validity in the absence of confounding method variance. Like the Campbell-Fiske scheme Jackson's multimethod factor analysis focuses on the examination of basic trait interrelationships. Whereas Campbell and Fiske examine trait covariation in the presence of method effects however, Jackson wishes to examine trait covariation in the absence of such effects. There are some basic problems with his attempts to do this.

As with the other techniques the utility of Jackson's procedures clearly rests on the appropriateness of his assumptions. In contrast to the other approaches it is clear from his statement of the problem that the assumptions he makes are unrealistic, especially his conception of method variance as "variance common only to measures within a single method of measurement" (1969, p. 37). Anticipating the problem of method intercorrelation Jackson recommends that "sound judgment in identifying distinctly different methods is important, however, for it should be recognized that a multimethod factor analysis employing quite similar methods may yield factors which are in part a function of method overlap" (1969, p. 41). This statement echoes Campbell and Fiske's admonition that "wherever possible, the several methods in one matrix should be completely independent of each other" (1959, p. 103). Such suggestions ignore the realistic research situation that social scientists often find themselves in, with a limited choice of methods, not to mention the virtual impossibility of knowing the extent to which they share variation a priori.

Assuming that it is possible to regulate the value of $\rho_{M_iM_j}$ methodologically so that its value is equal to zero, Jackson notes that the MTMM matrix prior to modification contains both trait and method covariation in the monomethod blocks but only trait covariation in the heteromethod blocks (1969, p. 39). With regard to the correlation of traits and methods Jackson cites a number of examples from the research literature in the general area of psychological testing (including some of his own), concluding that "method variance cannot be considered to be randomly distributed with respect to trait variance" (1969, p. 34). Besides questioning the assumptions underlying both the Campbell-Fiske and the Althauser-Heberlein approaches, these observations also question Jackson's own representation of trait and method factors in his discussion of the factorial composition of monomethod and heteromethod matrices (1969, p. 38). Jackson essentially portrays traits and methods as uncorrelated. We must therefore conclude that the multimethod factor-analysis approach assumes zero correlations among traits and methods, Jackson's own observations from the testing literature notwithstanding.

Prior to the proposed modification the matrix in which Jackson is interested involves MTHM values of the form

$$\rho_{X_iX_j} = \beta_{X_iX}\beta_{X_jX}$$

HTHM values of the form

$$\rho_{X_iY_j} = \beta_{X_iX}\beta_{Y_jY}\rho_{XY}$$

and HTMM values of the form

$$\rho_{X_iY_i} = \beta_{X_iX}\beta_{Y_iY}\rho_{XY} + \alpha_{X_iM_i}\alpha_{Y_iM_i}$$

If it were possible simply to delete the effects of methods from the HTMM values, the solution would be a simple one given the appropriateness of the assumptions made by Jackson. It would involve a p-factor oblique solution of the new MTMM matrix in which the pattern coefficients would be equivalent to the β_{X_iX} and the off-diagonal elements of the $E[FF']$ matrix would be the ρ_{XY}. It is the veritable impossibility of accomplishing this that stimulates Jackson's particular modification of the MTMM matrix.

As noted above, Jackson's modification of the MTMM matrix involves replacing the monomethod blocks with identity submatrices in order to delete the method effects from the monomethod submatrices. As Conger (1971) notes, this modification involves obviously contradictory assumptions—that variables are correlated between methods but uncorrelated within methods. This raises some questions regarding the status of the results of this ad hoc modification and analysis of the MTMM matrix. First the model being estimated is unclear since the posited relationships among the variables involved are not the same within and between methods of measurement. Second the meaning that should be attached to the estimates derived from the component analysis is uncertain. Finally the assumptions, particularly the assumption of uncorrelated methods, appear difficult to meet in practice.

DISCUSSION AND SYNTHESIS

The major focus of the concern that social scientists have had with random error of measurement has been on inferring the true relationships among variables from information about the correlations among their measures and the reliabilities of these measures. A similar focus is possible for the concern with nonrandom error of measurement. Until recently most social scientists would have asserted that in situations where nonrandom error is present, it would be virtually impossible to obtain an estimate of the true correlations among variables as they might if the measurement error were strictly random. The multitrait-multimethod approach allows for this possibility but until recently measurement models for evaluating the relationships in the MTMM matrix have not been developed and procedures for estimating these measurement models have been lacking. Recent path-analysis applications to unobserved-variable problems (Costner, 1969; Werts and Linn, 1970b; Althauser and Heberlein, 1970; Hauser and Goldberger, 1971) provide the basis for developing the necessary measurement models, and estimation procedures applicable to these models have recently been developed in a more general context (Jöreskog, 1970; Jöreskog, Gruvaeus, and Van Thillo, 1970). Jöreskog's confirmatory factor analysis procedure can be viewed as a general solution to the problem of estimating complex measurement models, including those involving nonrandom error.

We have reviewed four linear, additive models for the operation of nonrandom error in the MTMM matrix (excluding Jackson's multi-method factor analysis). First, the Costner (1969) overidentified model with no method factors and therefore no method effects. Second, the implicit Campbell-Fiske (1959) model in which method effects are present, but the method factors are uncorrelated with the trait factors and the effects of a given method of measurement are equal on all variables so measured. Third, the Althauser and Heberlein (1970) model in which the method factors are uncorrelated with the trait factors and the effects of a given method are not necessarily equal on all variables measured by that method.[10] And fourth, the Werts and Linn (1970b) full model, which allows for intercorrelated traits and methods and for unequal method effects.

In a given MTMM situation one of these models is likely to be more appropriate than the others. Since the type of error operating on one's variables depends largely on the type of content involved, it is unrealistic to argue in favor of any single model as the generally appropriate one. It is therefore necessary to develop a systematic strategy for deciding which model is most consistent with the data in a given MTMM situation. The researcher who confronts an MTMM matrix should have some a priori notions about how nonrandom measurement error might operate in the variables of interest. (Such considerations might even guide the collection of data on the variable measures.) Since this usually is not the case, the most general model (Werts and Linn) is perhaps the most useful initial model to attempt to fit. Of course this model is identifiable only when $p \geq 3$ and $m \geq 3$.

In the situation where $p = 3$ and $m = 3$, all four models are overidentified so they may all be compared for goodness of fit. As noted above perhaps the analyst's initial solution should be the general model (Werts and Linn); he would then move to the simpler models only if the estimates of the parameters of this model suggest such a strategy. For example, one might not wish to estimate the second model unless the

[10] I have ignored the variations of Althauser, Heberlein, and Scott (1971) on this model in the present discussion. These models differ from the third model in that within each MM and HM block of the MTMM matrix the methods involved are different time-orders in the presentation of the trait measures to the respondent, and the initial measurement can affect the subsequent measure. If the investigator can randomize the presentation of the relevant measures it is possible to minimize the problem. Indeed the variation that is then due to the time-order in the presentation of the measures is strictly random variation. In this manner the model involved becomes overidentified since one has two measures of each pm trait-method combination. This circumstance generates $2pm(2pm - 1)/2$ correlations and the original Althauser-Heberlein model in such a case involves $4pm + p(p - 1)/2 + m(m - 1)/2$ unknown parameters. Even the $p = 2$, $m = 2$ case is estimable in this situation. The doubling of the number of measures may provide a solution to the problem of underidentification in the models discussed in this section.

estimated correlations between traits and methods are near zero and unless the effects of a given method on all variables it measures are nearly equal in the full model. In this situation ($p = 3$, $m = 3$) the assumptions made by the Althauser-Heberlein approach and the implicit Campbell-Fiske model can be evaluated. Ironically the approach to checking the assumptions in the two models renders unnecessary the procedures based on them. The double goals of detecting the presence of method effects and of assessing the evidence for basic trait interrelationships in the presence of method effects are both accomplished with the Werts and Linn (1970b) approach.[11]

When $p \geq 3$ and $m = 2$ the alternatives are limited. Here only the first (Costner) and the second (implicit Campbell-Fiske) models are overidentified and thereby estimable by confirmatory factor analysis. The third and fourth models are underidentified in this situation. Only if the analyst believes either the Costner model or the implicit Campbell-Fiske model to be correct for his problem is there any possibility of testing his expectations. If he believes the third or fourth model to be a better representation of reality he must measure his variables with an additional method in a future sample in order to check his belief against empirical data. The Costner model is, in a sense, a null hypothesis that can always be tested for fit to the data. When $p = 2$ and $m = 2$ this is the only model that is estimable using confirmatory factor analysis—the other models are underidentified. Unfortunately the minimal MTMM situation does not allow us to test the appropriateness of the models that include nonrandom error, unless of course Costner's overidentified model fits the data, in which case an implicit test against all underidentified alternatives has been made. Perhaps the best strategy available when the Werts and Linn full model is underidentified is to fit the Costner overidentified model. If the fit is good, a number of alternative models can be eliminated from consideration. If the fit is not good, the implicit Campbell-Fiske model can be explored in the $p = 3$ and $m = 2$ situation but nothing can be done in the $p = 2$ and $m = 2$ case.[12] If the reality underlying the variable measures appears to be more com-

---

[11] A solution to Jackson's (1969) problem of assessing evidence for basic trait interrelationships in the absence of method effects is not readily seen with this approach, or with any other for that matter, owing to the impossibility of subtracting out method variance and the likelihood of correlated methods. Of course both these issues can be evaluated with confirmatory factor analysis procedures, but where they are applicable there is no need to use multimethod factor analysis.

[12] Analyses of some of the $p = 3$, $m = 2$ and $p = 4$, $m = 2$ MTMM matrices originally presented in Campbell and Fiske (1959) indicate that the implicit Campbell-Fiske model fits the data reasonably well in some cases. Thus the assumptions of the equality of certain method effects are not unreasonable.

plex than the range of permissible models the analyst will have to measure more variables or utilize more methods of measurement in a future sample.

It should be clear that even where the full model is underidentified, the use of confirmatory factor analysis as a way of checking the assumptions of identifiable models renders unnecessary the approaches which have been formulated on the basis of these models, namely, the Campbell-Fiske and the Althauser-Heberlein approaches. If we find that the implicit Campbell-Fiske model fits the data quite well in a particular situation, this suggests that the Campbell-Fiske criteria for discriminant validity would make the proper inferences. The application of their criteria would be superfluous, however, given the prior estimation of the model. The same argument applies in situations where the consistency criteria are applicable.

SUMMARY AND CONCLUSION

Since Campbell and Fiske's 1959 treatment of nonrandom error using a multitrait-multimethod (MTMM) matrix, there have been a number of critical evaluations of and proposed alternatives to their approach. This chapter has reviewed three of these alternative procedures, along with the original Campbell-Fiske criteria for convergent and discriminant validity, within a comparative framework. Utilizing a path-analytic framework I have pointed out the differences in the conceptualizations of nonrandom error that underlie the four approaches. I have attempted to clarify the assumptions involved in these approaches so that their implications for application and interpretation can be better understood. I have also attempted to point out what appear to be key differences in their analytic goals.

A major theme of this chapter has been that the meaning one attaches to the results of these procedures depends entirely on the veracity of the assumptions about nonrandom error on which the procedures themselves rest. Particularly with reference to the Campbell-Fiske criteria for convergent and discriminant validity and the Althauser-Heberlein application of Costner's consistency criteria, I have emphasized that the results of the procedures have questionable meaning outside the context of a particular set of assumptions. Althauser and Heberlein (1970) have made a similar point about the Campbell-Fiske criteria but some of their arguments have been shown to be wanting. Finally one approach, Jackson's multimethod factor analysis, was found to involve some internally contradictory assumptions that limit its utility altogether.

Three approaches—the Campbell-Fiske criteria, the use of consistency criteria by Althauser and Heberlein, and the confirmatory factor-analysis approach advanced by Werts and Linn—suggest four different models for the way in which nonrandom error operates to contaminate our measures of variables. Because there are at least these four ways of conceptualizing method error in a given case, the analyst is cautioned against seeking a generally acceptable model for nonrandom error in all MTMM situations. The nature of nonrandom error depends on the particular set of measured variables; the correct model underlying the variable measures may well differ from situation to situation.

Still the model for nonrandom error specified by Werts and Linn (1970b) is inclusive of the others; that is, the others are but special cases of this general model. This model allows trait and method factors to be correlated and method effects to be unequal over the effects of a given method. When $p = 3$ and $m = 3$ this general model, as well as the other three models, is overidentified and estimable using confirmatory factor analysis. This situation offers the analyst the opportunity to check each of the four models against his data, comparing their ability to reproduce the correlation matrix for the measured variables. Unfortunately, when $p = 3$ and $m = 2$ and when $p = 2$ and $m = 2$ the general model is underidentified and limits the analyst's flexibility. It is possible to estimate some other models in these situations, however.

I hope that this presentation has not appeared overly optimistic about the usefulness of the factor-analytic estimation procedures discussed. Perhaps none of the models specified here will provide an acceptable fit to the data in a given situation, even where several models are estimable. We can sometimes attribute responsibility for such occurrences to sampling error. However, one should also bear in mind that such models make a number of additional assumptions: linearity of all effects, additivity of method and trait effects, and essentially random effects of other variables on the entire set of observed variables. Therefore a final word should be added in the form of a caveat. If an investigator believes that such assumptions are not appropriate for his data (see Campbell and O'Connell, 1967), he should seek other solutions to the MTMM problem.

REFERENCES

ALTHAUSER, R. P. AND HEBERLEIN, T. A.
    1970 "A causal assessment of validity and the multitrait-multimethod matrix." In E. F. Borgatta and G. W. Bohrnstedt (Eds.), *Sociological Methodology 1970*. San Francisco: Jossey-Bass.

ALTHAUSER, R. P., HEBERLEIN, T. A. AND SCOTT, R. A.
    1971 "A causal assessment of validity: The augmented multitrait-multi-

method matrix." In H. M. Blalock, Jr. (Ed.), *Causal Models in the Social Sciences*. Chicago: Aldine-Atherton.

BLALOCK, H. M., JR.
1964 *Causal Inferences in Non-experimental Research*. Chapel Hill: University of North Carolina Press.
1969 "Multiple indicators and the causal approach to measurement error." *American Journal of Sociology* 75 (September):264–272.
1970 "Estimating measurement error using multiple indicators and several points in time." *American Sociological Review* 35 (February):101–111.

BLALOCK, H. M., JR., WELLS, C. S. AND CARTER, L. F.
1970 "Statistical estimation in the presence of random measurement error." In E. F. Borgatta and G. W. Bohrnstedt (Eds.), *Sociological Methodology 1970*. San Francisco: Jossey-Bass.

BOHRNSTEDT, G. W.
1969 "Observations on the measurement of change." In E. F. Borgatta (Ed.), *Sociological Methodology 1969*. San Francisco: Jossey-Bass.

BOHRNSTEDT, G. W. AND CARTER, T. M.
1971 "Robustness in regression analysis." In H. L. Costner (Ed.), *Sociological Methodology 1971*. San Francisco: Jossey-Bass.

CAMPBELL, D. T. AND FISKE, D. W.
1959 "Convergent and discriminant validation by the multitrait-multimethod matrix." *Psychological Bulletin* 56 (March):81–105.

CAMPBELL, D. T. AND O'CONNELL, E. J.
1967 "Methods factors in multitrait-multimethod matrices: Multiplicative rather than additive?" *Multivariate Behavioral Research* 2 (October):409–426.

CONGER, A. J.
1971 "Evaluation of multimethod factor analysis." *Psychological Bulletin* 75 (June):416–420.

COSTNER, H. L.
1969 "Theory, deduction, and rules of correspondence." *American Journal of Sociology* 75 (September):245–263.

CRONBACH, L. J. AND MEEHL, P. E.
1955 "Construct validity in psychological tests." *Psychological Bulletin* 52 (July):281–302.

DUNCAN, O. D.
1972 "Unmeasured variables in linear models for panel analysis." In H. L. Costner (Ed.), *Sociological Methodology 1972*. San Francisco: Jossey-Bass.

HAUSER, R. M. AND GOLDBERGER, A. S.
1971 "The treatment of unobservable variables in path analysis." In H. L. Costner (Ed.), *Sociological Methodology 1971*. San Francisco: Jossey-Bass.

HEBERLEIN, T. A.
1969 "The correction for attenuation and the multitrait-multimethod matrix: Some prospects and pitfalls." Unpublished M.A. thesis, University of Wisconsin, Madison.

HEISE, D. R.
1969 "Separating reliability and stability in test-retest correlation." *American Sociological Review* 34 (February):93–101.

JACKSON, D. N.
1969 "Multimethod factor analysis in the evaluation of convergent and discriminant validity." *Psychological Bulletin* 72 (July):30–49.

JÖRESKOG, K. G.
1969 "A general approach to confirmatory maximum likelihood factor analysis." *Psychometrika* 34 (June):183–202.
1970 "A general method for analysis of covariance structures." *Biometrika* 57 (2):239–251.

JÖRESKOG, K. G., GRUVAEUS, G. T. AND VAN THILLO, M.
1970 "ACOVS—A general computer program for analysis of covariance structures." *Educational Testing Service Research Bulletin*:70–15.

LORD, F. M. AND NOVICK, M. R.
1968 *Statistical Theories of Mental Test Scores*. Reading, Mass.: Addison-Wesley.

SIEGEL, P. M. AND HODGE, R. W.
1968 "A causal approach to the study of measurement error." In H. M. Blalock, Jr. and A. B. Blalock (Eds.), *Methodology in Social Research*. New York: McGraw-Hill.

SPEARMAN, C.
1927 *The Abilities of Man*. London: Macmillan.

WERTS, C. E. AND LINN, R. N.
1970a "Cautions in applying various procedures for determining the reliability and validity of multiple-item scales." *American Sociological Review* 35 (August):757–759.
1970b "Path analysis: Psychological examples." *Psychological Bulletin* 74 (September):193–212.

WERTS, C. E., LINN, R. L. AND JÖRESKOG, K. G.
1971 "Estimating the parameters of path models involving unmeasured variables." In H. M. Blalock, Jr. (Ed.), *Causal Models in the Social Sciences*. Chicago: Aldine-Atherton.

WILEY, D. E. AND WILEY, J. A.
1970 "The estimation of measurement error in panel data." *American Sociological Review* 35 (February):112–117.

5

INFERRING VALIDITY FROM THE MULTITRAIT-MULTIMETHOD MATRIX: ANOTHER ASSESSMENT

Robert P. Althauser
INDIANA UNIVERSITY

I am indebted to Duane Alwin (chapter in this volume) for the genesis and direction of my chapter. Conversations with Alwin and Thomas Heberlein have also proved helpful. I remain solely responsible for the contents of this chapter.

Campbell and Fiske's (1959) elaboration of discriminant validity and the multitrait-multimethod (MTMM) matrix creatively joined two among many conceptualizations of valid measurement. Variables purporting to measure one underlying trait should not be highly correlated with measures of supposedly different traits. Measures should not vary because of the methods of measurement used. These two conceptions were brought together by the device of confounding one trait and one method in each of several measures.

For Campbell and Fiske, assessing discriminant validity required an inference about the degree to which the observed correlations between measures corresponded to the relative magnitudes of correlations between traits. With measures confounding traits and methods, observed correlations were simultaneously the result not only of true trait correlations but also of two sorts of method effects: methods could lack independence from one another; and methods could produce spurious components in correlations between measures in concert with method dependence. In effect there were two foci of inference evident in Campbell and Fiske's paper. Given different kinds of observed correlations between measures in the MTMM matrix, one jointly made inferences about correlations between traits and about method effects.

The primary purpose of this chapter is to reassess the inference structure proposed by Campbell and Fiske in light of Alwin's discussion of Campbell and Fiske (1959), Althauser and Heberlein (1970), and Werts and Linn (1970). I assume familiarity with the different blocks of the matrix, with the three criteria Campbell and Fiske proposed for assessing the matrix (see Chapter Four; Althauser and Heberlein, 1970, pp. 153–157), and with the corresponding comparisons of observed MTMM correlations.

CAMPBELL AND FISKE: A REVIEW

Before turning to this reassessment, a brief comment on Alwin's discussion of this inference structure is needed to define a larger issue.

Alwin makes clear the need to maintain the analytical distinction between the two foci of inference. Heberlein and I and Campbell and Fiske did not consistently maintain the distinction, but this inconsistency is instructive.

Heberlein and I began our discussion with the distinction in mind. Indeed the causal model of MTMM measures which we set forth (and which Werts and Linn respecified for three methods and traits) clearly predicated this distinction. Yet we criticized two inferences about trait correlations proposed by Campbell and Fiske on the grounds that serious method effects could obtain just when the appropriate comparisons of correlations would lead some to infer that true trait correlations were modest or small, and that their measures thus possessed discriminant validity. This could happen when method effects were strong but virtually equal. This possibility led us to abandon inferences about true trait correlations and validity from the first and third comparisons of MTMM correlations.

The two passages Alwin cites[1] from Campbell and Fiske suggests that they consistently maintained the distinction between the two foci of inference throughout their discussion. Yet at several points, inferences about method effects accompanied and sometimes displaced inferences about trait correlations. When inspection of the matrix showed method effects to be apparently large, the conclusion that measures lacked validity followed without a separate inference about true trait correlations. The technical purity of their cautious statement (1959, p. 84) partially quoted by Alwin—that "in practice, perhaps all that can be hoped for is evidence for relative validity, that is, common variance specific to a trait, above and beyond method variance"—is not maintained.[2]

Thus we see in their inconsistency and ours a taken-for-granted connection between inferences about true trait correlations and method effects, on which the validity of our similar conclusions rest: that although one can narrowly define measures as having discriminant validity if modest or small true trait correlations can be inferred, such validity is meaningless if serious method effects can also be inferred from the same data.

In light of this review and Alwin's discussion, I conclude that we should independently attempt both types of inference, then link the outcomes of each inference according to this explicit rule: that measures possess discriminant validity when *both* modest or small true trait correlations *and* acceptably small method effects are inferred.

---

[1] One passage is quoted below in this paragraph. The other concerns an inference about method effects from a proposed (but neglected) comparison of monomethod and heteromethod correlations. It is odd that this comparison was not utilized by Campbell and Fiske. It is clear from Alwin's discussion (pp. 94–95) that this inference would have been unsupportable.

[2] The distinction between the two inferences is not maintained in their (Campbell and Fiske, 1959) discussion of a series of studies (Kelley and Krey, p. 85; Anderson, p. 86; Burwen and Campbell, p. 88; Borgatta p. 89; and Carroll, p. 93). On page 93 they write of the "sorry picture" of measure validity evident in the preceding illustrations, continuing: "The typical case shows an excessive amount of method variance, which usually exceeds the amount of trait variance." There is little neglect of the absolute amount of method variance in these examples and in the quotation. Only inferences that follow a strict comparison of correlations according to the proposed criteria would be consistent with pure "relative validity," as exemplified in their discussion of Borgatta's 1955 study (p. 90). Nor can one find the distinction between inferences made, or conclusions about validity referring to either inference, in two recent papers using the matrix approach (Armer and Schnaiberg, 1972; Summers and others, 1970; Jackman, 1973).

CRITERIA FOR DISCRIMINANT VALIDITY

This brings us back to the question of whether we can really make these two inferences as Campbell and Fiske proposed, by comparing selected correlations in a MTMM matrix.

To attempt such an inference is surely audacious. With two methods and traits we cannot identify eight distinct parameters (of four kinds); yet we desire to gauge the relative magnitudes of five of the eight (ρ_{yx} plus four method parameters). It is not an attempt some would make at all, given the extent, much less the mere presence, of under-identification.[3]

What follows is therefore offered with a few caveats and a bit of cynicism. The matrix has an intuitive appeal that is probably strong enough to continue to attract users, whatever criticisms may be offered. But we can at least be clear about the risks of error in the structure of inference Campbell and Fiske have proposed, and attempt to specify the circumstances (if any) under which such risks may be reduced to acceptable levels.

It will be useful to examine formally the bases for inferring either that method effects on MTMM measures are negligible or that the true correlation between traits is sufficiently modest. Both inferences begin with an inspection of the difference between two correlations in the case of the first two Campbell-Fiske criteria for discriminant validity, and with an inspection of a difference of differences between correlations in the case of the third criterion.[4] One concludes that the first or second criterion is satisfied when an appropriate difference of correlations (a

---

[3] Gauging relative magnitudes of parameters in the fashion of this and part of Alwin's chapter is obviously not equivalent to identifying parameters, though it partakes of most of the difficulties of the identification problem. It may also seem that I exclude cases of three or more methods and traits in the present discussion because I treat the case of two methods and traits. In the valuable hindsight of Werts and Linn's contribution, this is technically correct. In another sense, however, mine is also a general treatment. Campbell and Fiske were not aware that larger matrices would technically improve their inferences about method effects and true trait correlations (as Alwin and Werts and Linn point out), apart from an increased number of comparisons of correlations possible with larger matrices. The effective result is that their method of inference, from comparisons of paired correlations, always labors under the burden of underidentification regardless of the number of traits and methods. The method of CFA obviously does not.

[4] This view of the third criterion follows Althauser and Heberlein's earlier (1970) version of this criterion in contrast to Alwin's—that the rank orders of true correlations follow the same pattern in different blocks.

comparison I value or a *comparison II value*) is positive and greater than zero by an amount we shall call a just acceptable (minimum) difference ϵ_1 (or ϵ_2). The third criterion is met when a difference of differences of correlations (a *comparison III value*) is close enough to zero, that is, less than a just acceptable (maximum) difference ϵ_3. For the moment, we set aside issues of choosing ϵ_1, ϵ_2, and ϵ_3 for each comparison. The statistical significance of comparison values is also set aside.

Keeping both inferences separately in mind, let us consider the possibilities of two kinds of error. Our hypothesis is that measures are not valid; that is, either they do not discriminate or they are affected by methods or both. We could conclude after an inspection of each comparison that our measures are valid, but be wrong. We would be making a type 1 error if we accepted our measures as valid when for some reason they are not.

Conversely we could conclude that our measures are flawed, that they do not discriminate, or that method effects are not negligible, but be wrong. We would then be making a type 2 error by wrongly concluding that our measures are not valid. The probability of either type of error may depend, as we shall see, on the difference between the comparison values and the just acceptable differences ϵ_1.

The following discussion requires one essential assumption in addition to those already made in adopting the model for the matrix (see Alwin's Figure 2): uncorrelated errors of measurement and uncorrelated traits and methods. We assume that the signs of all coefficients in the model are positive. We make no assumption that the effects of the same method on different measures are equal.

Note also that the structure of inference which follows merely "details the logical consequences of those assumptions applied to a given body of data" (Werts and Linn, 1970, p. 120). Keep in mind, too, that we are discussing the possibility of making crude inferences about the relative magnitudes of some unknown parameters (true trait correlations, the effects of methods) based on observed comparison values. Such values, in any given case, could have been generated by many configurations of actual or hypothetical population values of all the parameters that determine comparison values (see Tables 1 and 2).

The sign and size of the observed inequality between a comparison value and its ϵ_i bear a different relationship to each of our twin foci of inference. Method effects may interfere with an inference that a difference between correlations is sufficiently large to conclude discriminant validity. Letting starred comparison-value symbols represent the differences between correlations that are solely a function of epistemic paths and true trait correlations, we may express this potential interference

TABLE 1
Hypothetical Comparison I Values

$$I = (\beta_1\beta_4 - \beta_2\beta_4\rho_{yz}) + (\alpha_1 - \alpha_2)\alpha_4\rho_{M_1M_2}$$

$\beta_i =$	0.4	0.8		0.6		0.4		0.4	
$\rho_{yz} =$	0.4	0.7	0.9	0.7	0.9			0.7	0.9
$\rho_{M_1M_2} = 0, \alpha_1 = 0$ or $\alpha_1 = \alpha_2$: I*	0.384	0.192	0.064	0.108	0.036	0.096		0.048	0.016
$\rho_{M_1M_2} = 0.3$									
α_4, α_1, or $\alpha_2 = 0.3$									
$\alpha_1 - \alpha_2 = 0.2$	0.402	0.210	0.082	0.126	0.054	0.114		0.066	0.034
$\alpha_1 - \alpha_2 = -0.2$	0.366	0.174	0.046	0.090	0.018	0.078		0.030	-0.002

Low $\rho_{M_1M_2}$, Low α_i

$\rho_{M_1M_2} = 0.3$									
α_4, α_1, or $\alpha_2 = 0.5$									
$\alpha_1 - \alpha_2 = 0.2$	0.414	0.222	0.094	0.138	0.066	0.126		0.078	0.046
$\alpha_1 - \alpha_2 = -0.2$	0.354	0.162	0.034	0.078	0.006	0.066		0.018	-0.014

Low $\rho_{M_1M_2}$, High α_i

$\rho_{M_1M_2} = 0.7$									
α_4, α_1, or $\alpha_2 = 0.3$									
$\alpha_1 - \alpha_2 = 0.2$	0.426	0.234	0.106	0.150	0.078	0.138		0.090	0.058
$\alpha_1 - \alpha_2 = -0.2$	0.342	0.150	0.022	0.066	-0.006	0.054		-0.006	-0.026

High $\rho_{M_1M_2}$, Low α_i

$\rho_{M_1M_2} = 0.7$									
α_4, α_1, or $\alpha_2 = 0.5$									
$\alpha_1 - \alpha_2 = 0.2$	0.454	0.262	0.134	0.178	0.106	0.166		0.118	0.086
$\alpha_1 - \alpha_2 = -0.2$	0.314	0.122	-0.006	0.038	-0.034	0.026		-0.022	-0.054

High $\rho_{M_1M_2}$, High α_i

TABLE 2
Hypothetical Comparison II Values

$$\text{II} = (\beta_1\beta_4 - \beta_1\beta_2\rho_{yz}) + \alpha_1(\alpha_4\rho_{M_1M_2} - \alpha_2)$$

$\beta_i =$	0.4	0.8	0.9	0.4	0.6	0.9	0.4	0.4	0.9
$\rho_{yz} =$		0.7			0.7			0.7	
				(II* values)					
$\rho_{M_1M_2}$ & $\alpha_i = 0$ or ($\rho_{M_1M_2}\alpha_4 = \alpha_2$)	0.384	0.192	0.064	0.216	0.108	0.036	0.096	0.048	0.016
				High $\rho_{M_1M_2}$, Low α_i					
$\rho_{M_1M_2} = 0.7$ $\alpha_1, \alpha_2, \text{or } \alpha_4 = 0.3$									
$\alpha_4 - \alpha_2 = 0.2$	0.399	0.207	0.079	0.231	0.123	0.051	0.111	0.063	0.031
$\alpha_4 - \alpha_2 = -0.2$	0.297	0.105	−0.023	0.129	0.021	−0.051	0.009	−0.039	−0.071
				Low $\rho_{M_1M_2}$, Low α_i					
$\rho_{M_1M_2} = 0.3$ $\alpha_1, \alpha_2, \text{or } \alpha_4 = 0.3$									
$\alpha_4 - \alpha_2 = 0.2$	0.339	0.147	0.019	0.171	0.063	−0.009	0.051	0.003	−0.029
$\alpha_4 - \alpha_2 = -0.2$	0.261	0.069	−0.059	0.093	−0.015	−0.087	−0.027	−0.075	−0.107
				High $\rho_{M_1M_2}$, High α_i					
$\rho_{M_1M_2} = 0.7$ $\alpha_1, \alpha_2, \text{or } \alpha_4 = 0.5$									
$\alpha_4 - \alpha_2 = 0.2$	0.409	0.217	0.089	0.241	0.133	0.061	0.121	0.073	0.041
$\alpha_4 - \alpha_2 = -0.2$	0.239	0.047	−0.081	0.071	−0.037	−0.109	−0.049	−0.097	−0.129
				Low $\rho_{M_1M_2}$, High α_i					
$\rho_{M_1M_2} = 0.3$ $\alpha_1, \alpha_2, \text{or } \alpha_4 = 0.5$									
$\alpha_4 - \alpha_2 = 0.2$	0.309	0.117	−0.011	0.141	0.033	−0.039	0.021	−0.027	−0.059
$\alpha_4 - \alpha_2 = -0.2$	0.179	−0.013	−0.141	0.011	−0.097	−0.169	−0.109	−0.157	−0.189

in an alternative way. Given that an observed I is greater than ϵ_i, the inference that I* is greater than ϵ_i is hazardous if there are method effects. The primary difference between the criteria (discussed later) is the extent to which the method-effect terms can oppose the dominance of the trait-epistemic terms.

First Criterion (Comparison I)

Using Alwin's notation we examine the equation for one example of the difference between the population values of a validity diagonal and heteromethod correlation ($\rho_{x_1 x_2} - \rho_{x_2 y_1}$), which comprises the first Campbell-Fiske criterion for discriminant validity. Taking I to represent the comparison I value, we can write

$$\begin{aligned} I &= (\beta_1\beta_4 + \alpha_1\alpha_4\rho_{M_1 M_2}) - (\beta_2\beta_4\rho_{yx} + \alpha_2\alpha_4\rho_{M_1 M_2}) \\ &= (\beta_1\beta_4 - \beta_2\beta_4\rho_{yx}) + \alpha_4(\alpha_1 - \alpha_2)\rho_{M_1 M_2} \end{aligned} \quad (1)$$

Let us also define the comparison I value on the additional assumption that the method term in Equation (1) is zero:

$$I^* = (\beta_1\beta_4 - \beta_2\beta_4\rho_{yx}) \quad (2)$$

Comparison I entails a trait-epistemic term composed of a difference of products of sizes two ($\beta_1\beta_4$) and three ($\beta_2\beta_4\rho_{yx}$). If the epistemic paths (βs) are comparable or modestly incomparable, this term is essentially a function of $(1 - \rho_{yx})$. A difference of unequal-sized products in this equation makes it possible for the trait-epistemic term to dominate the whole comparison because the method term is a product of size three and even includes one difference of method paths.

If we focus on the inference of relative magnitudes of ρ_{yx}, under what circumstances will I* exceed ϵ_1 when I does? And under what circumstances will I* be less than ϵ_1 when I is? Such circumstances clearly depend on the relative size of the two terms in the preceding equations. Assuming roughly comparable epistemic paths and setting aside the effect of dependent methods ($\rho_{M_1 M_2}$), their relative size is a function of $(1 - \rho_{yx})$ versus the difference in the effects of the same method on measures of hypothetically different traits, for example $(\alpha_1 - \alpha_2)$. In the case where $\alpha_1 = \alpha_2$ (which Alwin discusses), there is no apparent possibility of erroneous inference.[5] Otherwise, nonzero differences provide a small

---

[5] A danger remains, assuming that epistemic paths are comparable, that the measures of two traits discriminate too well: for example, ρ_{yx} is so small that it suggests that the variable chosen to validate the discriminatory power of our first variable was not conceptually close enough to that variable to provide a meaningful validation. See Althauser and Heberlein's comments about "theoretically relevant" variables (1970, p. 164).

margin of error to our inference about I* from an inspection of I. The larger the dependence of methods and the larger the method effect on the measure common to the correlations being compared (α_4 is the effect of M_2 on X_2), the greater this margin of error. Thus for I either greater or less than ϵ_1 but in the neighborhood of ϵ_1, there is some chance of a type 1 or type 2 error, although the chances would vary with the absolute difference between I and ϵ_1.[6] This is partially summarized in the following:

> A. When I is close to but greater than ϵ_1, the probability of a type 1 error relating to an inference about the true trait correlation is great; but in general[7] it decreases rapidly, the larger the positive difference is between I and ϵ_1.

Thus I would be greater than ϵ_1, but if α_1 is greater than α_2, I* could be less than ϵ_1, depending of course on the values of $\rho_{M_1 M_2}$, α_4, and the observed difference $(I - \epsilon_1)$. The summary is completed as follows:

> B. When I is close to but less than ϵ_1, the probability of a type 2 error relating to true trait correlations is great; but in general it decreases rapidly, the larger the positive difference is between ϵ_1 and I.

Thus I could be less than ϵ_1, but if α_1 is less than α_2, I* could be greater than ϵ_1, depending again on the unknown values of $\rho_{M_1 M_2}$ and α_4 and the observed difference $(\epsilon_1 - I)$. Notice that the distribution of comparison I values about corresponding I* values is symmetric and centered about I* values (see Table 1).

If we focus instead on inferences about method effects, we learn nothing from this comparison. Given their ability to disturb the inference about true trait correlations, the opposite might have been expected. The problem is that the value for the true correlation and the relative size of method effects (relative to epistemic paths and variance in measurement error) are independent of each other according to our model.[8] Thus serious method effects could accompany discriminating measures (for example, $1 - \rho_{yx}$ is modestly large). As pointed out in Althauser and Heberlein (1970, p. 158) method effects could be large and equal, can-

---

[6] Note that the adjectives describing probabilities of error ("great" and so on) are necessarily imprecise. I do not have a sampling theory for the distribution of comparison values under hypothesized I* or II* values. The reader can judge the propriety of these adjectives by inspecting Tables 1 and 2.

[7] "In general" because ϵ_i can be chosen to alter the probability of errors. See "choosing ϵ_1, ϵ_2" later in this chapter.

[8] That is, true trait correlations on the one hand and epistemic paths, method paths, and measurement errors on the other are independent of each other according to the model. The latter set of course completely determines variance in measures.

celing each other out ($\alpha_1 = \alpha_2$) and hence eliminating their impact on this comparison; yet they would still be present. In short this criterion, met or unmet, sheds no light on method effects.

Second Criterion (Comparison II)

Following Alwin's notation again, we examine the equation for one example of the difference between the population values of a validity diagonal and a monomethod correlation ($\rho_{x_1x_2} - \alpha_{x_1y_1}$), which comprises the second Campbell-Fiske criterion for discriminant validity. Denoting comparison II values by II, we have

$$\begin{aligned} \text{II} &= (\beta_1\beta_4 + \alpha_1\alpha_4\rho_{M_1M_2}) - (\beta_1\beta_2\rho_{yx} + \alpha_1\alpha_2) \\ &= (\beta_1\beta_4 - \beta_1\beta_2\rho_{yx}) + \alpha_1(\alpha_4\rho_{M_1M_2} - \alpha_2) \end{aligned} \quad (3)$$

In the event that the method term on the right is zero, the comparison II value is

$$\text{II}^* = (\beta_1\beta_4 - \beta_1\beta_2\rho_{yx}) \quad (4)$$

The second comparison again entails a trait-epistemic term composed of a difference of products of sizes two and three. A difference of unequal-sized products in this term does not result in its domination of the whole comparison because the same mix of products and differences is characteristic of the method-effect term. Just as comparably sized epistemic paths imply that the trait-epistemic term is primarily a function of $1 - \rho_{yx}$, so comparably sized method effects imply that the method term is primarily a function of $\rho_{M_1M_2} - 1$. Hence with the exception of some cases where α_4 is greater than α_2 and $\rho_{M_1M_2}$ is high, the method term tends to be negative. Its size increases, the more methods are independent of each other and the greater the method effects are. It is unfortunate that correlated methods help reduce the size of this term and thereby impede our detection of serious method effects.

Depending on the degree to which methods are independent, the method term in this comparison can nearly offset the trait-epistemic term. This increases the margin of error in our inferences about true correlations between traits, relative to that found for I and I* values. Also the distribution of comparison II values is neither symmetric nor centered about II* values as before.

Hence if we focus on inferences about true correlations among traits, observed comparison II values are more likely to be less than II* rather than greater, depending on the strength of $\rho_{M_1M_2}$ and of $\alpha_1\alpha_2$. Thus II may be less than ϵ_2 when in fact II* is greater than ϵ_2. Hence method effects can more easily produce type 2 than type 1 errors. In summary:

C. When comparison II values lie close to but are less than ϵ_2, the probability of a type 2 error relating to the true trait correlation is great, and decreases in general only modestly, the larger the positive difference is between ϵ_2 and II.

Hence we would wrongly conclude that the true trait correlation was too large (for example, $1 - \rho_{yx}$ was too small). Given the greater margin of error here, the risk of type 2 error is more invariant relative to the size of II $- \epsilon_2$ than was the case with the first comparison.[9]

Type 1 errors are much less likely to occur with this comparison and focus of inference. If comparison II values are greater than ϵ_2, then II* will be greater than ϵ_2 given the usually negative sign attending the method term. Positive terms can, however, result from configurations of great method dependence and modest differences in certain method paths (examples of this are in columns 1 and 5 of Table 2). Thus:

D. For comparison II values close to but just greater than ϵ_2, there is some probability of type 1 error although it decreases rapidly, the greater the positive difference (II $- \epsilon_2$).

Suppose our focus of inference is method effects. An inference that method effects are weak when comparison II values exceed some ϵ_2 is hazardous. Comparison II values can entail very high values of II* (for instance, strong epistemic paths and modest ρ_{yx}) with strong method effects.[10] Thus for modest values of ϵ_2 the risk of error is virtually invariant for much of the range of the difference (II $- \epsilon_2$). So we can proceed only with considerable difficulty to infer the absence of method effects from the satisfaction of this criterion. In summary:

E. When comparison II values are greater than but near ϵ_2, the probability of a type 1 error relating to method effects is great; it decreases in general slowly and inconsistently[11] the larger the positive difference between II and ϵ_2.

What about the other inference, that method effects are strong

---

[9] Moreover with values of ϵ_2 anywhere near zero (say 0.15 or less), large positive differences between ϵ_2 and IIs greater than zero are impossible; hence it becomes impossible to elude the region of error below ϵ_2 in order safely to conclude that a comparison II value less than ϵ_2 means that II* is less than ϵ_2. But we need not restrict ourselves to positive comparison II values for present purposes.

[10] Perhaps this is less true at the extremes of the difference (II $- \epsilon_2$). The joint determination of measures by epistemic paths, method paths, and measurement error suggests that at such extremes methods could be assumed weak. The probable rarity of such extremes makes this of little practical utility, however.

[11] The inconsistency is due to the possibility that when α_4 is greater than α_2 another set of comparison II values may exist for large differences between II and ϵ_2.

and present when comparison II values are less than ϵ_2 or even negative? In an earlier treatment (1970) Althauser and Heberlein suggest that the presence of method effects can be detected from comparison II values near zero, on the supposition that they lie near zero because method terms are likely to be negative and have (in this instance) virtually counteracted modest trait-epistemic terms. This suggestion should be qualified to take account of the margin of error present.

Suppose (see Table 2) we choose an ϵ_2 corresponding to some acceptable (but unknown) β_i and ρ_{yx}. For convenience set this $\epsilon_2 = \text{II}^*$. Consider the risks of a type 2 error that accompany the observation that II is less than ϵ_2. Could we falsely conclude that method effects were strong? A glance at columns 2, 4, 6, and 8 of Table 2 shows us that the size of the method paths is directly (and the strength of method dependence is inversely) proportional to the increasing difference ($\epsilon_2 - \text{II}$). Thus the risk of a false conclusion apparently decreases as comparison II values approach zero and become negative. The risk is great, however, in the region of II near ϵ_2. Examples can be found in Table 2 of such II values that accompany both weak and strong method effects. In short:

F. When a comparison II value is close to but less than ϵ_2, the probability of a type 2 error relating to method effects is great; in general it decreases slowly, the greater the positive difference between ϵ_2 and (positive or negative) comparison II values.[12]

Third Criterion (Comparison III)

We define an example of the comparison III below ($\rho_{x_1y_1} - \rho_{x_1z_1} = \rho_{x_1y_2} - \rho_{x_1z_2}$) following Alwin's notation, but following Althauser-Heberlein's version of this criterion as one requiring nearly constant differences between corresponding correlations across blocks.[13] The third criterion would be met here, in contrast with earlier cases, if comparison III values were less than some maximally acceptable amount ϵ_3:

$$\begin{aligned}\text{III} &= [(\beta_1\beta_2\rho_{yx} + \alpha_1\alpha_2) - (\beta_1\beta_3\rho_{xz} + \alpha_1\alpha_3)] \\ &\quad - (\beta_1\beta_5\rho_{yx} + \alpha_1\alpha_5\rho_{M_1M_2}) - (\beta_1\beta_6\rho_{xz} + \alpha_1\alpha_6\rho_{M_1M_2}) \\ &= \beta_1[\rho_{yx}(\beta_2 - \beta_5) - \rho_{xz}(\beta_3 - \beta_6)] \\ &\quad + \alpha_1[(\alpha_2 - \alpha_3) - \rho_{M_1M_2}(\alpha_3 - \alpha_6)]\end{aligned} \quad (5)$$

---

[12] One implication of this is that a choice of ϵ_2 in the region quite close to zero (less than 0.05, say) results in an inability to conclude from IIs near zero that method effects are present.

[13] Alwin's version of this criterion is incomplete. Suppose we observe that correlation A is greater than B and that correlation C is greater than D. In practice, if $(A - B)$ were greater than $(C - D)$ by very much (say 0.1 or more) we would begin to doubt the satisfaction of the criterion.

Analogous to II* or I* we define

$$\text{III}^* = \beta_1\{[\rho_{yx}(\beta_2 - \beta_5)] - [\rho_{xz}(\beta_3 - \beta_6)]\} \quad (6)$$

In this comparison the two trait-epistemic terms entail products of size three, and one element in every product is a difference of epistemic paths. Moreover the expression for III*, unlike that for I* or II*, involves an essential difference of true correlations ($\rho_{yx} - \rho_{xz}$) although each element of that difference is weighted by functions of epistemic paths. This implies that III* tends to be of a smaller order of magnitude than were I* or II* (which were functions essentially of $1 - \rho_{yx}$).[14]

In contrast the two method-effect terms in III entail products of sizes two and three. This makes it possible for the size two method product $[\alpha_1(\alpha_2 - \alpha_3)]$ to outweigh the other size three products; at the very least it may outweigh the other method product.

Generally we can see three reasons why III may depart from zero: first, there is a much dampened (by multiplication of epistemic paths) difference of true correlations (hence III* greater than zero); second, there is an inequality in the two method terms as mentioned immediately above; third, there is also the possibility that the two method terms, being of the same sign, could add or subtract from III* in combination. Thus method effects could disturb the otherwise modest but dampened differences between true correlations whatever the degree of method dependence ($\rho_{M_1M_2}$), but particularly if that dependence approaches one at the same time that α_2 is greater than α_3 and α_3 is less than α_6. Or, with independent methods, the remaining method term could disturb the inference about III* based on an observed III if α_2 were less than or greater than α_3 by a modest amount. Considering the comparatively smaller size of the trait-epistemic term in Equation (5), the potential disturbance of the comparison values by the method term rivals and perhaps exceeds that found in comparison II.

In short, if we focus on inferences about true trait correlations, a combination of possible circumstances involving the size of $\rho_{M_1M_2}$ and important differences in the size of positive signed method paths could easily produce an observed comparison III value greater than ϵ_3, when in fact III* is less than ϵ_3 or vice versa. Worse yet the likely dominance of one method term $[\alpha_1(\alpha_2 - \alpha_3)]$, particularly in combination with the second term, reduces the chances that errors will be less frequently made, the larger the absolute difference between III and ϵ_3. Both types of errors could occur. To summarize:

[14] But note one major qualification. If β_2 is greater than β_5 but β_3 is less than β_6, the desired difference of true correlations becomes a sum. This poses special problems for comparison III as seen later in this chapter.

G. The probability of a type 1 error relating to the comparison of two different trait intercorrelations is great and essentially invariant relative to the observed positive difference between ϵ_3 and III.

Thus III could be less than ϵ_3 but III* could be greater. We would have wrongly concluded that the criterion of the "same pattern of trait interrelationships" is met.

Conversely III could be greater than ϵ_3 but III* could be smaller. We would have wrongly concluded that the criterion is not met, when the pattern was actually acceptable (focusing exclusively on trait interrelationships). Hence:

H. The probability of a type 2 error relating to different trait intercorrelations is great and essentially invariant relative to the observed positive difference (III − ϵ_3).

Before moving on to inferences about method effects with comparison III, we should note an important characteristic of III*. Depending on which of two sets of assumptions about epistemic paths is most appealing, a conclusion that the third criterion is satisfied could correspond to the expectation that III* equals either zero or some small number greater than zero. III* should equal zero (if there are no method effects) on the assumption that $\beta_2 = \beta_5$ and $\beta_3 = \beta_6$. This assumption means that epistemic paths from different traits to measures made by the same method are equal. III* should equal some small number different from zero on the assumption that $\beta_2 = \beta_3$ and $\beta_5 = \beta_6$. Epistemic paths from the same trait to measures of the same trait made by different methods are equal. We can easily adjust our adopted value of ϵ_3 to either set of assumptions. But either way inequalities among these epistemic paths contrary to such assumptions can create an additional margin of error when inferring III* from III.

With this added problem and the apparent invariance of type 1 and 2 errors relative to the difference between observed comparison III values and ϵ_3, it seems appropriate to conclude that the already difficult inferences about trait intercorrelations based on comparisons I and II are, in the case of comparison III, hopelessly ensnarled in probable error. Use of this third criterion to infer the relative magnitudes and differences of trait correlations is therefore unwarranted.

One would think that the possible domination of the larger method term would predicate the detection of serious method effects, at least in the event that III exceeded ϵ_3. If α_2 were greatly different from α_3 and (for simplicity) $\rho_{M_1 M_2} = 0$, this would be conceivable. But on the whole such an inference is also unwarranted because (Althauser and Heberlein, 1970) method effects could be strong or weak but essentially equal, producing negligible method terms and an unwarranted inference about their effects. As with the proposed comparison I, comparison III should not be used to make inferences about the effects of methods.

Summary

In the preceding review of the proposed criteria for assessing discriminant validity, we have seen that comparisons I and II of MTMM correlations can help us decide whether the true correlations between traits are modest enough to allow us to conclude that their measures discriminate from one another, but that such inferences carry the risks of type 1 and 2 errors. Comparison II may support inferences about the danger of strong method effects, but such an inference is accompanied by a serious risk of type 1 and 2 errors. Neither inference can nor should be based on the proposed comparison III of differences of correlations.

To reiterate further, errors of inference about true correlations are especially likely when comparison I values are in the immediate region of some just acceptable (minimum) difference ϵ_1. Errors are distinctly less likely for larger absolute differences between I and ϵ_1.

Errors of inference about true correlations are much more likely when comparison II values are less than ϵ_2 as opposed to greater. Type 2 errors can particularly be expected. They also pose a serious problem: although they should decrease in probability for larger positive differences between ϵ_2 and II, setting ϵ_2 anywhere near zero rules out all but modest differences. Type 2 errors here are only moderately invariant with respect to comparison II values less than ϵ_2.

There is a highly likely error of type 1 for inferences about method effects based on comparison II. The risk declines only moderately and inconsistently as the comparison II value is increasingly greater than ϵ_2 and is reduced in direct proportion to the size of ϵ_2. A similar risk of type 2 errors exists. Again the risk declines moderately but consistently as the difference (ϵ_2 − II) is increasingly positive. This leaves inference about method effects based on the MTMM matrix in a less than wholly satisfactory state. We are not in a good position to conclude that they are present. There is little consolation in knowing we are in a slightly better position to conclude correctly that they are absent, despite the distinct chance of a type 2 error.

On balance, then, what can we conclude from these comparisons, taking the risks of error into account?

Comparison I. Values much larger than ϵ_1 or much smaller (if ϵ_1 is set far enough from zero) safely indicate measures that do or do not discriminate, respectively, focusing only on the likely range of values of ρ_{yx}. Nothing can be safely concluded about such correlations from comparison values closer to ϵ_1; for other reasons, nothing at all can be concluded about method effects. Note that strong method effects can accompany measures that discriminate assuming an exclusive focus on true correlations between traits.

Comparison II. Values much larger than ϵ_2 safely indicate measures that do discriminate, if we focus again on ρ_{yx}; values much less than ϵ_2 indicate the presence of strong method effects. Values smaller than ϵ_2 do not safely indicate that measures lack discriminatory power or that method effects are strong; values larger than ϵ_2 do not guarantee the absence of method effects unless ϵ_2 is set high.

Comparison III. Inferences about either ρ_{yx} or method effects are unwarranted here.

Choosing ϵ_1, ϵ_2

How would one go about choosing appropriate values for ϵ_1 or ϵ_2? Whatever strategy is adopted (some are suggested below), the ϵ_i should be set in the same spirit with which one chooses significance levels for most statistical tests: that is, before looking at the comparison values. The choices are not easy. Tables 1 and 2 of hypothetical comparison I and II values highlight the difficulty of attempting these inferences at all.

There are several possible decision-making strategies. With respect to ϵ_1, for example, one could first decide how strong the desirable but not minimal epistemic paths should be (say 0.6) and also what value for ρ_{yx} would correspond to the greatest ρ_{yx} that one would still be willing to interpret as indicating discriminant validity (say 0.7). One could then set ϵ_1 equal to the I* (here 0.108) corresponding to our standards for β_i and ρ_{yx}. Even if these standards corresponded to reality many combinations of dependent methods and weak to strong method paths could, in conjunction with the standard β_i and ρ_{yx}, produce observed comparison I values with a range centered on ϵ_1.[15]

But these standards may not correspond to reality for β_i and ρ_{yx}. In that likely event one must be prepared to accept more discriminating measures (ρ_{yx} less than 0.7) in a tradeoff for lesser epistemic paths. (This is seen if one graphs I* against ρ_{yx} for levels of β_i and then draws a horizontal line for the ϵ_1 value adopted.) If one is not so prepared, other strategies are possible.

[15] Note that the range is determined by the worst combination of dependent methods and strong method paths stipulated in the table. A greater or lesser range of error could be expected for higher or lower values of ρ_{yx} and ϵ_1, and could be calculated from the expression for comparison I. Keep in mind, however, the codetermination of measure variances by epistemic paths, method factors, and errors.

For example one can set ϵ_1 equal to the I* corresponding to an ambitious lower limit for β_i (say 0.7) such that, even with perfect measures ($\beta_i = 1.0$), ρ_{yx} falls no lower than a preset limit for discriminating ρ_{yx} (say about 0.7). The value of ϵ_1 would then be about 0.3. Finally one could set ϵ_1 equal to the I* corresponding to a lower limit on ρ_{yx} assuming perfect measures.

The procedure for selecting ϵ_2 is the same as that described above, although one obviously worries more about the greater range of error among comparison II values.

In general ϵ_i can be set lower than otherwise if one is willing to draw conclusions about ρ_{yx} or method effects on the assumption that lesser epistemic paths obtain, or (in the case of comparison I only) if one feels that methods are independent (in which case the method term in I goes to zero). As in setting a level of significance, the choice of ϵ_i depends on which error one most wishes to avoid. Setting ϵ_i equal to a I* or II* that corresponds to some combination of standards need not be an invariable rule. It is tempting, for example, to raise ϵ_2 slightly relative to the II* that corresponds to our standards, in an attempt to minimize the chance of a type 1 error relating to true correlations and to reduce the chances of type 1 errors relating to method effects.[16] In short one can set ϵ_i higher or lower than I* or II* to lessen chances for less acceptable errors in exchange for more acceptable errors.

SOME LARGER ISSUES

From the foregoing discussion, and from Alwin's emphasis on the greater dependence of assumptions by the Campbell-Fiske and consistency criterion approaches than by confirmatory factor analysis (CFA), it seems that we have both erected a great many signs reading "Beware of Assumptions." Let us reflect briefly on assumption dependence, referring both to the general subject of path analysis and the identification problem and to the specific problem of making MTMM inferences with fewer than three methods.

Ideally there would be consensus on what constitutes reasonable or unreasonable use of common-sense knowledge in making assumptions.[17] In the absence of such consensus, it is disturbing to find instances

[16] It is crucial to note that even setting ϵ_2 high does not save this inference from likely error if ρ_{yx} is too small, as when we fail to choose a meaningful variable to establish the discriminatory ability of a given measure. See footnote 5.

[17] One virtue of this consensus would be the realization by those who "expose" the assumptions of disputed studies that we are all in the same boat. For a recent example of such an exposé, see Taylor's (1973) criticism of Jencks and others' study of inequality. It focuses on the assumptions of path analysis.

where the assumptions are rationalized simply by necessity or convenience.[18] This situation suggests a criterion for reasonable usage of a priori knowledge: that assumptions be based as much as possible on rationales (substantive and methodological) that are independent of the immediate necessity or utility. To the degree that we adopt this criterion, we can get on with the development of arguments for and against assumptions in the contexts of different models, types of data, and purposes of inference.

How consistently is this criterion already observed in practice? Consider two sets of examples. The first appears in a small set of papers that responded to Heise's (1969) model of test-retest correlations. Heise assumed, among other things, constant reliability of measured scores over time. In contrast Wiley and Wiley (1970) reasoned from the character of at least some types of social processes that the variability of true scores should decline over time, and that a constant reliability of measures was thus too strong an assumption. Nestel (1970), though not responding to Heise, reasoned in a comparable situation that measurement error should decrease over time as respondents bring their answers closer to their true feelings. Land (1970) argues, prior to still another respecification of Heise's model, for Heise's constant reliability assumption on the grounds that certain variables remain in aggregate equilibrium over time. Despite the evident disagreement about assumptions, we can see examples here of the criterion being observed.

The same observation of the criterion may be found in different degrees in assumptions formally or informally made in interpreting the MTMM correlations. Knowledge about the independence or dependence of methods can simplify the process of making the inferences reviewed earlier. Assumptions that methods are dependent or independent in particular instances are frequent and their rationales are consistently non-utilitarian. Thus Summers, Seiler, and Wiley (1970) expect considerable dependence of different reputational methods for identifying community leaders. Campbell and Fiske (1959, pp. 86, 90) contrast examples of independent methods (obstruction box versus activity wheel; projection versus observation) and dependent methods (role-playing and free behavior versus observation).

Another assumption of great utility but one capable of predication on substantive grounds is that of uncorrelated traits and methods. The

[18] For example Juster (1970) complains that the assumption in recursive systems that covariances of disturbances are zero is made merely because it offers a "gain in the ease of estimation" of parameters; helps guarantee the consistency of OLS estimates; and results in computation convenience (obviously the most utilitarian of these rationales).

accuracy of this assumption surely varies with the type of data considered. For psychological data on such variables as IQ, traits and methods are not merely confounded in measures but are in all likelihood directly correlated. A priori reasoning along the same lines is more difficult with at least some sociological data. Who will make the case that true scores for (not measures of) anomie, crime rates, religiosity, and social class are directly correlated with variables for which observational methods or different survey methods are proxies? A strong case can sometimes be made for assuming uncorrelated traits and methods, then, independent of any necessity of making it.

We can certainly expect disputes as to whether the criterion in a certain case was met or not. What one researcher sees as an assumption of pure utility or necessity, another will base on a priori grounds. At least the adoption of the criterion makes the underlying issue of such disputes clear to both parties. A constructive response to the dispute can take the form of a reformulation of the problem that is less dependent on assumptions whether disputed on contrary substantive grounds or on substantive versus utilitarian grounds. This is evident in the papers responding to Heise. This chapter also serves as an example, being a reformulation of that part of Alwin's discussion of the first criterion in the case where the effects of the same method on the measures of different traits are assumed equal. My guess is that this assumption rarely makes sense in most concrete cases and would have to be made almost always on purely utilitarian grounds.

One final comment about the criterion. I do not mean to argue that one's willingness to make an assumption bears no relation whatsoever to necessity or utility, but only that the premises of an assumption should have some freedom from the demands of the immediate context. We find in practice that the autonomy of an assumption varies from context to context, and rightfully so. An assumption may be purely utilitarian in one context but retain its autonomy in another.[19]

A general issue of a different sort is raised by the sharp contrast between the sophisticated and systematic method of confirmatory factor

---

[19] Thus Althauser, Heberlein, and Scott (1971) are willing "for other purposes" to assume equality of method effects in a discussion of inference from a modified model of the matrix (one no longer confounding methods and traits) somewhat different from that assumed in this and Alwin's discussion. But this assumption was made in the context of a rough assessment of another source of invalidity—reactive effects—and not for the purpose of assessing the strength of method effects. This assumption makes sense in this model because the equality assumed is that of methods on two measures of the same underlying trait. The contrast in purposes and models should illustrate the principle of the varying autonomy of assumptions in differing contexts.

analysis, especially when applied to models containing three or more traits and methods,[20] and the inferences proposed by Campbell and Fiske, discussed earlier. The methods most suitable to the technical abilities and immediate needs of researchers (who, depending on how they conceptualize methods, may be lucky to obtain data by means of two methods) may not be the methods most suitable for efficient methodological research into MTMM methods.

For the latter purpose, there is no gainsaying the utility of the CFA approach. Its ability to not only estimate but test overidentified models will greatly advance the systematic study of similar and dissimilar methods as applied to different kinds of data. We may soon learn what assumptions are generally sound for diverse methods and types of data, in cases where only one or at best two methods are practically feasible. This should precede further theoretical work on making inferences from MTMM matrices.

But many researchers may find CFA difficult to set up, and few will utilize models with three or more methods (and three or more traits) for which CFA is especially attractive.[21] Less difficult if still demanding methods will remain, I would guess, in practical demand. The needs of most researchers should not be neglected because the models or methods they adopt are "special cases" of the more general models and method of CFA.

REFERENCES

ALTHAUSER, R. P. AND HEBERLEIN, T. A.
1970 "A causal assessment of validity and the multitrait-multimethod matrix." In E. F. Borgatta and G. W. Bohrnstedt (Eds.), *Sociological Methodology 1970*. San Francisco: Jossey-Bass.

ALTHAUSER, R. P., HEBERLEIN, T. A. AND SCOTT, R. A.
1971 "A causal assessment of validity: The augmented multitrait-multimethod matrix." In H. M. Blalock, Jr. (Ed.), *Causal Models in the Social Sciences*. Chicago: Aldine-Atherton.

[20] Of course, CFA can be employed on Costner's overidentified model (assuming no methods factors affect measures) or on Alwin's "implicit" Campbell and Fiske model (where $m = 2, p = 3$ and method effects are assumed equal), as Alwin's chapter points out.

[21] See K. G. Jorsekog (1970). A diffusion of CFA comparable to that of path analysis in the substantive literature of recent years seems unlikely, albeit desirable, given the greater technical demands made on students by its method of maximum likelihood estimation than made by ordinary least squares. One reason for the diffusion of path analysis, I suspect, is that many researchers have a minimally adequate comprehension of least squares estimation.

ANDERSON, E. E.
   1937 "Interrelationship of drives in the male albino rat, I. Intercorrelations of measures of drives." *Journal of Comparative Psychology*, 24:73–118.

ARMER, M. AND SCHNAIBERG, A.
   1972 "Measuring individual modernity: A near myth." *American Sociological Review* 37 (June):301–316.

BORGOTTA, E. F.
   1954 "Analysis of social interaction: Actual, role-playing, and projective." *Journal of Abnormal and Social Psychology*, 51:394–405.

BURWEN, L. S. AND CAMPBELL, D. T.
   1957 "The generality of attitudes toward authority and nonauthority figures." *Journal of Abnormal and Social Psychology*, 54:24–31.

CAMPBELL, D. T. AND FISKE, D. W.
   1959 "Convergent and discriminant validation by the multitrait-multimethod matrix." *Psychological Bulletin* 56 (March):81–105.

CARROLL, J. B.
   1952 "Ratings on traits measured by a factored personality inventory." *Journal of Abnormal and Social Psychology* 47:626–632.

HEISE, D. R.
   1969 "Separating reliability and stability in test-retest correlation." *American Sociological Review* 34 (February):93–101.

JACKMAN, M. R.
   1973 "Education and prejudice or education and response-set?" *American Sociological Review* 38 (June):327–339.

JENCKS, C. AND OTHERS
   1972 *Inequality: A Reassessment of the Effects of Family and Schooling in America*. New York: Basic Books.

JÖRESKOG, K. G.
   1970 "A general method for analysis of covariance structures." *Biometrika* 57:239–251.

JUSTER, R.
   1970 "Causal relations and structural models." *Proceedings of the Social Statistics Section*:81–91. Washington, D.C.: American Statistical Association.

KELLEY, T. L. AND KREY, A. C.
   1934 *Tests and Measurements in the Social Sciences*. New York: Scribner.

LAND, K.
   1970 "Some problems of statistical inference in dynamic sociological models." *Proceedings of the Social Statistics Section*:21–25. Washington, D.C.: American Statistical Association.

NESTEL, G.
   1970 "A longitudinal study of labor market behavior—Advantages and some methodological problems in analysis." *Proceedings of the Social Statistics Section*:26–31. Washington, D.C.: American Statistical Association.

SUMMERS, G. F., SEILER, L. H. AND WILEY, G.
  1970   "Validation of reputational leadership by the multitrait-multimethod matrix." In E. F. Borgatta and G. W. Bohrnstedt (Eds.), *Sociological Methodology 1970*. San Francisco: Jossey-Bass.

TAYLOR, H.
  1973   "Playing the dozens with path analysis: Methodological pitfalls in Jencks et al. inequality." Unpublished paper to appear in *Beyond Inequality*. New York: Carnegie Corporation Panel.

WERTS, C. AND LINN, R.
  1970   "Path analysis: Psychological examples." *Psychological Bulletin* 74 (September):193–212.

WILEY, D. E. AND WILEY, J. A.
  1970   "The estimation of measurement error in panel data." *American Sociological Review* 35 (February):112–117.

CORRELATION OF RATIOS OR DIFFERENCE SCORES HAVING COMMON TERMS

Glenn V. Fuguitt
UNIVERSITY OF WISCONSIN, MADISON

Stanley Lieberson
UNIVERSITY OF CHICAGO

This work has been supported by the Wisconsin Agricultural Experiment Station. The comments of Thomas Heberlein, the members of the fall 1972 methodology trainee seminar at the University of Wisconsin, and Judith Tanur are gratefully acknowledged.

Ratios and difference scores are often used in sociology, and correlations involving such measures frequently have a component in common in the independent and the dependent variable. There is scattered reference to this problem in the literature of many fields, and evidence of a growing awareness among social scientists that correlations of this sort deserve special attention in the research process. The purpose of this chapter is to review several major aspects of such statistical associations, and from this review to make some recommendations regarding appropriate procedures.

Generally we are considering correlations between functions of variables having some common elements. Of the possibilities here, however, our concerns are restricted to a few of the most frequently confronted ratio or difference correlations in which there is a common term. For ratios these are

$$r_{(Y/Z)Z} \qquad r_{(Y/Z)(X/Z)} \qquad r_{(Y/Z)(Z/X)}$$

For differences these are

$$r_{(Y-Z)Z} \qquad r_{(Y-Z)(X-Z)} \qquad r_{(Y-Z)(Z-X)}$$

Examples of variables from sociology for these correlations could be:

(1a) the association of the relative importance of the administrative component in an organization, with Z being organization size and Y administrative size.

(1b) the correlation of two sets of per capita figures such that each characteristic X, Y is divided by the same population Z, as total value of farm products sold divided by the number of farmers, correlated with the proportion of farmers belonging to a farm organization.[1]

(1c) the correlation of convictions Y per crimes Z with crimes Z per population X, to associate certainty of punishment with the crime rate.

(2a) the correlation of change between two points of time of a measure with its initial level, as change in a measure of ethnic group identification related to initial level of identification.

(2b) the association of two measures each standardized by a third through subtraction; for example Y own self-image, Z own ideal self-image, and X image of the person held by a significant other.

(2c) the association of change over one interval with change over the adjacent interval, as with X father's occupation, Z respondent's first occupation, and Y respondent's later occupation.

First we shall consider the idea of spurious correlation and how it has been measured through formulas expressing ratio and difference correlations as functions of the variances, means, and correlations be-

---

[1] The ratio or difference correlation problem considered in this chapter is distinct from the issue of ecological correlation suggested by this example. See Schuessler (1973).

tween the individual elements X, Y, and Z. Next we shall deal with the use of ratio or difference scores as a means of describing the association between two variables (1a and 2a above). After this the use of ratios or differences as a means of controlling in correlations (1b and 2b above) will be reviewed and related to corresponding partial correlations. Then we shall take up what Niefeld (1927), in his systematic development of possible ratio combinations, termed a *chain relative* (1c above), and the corresponding difference score (2c). In considering these we shall return to the issue of spurious correlation and how it may affect research procedures.

In general we assume that we are dealing with population parameters here, avoiding the difficult problems associated with statistical inference. Thus our emphasis is on description and interpretation of data that include ratio or difference scores.

There are other ratio and difference correlations found in the literature that we have not included because of the necessity to limit the scope of our discussion. Perhaps the most notable is the part-whole correlation $r_{(Y+X)X}$ (see Snedecor, 1956; Bartko and Pettigrew, 1968; Guilford, 1954). Similarly we cannot consider the implications of the fact that many functions are a combination of ratio and difference scores. For example not only does the correlation between the percentage of nonwhites and the percentage of the population having a high school education employ two ratios sharing a common denominator, but each numerator is also part of the denominator. Moreover one could consider the correlation of difference scores of percentages having common denominators. These complexities must be dealt with in future work.

COMPONENT FORMULAS AND SPURIOUS CORRELATION

In 1897 Karl Pearson presented an approximate formula for a correlation of ratios expressed in terms of the correlations and coefficients of variation of its individual elements:

$$r_{(Y/Z)(X/W)} = \frac{r_{YX}V_YV_X - r_{YW}V_YV_W - r_{XZ}V_XV_Z + r_{ZW}V_ZV_W}{\sqrt{V_Y^2 + V_Z^2 - 2r_{YZ}V_YV_Z}\sqrt{V_X^2 + V_W^2 - 2r_{XW}V_XV_W}}$$

By giving variables common terms or by substituting 1 for a variable where it is omitted, various ratio correlations may be derived from this basic formula. The results for the correlations considered here are as follows:

$$r_{(Y/Z)Z} = \frac{r_{YZ}V_YV_Z - V_Z^2}{V_Z\sqrt{V_Y^2 + V_Z^2 - 2r_{YZ}V_YV_Z}} \tag{3a}$$

$$r_{(Y/Z)(X/Z)} = \frac{r_{YX}V_YV_X - r_{YZ}V_YV_Z - r_{XZ}V_XV_Z + V_Z^2}{\sqrt{V_Y^2 + V_Z^2 - 2r_{YZ}V_YV_Z}\sqrt{V_X^2 + V_Z^2 - 2r_{XZ}V_XV_Z}} \quad (3b)$$

$$r_{(Y/Z)(Z/X)} = \frac{r_{YZ}V_YV_Z - r_{YX}V_YV_X - V_Z + r_{ZX}V_ZV_X}{\sqrt{V_Y^2 + V_Z^2 - 2r_{YZ}V_YV_Z}\sqrt{V_Z^2 + V_X^2 - 2r_{ZX}V_ZV_X}} \quad (3c)$$

Pearson derived his formula by using the binomial series expansion, under the assumption that third- and higher-order terms could be neglected. By straightforward algebra one may derive similar but exact formulas for the difference correlations. Results are

$$r_{(Y-Z)Z} = \frac{r_{YZ}\sigma_Y\sigma_Z - \sigma_Z^2}{\sigma_Z\sqrt{\sigma_Y^2 + \sigma_Z^2 - 2r_{YZ}\sigma_Y\sigma_Z}} \quad (4a)$$

$$r_{(Y-Z)(X-Z)} = \frac{r_{YX}\sigma_Y\sigma_X - r_{YZ}\sigma_Y\sigma_Z - r_{XZ}\sigma_X\sigma_Z + \sigma_Z^2}{\sqrt{\sigma_Y^2 + \sigma_Z^2 - 2r_{YZ}\sigma_Y\sigma_Z}\sqrt{\sigma_X^2 + \sigma_Z^2 - 2r_{XZ}\sigma_X\sigma_Z}} \quad (4b)$$

$$r_{(Y-Z)(Z-X)} = \frac{r_{YZ}\sigma_Y\sigma_Z - r_{YX}\sigma_Y\sigma_X - \sigma_Z^2 + r_{ZX}\sigma_Z\sigma_X}{\sqrt{\sigma_Y^2 + \sigma_Z^2 - 2r_{YZ}\sigma_Y\sigma_Z}\sqrt{\sigma_Z^2 + \sigma_X^2 - 2r_{ZX}\sigma_Z\sigma_X}} \quad (4c)$$

Note that the pairs of formulas in Equations (3) and (4) are almost the same except that coefficients of variation appear in the former and standard deviations in the latter. Note also that (3c) is the negative of (3b) and that (4c) is the negative of (4b).

In dealing with the correlation between Y/Z and X/Z [Equation (3b)], Pearson pointed out that if $r_{XY} = r_{XZ} = r_{YZ} = 0$, $r_{(Y/Z)(X/Z)}$ does not vanish but is equal to

$$V_Z^2/\sqrt{V_Y^2 + V_Z^2}\sqrt{V_X^2 + V_Z^2}$$

and this he termed a measure of the *spurious correlation*. Corresponding formulas follow immediately for Equations (3a) and (3c).

Regarding differences, if the correlations between the individual variables are all zero the spurious correlation may be expressed in terms of the individual variances. Thus if $r_{YZ} = 0$,

$$r_{(Y-Z)Z} = -\sigma_Z^2/\sqrt{\sigma_Y^2 + \sigma_Z^2}\,(\sigma_Z) = -\sigma_Z/\sqrt{\sigma_Y^2 + \sigma_Z^2}$$

The spurious correlation formulas, under the assumption that all component correlations are zero, would be positive for Equations (3b) and (4b) but negative for (3a), (4a), (3c), and (4c). In the latter cases the common term is in the denominator or the subtrahend for one variable but in the numerator or minuend for the other, so that its effect on the overall correlation is inverse.

In order to gauge the effect of spurious correlation for ratios, Pearson went on to compare correlations empirically obtained with those that would have been obtained from the same data if the component correlations were zero.

Recently Chayes (1971) followed Pearson's approach in developing correlations for types of ratios under the assumption that the component correlations are zero. He refers to these as null correlations, to be compared with correlations empirically obtained. Chayes gets around the problem of the approximate nature of the basic Pearson formula by using simulation as an alternative procedure for determining the null correlations.

Discussions of this problem have centered on the purpose and assumptions of the analysis to be undertaken. Several writers have regretted Pearson's choice of the word *spurious* to refer to this phenomenon. A number have pointed out that there is nothing intrinsically spurious about the correlation, though interpretations may indeed be spurious, as in inferring from a ratio correlation the size or direction of a component correlation or vice versa. A basic distinction here is whether the ratio or difference score is taken to be the basic variable describing the population under study or whether one's major interest really focuses on the component measures. If the former is the case, some authors argue that spurious correlation is not a problem (Yule, 1910; Kuh and Meyer, 1955; Rangarajan and Chatterjee, 1969). Logan (1972, p. 67) gives as an example the association of speed (miles per hour) with gasoline consumption (miles per gallon). The basic interest here is in whether cars that go faster burn gasoline at a greater rate, and not in the associations between component variables—miles traveled, time elapsed, or gasoline consumed. Just as this example utilizes a common numerator in the two ratios (miles), sociologists may likewise try to claim an inherent interest in ratios with a common denominator; for example, the correlation between per capita energy consumption of nations and their per capita gross national product.

As Schuessler (1972) concludes, this is why it is so important to specify the nature of the variables one is studying. Blau and Duncan (1967, pp. 194–199) criticize the use of difference-score correlations in the study of mobility, arguing that the research problems considered are better stated in terms of the component variables. In practice, however, it is not always easy to determine when the major interest is in the ratio or difference variable and when it is in the individual components.

Even if one's main concern is with ratio or difference variables, moreover, there may well be considerable interest in noting the relative importance of component correlations and variances on the ratio correlation. Bartko and Pettigrew (1968) present a nomograph relating r_{XY} with $r_{(Y-X)X}$ for different values of σ_Y^2/σ_X^2. Schuessler (1972, 1973) devotes a good deal of attention to the relation between ratio correlations and their components, and works out several examples by using the Pearson formulas and by taking logs.

Here we should note a caution from the literature, however. Pearson used the binomial expansion and neglected third- and higher-order terms.[2] In some empirical cases the deviation between the formula result and the ratio correlation may be large enough to render a component analysis relatively meaningless. On the other hand, as we have noted, the formulas for difference scores are exact.

To summarize, when ratios or difference scores are included in a correlation so that there is a common element in both the dependent and the independent variable, part of the correlation may be attributed to these common elements. Even if all the individual elements intercorrelate zero, the original ratio correlation would not be zero. Ratio or difference correlations may be expressed as functions of component correlations, and variances or coefficients of variation. These formulas may be useful in understanding the structure of the original relationship. Whether the correlation is spurious, however, depends on the nature of the variables and how they are treated, as well as on the goals and procedures of analysis for a particular research problem. Before drawing specific conclusions, therefore, it is necessary to examine the redundant correlations and their uses in more detail.

THE $r_{(Y/Z)Z}$ CORRELATION

The $r_{(Y/Z)Z}$ correlation is found widely in the literature. In addition to the example already given it is commonly used (as is the corresponding difference-score correlation) to associate a measure of change with the initial level of a variable. Thus change in population over a decade may be associated with initial size for a group of political units.[3]

---

[2] Thus Kunreuther (1966) points out that Pearson assumed $(Z - \bar{Z})/\bar{Z}$ would be small where Z is the common denominator (in a correlation of ratios with a common denominator) when in fact this assumption often is not the case. Kunreuther states in fact that if $|(Z - \bar{Z})/\bar{Z}| > 1$ for any observation, the series expansion does not converge. He concludes that an estimate based on the first few terms of the series expansion loses its accuracy as the mean of X/Z deviates from $\bar{X}/\bar{Z}$ and the coefficient of variation of Z increases; similarly for Y/Z.

[3] The correlation of percent change with size at the beginning of the period reduces to $r_{(Y/Z)Z}$. Percent change would be $[(Y - Z)/Z]100$ in our notation, or $[(Y/Z) - 1.0] 100$. Dividing this variable by 100 and adding 1.0 would not affect the correlation with Z.

Consider the linear equation $\hat{Y}_i = BZ_i + A$. If we divide through by Z_i (see Snedecor, 1956, p. 158) we obtain the following relation between the variables Y/Z and Z: $\hat{Y}_i/Z_i = B + (A/Z_i)$.

Several things are immediately evident from this equation that relate to the association between Y/Z and Z, and the corresponding correlation coefficient. The equation is not linear, but is linear in the parameters. That is, if $\hat{Y}/Z = \hat{U}$ and $1/Z = V$, we have a linear equation $\hat{U} = B + AV$. Thus the association between Z and Y/Z is curvilinear approaching B as an asymptote, and is positive if A is negative and negative if A is positive, regardless of the value of B. If A is zero, however, there is no association between Y/Z and Z.

This rather surprising result may seem more reasonable on reflection. If $A = 0$ the original equation is linear homogeneous, so there is a proportional relation between Z and Y not affected by the level of Z.

According to the least-squares solution $A = \bar{Y} - B\bar{Z}$. In a correlation-regression situation, the circumstances under which A will be negative or positive or zero are as follows:

If $A > 0$, $\bar{Y} > B\bar{Z}$, $B < \bar{Y}/\bar{Z} = (\Sigma Y/N)/(\Sigma Z/N) = \Sigma Y/\Sigma Z$
If $A < 0$, $\bar{Y} < B\bar{Z}$, $B > \bar{Y}/\bar{Z}$ $\hspace{4em} = \Sigma Y/\Sigma Z$
If $A = 0$, $\bar{Y} = B\bar{Z}$, $B = \bar{Y}/\bar{Z}$ $\hspace{4em} = \Sigma Y/\Sigma Z$

Thus the sign of A and hence the direction of the association between Y/Z and Z is determined by the size of B relative to the aggregate proportion of Y with respect to Z. This gives an interpretive basis for $r_{(Y/Z)Z}$. In terms of the original relation between Y and Z, we can conclude that if the slope based on the regression of the Y values on the Z values is steeper than that obtained by simply aggregating all the Zs and Ys, there will be a positive association between Y/Z and Z. Suppose Y is the 1970 population and Z is the 1960 population for a set of cities. If the slope of the regression of the 1970 population on the 1960 population is steeper than the overall ratio of the 1970 to 1960 population, larger cities will in this sense have more than a proportional increase in population.

R. A. Fisher (1947) presented results along the same lines using a covariance analysis of heart weights and body weights of cats. He found that for females the $B = 0.26$ was less than the aggregate ratio (0.39) and tested to see if A was significantly greater than zero. The result was almost significant, and he concluded that for females heart weight probably increases less than proportionally to body weight. For males the aggregate ratio was also 0.39 but the regression coefficient was 0.43; thus for males heart weight appears to increase more than proportionally but the results are not significant. The close agreement between sexes in the average percentage of body taken up by heart, masks differences in heart weight expected for a given body weight.

An implication of Fisher's conclusion is that the aggregate ratio may not be a good basis for prediction. This is emphasized with many examples from physiological research in a paper by Tanner (1949), who notes that using an aggregate ratio for prediction assumes that the correlation of Y/Z and Z is 0. These papers by Tanner and Fisher suggest a use for the $r_{(Y/Z)Z}$ correlation in evaluating the association of empirical data against the aggregate proportion as a norm.

A number of studies have looked into the association between some measure of organizational complexity and size, often through the $r_{(Y/Z)Z}$ correlation. In a recent paper Akers and Campbell (1970) cite several of these and report their own research on the relation between size and the proportion of members in administrative positions. They note the problem of correlating $r_{(Y/Z)Z}$ and turn instead to regression analysis between the log of the number of administrators Y and the log of organizational size Z. But they use a slope of 1 as a norm instead of the aggregate proportion with the original arithmetic variables Y and Z in comparing the regression to $r_{(Y/Z)Z}$. (In addition to articles cited by Akers and Campbell, related work includes Blau, 1970; Holdaway and Blowers, 1971; Klatzky, 1970; Pondy, 1969; and Rushing, 1967.)

Our conclusion is that $r_{(Y/Z)Z}$ is an appropriate means of considering one aspect of the possible relation between Z and Y. That is, assuming that this relation is linear, is the least-squares slope based on individual measures greater or less than that determined by simply aggregating all the observations? An unresolved question is that of how one would interpret the magnitude of $r_{(Y/Z)Z}$. If Z and Y are linearly related Y/Z and Z are not, unless $A = 0$. Also the effect of possible curvilinearity of the relation between Z and Y on the relation between Y/Z and Z needs to be considered.

THE $r_{(Y-Z)Z}$ CORRELATION

The results for the $r_{(Y-Z)Z}$ correlation parallel those of the preceding section. Again consider the linear equation $\hat{Y}_i = BZ_i + A$. Subtract Z_i from each side:

$$\hat{Y}_i - Z_i = BZ_i - Z_i + A$$
$$(\hat{Y}_i - Z_i) = (B - 1)Z_i + A$$

This indicates that the association between Z and $Y - Z$ is positive if $B > 1$, negative if $B < 1$, and zero if $B = 1$, regardless of the value of A. What are the conditions under which these values of B obtain? Since $r_{ZY} = B(\sigma_Z/\sigma_Y)$ ($B = b_{YZ}$ in conventional notation),

If $B = 1$, $r_{ZY} = \sigma_Z/\sigma_Y$
If $B > 1$, $r_{ZY} > \sigma_Z/\sigma_Y$
If $B < 1$, $r_{ZY} < \sigma_Z/\sigma_Y$

We conclude that another aspect of the possible relation between Z and Y may be gauged by the use of $r_{(Y-Z)Z}$. Assuming the relation between Z and Y to be linear, is the least-squares slope based on individual measures greater or less than 1.0? The relations for both types of associations may be summarized as in Table 1.

TABLE 1

Value of Ratio or Difference Correlation	Ratio Correlation $r_{(X/Z)Z}$	Difference Correlation $r_{(X-Z)Z}$
Zero	$A = 0, B = \Sigma Y/\Sigma Z, r_{ZY} = V_Z/V_Y$	$B = 1, r_{ZY} = \sigma_Z/\sigma_Y$
Positive	$A < 0, B > \Sigma Y/\Sigma Z, r_{ZY} > V_Z/V_Y$	$B > 1, r_{ZY} > \sigma_Z/\sigma_Y$
Negative	$A > 0, B < \Sigma Y/\Sigma Z, r_{ZY} < V_Z/V_Y$	$B < 1, r_{ZY} < \sigma_Z/\sigma_Y$

RATIOS AND DIFFERENCE SCORES AS CONTROLS

Ratios and difference scores are often used to determine the association between two variables while controlling for a third. In this mode of analysis one's basic interest would be in the association between two or more component variables, and the variable to be controlled is subtracted out or serves as a divisor. For example, $r_{(Y-Z)(X-Z)}$ or $r_{(Y/Z)(X/Z)}$. In both cases the basic interest is in the association between X and Y, controlling for Z. Associations are assumed between X,Z and Y,Z but are not considered by the researcher.

The spurious correlation derivation showed that it is risky to make inferences about component correlations from correlations of ratio or difference scores. How useful are these scores when one wishes to control a third variable? Here it is instructive to compare correlations using them with the conventional partial correlation coefficient. Using the Pearson approximation, Kuh and Meyer (1955) found that the minimum of $r_{(Y/Z)(X/Z)}$ with respect to V_Z was obtained when $r_{YZ} = V_Z/V_Y$ and $r_{XZ} = V_Z/V_X$, and that under these circumstances $r_{(Y/Z)(X/Z)} = r_{YX \cdot Z}$. From these conditions it also follows that both X and Y are linear homogeneous functions of Z and that $r_{(X/Z)Z} = r_{(Y/Z)Z} = 0$ (see Table 1).

Similarly we can take the exact formula for $r_{(Y-Z)(X-Z)}$ and show that it equals the partial correlation $r_{YX \cdot Z}$ when the slope of the association between Y and Z and between X and Z is 1, or $r_{YZ} = \sigma_Z/\sigma_Y$, $r_{XZ} = \sigma_Z/\sigma_X$, so that $r_{(Y-Z)Z} = r_{(X-Z)Z} = 0$:

$$r_{(Y-Z)(X-Z)} = \frac{r_{YX}\sigma_Y\sigma_X - r_{YZ}\sigma_Y\sigma_Z - r_{XZ}\sigma_X\sigma_Z + \sigma_Z^2}{\sqrt{\sigma_Y^2 + \sigma_Z^2 - 2\sigma_Y\sigma_Z r_{YZ}}\sqrt{\sigma_X^2 + \sigma_Z^2 - 2\sigma_X\sigma_Z r_{XZ}}}$$

If $r_{YZ} = \sigma_Z/\sigma_Y$ and $r_{XZ} = \sigma_Z/\sigma_X$, then

$$r_{(Y-Z)(X-Z)} = \frac{r_{YX}\sigma_Y\sigma_X - r_{YZ}r_{ZX}\sigma_X\sigma_Y - r_{XZ}r_{ZY}\sigma_Y\sigma_X + r_{ZY}\sigma_Y r_{ZX}\sigma_X}{\sqrt{\sigma_Y^2 + \sigma_Z^2 - 2\sigma_Z^2}\sqrt{\sigma_X^2 + \sigma_Z^2 - 2\sigma_Z^2}}$$

$$= \frac{\sigma_Y\sigma_X(r_{YX} - r_{YZ}r_{XZ})}{\sqrt{\sigma_Y^2 - \sigma_Z^2}\sqrt{\sigma_X^2 - \sigma_Z^2}}$$

$$= \frac{\sigma_Y\sigma_X(r_{YX} - r_{YZ}r_{XZ})}{\sqrt{\sigma_Z^2/r_{YZ}^2 - \sigma_Z^2}\sqrt{\sigma_Z^2/r_{XZ}^2 - \sigma_Z^2}}$$

$$= \frac{\sigma_Y\sigma_X(r_{YX} - r_{YZ}r_{XZ})}{\sqrt{\sigma_Z^2/r_{YZ}^2[1 - r_{YZ}^2]}\sqrt{\sigma_Z^2/r_{XZ}^2[1 - r_{XZ}^2]}}$$

$$= \frac{\sigma_Y\sigma_X(r_{YX} - r_{YZ}r_{XZ})}{\sigma_Z^2/r_{YZ}r_{XZ}\sqrt{1 - r_{YZ}^2}\sqrt{1 - r_{XZ}^2}}$$

$$= \frac{\sigma_Y\sigma_X(r_{YX} - r_{YZ}r_{XZ})}{\sigma_Y\sigma_X\sqrt{1 - r_{YZ}^2}\sqrt{1 - r_{XZ}^2}}$$

$$= r_{YX \cdot Z}$$

A single ratio or difference score may be considered a measure of one variable that controls or takes into account another. A change score, in which an observation at an initial time t_1 is subtracted from an observation of the same case at a later time t_2, is a good example of this. DuBois (1948) and Bohrnstedt (1969) consider such measures and note that if the effect of the control variable is really removed, the t_1 variable should correlate zero with the ratio or difference score. By transforming variables DuBois constructs ratio and difference scores so that these correlations are zero.

These writers also consider the residualized score $Y - \hat{Y}$ formed by least-squares regression so that $\hat{Y} = A + BZ$. Such scores meet the requirement that the correlation between the initial score Z and the residualized score is zero. If $B = 1$, a residual score would be $Y_i - Z_i - A$, identical to the difference score except for the constant term that would not affect any intercorrelations. Recall from Table 1 that, for difference scores, if $B = 1$, $r_{(Y-Z)Z} = 0$. In other words a difference score is equivalent to a residual score only if $B = 1$. Thus, consistent with the conclusion of Bohrnstedt, the residualized score is preferred for controlling purposes since it meets the requirement of zero correlation with the initial score regardless of the slope of B.

Bohrnstedt also discusses the part correlation coefficient—the correlation of a residualized score with another variable. Using the approach shown in making $r_{(Y-Z)(X-Z)}$ equivalent to $r_{YX \cdot Z}$, one can quickly determine $r_{(Y-Z)X} = r_{(Y \cdot Z)X}$ (the part correlation coefficient) under the condition that the slope of the regression of Z on Y is 1, and also show that $r_{(Y/Z)X} = r_{(Y \cdot Z)X}$ if $A = 0$ for the regression of Z on Y.

We should note also a connection with a related statistical technique. Gourlay (1953) contrasted the analysis of variance of difference scores with the analysis of covariance, using the intial measurement (Z in our notation) as the covariant. He reported, consistent with the other work mentioned here, that difference score ANOVA is approximately equivalent to covariance if $r_{ZY} = \sigma_Z/\sigma_Y$.

To summarize briefly, ratio correlations coincide with corresponding part correlations when the relation between the control variable and the dependent variable is linear homogeneous. Likewise ratio correlations coincide with corresponding partial correlations if the relation between the control variable and the independent variable is linear homogeneous, along with the relation between the control variable and the dependent variable. Difference-score correlations are equivalent to corresponding part correlations if the regression of the control variable on the dependent variable has a slope of 1. They are equivalent to corresponding partial correlations if in addition the regression of the independent variable and the control variable has a slope equal to 1.

Since only under these special conditions are ratio or difference-score correlations equivalent to corresponding part or partial correlations, one would seldom be justified in using the former as a substitute for the latter. In fact we could turn up only two arguments in favor of using ratio scores for such a research objective. Brown, Greenwood, and Wood (1914) compared $r_{(Y/Z)(X/Z) \cdot Z}$ with $r_{YX \cdot Z}$ and reported the former to be less affected by a few extreme scores. This may be due in part to nonlinearity of associations involving ratios. Kuh and Meyer (1955) contended that the use of $r_{(Y/Z)(X/Z)}$ with moderate departures from the conditions of linear homogeneous relations between Y and X with Z might be tolerated in order to correct a situation in which the error is directly proportional to X. If one's major interest is in the association between Y and X, correlation of ratios or difference scores could be misleading. To control the third variable, such measures might be occasionally justified only after determining that the extent of departure of the relation between Y,Z and X,Z from the criteria reviewed here are minimal.

THE $r_{(Y/Z)(Z/X)}$ CORRELATION

The $r_{(Y/Z)(Z/X)}$ correlation is sometimes employed in sociological research. A general circumstance of its use would be where a rate for a subpopulation is associated with the proportion that the subpopulation is of the total population. For example one might wish to correlate the proportion of black high school graduates with the proportion of the black population for different communities.

Recently there was an exchange in *Social Problems* concerned with such a correlation in criminology (Tittle, 1969; Chiricos and Waldo, 1970; Logan, 1971 and 1972; and Bailey, Gray, and Martin, 1971). This is the correlation of certainty of punishment with the crime rate, in which (using our notation) Y = admission to prison, Z = number of crimes, and X = total population.

Although there are exceptions, generally the correlation between Y/Z and X/Z is used when interest focuses on r_{YX} and Z is a control variable. Similarly with $r_{(Y/Z)Z}$ the problem can usually be stated in terms of the relation between Y and Z. With $r_{(X/Z)(Z/Y)}$, however, it is more difficult to reduce the research issue to the nature of a particular association between component variables so we must return to the points raised earlier in this chapter. The first approach to dealing with this problem comes out of the Pearson spurious correlation tradition. Thus in the criminology example Tittle's procedure, as well as that of Chiricos and Waldo, was to compare the empirical correlation $r_{(Y/Z)(Z/X)}$ with one obtained by a randomization technique. Their conclusions varied essentially because of different procedures of randomization.

Here the best procedure would seem to be to use Pearsonian correlations if at all possible in the research, rather than some other measure of association as done by Tittle and Chiricos and Waldo. Then one should compare the Pearson formula for ratio correlation (3c here) with that empirically obtained and, if the discrepancy is small, use the corresponding null formula. If the discrepancy is large one could obtain experimentally determined null correlations using the simulation approach of Chayes (1971, pp. 14–19), which takes the size of the coefficients of variation into account. Either way the null correlation is the value that would be obtained if $r_{YZ} = r_{XZ} = r_{XY} = 0$ given the coefficients of variation of the data at hand. The empirical correlation would need to depart from this to be meaningful.

Logan (1971) and Bailey, Gray, and Martin (1971), however, question this approach in the criminology example because they contend it is unrealistic to assume that the component rs are 0 and that therefore departures from the null would be expected. Would a difference between the correlation of Y/Z and Z/X and its null really indicate an association between the ratio variables that is not due to the common element Z? Here the difficulty seems to be in conceiving of the ratio correlations as functions of the component correlations and coefficients of variation. According to the Pearson formula any correlation greater than the null would have to be due to nonzero component correlations. We would expect some of these, for example the correlation between population and the number of crimes committed, to be nonzero. So what should we conclude about a ratio correlation that is greater than the null? It seems to us that from this approach one is either (a) forced back to the argument that if two ratios are theoretically meaningful as ratios, and hypotheses are stated as ratios, the results of a ratio correlation need not be considered as spurious; or (b) required to bring the component correlations explicitly into the development of the problem and (assuming that the Pearson approximation is good enough) examine the contribution of the components to the ratio correlation.

There is, however, another approach that deserves attention. Logan suggests computing the part correlation coefficient $r_{Y/Z(Z/X \cdot Z)}$ or $r_{Z/X(Y/Z \cdot 1/Z)}$ to remove the effect of the common term. (He notes that Z is not linearly related to Y/Z but $1/Z$ is). This, then, represents an effort to remove the effect of Z from one of the ratios and to correlate this residual with the other ratio. A similar solution was also considered years ago by Pearson (1910), by Brown, Greenwood, and Wood (1914), and by Neifeld (1927) using partial correlations to control the effect of a common element. A formal rationale for this approach is suggested by the work of Fleiss and Tanur (1971). Using expected values they show for a special case $\rho_{(X/Z)(Y/Z)}$ is not zero even though X, Y, and Z are independent. The same is true for $\rho_{(X/Z)(Y/Z) \cdot Z}$ but $\rho_{(X/Z)(Y/Z) \cdot (1/Z)}$ does equal zero under these assumptions. The same result holds for part correlations. One can also demonstrate, following their proof for the same special case, that $\rho_{(Y/Z)(Z/X)}$ does not equal zero but that both $\rho_{(Y/Z)(Z/X) \cdot Z}$ and $\rho_{(Y/Z)(Z/X) \cdot (1/Z)}$ do. This, then, would be a basis for Logan's analysis in the crime research, but under the assumption that Y, X, and Z are independent. Hence it is not clear that Logan has circumvented the objection that an independence assumption is unreasonable. Until more work is done on the rationale for part or partial correlations to remove the effect of a common term we prefer the straightforward Pearson procedure.

THE $r_{(Y-Z)(Z-X)}$ CORRELATION

The problem and procedures for the $r_{(Y-Z)(Z-X)}$ correlation closely parallel that for $r_{(Y/Z)(Z/X)}$. Thus one must argue that the difference scores have an intrinsic meaning, and so the correlation with a common term is not spurious, or else bring the component correlations into the formulation of the problem. In the latter case the exact component formula makes it possible to consider the contribution of component correlations to the difference-score correlation. It may be instructive to compare the empirically determined difference-score correlation with an appropriate null correlation, computed under the assumption that some or all of the component correlations are zero.

Blau and Duncan (1967) are quite critical of difference-score correlations in general, with or without common terms, and furnished the example of the $r_{(Y-Z)(Z-X)}$ correlation given earlier in this chapter, with X = father's occupation, Z = first occupation of son, and Y = later occupation of son. Their substantive interest in the component correlations leads them to refer to difference correlations as "tautological rearrangements" of information concerning the components. If $(Y - Z)$ and $(Z - X)$ are mobility variables, one might well expect a negative association between them. If $(Z - X)$ covers only a small part of a finite interval, there is a long portion remaining for the distance from Z to Y. The component formula shows this negative association to be an algebraic necessity if the three component correlations are positive and of similar magnitude. This they contend is close to being a spurious correlation.

A general conclusion is to interpret difference correlations with caution and to consider their relations with the component correlations. Beyond this, in situations where there is a basic interest in the components it might be preferable to reformulate the problem to obviate the use of difference scores. Thus research workers in stratification have tended to turn away from the analysis of mobility variables in order to focus on status attainment. Clearly a similar course may also be desirable for some problems involving ratio variables.

CONCLUSIONS AND GUIDELINES

We have considered the problem of correlating ratios or differences having common terms. We conclude by reviewing briefly the procedures one might follow in research.

First, an argument can be made that spurious correlation is not an issue in correlating ratios or differences having common terms, provided that one's interest is exclusively in the composite variables rather than in the components. We believe, however, that it is usually difficult to maintain that position; problems can be reformulated in terms of component variables, or in any event the relation between the components and the composite variables may be profitably explored.

Second, in considering the component variables we can identify two special types of ratio and difference correlations. The first, $r_{(Y/Z)Z}$ and $r_{(Y-Z)Z}$ are normally used when one's basic interest is in the nature of the association between Y and Z. We found that the direction of these ratio and difference correlations does tell us something specific about the nature of the association between Y and Z, assuming that Y and Z are linearly related. In terms of procedure, however, one might often prefer to examine the regression function for these two component variables, determining first whether the association between Y and Z is linear and if so estimating the parameters. The second special type of correlation involving a common term derives from interest in the association between two component variables Y and X, controlling for a third, Z. These are $r_{(Y/Z)(X/Z)}$ and $r_{(Y-Z)(X-Z)}$. Since they are equal to the corresponding partial correlation $r_{YX \cdot Z}$ only under special circumstances, generally it would be preferable to use the latter measure.

Third, if one's basic interest is not in the specific associations of components one may wish to examine the functional relation between ratio and difference correlations and their component correlations along with coefficients of variation or variances. For ratio correlations this is given in approximate form by the Pearson formula, but its use should be limited to empirical situations in which the approximation is good. The corresponding functions for difference scores are exact.

An important derivative of the component approach is to consider the implications of having a common term in both independent and dependent variables. This may be done by obtaining null correlations under the assumptions that the component correlations are zero. A similar procedure, which may be appropriate for ratios, uses part or partial correlations. Either way measurement of spurious correlation is based on the component perspective. This may give problems in interpreting the results, as when the reasonableness of the assumption that the component correlations are zero is questioned. In dealing with ratio and difference correlations, the researcher must as always state his problem clearly and recognize and work with the variables in which he has a primary interest.

REFERENCES

AKERS, R. L. AND CAMPBELL, F. L.
    1970 "Size and administrative component in occupational associations." *Pacific Sociological Review* (Fall):241–251.

BAILEY, W. C., GRAY, L. N. AND MARTIN, J. D.
    1971 "Communication." *Social Problems* 19 (Fall):284–289.

BARTKO, J. J. AND PETTIGREW, K. D.
  1968 "A note on the correlation of parts with wholes." *American Statistician* 22 (October):41. See also errata 22 (December):21.
BLAU, P. M.
  1970 "A formal theory of differentiation in organizations." *American Sociological Review* 35 (April):201–218.
BLAU, P. M. AND DUNCAN, O. D.
  1967 *The American Occupational Structure*. New York: Wiley.
BOHRNSTEDT, G. W.
  1969 "Some observations on the measurement of change." In E. F. Borgatta and G. W. Bohrnstedt (Eds.), *Sociological Methodology 1969*. San Francisco: Jossey-Bass.
BROWN, J. W., GREENWOOD, M., JR. AND WOOD, F.
  1914 "A study of index correlations." *Journal of the Royal Statistical Society* 77 (February):317–346.
CHAYES, F.
  1971 *Ratio Correlation: A Manual for Students of Petrology and Geochemistry*. Chicago: University of Chicago Press.
CHIRICOS, T. G. AND WALDO, G. P.
  1970 "Punishment and crime: An examination of some empirical evidence." *Social Problems* 18 (Fall):200–217.
DUBOIS, P. H.
  1948 "On the statistics of ratios." Paper presented at the annual meeting of the Psychometric Society.
FISHER, R. A.
  1947 "Analysis of covariance methods for the relation between the part and the whole." *Biometrics* 3:65–68.
FLEISS, J. L. AND TANUR, J. M.
  1971 "A note on the partial correlation coefficient." *American Statistician* 25:43.
GOURLAY, N.
  1953 "Covariance analysis and its application in psychological research." *British Journal of Statistical Psychology* 6 (May 1953):25–34.
GUILFORD, J. P.
  1954 *Psychometric Methods*. New York: McGraw-Hill.
HOLDAWAY, E. AND BLOWERS, T.
  1971 "Administrative ratios and organization size: A longitudinal examination." *American Sociological Review* 36 (April):278–286.
KLATZKY, S. R.
  1970 "Relationship of organizational size to complexity and coordination." *Administrative Science Quarterly* 15 (December):428–438.
KUH, E. AND MEYER, J. R.
  1955 "Correlation and regression estimates when the data are ratios." *Econometrica* 23:400–416.
KUNREUTHER, H.
  1966 "The use of the Pearsonian approximation in comparing deflated and undeflated regression estimates." *Econometrica* 34 (January):232–234.

LOGAN, C. H.
 1971 "On punishment and crime (Chiricos and Waldo, 1970): Some methodological commentary." *Social Problems* 19(Fall):280–284.
 1972 "General deterrent effects of imprisonment." *Social Forces* 51 (September):64–73.

NEIFELD, M. R.
 1927 "A study of spurious correlation." *Journal of the American Statistical Association* 22:331–338.

PEARSON, K.
 1897 "Mathematical contributions to the theory of evolution—On a form of spurious correlation which may arise when indices are used in the measurement of organs." *Proceedings of the Royal Society of London* 60:489–498.
 1910 "On the correlation of death rates." *Journal of the Royal Statistical Society* 73 (May):534–539.

PONDY, L. R.
 1969 "Effects of size, complexity, and ownership on administrative intensity." *Administrative Science Quarterly* 14 (March):47–60.

RANGARAJAN, C. AND CHATTERJEE, S.
 1969 "A note on comparison between correlation coefficients of original and transformed variables." *American Statistician* 23 (October): 28–29.

RUSHING, W. A.
 1967 "The effects of industry size and division of labor on administration." *Administrative Science Quarterly* 12 (September):273–295.

SCHUESSLER, K.
 1972 "Analysis of ratio variables: Opportunities and pitfalls." Paper presented at the annual meeting of the American Sociological Association, New Orleans, Louisiana.
 1973 "Ratio variables and path models." In A. S. Goldberger and O. D. Duncan (Eds.), *Structural Equation Models in the Social Sciences: Proceedings of a Conference.* New York: Seminar.

SEARLE, S. R.
 1969 "Correlation between means of parts and wholes." *American Statistician* 23 (April):23–24.

SNEDECOR, G. W.
 1956 *Statistical Methods.* (5th ed.). Ames: Iowa State University Press.

TANNER, J. M.
 1949 "Fallacy of per weight and per surface area standards, and their relation to spurious correlation." *Journal of Applied Physiology* 2 (July):1–12.

TITTLE, C. R.
 1969 "Crime rates and legal sanctions." *Social Problems* 16 (Spring):409–423.

YULE, G. U.
 1910 "On the interpretation of correlations between indices or ratios." *Journal of the Royal Statistical Society* 73 (June):644–647.

7

ALTERNATIVE APPROACHES TO ANALYSIS-OF-VARIANCE TABLES

Peter J. Burke
INDIANA UNIVERSITY

Karl Schuessler
INDIANA UNIVERSITY

It goes without saying, although it is usually said, that any errors in this chapter are the sole responsibility of the authors; the merits of the chapter, on the other hand, are the partial responsibility of the following persons who graciously supplied brief comments on a preliminary draft: T. A. Bancroft, O. D. Duncan, Holly Fuchs, and David Knoke. Our work was carried out under the auspices of an NIMH grant for training social scientists (MH10577), although that grant provided no direct financial support.

This discussion has a dual objective: to elucidate the statistical equivalence between conceptually different ways of doing an analysis of variance (AOV), and to assess criteria for selecting between these procedures in sociological research. The issue is whether extrastatistical considerations offer some basis for choosing one form of expression over another when statistical criteria are immaterial.

This undertaking had its inception in three distinct but related trends in sociology. First, the model of each measure as a linear combination of constants (parameters) and random error is very much in vogue today, having appeared explicitly or implicitly in at least one-fourth of all research papers in the *American Sociological Review*, the *American Journal of Sociology*, and *Social Forces* during the period from 1970 to 1972. Second, regression analysis of dummy variables, making its way into sociology from econometrics, is also becoming increasingly common today, with no less than 25 applications appearing in these journals for the same period. Third, also on the upswing in sociology is the use of models that ostensibly show the manner in which two or more variables are causally connected. The use of path diagrams to summarize what is no more than an analysis of variance is an instance of this trend.

None of these trends is free of complications and pitfalls. The linear model is sometimes not subject to statistical analysis because the conditions for such analysis have not been met; regression analysis of dummy variables appears to contradict dicta that attributes are not subject to algebraic analysis; path coefficients may be computed for an analysis-of-variance (AOV) table without regard for the causal assumptions implicit in that procedure.

Of the many crossed and nested classifications for which methods of analysis have been worked out, only the simplest are discussed here. These are divided into four parts, each comprising a somewhat distinct grouping of AOV tables: one-way and two-way tables with interval measures; one-way and two-way tables with a single covariable; one-way and two-way tables with a 0,1 dummy dependent variable; one-way tables with composite measures. In each case, alternative methods for getting sums of squares and alternative methods for presenting them are given with both numerical and substantive examples. Methodological implications, briefly noted in passing, are consolidated and discussed at the end of the chapter. Statistical references are limited largely to recent work having to do with AOV tables and their analysis; sociological references were selected for their specific illustrative value.

ANALYSIS OF VARIANCE

One-Way Table, Interval Measures

Fitting Constants. An analysis-of-variance table is a set of sample measures that have been sorted into two or more classes and whose variation may be represented by two or more sums of squares. Each measure is regarded as a linear combination of two or more terms with each term common to all measures in at least one class, except the error term, which differs from one measure to another.

In a one-way AOV table each measure is regarded as the sum of three parts:

$$Y_{ij} = \mu + \alpha_i + e_{ij} \tag{1}$$

where μ is common to all measures, α_i is common to all measures in the ith population (class), and e_{ij} is specific to the jth measure in the ith population. The usual object is to fit constants to the sample measures and on the basis of this fitting to test the hypothesis that the α_i are equal. Least-squares constants for sample measures are obtained by minimizing the function

$$F = \sum^{r} \sum^{n_i} (Y_{ij} - m - a_i)^2$$

(where r is the number of samples, or rows; n_i is the number of cases in the sample from the ith population; m is the constant fitted to all measures; a_i is fitted to all measures in the sample from the ith population), and solving the normal equations:

$$\begin{aligned} \partial F/\partial m &= 0 \\ \partial F/\partial a_i &= 0 \quad (i = 1, 2, \ldots, r) \end{aligned} \tag{2}$$

The solution of (2) requires an additional equation in some or all of the a_i, a requirement usually met by making their weighted sum equal to zero:[1]

$$n_1 a_1 + n_2 a_2 + \cdots + n_r a_r = 0 \tag{3}$$

Under this constraint, solution of (2) yields

$$\begin{aligned} m &= \bar{Y}_{.} \\ a_i &= \bar{Y}_i - \bar{Y}_{.} \end{aligned} \tag{4}$$

where $\bar{Y}_{.} = 1/\Sigma n_i \sum^{r} \sum^{n_i} Y_{ij}$ and $\bar{Y}_i = 1/n_i \sum^{n_i} Y_{ij}$.

The hypothesis that the α_i do not differ is tested by the ratio of sample variances based respectively on the differences among the α_i and the deviations of individual measures from the respective a_i within samples. In hypothesis-testing it is assumed that the e_{ij} are normally and independently distributed with zero mean and common variance σ^2.

The procedure is to calculate in succession the sum of the squared Y_{ij},

$$SS(Y) = \sum^{r} \sum^{n_i} Y_{ij}^2 \tag{5}$$

[1] This requirement may also be met by setting $a_i = 0$ or $\Sigma a_i = 0$.

TABLE 1
Analysis of Variance of One-Way Table

Source	Sum of Squares	DF
Total	$SS(Y) - SS(m) = SS(y) = \sum^{r}\sum^{n_i}(Y_{ij} - \bar{Y}_{..})^2$	$N - 1$
Between	$SS(m,a) - SS(m) = SS(a) = \sum^{r} n_i(\bar{Y}_i - \bar{Y}_{..})^2$	$r - 1$
Within (error)	$SS(Y) - SS(m,a) = SS(e) = \sum^{r}\sum^{n_i}(Y_{ij} - \bar{Y}_i)^2$	$N - r$

The sum of squares for m and a_i fitted together,[2]

$$SS(m,a) = \sum^{r}\sum^{n_i} (m + a_i)^2 \qquad (6)$$

and the sum of squares for m fitted alone, as if measures had not been sorted into samples,

$$SS(m) = N\bar{Y}^2 \qquad (7)$$

where $N = \Sigma n_i$.

Subtracting $SS(m)$ from $SS(Y)$ gives the total sum of squares corrected for the mean: $SS(y) = SS(Y) - SS(m)$. Deducting $SS(m,a)$ from $SS(Y)$ gives the sum of the squared errors:

$$SS(e) = SS(Y) - SS(m,a) \qquad (8)$$

Finally, subtracting $SS(m)$ from $SS(m,a)$ gives the sum of squares attributable to the main classification, mean corrected:

$$SS(a) = SS(m,a) - SS(m) \qquad (9)$$

It is pertinent that Equation (8) may be obtained by adding sums of squared deviations from sample means, and that Equation (9) may be obtained by adding weighted (by sample frequencies) squared differences between sample means and the overall mean. These identities are displayed in Table 1.

By virtue of these identities it is possible to move directly to a test of the hypothesis that the α_i do not differ, without the bother of fitting constants to sample measures. Nevertheless the fitted constants are the elements of which the final results consist, even though they may be sidestepped in running significance tests (Bancroft, 1968).

To illustrate numerically the fitting of constants, we drew a random sample of 90 measures (see Table 22 in the appendix) from a normal population with mean 12.00 and variance 5.00, adding $\alpha_1 = +1.00$ to

---

[2] Denoted $R(\mu,\alpha)$ by many writers. This notation calls attention to the reduction in sum of squares brought about by fitting a specific population model, for example $Y_{ij} = \mu + \alpha_i + e_{ij}$.

TABLE 2
Means and Variances for Random Groups

	Category			
	A_1	A_2	A_3	Total
$\bar{Y}_i$	13.81	11.35	11.08	12.08
s_i^2	5.11	4.81	4.61	6.25
n_i	30	30	30	90

TABLE 3
Analysis of Variance of Simulated Measures, One-Way Table

Source	Sum of Squares	DF	Mean Square	F	p
Total	$SS(y) = 556.24$	89			
Between	$SS(a) = 135.11$	2	67.55	13.96	<0.01
Error	$SS(e) = 421.12$	87	4.84		

$$\eta^2 = 135.11/556.24 = 0.24$$

each measure in the first group of 30, $\alpha_2 = -0.20$ to each in the second group, and $\alpha_3 = -0.80$ to each measure in the third group. Sample means and variances are given in Table 2.

Substituting in Equation (4) gives these fitted constants: $m = 12.08$, $a_1 = 1.73$, $a_2 = -0.73$, $a_3 = -1.00$. Substituting in Equations (5) to (7) gives the following sums, which are manipulated for the entries in Table 3:

$$SS(Y) = 13{,}687.44$$
$$SS(m,a) = 30(12.08 + 1.73)^2 + 30(12.08 - 0.73)^2$$
$$+ 30(12.08 - 1.00)^2 = 13{,}266.32$$
$$SS(m) = \sum^{r}\sum^{n_i} (12.08)^2 = 13{,}131.21$$

Tests of significance are carried out in the usual manner;[3] the correlation ratio squared (η^2), defined as the between-groups sum of squares divided by the total sum of squares, may be computed if required.

Regression Analysis of Dummy Variables. We may change Equation (1) into a regression model by substituting $\mu(U)$ for μ, and $\alpha_i(Z_i)$ for α_i, and leaving the e_{ij} unchanged:

$$Y_{ij} = \mu(U) + \alpha_1(Z_1) + \cdots + \alpha_r(Z_r) + e_{ij} \qquad (10)$$

---

[3] Testing procedures presented here hold for fixed effects (model 1) but not necessarily for random effects (model 2), a restriction justified by the virtual absence of tables of random effects in sociological writing.

where $U = 1$ for all cases, $Z_i = 1$ for all cases in the ith population and zero otherwise, and so on. Equation (10) is the basis for the statement that the parameters of (1) may be construed as regression coefficients on dummy variables. This interpretation has been commonplace among statisticians for over 40 years (Yates, 1933).

Least-squares regression coefficients in the sample are given by minimizing the function

$$F = \sum_{}^{r}\sum_{}^{n_i}[Y_{ij} - m(U) - a_1(Z_1) - \cdots - a_r(Z_r)]^2$$

and solving the normal equations. As with (2) the solution of the normal equations requires an additional equation in one or more of the unknown coefficients. Although Equation (3) might be used, a procedure of considerable practicality is to make any a_i, say a_1, equal to zero (Suits, 1957). Under this constraint the normal equations have these solutions:

$$m = \bar{Y}_1$$
$$a_i = \bar{Y}_i - \bar{Y}_1 \qquad (i = 1, 2, \ldots, r) \tag{11}$$

consistent with the requirement that a_1 equal zero.[4] If Y is correlated with its regressors, predictions based on the equation

$$\hat{Y}_{ij} = m(U) + \Sigma a_i(Z_i) \tag{12}$$

are more efficient than those based on the overall mean of the Ys; otherwise predictions are no better. Efficiency of prediction in a sample of measures is usually gauged by the multiple correlation squared, $R^2_{y \cdot a}$.[5] Testing the significance of regression runs parallel to testing the significance of the differences among the a_i as calculated in the analysis of variance and is of course subject to the same assumptions. One first gets

$$SS(Y) = \Sigma\Sigma Y^2_{ij}$$

Next the sum of the squared predicted $\hat{Y}$ values:

$$SS(m,a) = \sum_{1}^{r} n_i[m(U) + \Sigma a_i(Z_i)]^2$$

Correcting $SS(Y)$ and $SS(m,a)$ by $SS(m) = N\bar{Y}^2$ gives the total sum

---

[4] Subtracting $(1/N)\Sigma n_i a_i$ from each of these estimates gives estimates under the constraint that $\Sigma n_i a_i = 0$. This is equivalent to shifting the scale origin of the a_i from $\bar{Y}_1$ to $\bar{Y}_.$; it is also equivalent to changing the design, or incidence, matrix so as to express regression coefficients as deviations from the overall sample mean. For a discussion see Morrison (1967).

[5] Used here to denote the squared product-moment correlation between the predicted values $\hat{Y}_{ij}$ and the observed values Y_{ij}.

of squares and the regression sum of squares:

$$SS(y) = SS(Y) - SS(m)$$

$$SS(a) = SS(m,a) - SS(m)$$

Taking $SS(m,a)$ from $SS(Y)$ gives the sum of the squared deviations from regression:

$$SS(e) = SS(Y) - SS(m,a)$$

The squared multiple correlation between Y and the r dummy variables is obtained by dividing the total sum of squares into the regression sum of squares:

$$R_{y.a}^2 = SS(a)/SS(y) \qquad (13)$$

In this instance $R_{y.a}^2$ is merely a different symbol for the squared correlation ratio η_{ya}^2. Note that $SS(a)$ may be obtained by multiplying $SS(y)$ by $R_{y.a}^2$ and that $SS(e)$ is the product of $SS(y)$ and $1 - R_{y.a}^2$. These identities are shown in Table 4.

To exemplify by numbers the fitting of regression coefficients, we draw again on the 90 measures summarized in Table 2. Substituting solutions obtained by Equation (11) into (12) gives the prediction equation:

$$\hat{Y}_i = 13.81(U) + 0(Z_1) - 2.46(Z_2) - 2.73(Z_3)$$

Substituting sums of squares from Table 3 into Equation (13) gives the predictive efficiency of A: $R_{y.a}^2 = 0.24$, which may be tested for significance by the entries in Table 3.

Path Analysis. We may express Equation (1) as a path model by measuring each variate from its mean in units of its standard deviation, that is, by converting all variables into standard form. With these changes the coefficients on α_i and e_{ij} must be made explicit since they generally differ from unity:

$$y'_{ij} = p_{y\alpha}\alpha'_i + p_{ye}e'_{ij}$$

where $y'_{ij} = (Y_{ij} - \mu)/\sigma_y$, $\alpha'_i = \alpha_i/\sigma_\alpha$, and so on. The constants $p_{y\alpha}$ and p_{ye} have come to be known as "path coefficients," a terminology sug-

TABLE 4
Regression Analysis of One-Way Table

Source	Sum of Squares	DF
Total	$SS(y) = SS(y)(1)$	$N - 1$
Between	$SS(a) = SS(y)(R_{y.a}^2)$	$r - 1$
Error	$SS(e) = SS(y)(1 - R_{y.a}^2)$	$N - r$

gested by the diagrammatic version of the algebraic model; for an example, see Figure 1 (p. 162).

Carrying out corresponding operations on sample measures, we get the empirical path equation:

$$y'_{ij} = p_{ya}a'_i + p_{ye}e'_{ij} \tag{14}$$

where $y'_{ij} = (Y_{ij} - \bar{Y}.)\sqrt{N}/\sqrt{SS(y)}$, $a = a'_{ii}\sqrt{N}/\sqrt{SS(a)}$, and $e'_{ij} = e_{ij}\sqrt{N}/\sqrt{SS(e)}$ by definition, and, hence,

$$p_{ya} = [SS(a)/SS(y)]^{\frac{1}{2}}$$

$$p_{ye} = [SS(e)/SS(y)]^{\frac{1}{2}}$$

Furthermore, since both p_{ya}^2 and $R_{y.a}^2$ equal η_{ya}^2 it follows that p_{ya}^2 and $R_{y.a}^2$ are equal to each other and that each has the same statistical significance.

For the 90 measures summarized in Table 3, $p_{ya} = 0.49$ and $p_{ye} = 0.87$. The interpretation to be placed on these "findings" depends on the causal assumptions one is willing to make. One may interpret 0.49 as a measure of A's causal force if one assumes that A causes Y but not the reverse, and that none of the omitted causal variables is correlated with A. Although this assumption may be tenable for treatments randomly assigned to units, it may be debatable for many samples of nonexperimental data. For that reason, explained and unexplained sums of squares for survey data should not as a rule be represented by path coefficients and path diagrams unless there are compelling reasons to the contrary.

One-way tables with interval measures are fairly common in sociology but they usually contain complications that militate against significance-testing and the drawing of causal inferences. Gaston's (1970) analysis of variance of individual measures of scientific productivity grouped by prestige of one's current institutional affiliation is a case in point. Institutions of low, middle, and high prestige had productivity means of 12.6, 16.4, and 18.5. Because these averages rest on an enumeration of nearly all cases ($N = 203$) in the target universe ($N = 220$), significance-testing requires special justification; moreover, because units were not randomly assigned to institutions the F-ratio provides no demonstration that institutional prestige causes scientific productivity, or the reverse, or both.

However, it should not be concluded that one-way tables are never subject to causal interpretation. An example may be abstracted from Featherman's (1971) report on the relation between religious background and social achievement. A rough version of his hypothesis is that a family's religion, as well as its income, affects the formal schooling it provides its children. This hypothesis may be represented by a path diagram with the understanding that the dependent variable—years of schooling—has been adjusted for the effects of family income:

$$\boxed{\text{Religion}} \longrightarrow \boxed{\text{Schooling}} \longleftarrow \boxed{\text{Error}}$$

From a one-way table showing years of schooling by religion it would be possible to calculate p_{ya} and thereby to measure the direct effect of religion (A) on education (Y).

The path analysis of ordinal data, where each ordered class is represented by a dummy variable, has been considered by Boyle (1970); the discussion of this matter has been carried forward by Lyons and Carter (1971).

Two-Way Table, Interval Measures

Fitting Constants. In the two-way analysis of variance, each measure is regarded as the sum of five parts:

$$Y_{ijk} = \mu + \alpha_i + \beta_j + \gamma_{ij} + e_{ijk} \tag{15}$$

where μ is common to all measures, α_i to all measures in the ith population (row), β_j to all measures in the jth population (column), and γ_{ij} to all measures in the ijth subpopulation (ith row, jth column).

As with the one-way table, the problem is to fit constants and to test the hypothesis that populations do not differ in their constants. And as with the one-way table, the general procedure is to allocate the total sum of squares to its respective components by fitting a succession of reduced models and testing specific hypotheses by the results of these fittings. Although this procedure of comparing successively reduced models holds for all two-way tables, particular operations differ according to whether cell frequencies are proportional or disproportional. In the latter case, factors become correlated and that correlation must be taken into account in testing their significance. Since disproportional frequencies are likely to be the rule rather than the exception in sociology, the special methods for handling them will be of particular interest to sociologists.

The procedure is to fit a succession of analysis-of-variance models to sample measures:

$$\begin{aligned}
Y_{\cdot jk} &= \mu + \alpha_i + \beta_j + \gamma_{ij} + e_{ijk} \\
Y_{ijk} &= \mu + \alpha_i + \beta_j + e_{ijk} \\
Y_{ijk} &= \mu + \alpha_i + e_{ijk} \\
Y_{ijk} &= \mu + \beta_j + e_{ijk} \\
Y_{ijk} &= \mu + e_{ijk}
\end{aligned}$$

With equal n_{ij} and subject to the constraint that $\sum^r a_i = \sum^c b_j =$

$\sum^{r} c_{ij} = \sum^{c} c_{ij} = 0$, least-squares constants for the full model are $m = \bar{Y}_{..}$, $a_i = \bar{Y}_{i.} - \bar{Y}_{..}$, $b_j = \bar{Y}_{.j} - \bar{Y}_{..}$, $c_{ij} = \bar{Y}_{ij} - \bar{Y}_{i.} - \bar{Y}_{.j} + \bar{Y}_{..}$. It is of interest, if not remarkable, that these least-squares constants remain identical from one fitting to the next (provided that constraints are left unchanged).

Sums of squares for fitted constants may be calculated by the computing formulas given in Table 5. Sums of squares for the a_i, b_j, and c_{ij} (mean corrected) are next calculated as

$$SS(a) = SS(m,a,b) - SS(m,b) = SS(m,a) - SS(m)$$
$$SS(b) = SS(m,a,b) - SS(m,a) = SS(m,b) - SS(m) \quad (16)$$
$$SS(c) = SS(m,a,b,c) - SS(m,a,b) = SS(m,c) - SS(m)$$

The simplified relations on the extreme right hold by virtue of the equal n_{ij}, which cause factors to be uncorrelated (orthogonal) and component sums of squares to be additive. Finally the total sum of squares and the sum of squares for error are calculated:

$$SS(y) = \Sigma\Sigma\Sigma Y_{ijk}^2 - SS(m)$$
$$SS(e) = \Sigma\Sigma\Sigma Y_{ijk}^2 - SS(m,a,b,c)$$

Now it can be demonstrated that $SS(a)$ and $SS(b)$ may be obtained by adding weighted squared differences between marginal means

TABLE 5
Sums of Squares for Constants

Representation	Definition	Computational Formulas (for equal cell frequencies)
$SS(m,a,b,c)$	$\Sigma\Sigma(m + a_i + b_j + c_{ij})^2$	$\Sigma\Sigma n_{ij} \bar{Y}_{ij}^2$
$SS(m,a,b)$	$\Sigma\Sigma(m + a_i + b_j)^2$	$\Sigma n_{i.} \bar{Y}_{i.}^2 + \Sigma n_{.j} \bar{Y}_{.j}^2 - N\bar{Y}_{..}^2$
$SS(m,a)$	$\Sigma\Sigma(m + a_i)^2$	$\Sigma n_{i.} \bar{Y}_{i.}^2$
$SS(m,b)$	$\Sigma\Sigma(m + b_j)^2$	$\Sigma n_{.j} \bar{Y}_{.j}^2$
$SS(m)$	$\Sigma\Sigma(m)^2$	$N\bar{Y}_{..}^2$

and the overall mean, and that $SS(c)$ may be obtained by adding weighted squared differences between observed cell means and those expected from marginal means. Tests of significance are carried out in the usual manner (illustrated in Table 7).

If interaction is present Equation (15) is taken as the population model. Although row effects are now recognized as dependent on column effects and vice versa, the procedure for testing their significance is uncomplicated since $SS(a)$ and $SS(b)$, as obtained by Equation (16), are free of the effect of interaction.

In the case of disproportional n_{ij}, factors are no longer orthogonal and it becomes necessary to take into account their joint effects as well as the direct effect of each one. As in the case of equal n_{ij}, we begin by fitting the full model and the additive model in that order. With disproportional n_{ij}, however, the fitted constants m, a_i, b_j, and c_{ij} do not remain identical from fitting to fitting nor can they be represented as simple differences between marginal and cell means. Moreover, with disproportionality sums of squares are no longer additive, and the simplified computational formula for $SS(m,a,b)$ in Table 5 cannot be applied. To calculate sums of squares for constants, the normal equations for each model must be solved for the fitted constants, and solutions substituted into the definitional formulas of Table 5. From these, sums of squares for interaction and error sums of squares may be calculated:

$$SS(c) = SS(m,a,b,c) - SS(m,a,b)$$
$$SS(e) = \Sigma\Sigma\Sigma Y_{ijk}^2 - SS(m,a,b,c)$$

At this juncture our procedure is determined by the inferred presence or absence of interaction.[6] In the event of no interaction we proceed to get solutions of one-factor models and corresponding sums of squares. However, actual fitting may be foregone because (as in Table 5)

$$SS(m,a) = \Sigma n_{i.} \bar{Y}_{i.}^2$$
$$SS(m,b) = \Sigma n_{.j} \bar{Y}_{.j}^2$$

With these sums in hand we proceed to calculate the sum of squares for rows (A) net of the effect of columns (B), and the sum of squares for columns net of the effect of rows:

$$SS(a) = SS(m,a,b) - SS(m,b)$$
$$SS(b) = SS(m,a,b) - SS(m,a)$$
(17)

A finding of interaction would dictate acceptance of Equation (15) as the population model and correspondingly a modification in testing procedures. In the presence of interaction, row and column sums of squares as obtained by Equation (17) are confounded with interaction. To disentangle these effects, constants may be fitted to

$$Y_{ijk} = \mu + \alpha_i + \gamma_{ij} + e_{ijk}$$
$$Y_{ijk} = \mu + \beta_j + \gamma_{ij} + e_{ijk}$$

subject to the restriction that $\Sigma^r \gamma_{ij} = \Sigma^c \gamma_{ij} = 0$ in the population. After solving the normal equations one proceeds to calculate

$$SS(m,a,c) = \Sigma\Sigma(m + a_i + c_{ij})^2$$

---

[6] Bancroft (1968) advises that, in an incompletely specified model, interaction should be tested at the 0.25 level if main effects are to be tested at the 0.05 level.

$$SS(m,b,c) = \Sigma\Sigma(m + b_j + c_{ij})^2$$

From these calculations the sum of squares for rows net of the effects of columns and interaction, and the sum of squares for columns net of the effects of rows and interaction, are computed:[7]

$$SS(a) = SS(m,a,b,c) - SS(m,b,c)$$
$$SS(b) = SS(m,a,b,c) - SS(m,a,c) \tag{18}$$

As stated before, with disproportional data the analysis is complicated by the presence of correlational (joint) terms in both $SS(m,a,b,c)$ and $SS(m,a,b)$. For example, in disposing of the single correlational term in $SS(m,a,b)$ one may limit the analysis to the effect of each factor net of the others as was done above; or, if warranted, one may construe the joint effect as an indirect effect with either A or B dependent but not both. In the latter event the difference between $SS(m,a,b)$ and the sum of $SS(a)$ and $SS(b)$, each calculated by Equation (17), is allocated to A if B is dependent, or to B if A is dependent. (This possibility is represented by a path diagram later in this chapter; strictly speaking, it entails dropping the AOV model and substituting a recursive system.)

Similarly one may ignore the three correlational terms in $SS(m,a,b,c)$ and restrict the analysis to the effect of each factor net of the other two, as was done above. Or, if warranted, one may interpret the correlation terms as measures of indirect effects. In the latter case, which entails causal assumptions, joint effects are assigned to whichever factor is presumed to exert an indirect effect through the other two.

To illustrate the two-way analysis with equal n_{ij}, we divided each sample of 30 measures (Table 2) into three subsamples of ten each, adding $\beta_1 = 1.20$ to the first set of ten measures, $\beta_2 = -0.40$ to the second, and $\beta_3 = -0.80$ to the third. The γ_{ij} are identically zero and no interaction is present in the population. Marginal and cell means, from which fitted constants may easily be obtained, are given in Table 6. Sums of squares based on fitted constants and tests of significance are given in Table 7.

To illustrate the two-way analysis with disproportional n_{ij}, the same row and column constants as used above were assigned to the 90 measures arranged disproportionally among cells (see Table 22 in the appendix). Frequencies and means are given in Table 8. Fitted constants for the full model of four terms and for models having one fewer term, each set of constants subject to the constraint that $\Sigma a_i = \Sigma b_i = \sum^r c_{ij} = \sum^c c_{ij} = 0$, are given in Table 9.

In Table 10, right side, we give the effect of A (rows) net of B

---

[7] An alternative testing procedure, Yates's (1934) method of weighted squares of means, yields identical results in the present case.

(columns), and the effect of B net of A as calculated by Equation (17) on the assumption of no interaction; in the same table, left side, we give the effect of A net of B and C (interaction), the effect of B net of A and C, and the effect of C net of A and B as calculated by Equation (18) on the assumption that interaction is present.

TABLE 6
Means and Frequencies, Simulated Measures

	B_1	B_2	B_3	
A_1	15.11 (10)	12.98 (10)	13.32 (10)	13.81 (30)
A_2	12.83 (10)	10.99 (10)	10.23 (10)	11.35 (30)
A_3	12.35 (10)	11.56 (10)	9.34 (10)	11.08 (30)
	13.43 (30)	11.84 (30)	10.97 (30)	12.08 (90)

TABLE 7
Analysis of Variance of Simulated Measures, Two-Way Table with Equal Cell Frequencies

Source	Sum of Squares	DF	MS	F
Total	$SS(y) = 645.58$	89		
Subclasses	$SS(a,b,c) = 245.79$	8	31.72	6.22
Rows	$SS(a) = 135.11$	2	67.55	13.67
Columns	$SS(b) = 93.80$	2	46.90	9.49
Interaction	$SS(c) = 16.88$	4	4.22	0.85
Error	$SS(e) = 399.79$	81	4.94	

TABLE 8
Means and Frequencies, Simulated Measures

	B_1	B_2	B_3	
A_1	15.78 (5)	12.98 (10)	13.03 (15)	13.47 (30)
A_2	12.83 (10)	10.87 (15)	10.24 (5)	11.42 (30)
A_3	12.22 (15)	12.77 (5)	9.34 (10)	11.35 (30)
	13.01 (30)	11.89 (30)	11.34 (30)	12.08 (90)

Regression Analysis of Dummy Variables. Replacing the constants of Equation (15) by coefficients on dummy variables gives the regression equation:

$$Y_{ijk} = \mu(U) + \cdots + \alpha_i(Z_i) + \cdots + \beta_j(X_j)$$
$$+ \cdots + \gamma_{ij}(W_{ij}) + \cdots + e_{ijk} \quad (19)$$

Since dummy variables alter only the appearance of the model and not its essential nature, procedures for testing their predictive efficiency are the same as those for testing the significance of fitted constants. Least-squares regression coefficients are obtained for the full model [Equation 19)] and for the following reduced models with one or more fewer terms:

$$Y_{ijk} = \mu(U) + \Sigma\alpha_i(Z_i) + \Sigma\beta_j(X_j) + e_{ijk}$$
$$Y_{ijk} = \mu(U) + \Sigma\alpha_i(Z_i) \qquad\qquad + e_{ijk}$$
$$Y_{ijk} = \mu(U) \qquad\qquad + \Sigma\beta_j(X_j) + e_{ijk}$$

Solving the normal equations under the usual constraints, namely, $\sum^r a_i = \sum^c b_j = \sum^r c_{ij} = \sum^c c_{ij} = 0$, one gets these formulas for the full model: $m = \bar{Y}_{..}$, $a_i = \bar{Y}_{i.} - \bar{Y}_{..}$, $b_j = \bar{Y}_{.j} - \bar{Y}_{..}$, and $c_{ij} = \bar{Y}_{ij} - \bar{Y}_{i.} - \bar{Y}_{.j} + \bar{Y}_{..}$. These formulas also hold for each of the reduced models provided that constraints are left unchanged.

Sums of squares due to regression (uncorrected for the mean) are next calculated for each model:

$$SS(m,a,b,c) = \Sigma\Sigma n_{ij}[m(U) + \Sigma a_i(Z_i) + \Sigma b_j(X_j) + \Sigma\Sigma c_{ij}(W_{ij})]^2$$
$$SS(m,a,b) = \Sigma\Sigma n_{ij}[m(U) + \Sigma a_i(Z_i) + \Sigma b_j(X_j)]^2$$
$$SS(m,a) = \Sigma n_{i.}[m(U) + \Sigma a_i(Z_i)]^2$$
$$SS(m,b) = \Sigma n_{.j}[m(U) + \Sigma b_j(X_j)]^2$$

Subtracting $SS(m) = N\bar{Y}^2$ (the correction for the mean) from each of the above and dividing by $SS(y)$ gives

$$R^2_{y.abc} = SS(a,b,c)/SS(y)$$
$$R^2_{y.ab} = SS(a,b)/SS(y)$$
$$R^2_{y.a} = SS(a)/SS(y)$$
$$R^2_{y.b} = SS(b)/SS(y)$$

Inverting this procedure gives sums of squares in terms of correlation coefficients, as shown in Table 11.

With uncorrelated factors, multiple correlations may be obtained by adding up zero-order correlations:

$$R^2_{y.ab} = R^2_{y.a} + R^2_{y.b}$$

TABLE 9

Fitted Constants for Four Models, Two-Way Table with Disproportional Frequencies

Model	m	a_1	a_2	b_1	b_2	c_{11}	c_{12}	c_{21}	c_{22}
$\mu + \alpha_i + \beta_j + \gamma_{ij}$	12.23	1.70	−0.92	1.38	−0.02	0.47	−0.93	0.14	−0.42
$\mu + \alpha_i + \beta_j$	12.08	1.82	−0.82	1.41	−0.22				
$\mu + \alpha_i + \gamma_{ij}$	12.23	1.20	−0.55			0.09	−0.43	0.02	−0.80
$\mu + \beta_j + \gamma_{ij}$	12.23			0.85	0.11	−0.08	−0.75	0.51	−0.97

[a] Omitted constants may be obtained by algebraic addition.

TABLE 10

Analysis of Variance of Simulated Measures, Two-Way Table with Disproportional Frequencies

	Interaction Assumed Present				Interaction Assumed Absent			
Source	SS	DF	MS	F	SS	DF	MS	F
Total	596.72	89			596.72	89		
Subclasses	212.49	8	26.56	5.60	212.49	8	26.56	5.60
Rows	106.97	2	53.48	11.28	137.76	2	68.88	14.11
Columns	92.16	2	46.08	9.72	94.39	2	47.18	9.67
Interaction	30.76	4	7.69	1.62				
Error	384.23	81	4.74		414.99	85	4.88	

TABLE 11
Regression Analysis of Two-Way Table

Source	Sum of Squares	DF
Total	$SS(y)(1.00)$	$N-1$
Subclasses	$SS(y)R^2_{y.abc}$	$rc-1$
Row	$SS(y)R^2_{y.a}$	$r-c$
Column	$SS(y)R^2_{y.b}$	$c-1$
Interaction	$SS(y)R^2_{y.c}$	$(r-1)(c-1)$
Error	$SS(y)(1-R^2_{y.abc})$	$N-rc$

$$R^2_{y.abc} = R^2_{y.ab} + R^2_{y.c}$$

Regression analysis, like the analysis of variance, is less convenient when applied to disproportional, or unbalanced, data: estimates of parameters can no longer be gotten from sample and subsample means; squared zero-order correlation coefficients can no longer be added up to get squared multiple correlations; the regression sum of squares may be allotted to both direct and joint effects. All these complications come from the correlations among factors inhering in the disproportional cell numbers. Dealing with them entails more numerous computations but no new statistical principles. For that reason the essential procedure is unchanged.

First calculate $SS(Y)$ and $SS(m,a,b,c)$ and the difference between them for $SS(e)$—the sum of the squared residuals around regression. Reducing both $SS(Y)$ and $SS(m,a,b,c)$ by the correction for the mean $n\bar{Y}^2$ and dividing the latter by the former gives

$$R^2_{y.abc} = SS(a,b,c)/SS(y)$$

Next, by comparable methods calculate

$$R^2_{y.ab} = SS(a,b)/SS(y)$$

where $SS(a,b) = SS(m,a,b) - SS(m)$.

The hypothesis of no interaction is tested by the difference between $R^2_{y.abc}$ and $R^2_{y.ab}$. If it is not rejected one proceeds to calculate the contribution of A net of B and vice versa:

$$R^2_{y.ab} - R^2_{y.b}$$
$$R^2_{y.ab} - R^2_{y.a}$$

If the hypothesis of no interaction is rejected, one proceeds to calculate

$$R^2_{y.abc} - R^2_{y.bc}$$

and
$$R^2_{y.abc} - R^2_{y.ac}$$
for the net contributions of A and B.

To illustrate these procedures, regression analyses were carried out separately on the equal frequencies of Table 6 and the disproportional frequencies of Table 8. The prediction equation for balanced frequencies,

$$\hat{Y}_{ij} = 12.08(U) + 1.73(Z_1) - 0.73(Z_2) - 1.00(Z_3) + 1.35(X_1)$$
$$- 0.24(X_2) - 1.11(X_3) - 0.04(W_{11}) - 0.59(W_{12})$$
$$+ 0.63(W_{13}) - 0.13(W_{21}) - 0.12(W_{22}) - 0.01(W_{23})$$
$$- 0.09(W_{31}) + 0.71(W_{32}) - 0.62(W_{33})$$

may be contrasted with the equation for unbalanced frequencies,

$$\hat{Y}_{ij} = 12.23(U) + 1.70(Z_1) - 0.92(Z_2) - 0.78(Z_3) + 1.38(X_1)$$
$$- 0.02(X_2) - 1.36(X_3) + 0.47(W_{11}) - 0.93(W_{12})$$
$$+ 0.46(W_{13}) + 0.14(W_{21}) - 0.42(W_{22}) + 0.28(W_{23})$$
$$- 0.61(W_{31}) + 1.35(W_{32}) - 0.74(W_{33})$$

Note that all dummy variables are present in the prediction equation when each set of regression coefficients sums to zero.

To measure the predictive efficiency of factors A, B, and C separately and jointly, squared multiple correlations were computed. For equal frequencies we find $R^2_{y.abc} = 0.38$, $R^2_{y.a} = 0.21$, $R^2_{y.b} = 0.15$, and $R^2_{y.c} = 0.03$. For significance-testing, since multiple correlations and mean squares have the same F-ratios we may use the results of Table 7. With disproportional frequencies the correlations are found to be $R^2_{y.abc} = 0.36$, $R^2_{y.ab} = 0.31$, $R^2_{y.ac} = 0.21$, and $R^2_{y.bc} = 0.18$. The significance of the net predictive efficiencies of factors A, B, and C is tested by the variance ratios given in Table 10.

Path Analysis. Standardizing means and variances of all variables at 0 and 1 gives the fitted path equation:

$$y'_{ijk} = p_{ya}a'_i + p_{yb}b'_i + p_{yc}c'_{ij} + p_{ye}e'_{ijk}$$

In the case of equal cell frequencies, factors are uncorrelated and

$$p^2_{ya} = R^2_{y.a}$$
$$p^2_{yb} = R^2_{y.b}$$

$$p_{yc}^2 = R_{y.c}^2$$
$$p_{y.e}^2 = 1 - R_{y.abc}^2$$

By the same token the path diagram contains no curved arrows (Figure 1).

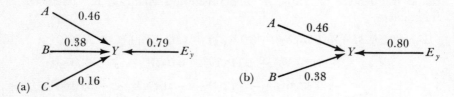

Figure 1. Diagrams for full model (a) and additive model (b), uncorrelated factors.

For our table of equal frequencies (Table 6), path coefficients are $p_{ya} = 0.46$, $p_{yb} = 0.38$, $p_{yc} = 0.16$, and $p_{ye} = 0.79$. These are entered alongside paths in Figure 1(a). If the interaction term is ignored, p_{ya} and p_{yb} remain unchanged; however, p_{ye}^2 becomes $1 - R_{y.ab}^2$. For our example $p_{ye} = 0.80$ with interaction disregarded. These results are displayed in Figure 1(b).

Correlated factors, as intimated above, provide an opportunity to consider alternatives to the standard AOV model although none of these alternatives may be realistic and some may be fanciful. For instance the assignment of causal priority to interaction has logical difficulties since interaction is no more than the failure of main effects to account for the variation of subclass means. It is left-over variation. Figure 2(a) represents the standard model in which no factor has causal priority.

The possibility that C is dependent on B and B on A may be expressed by path equations,

$$c'_{ij} = p_{cb}b'_j + p_{ce}e'_{ij}$$
$$b'_j = p_{ba}a'_i + p_{be}e'_j$$

or by a diagram as in Figure 2(b). The alternative possibility that both A and B are exogenous and that C is dependent on both similarly is expressible in equational form,

$$c'_{ij} = p_{cb}b'_j + p_{ca}a'_i + p_{ce}e'_{ij}$$

or as a path diagram as in Figure 2(c).

If no factor has causal priority, the analysis is necessarily re-

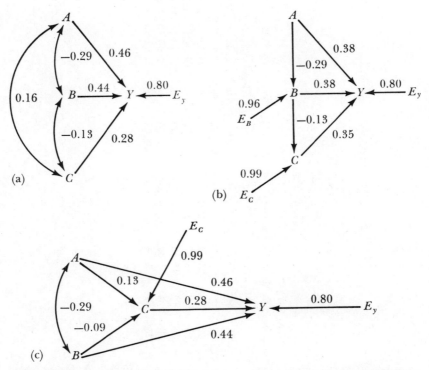

Figure 2. Diagrams for AOV model (a) and recursive models (b, c), correlated factors.

stricted to net effects since no indirect effects are present. The entries in Table 12(a) exemplify this possibility.

With causal priorities, sums of squares may cover both direct and indirect effects. In the second example, where C is dependent on B and B is dependent on A, the procedure is to assign to C the difference between the sum of squares for the full model and the sum of squares for the additive (C excluded) model; assign to B the difference between the sum of squares for the additive model and the total sum of squares for A; and assign to A the difference between the sum of squares for the additive model and the net sum of squares for B. This procedure is illustrated in Table 12(b).

In the third example, where A and B have the same causal priority and C is dependent on both, the analysis is again limited to net effects: the effect of C net of A and B; the effect of B net of A; and the effect of A net of B. This possibility is shown in Table 12(c).

K. Hope (1971) has provided an instructive example of the flexi-

TABLE 12

Analysis of Variance for Path Models in Figure 2

Source	Model (a)				Model (b)				Model (c)			
	SS	DF	MS	F	SS	DF	MS	F	SS	DF	MS	F
Total	596.72	89			596.72	89			596.72	89		
Subclasses	212.49	8	26.56	5.60	212.49	8	26.56	5.60	212.49	8	26.56	5.60
Rows	106.97	2	53.48	11.28	87.34	2	43.67	9.21	137.76	2	68.88	14.53
Columns	92.16	2	46.08	9.72	94.39	2	47.20	9.96	94.39	2	47.20	9.96
Interaction	30.76	4	7.69	1.62	30.76	4	7.69	1.62	30.76	4	7.69	1.62
Error	384.23	81	4.74		384.23	81	4.74		384.23	81	4.74	

bility of the method of fitting constants to a two-way table of nonexperimental data with disproportional cell frequencies. His general object was to determine whether social mobility has an effect on family fertility, net of husband's class of origin and class of destination; his general procedure was to compare the explanatory power of the full model (mobility included) with that of the reduced model (mobility excluded). The substantive significance of his analysis aside, it is especially recommended as a demonstration of the versatility of the method of fitting constants (or regression analysis of dummy variables) and of the additional opportunities for analysis that arise when classes (such as social class) may be ordered from low to high.

Another example of the method of fitting constants is contained in a report by Yancey, Rigsby, and McCarthy (1972). They applied it to a six-way AOV table to gauge the effect of marriage, work, sex, age, race, and education, each net of the others, on number of psychosomatic symptoms. Since they included no interaction terms in their population models, their application is somewhat specialized; it does exemplify the case of fitting constants to a succession of models from which interaction terms have been a priori excluded and is therefore of interest when such an analysis is contemplated. Other recent examples include those of Beattie and Spencer (1971) and Laslett (1971).

ANALYSIS OF COVARIANCE

One-Way Table, Single Covariate

Fitting Constants. Adding the regression of Y on the continuous variable V to Equation (1) gives the standard covariance model for a one-way table:

$$Y_{ij} = \mu + \alpha_i + \delta(v_{ij}) + e_{ij} \qquad (20)$$

where δ is the unit change in Y per unit change in V, and $v_{ij} = V_{ij} - \bar{V}_{..}$. As in the analysis of variance, the main problem is to fit constants and to test the hypothesis that the α_i are equal. To avoid ascribing to the factor A what may be due to the covariate V, the effect of the latter is statistically removed before testing the hypothesis. Least-squares constants, chosen to minimize the function

$$F = \Sigma\Sigma[Y_{ij} - m - a_i - d(v_{ij})]^2$$

and subject to the constraint that $\sum r_i a_i = 0$, are

$$m = \bar{Y}_{..}$$
$$a_i = (\bar{Y}_i - \bar{Y}_.) - d(\bar{V}_i - \bar{V}_.)$$
$$d = \Sigma\Sigma(V_{ij} - \bar{V}_i)(Y_{ij} - \bar{Y}_i)/\Sigma\Sigma(V_{ij} - \bar{V}_i)^2$$

To test the null hypothesis that the α_i are equal, we first calculate the total sum of squares (mean corrected):

$$SS(y) = SS(Y) - SS(m)$$

Next the sum of squares attributable to both A and V is obtained:

$$SS(a,v) = \Sigma\Sigma[a_i + d(v_{ij})]^2$$

Subtracting $SS(a,v)$ from $SS(y)$ gives the sum of the squared errors:

$$SS(e) = SS(y) - SS(a,v)$$

The sum of squares attributable to A after eliminating the effect of V is

$$SS(a) = SS(a,v) - SS(v)$$

where $SS(v) = \Sigma\Sigma[d(v_{ij})]^2$ and $d = \Sigma\Sigma(V_{ij} - \bar{V}.)(Y_{ij} - \bar{Y}.)/\Sigma(V_{ij} - \bar{V}.)^2$ as if cases had not been sorted into classes.

Similarly the sum of squares attributable to V after eliminating the effect of A is

$$SS(v) = SS(a,v) - SS(a)$$

where $SS(a) = \Sigma n_i(a_i)^2$ and $a_i = (\bar{Y}_i - \bar{Y}.)$ as if there were no covariate.

Dividing $SS(a)$ by its $r - 1$ df, and $SS(e)$ by its $n - r - 1$ df gives mean squares whose ratio has a central F distribution when the null hypothesis that the α_i are equal is true. However, caution must be exercised in interpreting this result owing to possible correlation between the covariate and the factor whose effect on Y is in question. The effect of such a correlation is to reduce $SS(a)$ relative to $SS(e)$ and thereby to increase the risk of accepting a false hypothesis. In this situation statisticians (for example, Sprott, 1970) suggest, not that the analysis of variance be abandoned, but that $SS(a)$ be taken for what it is: a sum of squares adjusted for both regression and the presumed indirect effect of A transmitted via V. For a discussion of this and related issues see Mallios (1970).

For a numerical example we added a covariate randomly selected from a normal population with zero mean and variance 1.00 to each measure in Table 2 (see Table 22 in the appendix). Fitted constants for these measures and the analysis of variance of the adjusted measures are shown in Table 13.

Regression Analysis. Substituting $\mu(U)$ for μ, and $\alpha_i(Z_i)$ for α_i, and leaving the $\delta(v_{ij})$ and e_{ij} unchanged gives the regression model:

$$Y_{ij} = \mu(U) + \alpha_1(Z_1) + \cdots + \alpha_r(Z_r) + \delta(v_{ij}) + e_{ij} \quad (21)$$

where $U = 1$ for all cases; $Z_i = 1$ for all cases in the ith population and zero otherwise; and δ is the change in Y per unit change in V.

TABLE 13
Analysis of Covariance of Simulated Measures, One-Way Table

Source	Sum of Squares	DF	MS	F
Total	$SS(y) = 623.92$			
Rows	$SS(a) = 134.03$	2	67.02	13.68
Covariate	$SS(v) = 87.56$	1	87.56	17.87
Error	$SS(e) = 421.10$	86	4.90	

$m = 12.08 \quad a_1 = 1.73 \quad a_2 = -0.73 \quad a_3 = -1.00 \quad d = 1.02$

Solving the normal equations under the constraint that a_1 equals zero[8] gives

$$m = \bar{Y}_1$$
$$a_i = (\bar{Y}_i - \bar{Y}_1) + d(\bar{V}_i - \bar{V}_1) \qquad (22)$$
$$d = \Sigma\Sigma(V_{ij} - \bar{V}_i)(Y_{ij} - \bar{Y}_i)/\Sigma\Sigma(V_{ij} - \bar{V}_i)^2$$

The squared multiple correlation of Y on A and V is

$$R^2_{y.av} = SS(a,v)/SS(y)$$

where $SS(y) = SS(Y) - SS(m)$ and $SS(a,v) = SS(m,a,v) - SS(m)$.

The squared correlation of Y on V is $R^2_{y.v} = SS(v)/SS(y)$ as if cases had not been sorted into classes. Similarly the squared correlation of Y on A is $R^2_{y.a} = SS(a)/SS(y)$ as if there were no covariate.

Subtracting $R^2_{y.v}$ and $R^2_{y.a}$ each from $R^2_{y.av}$ gives, respectively, the proportion of variance in Y attributable to A net of V, and the proportion of variance in Y attributable to V net of A. These are squared part correlations:[9] one between unadjusted A and Y adjusted for V; the other between unadjusted V and Y adjusted for A. Multiplying the total sums of squares $SS(y)$ by these squared part correlations gives $SS(a)$ and $SS(v)$, as obtained in the analysis of covariance. Part correlations and the $SS(a)$ and $SS(v)$ yield exactly the same F-ratios and therefore the same statistical inferences. Literal results are summarized in Table 14.

To illustrate procedures we draw on the measures given in the previous section. Substituting estimates obtained by Equation (22) into (21) gives the prediction equation:

$$\hat{Y} = 13.81 + 0(Z_1) - 2.46(Z_2) - 2.73(Z_3) + 1.02(V)$$

[8] To convert the a_i obtained by Equation (22) to the a_i under the constraint that $\Sigma n_i a_i = 0$, add the quantity $[(\bar{Y}_1 - \bar{Y}_.) + d(\bar{V}_1 - \bar{V}_.)]$ to each one.

[9] When one of two variables X and Y is adjusted for its regression on a third variable Z, the correlation between the unadjusted variable and the adjusted variable is termed a *part correlation*. Similarly the correlation between X adjusted for Z alone, and Y adjusted for both Z and W, is a part correlation.

TABLE 14
Regression Analysis of One-Way Table with Single Covariate

Source	Sum of Squares	DF
Total	$SS(y) = SS(y)(1)$	$N - 1$
Rows	$SS(a) = SS(y)(R_{y.av}^2 - R_{y.v}^2)$	$r - 1$
Covariate	$SS(v) = SS(y)(R_{y.av}^2 - R_{y.a}^2)$	1
Error	$SS(e) = SS(y)(1 - R_{y.av}^2)$	$N - r - 1$

To assess the predictive efficiency of both A and V, we calculate

$$R_{y.av}^2 = 0.33$$

To assess the predictive efficiency of A net of V, we calculate

$$R_{(y.v)a}^2 = R_{y.av}^2 - R_{y.v}^2$$

$$= 0.33 - 0.11 = 0.22$$

Similarly the predictive efficiency of V net of A is given by

$$R_{(y.a)v}^2 = R_{y.av}^2 - R_{y.a}^2$$

$$= 0.33 - 0.18 = 0.15$$

The significance of these part correlations is tested by the variance ratios given in Table 13.

Path Analysis. We may put Equation (20) in the form of a path model by reducing all variables to standard form:

$$y_{ij}' = p_{ya}\alpha_i' + p_{yv}v_{ij}' + p_{ye}e_{ij}'$$

To diagram this model or its sample counterpart, we connect A and V by a curved arrow to accommodate a possible correlation between them as in Figure 3(a). In the ideal experiment A and V are uncorrelated (orthogonal), so that no indirect effects are present. In this case the effects of A and V are gauged respectively by $p_{ya} = R_{y.a}$ and $p_{yv} = R_{y.v}$.

If A and V are correlated, we may either limit the analysis to direct paths running from A to Y and V to Y, or replace the AOCOV model by one that provides for indirect effects. For example, if we specify that Y is dependent on both A and V and that V is dependent on A our model becomes

$$y_{ij}' = p_{ya}\alpha_i' + p_{yv}v_{ij}' + p_{ye}e_{ij}'$$

$$v_{ji}' = p_{va}\alpha_i' + p_{ve}e_{ij}'$$

The path diagram of this model entails dropping a curved arrow and adding two straight ones as in Figure 3(b). With this recursive scheme

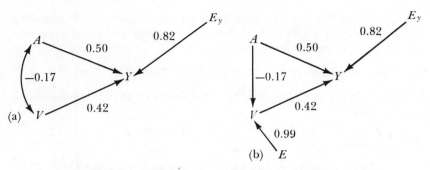

Figure 3. Diagrams for covariance model (a) and recursive model (b).

TABLE 15
Analysis of Covariance for Path Model in Figure 3

Model (a)					Model (b)				
Source	SS	DF	MS	F	Source	SS	DF	MS	F
Total	623.92	89			Total	623.92	89		
Rows	134.03	2	67.02	13.68	Rows	115.26	2	57.63	11.76
Covariate	87.56	1	87.56	17.87	Covariate	87.56	1	87.56	17.87
Error	421.10	86	4.90		Error	421.10	86	4.90	

one takes $R^2_{y.a}$ as the percentage variation in Y attributable to A, and $R^2_{y.av} - R^2_{y.a}$ as the percentage variation attributable to V.

Since A and V are correlated ($r_{av} = -0.17$) in our sample of measures, it becomes necessary (unless one assumes there is no correlation in the population) to choose between the standard AOCOV model in which neither A nor V has causal priority, and the illustrative recursive model in which causal priority is assigned to A. Calculations made under both assumptions are given in Table 15.

Two-Way Table

Regression Analysis. Adding β_i and γ_{ij} to Equation (20) gives the full covariance model for a two-way table with a single covariate:

$$Y_{ijk} = \mu + \alpha_i + \beta_j + \gamma_{ij} + \delta(v_{ijk}) + e_{ijk} \qquad (23)$$

To shorten the discussion, and since no new principles are involved in testing, we limit ourselves to dummy variables, omitting synonymous procedures for fitted constants and path coefficients. The regression model is

$$Y_{ijk} = \mu(U) + \Sigma\alpha_i(Z_i) + \Sigma\beta_j(X_j) + \Sigma\Sigma\gamma_{ij}(W_{ij}) + \delta(v_{ijk}) + e_{ijk} \quad (24)$$

where $U = 1$ for all cases, $Z_i = 1$ for all cases in the ith population, $W_{ij} = 1$ for all cases in the ijth subpopulation, and so forth.

Substituting least-squares solutions into Equation (24), squaring and summing, and subtracting the correction for the mean gives the sum of squared regression values:

$$SS(a,b,c,v) = \Sigma\Sigma\Sigma[m + \Sigma a_i(Z_i) + \Sigma b_j(X_j) + \Sigma\Sigma c_{ij}(W_{ij}) + d(v)]^2 - N\bar{Y}^2$$

Dividing this result by the total sum of squares gives the squared multiple correlation

$$R^2_{y.abcv} = SS(a,b,c,v)/SS(y) \qquad (25)$$

Next calculate

$$SS(b,c,v) = \Sigma\Sigma[m + \Sigma b_j(X_j) + \Sigma\Sigma c_{ij}(W_{ij}) + d(v_{ijk})]^2 - N\bar{Y}^2$$

Dividing this result by the total sum of squares gives

$$R^2_{y.bcv} = SS(b,c,v)/SS(y)$$

Subtracting this result from (25) gives the part correlation between A and Y with the influence of B, C, and V eliminated, or the proportion of variance attributable to A net of all other effects:

$$R^2_{(y.bcv)a} = R^2_{y.abcv} - R^2_{y.bcv}$$

By multiplying this coefficient by $SS(y)$, one gets $SS(a)$ as obtained in the standard analysis of covariance.[10] The same procedure is used to calculate

$$R^2_{(y.acv)b} = R^2_{y.abcv} - R^2_{y.acv}$$
$$R^2_{(y.abv)c} = R^2_{y.abcv} - R^2_{y.abv}$$
$$R^2_{(y.abc)v} = R^2_{y.abcv} - R^2_{y.abc}$$

These procedures, along with those for calculating effects in the absence of interaction, are given in Table 16.

To exemplify procedures, an AOCOV via dummy variables was carried out on the balanced frequencies of Table 6 and the disproportional frequencies of Table 8, adding to each measure the covariate described earlier. Component sums of squares and part correlations are shown in Table 17; they are tested for significance in the usual way.

Examples of the analysis of covariance in sociology could be met only rarely a few years ago (before 1965) but today they are regularly encountered. Perrucci and Perrucci (1970) used the analysis of covariance to measure the effect of social origin A on career mobility Y net of educational context B and work experience V. However, in their analysis they did not separate main effects (A and B) and interaction (AB)

---

[10] In carrying out these operations it is necessary to impose $r + c - 1$ constraints on interaction. For an explanation, see Searle (1971, pp. 300–301).

TABLE 16
Regression Analysis of Two-Way Table with Single Covariate

Source	With Interaction	DF	Without Interaction	DF
Total	$SS(y) = SS(y)(1)$	$N-1$	$SS(y) = SS(y)(1)$	$N-1$
Rows	$SS(a) = SS(y)(R^2_{y.abcv} - R^2_{y.bcv})$	$r-1$	$SS(a) = SS(y)(R^2_{y.abv} - R^2_{y.bv})$	$r-1$
Columns	$SS(b) = SS(y)(R^2_{y.abcv} - R^2_{y.acv})$	$c-1$	$SS(b) = SS(y)(R^2_{y.abv} - R^2_{y.av})$	$c-1$
Interaction	$SS(c) = SS(y)(R^2_{y.abcv} - R^2_{y.abv})$	$(r-1)(c-1)$		
Covariate	$SS(v) = SS(y)(R^2_{y.abcv} - R^2_{y.abc})$	1	$SS(v) = SS(y)(R^2_{y.abv} - R^2_{y.ab})$	1
Error	$SS(e) = SS(y)(1 - R^2_{y.abcv})$	$N - rc - 1$	$SS(e) = SS(y)(1 - R^2_{y.abv})$	$N - r - c$

TABLE 17
Regression Analysis of Simulated Measures, Two-Way Table with Single Covariate

(a) Equal Cell Frequencies

Interaction Assumed Present

Source	SS	DF	MS	F	Squared Part Correlation
Total	706.21	89			
Rows	133.16	2	66.58	13.32	0.19
Columns	93.57	2	46.79	9.36	0.13
Interaction	16.89	4	4.22	0.84	0.02
Covariate	75.70	1	75.70	15.14	0.11
Error	399.76	80	5.00		

Interaction Assumed Absent

Source	SS	DF	MS	F	Squared Part Correlation
Total	706.21	89			
Rows	133.92	2	66.96	13.50	0.19
Columns	93.76	2	46.88	9.45	0.13
Covariate	86.19	1	86.19	17.38	0.12
Error	416.65	85	4.96		

(b) Disproportional Cell Frequencies

Interaction Assumed Present

Source	SS	DF	MS	F	Squared Part Correlation
Total	671.88	89			
Rows	135.32	2	67.66	14.10	0.20
Columns	94.67	2	47.34	9.86	0.14
Interaction	31.17	4	7.79	1.62	0.05
Covariate	64.90	1	64.90	13.52	0.10
Error	383.82	80	4.80		

Interaction Assumed Absent

Source	SS	DF	MS	F	Squared Part Correlation
Total	671.88	89			
Rows	136.73	2	68.37	13.84	0.20
Columns	94.34	2	47.17	9.54	0.14
Covariate	83.77	1	83.77	16.96	0.12
Error	414.99	84	4.94		

after adjusting for the covariable because, as they acknowledge, no program for handling disproportional data was available. Hauser's (1971) path diagram of the covariance model is an alternative to the one given here; both necessarily lead to the same statistical inferences. Other recent sociological applications of AOCOV include Gurin (1970), Beattie and Spencer (1971), and Wilson (1971).

DUMMY (0,1) DEPENDENT VARIABLE

One-Way Table

At this juncture our inquiry shifts to the case of a dummy dependent variable Y restricted to the values of 0 and 1. Although this restriction leaves procedures for fitting constants unchanged, it may require, in specific instances, that testing procedures be modified or even discarded.

The population model for the analysis of variance of binary dummy measures arranged in a single classification is Equation (1). Least-squares estimates of constants are expressible as functions of marginal proportions

$$m = p = \sum^r n_i p_i / N$$

$$a_i = p_i - p$$

because $p_i n_i = \sum^{n_i} Y_{ij}$ and $pN = \sum\sum_1^r Y_{ij}$ when $Y_{ij} = 1$ or 0. Then the total sum of squares in Y (mean corrected) is $SS(y) = Npq$, where $q = 1 - p$. Similarly the error sum of squares is $SS(e) = \sum^r n_i p_i q_i$ and the sum of squares due to A is

$$SS(a) = SS(y) - SS(e) = \sum^r n_i (p_i - p)^2$$

Although one may set up the F-ratio

$$F = \frac{SS(a)/r - 1}{SS(e)/n - r} = \frac{BSS/r - 1}{WSS/N - r} \qquad (26)$$

the F-table should not be used unreservedly for testing significance, since the assumption that errors are normally distributed with a common variance cannot be met. (For a discussion of F's robustness when the usual assumptions of the analysis of variance are violated, readers should consult Kendall and Stuart, 1966.)

A statistic for testing the significance of differences between G groups when the dependent variable consists of I unordered classes has been proposed by Light and Margolin (1971): $C = (N - 1)(I - 1)(BSS)/TSS$, where $N = $ the total number of observations, $BSS = $

between-group sum of squares, and TSS = total sum of squares. This statistic, C, is asymptotically approximated as $\chi_{(I-1)(G-1)}$ under the null hypothesis that all G groups have the same probability structure. When $I = 2$ or when the dependent variable is a 0,1 dummy, as in our case, C reduces to

$$C = N - 1(BSS/TSS) \qquad (27)$$

Light and Margolin remark that the F-ratio [Equation (26)] and the specialization of C [Equation (27)] are monotonically related, but they provide no guidelines for choosing between F and C. They remark (p. 544) that "while the test statistics are monotonically related, the reference distributions do not obey the same relationship. . . . How important this difference is, especially for $I > 2$, we leave as an unresolved question." Unresolved issues apart, Light and Margolin's method may have special utility in sociology where unordered classes are regularly encountered.

To illustrate procedures we did an analysis of variance of Coleman's (1970) table of frequencies (Table 18), representing the equilibrium of a process in which the probability of a person's moving from one state to another is subject to the influence of an independent variable. The null hypothesis to be tested is that the independent variable has no effect on the tendency of a person to move from one category to the other. The analysis of variance of Table 18 is given in Table 19, together with the C, χ^2, and F. Since C is a function of χ^2 when $I = 2$ (that is, when $Y_{ij} = 0,1$), it necessarily leads to the same decision with respect to the null hypothesis. Although the F-ratio may lead coincidentally to

TABLE 18
Distribution of Y by A_1 and A_2

Value of Y	A_1	A_2	Total
1	0.619(317)	0.744(363)	0.680(680)
0	0.383(195)	0.256(125)	0.320(320)
Total	1.000(512)	1.000(488)	1.000(1000)

TABLE 19
Analysis of Variance of Table 18

Source	SS	DF	MS	F
Total	$SS(y) = 217.600$	999		
Between	$SS(a) = 3.904$	1	3.904	18.24
Error	$SS(e) = 213.696$	998	0.214	

$\chi^2 = 17.86$ $C = 17.92$ $m = 0.680$ $a_1 = -0.061$ $a_2 = 0.064$

the same decision, it is not an equivalent test. For a discussion consult Light and Margolin (1971).

Two-Way Table

Fitting constants to a two-way table with a 0,1 dependent variable involves no new principles, only more detail.[11] The population model is Equation (15).

In running F-tests we first calculate the sum of squares for the full model. This works out to

$$SS(m,a,b,c) = \Sigma\Sigma n_{ij}(p_{ij})^2 \qquad (28)$$

where p_{ij} is the mean of the ijth subsample.

Subtracting Equation (28) from $SS(Y) = \Sigma\Sigma Y_{ij}^2$ gives the sum of squares for error:

$$SS(e) = SS(Y) - SS(m,a,b,c)$$

The additive model is next fitted and its corresponding sum of squares is subtracted from (28) for the sum of squares due to interaction:

$$SS(c) = SS(m,a,b,c) - SS(m,a,b)$$

A finding of no interaction would require the calculation of

$$SS(a) = SS(m,a,b) - SS(m,b)$$

and

$$SS(b) = SS(m,a,b) - SS(m,a)$$

to test, respectively, for the effect of A with B eliminated and the effect of B with A eliminated.

A finding of interaction would pose the usual problem of whether to discontinue the analysis on the grounds that main effects are ambiguous and difficult to interpret; or to continue and to test for the significance of A net of B and C, and the significance of B net of A and C. If the decision is to continue, one may obtain $SS(a) = SS(a,b,c) - SS(b,c)$, and $SS(b) = SS(a,b,c) - SS(a,c)$ by either the method of fitting constants (with the required constraints) or by the method of weighted squares of means.

To illustrate numerically the foregoing procedures, we applied them to Coleman's (1970) table of frequencies, representing the equilibrium of a process in which a person's potential for moving is subject to the influence of two factors rather than one. Cell and marginal propor-

---

[11] In the future this approach may be largely superseded by Goodman's (1972) work on dichotomous variables. In this connection see also Grizzle, Starmer, and Koch (1969).

tions (means) and corresponding frequencies are given in Table 20; the analysis of variance is given in Table 21; also given are constants fitted under the constraints that $\sum^r a_i = \sum^c b_j = \sum^r c_{ij} = \sum^c c_{ij} = 0$. These elaborate results may be compared with the simpler ones given by Coleman.

Whereas AOV tables with 0,1 measures are fairly common in sociology, they are seldom subjected to an analysis of variance. Horan's (1971) study of voting behavior is an exception. To determine whether a person refrains from voting because of the cross-pressures to which he is subject, Horan set up the model

$$Y_{ijk} = \mu + \alpha_i + \beta_j + \gamma_g + e_{ijk} \tag{29}$$

where α_i is common to all persons having the ith occupation, β_j is common to all with the jth religion, and γ_g is common to all persons exposed to the same (gth) political cross-pressures. In assessing cross-pressures Horan's procedure was to get the difference between the sum of squares for Equation (29) and the sum of squares for the reduced model,

$$Y_{ijk} = \mu + \alpha_i + \beta_j + e_{ijk}$$

and to test the significance of that difference. Horan's paper is particularly valuable in directing attention to the use of AOV procedures in model-testing when variables are measured on nominal scales.

0,1 DEPENDENT VARIABLE

Discriminant Function

Discriminatory analysis is a technique for assigning cases to qualitative classes on the basis of quantitative measures. In carrying out such an analysis, one starts with a one-way table of N cases, each measured on m quantitative variables. Measures are weighted and summed according to the criterion that such sums will show the largest possible between-group sum of squares. These same weights may be applied to cases for which measures are available but whose classification is unknown.

TABLE 20
Cell and Marginal Proportions

	B_1	B_2	Total
A_1	0.444 (250)	0.786 (262)	0.619 (512)
A_2	0.598 (244)	0.889 (244)	0.744 (488)
Total	0.520 (494)	0.836 (506)	0.680 (1000)

TABLE 21
Analysis of Variance of Table 20

	Interaction Assumed Present					Interaction Assumed Absent			
Source	SS	DF	MS	F	Source	SS	DF	MS	F
Total	217.60	999			Total	217.60	999		
Subcells	29.20	3	9.73	51.21	Subcells	29.20	3	9.73	51.21
Rows	3.07	1	3.07	16.16	Rows	3.86	1	3.86	20.32
Columns	25.03	1	25.03	131.74	Columns	24.78	1	24.78	130.42
Interaction	0.16	1	0.16	0.84					
Error	188.40	996	0.19		Error	188.56	997	0.19	

$m = 0.6795$
$a_1 = -a_2 = -0.0644$
$b_1 = -b_2 = -0.1583$
$c_{11} = -c_{12} = -c_{21} = c_{22} = -0.0128$

$m = 0.6796$
$a_1 = -a_2 = -0.0642$
$b_1 = -b_2 = -0.1586$

When the classification is a dichotomy, it may be treated as a 0,1 dummy variable and the efficiency of prediction gauged by either an analysis of variance of the weighted sum or by a regression analysis of the dummy variable on its m regressors.

The sum of m measures, each weighted according to this criterion, has come to be known as the *linear discriminant function*, a term from Fisher (1936).[12] If an analysis of variance of this sum

$$Y = \lambda_1 X_1 + \cdots + \lambda_m X_m \qquad (30)$$

where the λ_i are the required weights, leads to a significant F-ratio the inference is drawn that predictive efficiency cannot be attributed to random sampling variation. Alternative interpretations are discussed by Kendall (1961).

The F-ratio in which the analysis culminates is arrived at in three steps: finding the λ_i that jointly maximize the variance ratio; weighting the observed X_i and summing for the composite measure; running an analysis of variance on these composite measures.

It has been shown (Fisher, 1936) that the a_i in Equation (31) are proportional to the λ_i in (30):

$$\bar{X}_{i1} - \bar{X}_{i2} = \sum_{i=1}^{m} a_i S_{ij} \qquad (31)$$

where $\bar{X}_{i1}$ is the mean of the ith variable for the first group, $\bar{X}_{i2}$ is the mean of the ith variable for the second group, and S_{ij} is the sum of the products (mean corrected) between X_i and X_j ($i, j = 1, 2, \ldots, m$). Therefore, since any multiple of the λ_i yields the same variance ratio as the λ_i themselves, it suffices to solve Equation (31) and use the resulting a_i as weights. This is standard practice.

The analysis of variance of composite measures differs from the standard method for a dichotomy in this respect: the between-groups sum of squares is divided by m df instead of 1 df; the within-groups sum of squares is divided by $N - m - 1$ df instead of $N - 2$ df. This reduction in degrees of freedom for the error term corresponds to the increase in the number of fitted constants.

Regression Analysis

No dummy variable is used in getting the discriminant function; however, the method of regression requires that a dummy be introduced. Then the squared multiple correlation gives the percentage variance ex-

---

[12] The *multiple discriminant function* meets the same criterion for three or more groups.

plained by the m independent regressors, or the percentage reduction in error that may be ascribed to them.

Setting up the normal equations under the restriction that $Y = 1$ for the n_1 cases in the first group and $Y = 0$ for the n_2 cases in the second group gives the product-sum of Y and X_j in terms of weighted product-sums for X_i and X_j ($i,j = 1, 2, \ldots, m$):

$$S_{yj} = b_1 S_{1j} + b_2 S_{2j} + \cdots + b_m S_{mj} \tag{32}$$

Solving the m normal equations (32) and manipulating the b_i leads to R^2, or the predictive efficiency of the regression coefficients relative to that of the overall mean of the dependent variable.

Relevant to this discussion is the proportionality between the least-squares partial regression coefficients in Equation (32) and the least-squares constants in (31). Multiplying Equation (31) by $k = S_{yi}/(\bar{X}_{i1} - \bar{X}_{i2})$ gives the b_i as a function of the a_i; inverting this procedure we get the a_i as a function of the b_i.

Since least-squares coefficients in Equations (31) and (32) are proportional to one another, it is necessarily the case that the squared correlation ratio is equal to the squared multiple correlation between the 0,1 dummy and its m regressors:

$$R^2_{y.1\ldots m} = \eta^2_{ya}$$

Both models may be represented by a path diagram, a procedure that may clarify relations between them. In Figure 4(a) the discriminant function is shown as a function of the classification factor and random error; in Figure 2(b) the 0,1 dependent variable, corresponding to the dichotomous classification, is shown as a function of its m regressors plus error.

Contrary to expectation (since it deals with the distinguishing characteristics of groups), the discriminant function is used only infrequently in sociology—at least it seldom appears in the research litera-

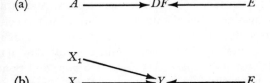

Figure 4. Diagrams of 0,1 dependent variable: (a) discriminant function (b) regression equation.

ture. Loy (1969) has used it to differentiate among swimming coaches, grouped according to number of years between the availability of a new training device and their adoption of it in their programs. Kornberg and Brehm (1971) have used it to differentiate between students and faculty sympathetic or unsympathetic toward a college campus protest incident. An example of the discriminant function in economic research is supplied by Higgins (1970). Statistical work by Warner (1963, 1967) should be consulted by sociologists planning to use the discriminant function or an equivalent method.

DISCUSSION AND CONCLUSIONS

In analyzing measures in an AOV table, it makes no difference statistically whether sums of squares are expressed in terms of fitted constants, regression coefficients, or path coefficients. However, these terms answer to somewhat different purposes; they are liable to different abuses; they carry somewhat different connotations and imagery; and since they differ in nuance, one may be mistakenly used when another is called for. This tendency toward imprecise and misleading expression may be especially marked in sociology whose methodology is so heavily borrowed from other fields.

Fitted constants answer to the question of whether two or more populations differ in their characteristics; regression coefficients answer to the predicted change in one variable per unit change in another; path coefficients answer to the question of causal effects. Accordingly, fitted constants might be chosen when emphasis is on differences among population characteristics; regression coefficients when the emphasis is on prediction; and path coefficients when the emphasis is on direct and indirect causal influences.

The infrequent use of the analysis of variance in sociological research is usually laid to its restrictive assumptions about populations and samples. And when it is used, note is usually taken of the robustness of the F-test in the face of violated assumptions. Assumptions are not relaxed by expressing sums of squares in terms of path coefficients or regression coefficients; yet there is a tendency to disregard assumptions when doing an analysis of variance under a different name, such as *multiple classification analysis* (Andrews, Morgan, and Sonquist, 1967). The fault lies with those users who proceed as if hypothesis-testing in the analysis of variance under an alternate name were free of sampling assumptions. The language of experimental design has the virtue of calling to mind assumptions about significance-testing that may go unnoticed in the hands of a vocabulary (such as path analysis) that tends to dwell on other matters (such as causal links).

As is well known, the analysis of variance was devised to give a systematic answer to the question of whether plants flourish more under one experimental treatment than under another, other things being equal. The condition that other things be equal is met by the random assignment of treatments to experimental units. Randomization is not required to carry out the arithmetic of the analysis of variance; without it, however, inferences about the cause of the differences between groups are necessarily quite tentative.

Sociologists usually find themselves in the position of having to compare groups produced by survey sampling (for example, men and women) rather than groups produced by the random assignment of treatments to individuals (for example, experimental and control). With samples of predetermined populations, one may as a first possibility skirt the issue of causation and merely conclude, as in a descriptive survey, that subpopulations (for example, blacks and whites) are alike or unlike in their characteristics. That procedure suffices if inferences about the causal forces producing those differences are not required; otherwise, one must undertake to sort out the causes of a given effect. Although the analytic sample survey has such a sorting as its goal, techniques for doing that in particular problems have not been worked out and writing on this topic tends to dwell on unresolved issues.

Second, from a statistically significant finding and possibly other evidence one may conclude that the classificatory factor has a causal role, leaving unspecified what it is and its net effect. One may decide, for example, that a scientist's laboratory (including his colleagues) has an effect on his or her productivity, without specifying the structural system of which that effect is one element. Such a conclusion is more a reasoned judgment about the presence of causality than a strictly drawn inference about its direction and strength. Many sociological conclusions based on crossed and nested classifications of survey data are broad judgments of this kind, rather than rigorous causal inferences.

Third, one may make the assumption that the effect of the classificatory factor on the dependent variable is independent of all variables except those explicitly included in the analysis. This assumption would justify the use of the path model (or structural equation). However, since the relations between the classificatory factor and the omitted variables are generally unknown, estimates obtained on the assumption that they are nil might better be regarded as working hypotheses to be tested than as measures of structural effects. This point is worthy of mention because of the tendency of sociologists to express results in terms of path coefficients, without giving much thought to the assumptions and implications of that procedure.

At several points we have noted that, to solve uniquely the normal equations, constraints must be imposed on the solutions for fitted constants or regression coefficients. Three alternatives were illustrated for the one-way table, and it was pointed out that the effect of each was to fix the scale origin for the constants. For example the constraint that $a_i = 0$ fixes the scale origin at $\bar{Y}_i$; $\Sigma n_i a_i = 0$ fixes the origin at $\bar{Y}_.$; and $\Sigma a_i = 0$ fixes the origin at the unweighted mean of class means. Sums of squares and hypothesis-testing, it was noted, were unaffected by changes in origin.

With the two-way table, however, the situation is a trifle different: to fit the full model it is necessary to impose $r + c + 1$ constraints—one on the a_i, one on the b_i, and $r + c - 1$ on the c_{ij}. These latter constraints affect more than the scale origin of the c_{ij}. They also affect the correlation between factors A (rows) and C (interaction), and between B (columns) and C; and, because of this contingency, the assessment of the effects of A and B net of C (on the assumption of interaction) depend on the constraints imposed on the c_{ij}.

If in this situation it is possible to specify the way in which the population model is restricted, constraints on the solution may be selected to correspond to those restrictions (Searle, 1971, pp. 314–315). Since, by definition, restrictions hold in the population, they depend on theoretical considerations or on prior knowledge about the population. For example the restriction that $\sum^r n_{ij}\gamma_{ij} = \sum^c n_{ij}\gamma_{ij} = 0$ suggests that the magnitudes of the γ_{ij} change as population subclass frequencies change. Such a restriction does not seem reasonable for dynamic models where subclass frequencies may change from one trial to the next, as for example in stayer-mover models. Neither does it seem reasonable to restrict arbitrarily one or more of the γ_{ij} to zero, as this would imply the absence of interaction in those cells; however, such a restriction on the γ_{ij} may be called for in certain problems (see Hope, 1971). Under the restriction that $\sum^r \gamma_{ij} = \sum^c \gamma_{ij} = 0$, interaction may be present in each subclass and does not necessarily change as subclass frequencies change. These restrictions are implied by our choice of constraints.

The arbitrary origin of constants represents an advantage that may be realized in certain cases. As pointed out earlier, constants, or regression coefficients, on dummy variables represent differences between fitted means, for example $[(a_i + m) - (m)]$. If the analysis is limited to the hypothesis that all constants are equal, as in a conventional analysis of variance, the point of origin is immaterial. If deviations of constants from a particular point are of substantive interest, however, it is logical to select that point as the origin. For example, if the only differences of interest are between a given class and every other class, as in the case of a control group and several experimental groups, the mean of the control group is the logical point of origin. When a constant on a dummy variable corresponds to a difference between class means, it provides a test of the significance of that difference or contrast, assuming that necessary assumptions are met. For an example see Horan (1971).

One caution on this approach is perhaps in order. Such tests of particular contrasts are not a substitute for the full analysis of variance. These regression coefficients measure specific contrasts that are but a subset of all possible contrasts. It is thus possible that the contrasts chosen by selecting one origin may be nonsignificant although the analysis of variance shows that differences (other than those selected for test) exist. It is similarly possible that the particular contrasts represented by regression coefficients are statistically significant although the overall analysis of variance indicates that differences do not exist. In either case care must be exercised in interpreting the results, as Cramer (1972) has succinctly pointed out; on this same point see also Jennings (1967).

Misunderstandings about data and their relationships are likely to arise when a previously narrow technical term begins to take on loose meanings. The trouble is that words are taken to mean one thing when they actually mean something else. For example the term *analysis of variance* may be taken to mean an analysis that answers to the question of whether differences between groups are due to differences between treatments; however, an analysis of survey data does not necessarily yield an answer to that question. As intimated above, an analysis of variance of survey data may justify the inference that populations differ but permit no inference about the causal forces behind those differences.

Another example: the term *regression coefficient* is usually taken to mean the slope of a fitted line on coordinate axes, and interpreted as the change in Y per unit change in X in the absence of random disturbances. That interpretation is somewhat forced with dummy variables, however, since a regression coefficient on a dummy variable reflects not concomitant variation but the difference between two constants, such as $a_i - a_1$, $[(a_i + m) - m]$, and so forth. To construe that difference as slope is to convey the impression that dummy variables are subject to the same operations as continuous variables or interval measures; in particular, that a dummy variable may be plotted by cartesian coordinates. Since the term *fitted constant* carries no such connotation and merely denotes an element common to a given class, it may be less subject to misinterpretation.

Still another example: the term *path analysis* refers to a method for testing causal assumptions; nevertheless sums of squares from an AOV table may be expressed in the symbolism of path analysis even though causal assumptions were never drawn. In the latter event, results might better be presented as the outcome of a regression analysis since such analysis is free of causal assumptions. Pertinent in this connection is Goldberger's (1973) comment on the distinction between regression and structural models: "In a structural equation model each equation represents a causal link rather than a mere empirical association. In a regression model, on the other hand, each equation represents the conditional mean of a dependent variable as a function of explanatory variables. It is this distinction which makes conventional regression analysis an inadequate tool for estimating structural equation models" (p. 2).

The implication of the foregoing examples is that misleading language ought to be avoided in reporting results based on measures sorted into classes: in particular, that the language of experimental design be used guardedly in the absence of randomization; that the language of regression be used advisedly with 0,1 dummy variables; that the symbolism of path analysis not be used when no more than a regression analysis has been carried out. These points take on added significance today because of the tendency of social researchers to adopt the language in which a particular algorithm is given, whether appropriate to the analysis or not.

In conclusion, this discussion has sought to substantiate that sums of squares for AOV tables may be expressed in terms of constants, regression coefficients, or path coefficients. It was also brought out that it makes no difference in significance-testing which form of expression is adopted. Even so, one concept does not necessarily serve as well as another in a given investigation. As noted above, these concepts represent somewhat different perspectives; they are not equally vulnerable to the same complications; they provide different interpretations of the same data; consequently one concept may convey accurately the purposes of a study that will be misrepresented by another. Since the term *constant* is relatively free of connotations about the level of measurement and causal connections, that terminology might normally be adopted. In studies of predictive efficiency, the language of correlation and regression might be apt; similarly, in studies of causal links the language of path analysis might be justified and even required. Unless these concerns are made explicit, however, and to avoid possible misunderstandings, it would seem generally best to express sums of squares and means squares in terms of fitted constants within the conventional format of the analysis of variance.

APPENDIX

TABLE 22
Basic Variate Y and Covariate V

	B_1		B_2		B_3	
	Y_{11k}	V_{11k}	Y_{12k}	V_{12k}	Y_{13k}	V_{13k}
	10.03[a]	−0.74[a]	9.43	0.01	12.74	0.54
	14.88[a]	1.78[a]	13.63	0.24	13.92	2.16
	11.02[a]	−1.34[a]	7.53	−0.19	9.72	−1.31
	11.15[a]	−1.51[a]	13.30	−1.34	13.30	−1.46
A_1	14.15[a]	0.20[a]	10.81	−0.72	14.37	0.81
	15.85	1.75	13.25	0.19	10.90	−0.46
	13.86	−0.47	18.06	−0.95	15.35	−0.10
	11.73	0.11	11.49	−0.34	12.92	−0.22
	13.16	0.45	12.87	−0.89	11.17	−1.18
	13.32	1.69	13.41	−0.00	16.83	0.03
	Y_{21k}	V_{21k}	Y_{22k}	V_{22k}	Y_{23k}	V_{23k}
	9.81	0.17	13.92	2.05	6.25[a]	1.63[a]
	10.37	1.57	11.33	−0.49	13.81[a]	0.60[a]
	10.84	0.52	9.81	−1.85	14.17[a]	−1.97[a]
	11.73	−0.12	15.00	0.93	12.47[a]	−0.44[a]
A_2	13.07	−1.18	10.77	0.57	9.41[a]	0.60[a]
	12.72	−0.31	13.79	−0.74	12.11	−0.89
	12.36	−1.74	11.51	−0.30	11.69	−0.28
	11.22	0.53	9.16	0.82	14.68	−0.18
	11.11	0.05	10.55	0.94	11.28	−1.53
	15.09	−1.73	10.05	0.33	6.41	−0.68
	Y_{31k}	V_{31k}	Y_{32k}	V_{32k}	Y_{33k}	V_{33k}
	9.12	−0.47	13.36[a]	0.33[a]	10.66	1.40
	13.59	−0.39	13.30[a]	0.45[a]	14.24	−0.12
	12.94	−0.20	10.81[a]	−0.47[a]	10.41	0.71
	11.55	−0.46	9.50[a]	1.41[a]	9.50	−1.50
A_3	16.20	−0.62	10.77[a]	0.70[a]	8.42	0.67
	8.69	−0.47	14.10	1.41	11.82	1.91
	12.83	−0.54	16.11	0.46	13.12	−1.09
	13.63	−0.32	12.98	0.22	8.53	−0.64
	10.12	1.66	12.63	0.82	10.10	1.62
	10.81	0.27	14.01	0.13	12.63	1.12

[a] To create disproportional frequencies, these measures were moved to another column within the same row to give the distribution shown in Table 8.

REFERENCES

ANDREWS, F., MORGAN, J. AND SONQUIST, J.
    1967 *Multiple Classification Analysis.* Ann Arbor: University of Michigan Institute for Social Research.

BANCROFT, T. A.
1968 *Topics in Intermediate Statistical Methods*. Ames: Iowa State University Press.

BEATTIE, C. AND SPENCER, B. G.
1971 "Career attainment in Canadian bureaucracies: Unscrambling the effects of age, seniority, education, and ethnolinguistic factors on salary." *American Journal of Sociology* 77 (November):472–490.

BOYLE, R. P.
1970 "Path analysis and ordinal data." *American Journal of Sociology* 75 (January):461–480.

COLEMAN, J. S.
1970 "Multivariate analysis for attribute data." Pp. 217–224 in E. F. Borgatta and G. W. Bohrnstedt (Eds.), *Sociological Methodology 1970*. San Francisco: Jossey-Bass.

CRAMER, E. M.
1972 "Significance tests and test of models in multiple regression." *American Statistician* 26 (October):26–30.

FEATHERMAN, D. L.
1971 "The socioeconomic achievement of white religioethnic subgroups: Social and psychological explanations." *American Sociological Review* 36 (April):207–222.

FISHER, R. A.
1936 "The use of multiple measurements in taxonomic problems." *Annals of Eugenics* 7:179–188.

GASTON, J.
1970 "The reward system in British science." *American Sociological Review* 35 (August):718–732.

GOLDBERGER, A. S.
1973 "Structural equation models: An overview." Chap. 1 in A. S. Goldberger and O. D. Duncan (Eds.), *Structural Equation Models in Social Science: Proceedings of a Conference*. New York: Seminar.

GOODMAN, L.
1972 "A modified multiple regression analysis approach to the analysis of dichotomous variables." *American Sociological Review* 37 (February):28–46.

GRIZZLE, J. E., STARMER, C. F. AND KOCH, G. G.
1969 "Analysis of categorical data by linear models." *Biometrics* 25 (September):489–504.

GURIN, P.
1970 "Motivation and aspirations of Southern Negro college youth." *American Journal of Sociology* 75 (January):607–631.

HAUSER, R. M.
1971 *Socioeconomic Background and Educational Performance*. Washington, D.C.: American Sociological Association.

HIGGINS, G. F.
  1970 "A discriminant analysis of employment in defense and nondefense industries." *Journal of the American Statistical Association* 65 (June): 613–622.
HOPE, K.
  1971 "Social mobility and fertility." *American Sociological Review* 36 (December):1019–1032.
HORAN, P. M.
  1971 "Social positions and political cross-pressures: A re-examination." *American Sociological Review* 36 (August):650–660.
JENNINGS, E.
  1967 "Fixed effects analysis of variance by regression methods." *Multivariate Behavioral Research* 2 (January):95–108.
KENDALL, M. G.
  1961 *A Course in Multivariate Analysis*. London: Griffin.
KENDALL, M. G. AND STUART, A.
  1966 *The Advanced Theory of Statistics*. Vol. 3. New York: Hafner.
KORNBERG, A. AND BREHM, M. L.
  1971 "Ideology, institutional identification, and campus activism." *Social Forces* 49 (March):445–459.
LASLETT, B.
  1971 "Mobility and work satisfaction: A discussion of the use and interpretation of mobility models." *American Journal of Sociology* 77 (July):19–35.
LIGHT, R. J. AND MARGOLIN, B. H.
  1971 "Analysis of variance for categorical data." *Journal of the American Statistical Association* 66 (September):534–544.
LOY, J. W., JR.
  1969 "Social psychological characteristics of innovations." *American Sociological Review* 34 (February):73–82.
LYONS, M. AND CARTER, T. M.
  1971 "Comments on Boyle's 'Path analysis and ordinal data.'" *American Journal of Sociology* 76 (May):1112–1132.
MALLIOS, W. S.
  1970 "The analysis of structural effects in experimental design." *Journal of the American Statistical Association* 65 (June):808–827.
MORRISON, D. F.
  1967 *Multivariate Statistical Methods*. New York: McGraw-Hill.
PERRUCCI, C. C. AND PERRUCCI, R.
  1970 "Social origins, educational contexts, and career mobility." *American Sociological Review* 35 (June):451–463.
SEARLE, S. R.
  1971 *Linear Models*. New York: Wiley.
SPROTT, D. A.
  1970 "Note on Evans and Anastasio on the analysis of covariance." *Psychological Bulletin* 73 (April):303–306.

SUITS, D. B.
- 1957 "Use of dummy variables in regression equations." *Journal of the American Statistical Association* 52 (December):548–551.

WARNER, S. L.
- 1963 "Multivariate regression of dummy variates under normality assumptions." *Journal of the American Statistical Association* 58 (December):1054–1063.
- 1967 "Asymptotic variances for dummy variate regression under normality assumptions." *Journal of the American Statistical Association* 62 (December):1305–1314.

WILSON, R. A.
- 1971 "Anomie in the ghetto: A study of neighborhood type, race, and anomie." *American Journal of Sociology* 77 (July):66–88.

YANCEY, W. L., RIGSBY, L. AND MCCARTHY, J. D.
- 1972 "Social position and self-evaluation: The relative importance of race." *American Journal of Sociology* 78 (September):338–359.

YATES, F.
- 1933 "The principles of orthogonality and confounding in replicated experiments." *Journal of Agricultural Science* 23:108–145.
- 1934 "The analysis of multiple classifications with unequal numbers in the different classes." *Journal of the American Statistical Association* 29:51-66.

8

HIERARCHICAL MODELS FOR SIGNIFICANCE TESTS IN MULTIVARIATE CONTINGENCY TABLES: AN EXEGESIS OF GOODMAN'S RECENT PAPERS

James A. Davis
National Opinion Research Center
UNIVERSITY OF CHICAGO

I wish to thank Stephen Fienberg, Leo Goodman, Avery Guest, and Howard Schuman for their comments, corrections, and criticisms. I am also most grateful to Edmund D. Meyers, Jr., and the Kiewit Computation Center of Dartmouth College for generous assistance.

In a flurry of recent papers (1970, 1971, 1972a, 1972b, 1972c), Leo Goodman presents and elaborates a system for the analysis of contingency tables (cross-classifications of nominal and ordinal variables) that promises to be extremely useful to sociologists. The papers are.

however, extremely compressed, heavily salted with the cumbersome notation of contingency analysis, and are not easily accessible to the student and average research worker. The aim of this chapter is to explain the logic and procedures of the system in terms the reader (and writer) may find more comfortable.

The Goodman system consists of two parts: a scheme for making significance tests by means of "hierarchical models" and an extensive discussion of a set of techniques known as "log linear models." The two parts are logically and practically distinct. I shall treat only the former.

Among the important uses of hierarchical models are the following: tests for the significance of partial correlations; tests for interactions (specifications) where the control variable has as many categories as one pleases; tests for higher-order (three or more variable) interactions; succinct statements of what is and what is not going on in a contingency table. Since none of these tools has been easily available to the average sociologist, the Goodman system is well worth learning—especially because it provides considerable insight into the properties of cross-classifications and the logic of significance tests.

My explanation of the Goodman system is nontechnical but it does assume some exposure to contingency table analysis. In particular the reader should be familiar with the following concepts: marginals, expected cell values, statistical independence, the chi square test for differences between expected and observed frequencies, and degrees of freedom (see Davis, 1971, Chap. 3, or any elementary statistics textbook).

BACKGROUND

To understand how to use the Goodman system, the reader should be familiar with three concepts: *odds ratios*, *effects*, and *models*.

Odds Ratios

An odds ratio is the ratio of frequencies for two categories of some variable. The concept, which may be unfamiliar, is extremely useful in defining the models that are the heart of Goodman's system, and it also gives us a common language for talking about a variety of statistical properties, such as skewed distributions, partial associations, specifications, and interactions.

Consider the hypothetical fourfold table shown in Table 1. Looking at the column totals, we observe that 30 cases are Yes on variable B and 70 cases are No. The odds are 30 to 70 that a case in Table 1 is a Yes on variable B and the odds are 70 to 30 that a case in Table 1 is a No on variable B. Taking the ratio $30:70 = 0.429$, we can say that the

TABLE 1
Hypothetical Fourfold Table

		Variable B		
		Yes	No	Total
Variable A	High	15	35	50
	Low	15	35	50
	Total	30	70	100

odds ratio for Yes versus No on variable B is 0.429. We can symbolize such calculations (although this is not Goodman's notation) as follows:

$$\begin{pmatrix} \text{Yes} \\ B \\ \text{No} \end{pmatrix} = \text{Odds ratio for } B = 30:70 = 0.429$$

$$\begin{pmatrix} \text{High} \\ A \\ \text{Low} \end{pmatrix} = \text{Odds ratio for } A = 50:50 = 1.000$$

The category frequency appearing above the letter is divided by the category frequency below the letter. Which category frequency we choose to put above and which we choose to put below is perfectly arbitrary. We can decide to say that

$$\begin{pmatrix} \text{Yes} \\ B \\ \text{No} \end{pmatrix} = 0.429$$

or to say that

$$\begin{pmatrix} \text{No} \\ B \\ \text{Yes} \end{pmatrix} = 2.333$$

but the decision is irrevocable in a particular analysis.

The odds ratio is 1.000 for a situation in which the two categories are equal (such as variable A in Table 1) regardless of which ratio we calculate. Its minimum is zero (for example, $0:70 = 0$) but it has no defined upper limit. At the extreme, where a frequency is divided by zero (say, $70:0$), the odds ratio has no specific numerical value. This property makes it necessary to make certain adjustments in the data when one is calculating Goodman's measures of association, but it has no importance for the significance tests discussed in this chapter.

The concept of odds ratios can be extended to conditional odds ratios and then to relative odds ratios. The odds ratio

$$\begin{pmatrix} \text{Yes} \\ B \\ \text{No} \end{pmatrix}$$

was based on all the cases in Table 1, that is, on the marginals for item B. One can also calculate these ratios for particular categories of another variable; for example, calculating

$$\begin{pmatrix} \text{Yes} \\ B \\ \text{No} \end{pmatrix}$$

when A is high, using the frequencies in the top row of Table 1. We call such results *conditional odds ratios* and use the conventional vertical line to indicate a condition. Thus

$$\left[\begin{pmatrix} \text{Yes} \\ B \\ \text{No} \end{pmatrix} \mid A = \text{high} \right] = 15:35 = 0.429$$

in Table 1. Conditional odds ratios lead directly to the notion of independence and association. Many of us would evaluate independence in Table 1 by means of the *cross-product difference* (Davis, 1971, pp. 34–50). Thus $(35*15 - 35*15) = (525 - 525) = 0$. Since equality of the cross-products is a definition of independence, we would conclude that Table 1 shows independence for A and B. Exactly the same destination can be reached through conditional odds ratios and the notion of relative odds ratios.

TABLE 2
Cell Frequencies in Fourfold Table

	y	
	−	+
x +	a	b
x −	c	d

Table 2 represents a diagram of cell frequencies in a fourfold table. Designating the cell frequencies in a fourfold table as in Table 2, we call $(b/d)/(a/c)$, the ratio of two conditional odds ratios, a *relative odds ratio*:

$$\overset{+}{X} \overset{+}{Y} = \frac{\overset{+}{X} \mid Y = +}{\overset{+}{X} \mid Y = -} = \frac{b/d}{a/c} \tag{1}$$

From high school algebra:

$$\frac{b/d}{a/c} = \frac{bc}{ad} = \frac{b/a}{d/c} = \overset{+}{\underset{-}{X}}\ \overset{+}{\underset{-}{Y}} = \overset{+}{\underset{-}{Y}}\ \overset{+}{\underset{-}{X}} \tag{2}$$

Equation (2) tells us two things. First it says that the ratio of the cross-products (not their difference) is identical in value to the ratio of the two conditional odds ratios. In particular, whenever the cross-products are equal in magnitude, their ratio, the relative odds ratio, must equal 1.000. Second it says that one gets the same number whether one takes the ratio of the two X conditionals or the ratio of the two Y conditionals. The relative odds ratio is symmetrical. (But remember, one does not get the same number if one reverses plus and minus for one of the variables. The effect of reversing the signs for one of the items is to change the odds ratio to its reciprocal.)

Thus there are two new definitions of lack of independence in a fourfold table: the conditional odds ratios are not equal; the relative odds ratio does not equal 1.000. The identical concepts apply to larger tables but the number of possibilities increases rapidly. Taking the odds ratio for B in Table 3, we see that there are six ratios we can examine (ignoring which letter is at the top and which is at the bottom):

$$\begin{pmatrix} i \\ B \\ j \end{pmatrix}\begin{pmatrix} i \\ B \\ k \end{pmatrix}\begin{pmatrix} i \\ B \\ l \end{pmatrix}\begin{pmatrix} j \\ B \\ k \end{pmatrix}\begin{pmatrix} j \\ B \\ l \end{pmatrix}\begin{pmatrix} k \\ B \\ l \end{pmatrix}$$

one for each pair of categories. And each has a relative odds ratio for each possible pair of categories on the other variable:

High	High	Medium
A	A	A
Medium	Low	Low

TABLE 3
Hypothetical 3 × 4 Table

		B: i	j	k	l
	High				
A	Medium				
	Low				

Since a variable with K categories has $(K)(K-1)/2$ pairs of categories, we can put it more generally. For an $R \times C$ table (where R

is rows and C is columns):

$$\left(\frac{(R)(R-1)}{2} \cdot \frac{(C)(C-1)}{2}\right) = \left(\frac{(R)(C)(R-1)(C-1)}{4}\right) \quad (3)$$

$$= \text{Number of relative odds ratios}$$

Table 3 has $(4)(3)(3)(2)/4 = 18$ different (though not mathematically independent) relative odds ratios. A fourfold table has $(2)(2)(1)(1)/4 = 1$. Equation (3) and its discussion leads to a generalization of the second of our new definitions of lack of independence: an $R \times C$ table lacks independence if any relative odds ratios do not equal 1.000.

This concept can also be extended to tables with more than two variables, which leads us to "relative relative" or higher-order odds ratios. To avoid cumbersome phrases like "super" or "relative relative," we define the order of an odds ratio as the number of variables involved in its calculation. $\overset{+}{A}$ is a first-order odds ratio, $\overset{++}{\underset{--}{AB}}$ is a second-order odds ratio, $\overset{+++}{\underset{---}{ABC}}$ is a third-order odds ratio, and so on. The phrase "in its calculation" implies that conditional variables are not counted in assessing order. $\overset{++}{\underset{--}{BC}}|A = +$ is a second-order conditional odds ratio.

Let us consider the third-order odds ratio $\overset{+++}{\underset{---}{ABC}}$ in this hypothetical table (Table 4). We may think of it as calculating the second-order odds ratio (cross-product ratio) for A and B within each category of C and then finding the ratio of these two conditional results. In algebra:

$$\frac{\overset{+\;+}{\underset{-\;-}{A\;B}}|C = +}{\overset{+\;+}{\underset{-\;-}{A\;B}}|C = -} = \frac{fg/eh}{bc/ad} = \frac{fgad}{ehbc} = \overset{+\;+\;+}{\underset{-\;-\;-}{A\;B\;C}} \quad (4)$$

TABLE 4
Diagram of Third-Order Odds Ratio

	$C = -$				$C = +$	
		B				B
		−	+			−	+
A	+	a	b	A	+	e	f
	−	c	d		−	g	h

The third-order and all higher-order results are symmetrical in the sense that one gets the same answer whatever order one picks for the ratios. Thus $\overset{+++}{\underset{---}{BCA}}$ implies that we calculate the $\overset{++}{\underset{--}{BC}}$ odds ratios within levels of A and find their ratio as in Equation (5).

$$\frac{\overset{+\ +}{\underset{-\ -}{B\ C}}|A = +}{\overset{+\ +}{\underset{-\ -}{B\ C}}|A = -} = \frac{fa/be}{ch/dg} = \frac{fadg}{bech} = \frac{fgad}{ehbc} \qquad (5)$$

A third-order odds ratio of 1.000 means that all the two-variable associations are identical in magnitude across categories of the third item. (It does not imply that all three—AB, AC, BC—have the same strength or that any of them depart from independence.)

A third-order odds ratio other than 1.000 means that for each of the three associations (AB, AC, BC) the magnitudes in the two conditions differ. It also implies that at least one of the two conditional tables for each association shows lack of independence. If both conditional tables showed independence, the two conditional odds ratios would be 1.000 and so would the third-order coefficient.

When interpreting third-order odds ratios other than 1.000, we usually view the result as a *specification* or an *interaction* (Davis, 1971, pp. 99–103), saying, for example, that the degree of correlation between A and B varies, depending on the category of C. This is a useful way to wrench some sense from the data, but it is important to remember that higher-order effects are interchangeable. When the third-order odds ratio for ABC differs from 1.000, it is equally correct to say that the correlation between A and B varies, depending on the category of C; or that the correlation between A and C varies, depending on the category of B; or that the correlation between B and C varies, depending on the category of A.

A specific example may help clarify the concept of higher-order odds ratios or interactions. Table 5 gives multivariate data on employed persons from the 1960 U.S. Census rounded to the nearest thousand (figures are from Davis, 1971, p. 157). All variables are dichotomies: A is 1959 earnings, dichotomized as $+$ = $4000 or more, $-$ = less than $4000; B is occupation, with $+$ = white collar and $-$ = blue collar and farm; C is education, with $+$ = high school graduate and $-$ = less than high school graduate; and D is sex, with $+$ = male and $-$ = female.

Column I lists eight conditional first-order odds ratios for A, the high-income frequencies divided by low-income frequencies within the various combinations of the other three variables.

TABLE 5
Sex, Education, Occupation, and 1959 Earnings

		Frequencies	B Occupation	C Education	D Sex	Odds Ratios			
A Earnings						I + − $A\|B,C,D$	II + + − − $AB\|C,D$	III + + + − − − $ABC\|D$	IV + + + + − − − − $ABCD$
3,451		7,294	+	+	+	2.114	2.321	1.235	1.043
4,188		3,817	−	+	+	0.911			
2,397		1,986	+	−	+	0.829	1.880		
13,303		5,871	−	−	+	0.441			
6,982		1,150	+	+	−	0.165	4.342	1.184	
2,005		76	−	+	−	0.038			
2,538		168	+	−	−	0.066	3.667		
6,063		107	−	−	−	0.018			

Column II lists four conditional second-order odds ratios, $AB|C,D$ (with ++/−− signs). In each the result in Column I for plus on occupation was divided by the result for minus on occupation. All four exceed 1.000. This is equivalent to saying that there is a nonzero partial correlation between occupation and income, controlling for education and sex. If there were no partial association, the second-order odds ratios would all be 1.000.

Column III compares the second-order results for plus on education with those for minus on education. It asks whether the occupation-income relationship is the same within levels of education. Because both third-order odds ratios exceed 1.000, we infer that the association between occupation and income is stronger among the better-educated. There is a specification or interaction.

Column IV is the fourth-order odds ratio. Its value, 1.043, is quite close to 1.000, and without a significance test one would not wish to draw a firm conclusion (more on this later). Assuming for the sake of discussion only that it is greater than 1.000, it could be described as a specification of a specification or as an interaction of an interaction. One English translation would be: "The tendency for high education to accentuate the occupation-income correlation is greater among men."

The concept of higher-order interactions can be extended indefinitely, although plausible substantive interpretations seem to decrease geometrically with the order of the effect. We can summarize our discussion and illustrate the utility of the odds ratio concept by the following statements:

Odds Ratio Statement	Statistical Property
1. Odds ratio	1. Ratio of two category frequencies for some variable
2. The first-order (nonconditional) odds ratio $\neq 1.000$	2. The marginal frequencies for the two categories are not identical
3. The second-order odds ratio $\neq 1.000$	3. The two items are associated (not independent) at the zero-order level
4. The second-order conditional odds ratio $\neq 1.000$	4. The two items have a nonzero partial association
5. The third-order odds ratio $\neq 1.000$	5. The three items show an interaction or specification
6. The fourth-order odds ratio $\neq 1.000$	6. The four items show an interaction (the third-order interaction is specified)

Effects

The second concept in Goodman's system discussed here is *effects*, another term that may be unfamiliar. It is a point of view rather than a statistical property but it helps glue the system together. In a manner of speaking, the analyst working with the Goodman system views the cell frequencies in his cross-tabulation as a dependent variable. His data analysis is an attempt to account for variation in cell frequencies. The broad concept is a familiar one. We are all used to the idea that in multiple regression the analyst attempts to account for variation in scores on a dependent variable through scores on predictor variables. But the analogy is rough and can be misleading. In Goodman analysis we are not accounting for scores on a particular variable but for joint frequencies on a number of variables: our predictors are not scores on a variable but statistical properties involving sets of variables. The specific statistical properties are defined precisely later in this chapter, but for an introduction we can sketch them as follows.

A *single*-variable effect is a difference in cell frequencies that reflects the marginal distributions for one or more items. For example, in a cross-tabulation involving race the cells associated with race = black may be systematically smaller because there are many fewer blacks than whites in the total sample.

A *two*-variable effect is a difference in cell frequencies that reflects an association between a pair of variables. For example, in a cross-tabulation involving occupation and income, cells for the combination of high occupation and high income may be relatively larger because occupation is correlated with income.

A *three*-variable effect is a difference in cell frequencies that reflects an interaction or specification of three variables. For example, in a cross-tabulation involving race, region, and attitudes toward civil rights, cells for the combination of white, Southern, and anti-civil rights may be especially large if it is the case that race differences in attitudes toward civil rights are stronger in the South.

Four-, five-, ..., N-variable effects can be described in a similar fashion. (The reader has undoubtedly noticed a similarity between the kinds of effects listed and the kinds of odds ratios defined above. They are really the same thing. One uses odds ratios to talk concretely about various kinds of effects. *Effect* is the abstract concept and *odds ratios* are its concrete language.)

Readers familiar with analysis of variance will see an obvious analogy and may find it comfortable to think of the Goodman procedure as akin to carrying out analysis of variance on cell frequencies. There are some potentially confusing semantic problems with this analogy also. In analysis of variance, the term *interaction* applies to effects involving two or more variables. In the statistical tradition of contingency table analysis, two-variable effects are called *associations* or *correlations* and the term *interaction* is reserved for higher-order effects. We shall take the latter position and speak of *single-variable or marginal effects, two-variable or association effects*, and *three or more variable or interaction effects*.

Models

The final concept necessary to understand the Goodman system is a more familiar word, *models*. The central operation in the system is constructing and testing models—sets of semiartificial data created by the analyst and having some statistical property. The analyst creates a series of models, compares them with actual data, and uses the discrepancies or lack of discrepancies to assess the presence of various statistical effects.

The reader is already familiar with the concept of models, but not the word, from standard tests for association. Although we do not usually think of it this way, the standard test for significant association between two variables is an instance of modeling. We create a set of semiartificial data that has some properties identical to the real data (the same marginals and same grand total) and one big difference—in our model the two variables are forced to be statistically independent. We then compare our model with the real data, and if there is a significant discrepancy—if our model does not fit—we say that there is an association between the variables. Goodman's system extends this idea backward and forward: backward to an even more primitive model and forward to models involving many variables and their interactions.

The three background concepts—odds ratios, effects, and models—all fit together. We can summarize this section as follows: in the Goodman system the analyst attempts to account for the cell frequencies in his cross-tabulation by hypothesizing effects, by building models that embody the presence and absence of various effects through setting the odds ratios to appropriate values, and by comparing the model with the actual data.

SPECIFIC MODELS

This section considers the specific models one can build, how such models are constructed and tested, and the inferences that follow from various outcomes. The broader questions of when an analyst should use various models, what the results mean, and how all of this fits into conventional data analysis are considered in the following section. I shall treat the following kinds of models, classified in terms of the effects at issue: no effects, single-variable effects, two-variable effects, three-variable effects, higher-order effects, and mixed models.

Equal-Probability Model: No Effects

Is there a contingency table so devoid of interest, a concatenation of figures so nonproblematical that it could not even arouse the interest of a statistics graduate student seeking a thesis topic? One never knows until he tries, but one candidate is Table 6. The crucial statistical property in Table 6 is not very subtle. Each of the 24 cells in the table has exactly 149 cases. Is the table interesting? If it turned up as the result of a run on actual data, it would be very interesting—one would immediately ask what went wrong with the computer. But as a sort of Platonic "ideal table," it is the essence of nothingness since there is absolutely nothing going on of any statistical interest. Table 6 is an example of the first and most primitive of Goodman's nested set of models, the model assuming equal probability or no effects.

There is more (or perhaps less) to equal-probability tables than meets the eye when we consider their properties in terms of odds ratios and effects. Thus:

1. All first-order odds ratios are 1.000. If we sum the cell frequencies in Table 6 to obtain the item marginals, we find that all the dichotomies have marginal frequencies of 1788 in each category and that the trichotomous variable has a frequency of 1192 in each of its three categories. Equal sizes of all marginal categories is equivalent to saying that all first-order odds ratios are 1.000.
2. All second-order odds ratios are 1.000. A second-order odds ratio is a fourfold table, and we see that any fourfold table we define within Table 6 has cell frequencies of 149, 149, 149, and

TABLE 6
Equal-Probability $2 \times 3 \times 2 \times 2$ Table ($N = 3576$)

	Variable A										
	Something						Something Else					
Variable B	This		That		The Other		This		That		The Other	
Variable C	Yes	No	Yes	No	Yes	No	Yes	No	Yes	No	Yes	No
Variable D												
High	149	149	149	149	149	149	149	149	149	149	149	149
Low	149	149	149	149	149	149	149	149	149	149	149	149

149. The fourfold table shows independence, which is equivalent to saying that the second-order odds ratio is 1.000.
3. All higher-order odds ratios are 1.000. Since all fourfold tables have odds ratios of 1.000, all second-order odds ratios are 1.000:1.000 or 1.000. And, by a similar argument, it follows that odds ratios of any order are all 1.000.
4. Therefore all odds ratios are 1.000 in an equal-probability table.

Since an effect is defined as an odds ratio that departs from 1.000 (to be discussed later), the equal-probability table has no effects. Both intuition and the properties of odds ratios tell us that in an equal-probability table (no-effect table) absolutely nothing is going on.

To construct an equal-probability model one finds the total number of cells in the table (here 24) and then divides N (the total cases) by that number (3576/24 = 149). More abstractly the cell values in an equal-probability model with variables A, B, C, and so on such that A has a total of A categories, B has a total of B categories, and so on, are

$$\text{Cell value} = N/A * B * C \ldots \qquad (6)$$

The values in an equal-probability model tell us nothing until we compare them with actual data. The figures in Table 6 are in fact the equal-probability model for a particular table adapted from M. A. Schwartz (1967, Table 8, p. 133). Schwartz compares a number of surveys from 1942 to 1963 to trace trends in white attitudes toward Negroes. There is no reason why we cannot treat time (year of study) as a variable—provided that each study contains the same questions—and the Goodman system is especially useful for this purpose. Schwartz's variables are as in Table 7. The raw frequencies in her real-data table

TABLE 7
Schwartz's Variables

Variable	Content	Categories	
Time (T)	Year of study	1946	1963
Education (E)	Respondent's educational attainment	Grade school, high school, college	
Region (R)	Respondent's region	South	Other (North)
Jobs (J)	"Do you think Negroes should have as good a chance as white people to get any kind of job or do you think white people should have the first chance at any kind of job?"	Negroes should have as good a chance	Other

(calculated from the percentages and bases she reports) are presented in Table 8. The actual data seem pretty far from the model. Only a few of the cells are anywhere near the predicted value of 149, some are as high as 300 or 400, and some are as small as 50.

The discrepancies between model and data might be accounted for by chance fluctuations—sampling or measurement error. The well-known chi square test enables us to check this possibility. For each cell we first compare the observed (raw data) and expected (model) values (for example, 52 versus 149 in the upper left-hand corner). We next square the discrepancy $(52 - 149 = -97; -97^2 = 9409)$, divide the squared discrepancy by the expected (model) value $(9409/149 = 63.15)$, and then sum the cell chi square values to give a total chi square for the table. In practice the model data should be run out a decimal or two. For example, $3579/24$ is really 149.12. I used whole numbers here for simplicity of explanation only.

As is usual in chi square tests, we need to know the degrees of freedom (DF) or number of independent pieces of information. When 23 cell discrepancies have been computed, we can obtain the 24th by subtraction—since the discrepancies in the table must sum to zero. Only one of the chi square values is redundant. Here, and in general, the degree of freedom for the equal-probability model equals

$$(A * B * C * D \ldots) - 1$$

[see Equation (7)]. In our example $24 - 1 = 23$. In a fourfold table we would get $(2 * 2) - 1 = 3$.

$$\text{DF for variables } A, B, C \ldots = (A * B * C \ldots) - 1 \tag{7}$$

We obtained a chi square value of 2798.49 for the discrepancy between Table 6 (the model) and Table 8 (the data). The standard chi square table (at the back of any statistics book) tells us that for 23 degrees of freedom, a chi square value of 40.3 would be significant at the 0.01 level. This exceeds the alpha level of 0.01 that I shall use throughout this chapter. We conclude that our model does not fit.

What have we learned? It depends on how the test comes out. If the equal-probability model fits (if the chi square is not significant): there is nothing going on in the table. There are no effects to analyze. We cannot reject the hypothesis that all odds ratios are 1.000. If the equal-probability model does not fit (if the chi square is significant): something is going on in the table. The cell frequencies in the data differ from each other more than chance can account for. However, we do not know *what* is going on. It is not the case that all odds ratios are 1.000, but we cannot point to any specific odds ratios that differ from 1.000.

TABLE 8
Cell Frequencies in Schwartz's Data

	Grade		1946 High		College		Grade		1963 High		Other	
	South	Other	South	Other	South	Other	South	Other	South	Other	South	Other
As good	52	311	64	439	42	204	71	148	126	410	55	201
Other	206	365	163	374	51	83	44	61	31	56	14	8

203

Single-Variable Effects: No Associations

The failure of the equal-probability model tells us that there are some effects in the data. Following the principle of parsimony, we next try to fit the data with the simplest possible alternative. It can be described alternatively as:

1. A model in which first-order odds ratios are allowed to depart from 1.000, but all higher-order odds ratios are set to 1.000
2. A model in which cell frequencies are not necessarily identical, but there are no partial associations or interactions
3. A model in which the cell frequencies are exactly proportional to the marginal frequencies for the items
4. A model that allows single-variable effects only
5. A model that tests the hypothesis that all differences in cell frequencies can be accounted for by the single-variable category distributions of the items

The familiar chi square test for significant association in an $R \times C$ table is an example of a marginal-only model. We do not usually dignify such calculations with the awesome term *model*, but testing for a significant association can be viewed as building a model in which cell frequencies are proportional to the marginal frequencies but no higher-order (two-variable, correlational) effects are permitted.

Less familiar is the extension of this idea to any number of variables, as in our example of the Schwartz data. Table 9 gives us her marginals. How many cases should our model have for a particular cell, say, 1946/high school/South/as good, under the hypothesis that cell frequencies are a function of marginal frequencies? Using a not unfamiliar logic, we multiply odds or probabilities like this:

$$\frac{2354}{3579} * \frac{1663}{3579} * \frac{919}{3579} * \frac{2123}{3579} * 3579 = \frac{7,637,728,445,974}{164,076,654,996,081} * 3579$$

$$= 0.0466 * 3579 = 166.8 = 0.658 * 465 * 0.257 * 0.593 * 3579$$
$$= 0.0467 * 3579 = 167.1$$

Using the actual frequencies we get an expected value of 166.8 for that cell; using proportions we get 167.1; the difference is due to rounding. When working by hand, the proportional approach keeps the number of figures within practical limits, but with computer programs the frequency approach is more accurate.

The same calculations are made for each cell, giving the following general formula (we use here the conventional summation sign Σ to indicate a sum or total, and use the notation $A_iB_jC_k$ to name the cell

TABLE 9
Single-Variable Marginal Frequencies for Data in Table 8

Variable	Categories	Frequency	Proportion
Time (T)	1963	1225	0.342
	1946	2354	0.658
		3579	1.000
Education (E)	Grade	1258	0.351
	High school	1663	0.465
	College	658	0.184
		3579	1.000
Region (R)	South	919	0.257
	Other	2660	0.743
		3579	1.000
Jobs (J)	As good	2123	0.593
	Other	1456	0.407
		3579	1.000

defined by the ith category of variable A, the jth category of variable B, and so on):

$$\Sigma(A_i B_j C_k \cdots) = \left(\frac{\Sigma A_i}{N} * \frac{\Sigma B_j}{N} * \frac{\Sigma C_k}{N} \cdots \right) * N \qquad (8)$$

Canceling the Ns we obtain an alternate version that is easier for calculations:

$$\Sigma(A_i B_j C_k \cdots) = \frac{(A_i * B_j * C_k \cdots)}{N^{v-1}} \qquad (9)$$

where N means the number of variables.

As before, we compare each cell in the model with its mate in the actual data, square the discrepancy, divide by the expected (model) value, and sum the terms to obtain a total chi square for the model.

How many degrees of freedom do we use? The answer is simple. Starting with $(A * B * C \ldots) - 1$, we subtract for each variable $K - 1$, where K equals the total number of categories in the variable. Because matters become more complex as we move on to more elaborate models, it is worth the time to consider the reasoning behind this magic number. Consider first a single variable A with three categories I, II, and III. If we were to test the equal-probability model in the previous section, we could make our calculations for any two of the three cells in the distribution and then fill in the observed and expected in the last cell by subtraction, since both the observed and expected cell values must sum to N. It makes no difference which cell we treat as the last or redundant cell, but call it III and diagram the situation in Figure 1, where numbers indicate an empirical result and cross-hatching the redundant cell.

Can we apply the single-variable model to our hypothetical A? Of course not. The cell value *is* the category total ($\Sigma A_i = \Sigma A$) and there cannot be discrepancy between observed and predicted. The degrees-of-freedom rule for single-variable effects gives us the same answer. In Figure 1, $(A*B*C\ldots) - 1$ equals $(A) - 1$. We get $3 - 1 = 2$. Since $K = 3$, $K - 1 = 2$. And there is general agreement that $2 - 2 = 0$. When we apply the single-variable model to a lone item, the degrees of freedom are zero. This is an instance of a general property of the Goodman system. To test a model one must have at least one more variable than the level being tested. A single-variable model requires at least two variables in the data. So we add a second variable B with categories i, j, k, and l (see Figure 2). As before, the expected cases must sum to N as well as the observed cases. Consequently there will again be a redundant cell. I have arbitrarily put it down in the lower right-hand corner.

In moving from the equal-probability model to the single-variable model, I have introduced some new restrictions. Not only must both observed and expected cases sum to N but the expecteds in each category also must sum to the actual marginals. In other words: the model always has the same marginals and total as the data, whereas the previous equal-probability model had the same total but different category marginals (except in the special case where it fit). Figure 3 adds these new restrictions.

Let us arbitrarily begin our analysis in the upper left-hand corner and move from left to right across rows. After calculating chi squares for the cells marked 1 and 2, we find that the next result (B_iA_{III}) can be obtained by subtraction since the three cells are required to sum to ΣB_i. I have shaded that cell to indicate that it is redundant. The same thing

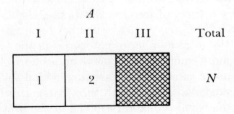

Figure 1. Schematic notion of degrees of freedom in an equal-probability model.

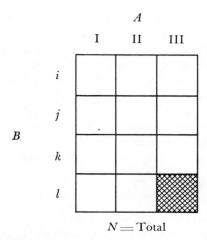

Figure 2. Two-variable model with an arbitrarily chosen redundant cell.

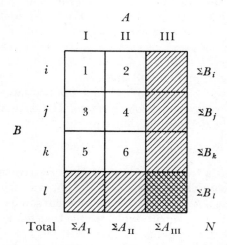

Figure 3. Schematic notion of Degrees of Freedom in a single-variable model.

happens in the second and third rows giving us two more shaded redundant cells in the right-hand column of Figure 3. Moving down to the fourth row we find that the first two cells can also be obtained by subtraction because of the column sum restrictions given by ΣA_I and ΣA_{II}.

Finally we reach the lower right-hand corner where we find the redundant cell from the equal-probability model. This cell is triply redundant. We could obtain its results from the row restriction ΣB_l or the column restriction ΣA_{III} or from N. The cell is surely redundant but the single-variable restrictions do not make it more redundant. This is the reason for the minus one in the $K - 1$ formula. Any variable added in a single-variable model adds only $K - 1$ new redundant cells.

In fact the diagrams are illustrative rather than rigorous, since one need not start at the upper left-hand corner and work across the rows. But the principle is quite general, as the reader will see if he tries various schemes for filling in cells that cannot be obtained by subtraction.

Stating the rule more explicitly to allow for the fact that one may wish to create models where some variables are set for equal-probability and others for single-variable, we obtain Equation (10):

$$DF = (A*B*C*D*E*F) - (1) - [(A - 1) + (B - 1) + (C - 1)] \quad (10)$$

where DF equals degrees of freedom for model with single-variable effects A, B, C and equal-probability predictions D, E, F. For Figure 3 we would get $DF = (4*3) - (1) - (3 + 2) = 6$.

We are all familiar with a different formula for degrees of freedom in a two-variable contingency table $(R - 1)(C - 1)$, and $(4 - 1)(3 - 1)$ does equal 6. But this is a happy coincidence. Multiplication of $K - 1$ beyond two variables does not give the same answer as Equation (10). For example when $A = 3$, $B = 4$, and $C = 5$; $(A - 1)(B - 1)(C - 1)$ equals 24, whereas Equation (10) gives 50.

In the Schwartz data (Table 9) time has two categories, education has three, region has two, and jobs has two. The degrees of freedom for a single-variable model using all four are

$$DF = (2*3*2*2) - (1) - (1 + 2 + 1 + 1) = 18$$

After constructing a model in which the cell frequencies are given by multiplying the marginal frequencies of the four variables, we compared the model with the data and obtained a total chi square value of 823.53. Looking this up in a chi square table, we see that for 18 degrees of freedom a value of 34.805 is significant at the 0.01 level. The model does not fit.

How shall we interpret the result? If the single-variable model fits (if the chi square is not significant): (1) There are no two-variable or higher-order effects. (2) There may or may not be single-variable effects. If the single-variable model does not fit (if the chi square is significant): (1) There are some two-variable or higher-order effects, but we do not know which ones unless we are analyzing a two-variable table. (2) There may or may not be single-variable effects.

The results of testing a single-variable model are not terribly informative by themselves. Failure to fit, as in the failure of an equal-probability model, may be construed as a hunting license but this time it is a little more specific. The difference between the two failures may be put this way: failure of the equal-probability model indicates that something is going on; failure of the single-variable model indicates that something is going on that cannot be accounted for by the marginals of the variables—therefore it must involve pairs, triplets, or larger combinations of variables.

And, contrary to expectations, testing a single-variable model tells us nothing about the presence or absence of single-variable effects. If the reader refers to the five alternative definitions at the beginning of this section, he will see important qualifiers such as "allowed" in (1), "not necessarily" in (2), and "allows" in (4). The explanation is simple. We build the model from the single-item marginals. If the item has unequal category frequencies (first-order odds ratios differing from 1.000), so will the model. But if the item should have equal category frequencies, equal probability for the item will be built into the model.

The point is a general property of the Goodman system and can be summarized by the following generalization: an X-variable model is one that allows but does not require effects of level X, $X - 1$, $X - 2$, and so on, whereas it forbids effects of level $X + 1$, $X + 2$, and so forth.

Two-Variable Models: No Interactions

If a single-variable model permits single-variable effects but prohibits higher-order differences, the suspicion arises that a two-variable model permits two-variable effects but prohibits all higher-order effects. Correct. A two-variable model can be described alternatively as:

1. A model in which first- and second-order odds ratios are allowed to depart from 1.000 but all higher-order odds ratios are set to 1.000
2. A model in which partial associations between pairs of variables may be present but there are no interactions or higher-level variations in the associations
3. A model that allows only single- and two-variable effects
4. A model that tests the hypothesis that all the differences in cell frequencies can be accounted for by partial correlations constant in magnitude from condition to condition.

How does one construct a two-variable model? The rules are as follows. The data must sum to N. The item marginals must agree with the raw data. The zero-order cross-tabulations for the pairs of variables in question must agree with the raw data. All third-order and higher odds ratios must be 1.000.

It is not obvious how such a model might be formed but there is an algorithm or mathematical strategy for constructing these tables by iteration (successive approximation). The procedure is not very difficult—three or four variables can be done by hand in about 30 minutes once one learns the technique. This task is clearly appropriate for a computer, however, and no one will go broke computing the model, since it has been proved that the iterations must converge at a rapid rate.

The process itself is not illuminating and I have relegated it to the appendix. Instead I wish to give the results of hand calculations for the Schwartz data to show what a three-item, two-variable model looks like. For simplification, in Table 10 I arbitrarily excluded time from the analysis, leaving a three-item, twelve-celled table $[(3) * (2) * (2) = 12]$. To see whether the modeled data meet the criteria, we first check whether we can reproduce the zero-order correlations for the variables. Taking region and education, for example, we get Table 11.

Although the model and raw data results are very close, if the reader looks back to Table 10 he will see that some cells there differ quite a bit between the raw data and the model. Did we also succeed in meeting the single-variable marginal and N restrictions? Of course. If we can reproduce the zero-order cross-tabulation to a desired level of accu-

TABLE 10
Original Data and Two-Variable Model for Schwartz Variables
of Region, Education, and Jobs

(a) Raw Data ($N = 3597$)

		Grade School		High School		College	
		South	Other	South	Other	South	Other
Jobs	+	123	459	190	849	97	405
	−	250	426	194	430	65	91

(b) Two-Variable Model

		Grade School		High School		College	
		South	Other	South	Other	South	Other
Jobs	+	122.3	459.8	183.2	856.4	104.5	397.5
	−	250.6	425.4	200.7	422.8	57.5	98.5

TABLE 11
Zero-Order Association between Region and Education
in Raw Data and Two-Variable Model

Region	Grade School		High School		College	
	Raw	Model	Raw	Model	Raw	Model
South	373	372.9	384	383.9	162	162.0
Other	885	885.2	1279	1279.2	496	496.0

racy, we must match the marginal and N restrictions as well. Let us see whether the data are free of higher-order interactions. Table 12 gives the figures.

For region and jobs, the top three lines in Table 12, we observe values close to 0.45 for all three education conditions. This is odds ratio language for saying that there is a negative partial between region (South) and jobs, or, in English, Southerners are less likely to endorse equality of employment. If the partials had vanished, the odds ratios would have been 1.000 or close to it. The reader may find the following rule helpful: in a second-order odds ratio, a value less than 1.000 is a negative correlation; a value greater than 1.000 is a positive correlation—under the convention that plus is assigned to the top category of the first item (for example, S for region) and the left category of the second item (for example, plus for jobs). Since all three conditional values are close

TABLE 12
Higher-Order Odds Ratio for Modeled Data in Table 10

Second-Order Odds Ratio	Condition		Third-Order Odds Ratios	
Region (R) and Jobs (J)				
$\quad S \ +$	Grade school	0.452	} 1.002	
$\quad R \ \ J\|E$	High school	0.451		1.002
$\quad O \ -$	College	0.450	} 1.002	
Education (E) and Jobs (J)				
$\quad G \ +$	South	0.535		
$\quad E \ \ J\|R$			1.002	
$\quad H \ -$	Other	0.534		
$\quad G \ +$	South	0.268		
$\quad E \ \ J\|R$			1.000	
$\quad C \ -$	Other	0.268		
$\quad H \ +$	South	0.502		
$\quad E \ \ J\|R$			1.000	
$\quad C \ -$	Other	0.502		
Region (R) and Education (E)				
$\quad S \quad G$	Jobs $-$	1.241		
$\quad R \ \ E\|J$			0.998	
$\quad O \quad H$	Jobs $+$	1.243		
$\quad S \quad H$	Jobs $-$	0.813		
$\quad R \ \ E\|J$			0.999	
$\quad O \quad C$	Jobs $+$	0.814		
$\quad S \quad G$	Jobs $-$	4.319		
$\quad R \ \ E\|J$			0.998	
$\quad O \quad C$	Jobs $+$	4.359		

to 0.45, the three higher-order odds ratios are all very close to 1.000. The degree of correlation between region and jobs is the same in each level of schooling in this model.

Turning to the second pair of variables, education and jobs, we see that each of the three possible odds ratios is negative and the higher-order odds ratios are all close to 1.000. The reason education has a negative correlation with job attitudes is that we assigned the *lower* level of education to the top of the notation. The matter is quite arbitrary, but it would probably have been better craftsmanship to reverse the categories in these odds ratios.

The last pair, region and education, shows the same pattern but is of some interest in that one of the conditional odds ratios is negative whereas the others are positive. Inspection of the original data shows that when considering only the high school and college groups, Southerners have a slightly greater proportion of persons reporting some college. The point has no particular importance for the Goodman system, but it does illustrate how decomposing a relationship into all possible odds ratios can show us properties we would otherwise miss.

Tables 11 and 12 have now convinced us that our iteration did deliver the goods: a model where all zero-order relationships are identical with those in the raw data, where nonzero partial associations can appear, and where all third-order odds ratios are 1.000.

To test the model we compare the observed and expected values in each cell and calculate the total chi square, just as in the previous examples. For the total four-variable Schwartz data, a computer program generated the complete model and obtained a total chi square value of 31.35.

How many degrees of freedom do we use? The restrictions are given by the cell frequencies in each of the zero-order tables, and we have one redundant calculation for each such cell. Referring to Figure 3, however, we see that not all of these $R \times C$ restrictions are new since the N and the single-variable restrictions are included. Thus each two-variable hypothesis adds only $(R-1)(C-1)$ new restrictions, just as each marginal added only $K-1$ new restrictions when we moved from the equal-probability to the single-variable model.

Goodman provides a handy scheme for talking about his higher-order models and I shall use it to specify the degrees of freedom. He simply assigns a letter to each variable, describes a two-variable hypothesis by a pair of letters in parentheses, describes a single-variable hypothesis by a single letter in parentheses but only if it does not appear in a two-variable hypothesis, and ignores a variable treated only as equal-probability.

Consider, for example, a five-variable model with items A, B, C, D, and E in which A and C are set for two-variable, A and D for two-variable, C and D for two-variable, B for single-variable, and E for equal-probability. In shorthand we can describe the model in this way:

$$(A,C)\ (A,D)\ (C,D)\ (B)$$

Our two-variable model for the Schwartz data can be described like this:

$$(T,E)\ (T,R)\ (T,J)\ (E,R)\ (E,J)\ (R,J)$$

To calculate degrees of freedom, apply the following rules for degrees of freedom in two-variable models:
1. Obtain the total by multiplying $A * B * C * D * E \ldots$
2. Subtract one degree of freedom for N regardless of the number of equiprobable variables
3. Subtract $(K - 1)$ for each different letter that appears anywhere in the list [in our hypothetical example: $(A - 1) + (B - 1) + (C - 1) + (D - 1)$]
4. Subtract $(R - 1)(C - 1)$ for each pair of letters within parentheses [in our hypothetical example: $(A - 1)(C - 1) + (A - 1)(D - 1) + (C - 1)(D - 1)$]

Remembering that in these data $K = 2$ for all items except education (which has three categories), the degrees of freedom are as follows:
1. $(2 * 3 * 2 * 2) = 24$
2. 1
3. $(1 + 2 + 1 + 1) = 5$ ⎫
4. $(1 * 2) + (1 * 1) + (1 * 1) + (2 * 1) + (2 * 1) + (1 * 1) = 9$ ⎬ 15
   DF $= 24 - 15 = 9$

The chi square table tells us that for nine degrees of freedom a total chi square of 21.666 is significant at the 0.01 level. Our chi square value of 31.35 is statistically significant. This third model does not fit either.

The interpretation rule for a two-variable model goes like this. If the two-variable model fits (if the chi square is not significant): (1) There are no significant three-variable or higher-level interactions (no specifications). (We cannot reject the hypothesis that all third-order or higher odds ratios are 1.000.) (2) There may or may not be item skews and nonzero partial associations among the variables. If the two-variable model does not fit (if the chi square is significant): (1) It is not the case that all third-order and higher odds ratios are 1.000, but we do not know whether any particular higher-order effects are significant. (2) There may or may not be item skews and nonzero partial associations among the variables. Special situation: In a three-variable table, a significant chi square for the two-variable model implies that the lone possible higher-order effect, the three-way interaction, is significant.

The significant chi square for our two-variable model means that we must proceed to higher-order models because we cannot account for the cell frequencies by the simple effects so far introduced.

Higher-Order Models

The logic of increasingly complicated models including all prior effects should be clear by now, so it is not necessary to consider higher-order models in detail. Rather I shall review the properties of three-variable models and then sketch the rationale for higher-order models. A three-variable model may be defined alternatively as one that permits skews, partial associations, and three-variable interactions but no higher-order effects; or as one that sets fourth-order and higher odds ratios to 1.000 but allows lower-order odds ratios to depart from 1.000.

Construction of three-variable models is a surprisingly simple extension of the iteration scheme described in the appendix of this chapter. One proceeds in exactly the same fashion as before, except for this data restriction: the model cell frequencies must sum to the cell frequencies of the relevant three-variable cross-tabulations.

Consider variables A, B, C, and D. The complete two-variable model required that the model data match the cell frequencies for the zero-order cross-tabulations AB, AC, AD, BC, BD, and CD. For these four variables we can make four three-variable cross-tabulations: ABC, ABD, ACD, and BCD. For the data in the Schwartz table we could tabulate region by time by jobs, region by education by jobs, time by jobs by education, and time by region by education. The first would have $2 \times 2 \times 2 = 6$ cells, the second $2 \times 3 \times 2 = 12$ cells, and so on. Following the steps given in the appendix, we proceed to create a set of data such that we can sum the cell frequencies in the model data and obtain the raw data cell values for each of the three-way tables. Such a model has all odds ratios of fourth-order or higher equal to 1.000, just as the two-variable model had all odds ratios of third-order or higher equal to 1.000. As usual the model can be compared with the data, provided of course that there are four or more variables. With three variables, a three-variable model *is* the raw data and no discrepancy can occur.

Degrees of freedom are calculated by a straightforward extension of the rules presented in the preceding section. I shall present them in a general form that should enable the reader to calculate easily the degrees of freedom for models of any order. Given models stated in paren-

theses, for example (I,J,K,L) (R,S,T) (P,Q):
1. Obtain the total by multiplying all distinct letters; for example, $I * J * K * L * R * S * T * P * Q$.
2. Subtract 1 for the N restriction.
3. Subtract $K - 1$ for each different letter that appears anywhere in the set.
4. Subtract $(R - 1)$ $(C - 1)$ for each pair of letters within parentheses; for example, IJ, IK, IL, JK, JL, KL, RS, RT, ST, PQ. Note: Subtract a particular product only once, no matter how many sets of parentheses include it. Do not subtract a product if the letters are not in the same parentheses (for example, L and R in the sample above).
5. Subtract $(R - 1)$ $(S - 1)$ $(T - 1)$ for each triplet within parentheses, applying the note in rule 4.
6. Subtract $(I - 1)$ $(J - 1)$ $(K - 1)$ $(L - 1)$ for each set of four letters within parentheses, applying the note in rule 4.
7. And so on, for each subset of increasing size up to the total number of variables minus 1.

Degrees of freedom for a complete three-variable model of the Schwartz data can be calculated as follows, using $E = 3$, $R = 2$, $J = 2$, and $T = 2$ for the four variables education, region, jobs, and time. The complete three-variable model is: (E,R,J) (E,R,T) (E,J,T) (R,J,T)—in other words, all possible combinations of three variables. We proceed as follows:

1. Total DF $= 3 * 2 * 2 * 2 = 24$.
2. Subtracting 1 for N gives 23.
3. Since each letter appears, we subtract $(E - 1 = 2) + (R - 1 = 1) + (J - 1 = 1) + (T - 1 = 1) = 5$ for single-variable effect restrictions, giving $23 - 5 = 18$.
4. Since each pair appears at least once (for example, R and T occur in the second and fourth set of parentheses) we further subtract:

$$(E - 1)(R - 1) = 2$$
$$(E - 1)(J - 1) = 2$$
$$(E - 1)(T - 1) = 2$$
$$(R - 1)(J - 1) = 1$$
$$(R - 1)(T - 1) = 1$$
$$(J - 1)(T - 1) = 1$$
$$\overline{}$$
$$18 - 9 = 9$$

5. And for the four triplets:
$$(E - 1)(R - 1)(J - 1) = 2$$
$$(E - 1)(R - 1)(T - 1) = 2$$
$$(E - 1)(J - 1)(T - 1) = 2$$
$$(R - 1)(J - 1)(T - 1) = 1$$
$$\overline{}$$
$$9 - 7 = 2$$

We end up with two degrees of freedom for the model.[1]

Our computer program constructed and tested the three-variable model, obtaining a total chi square of 6.91, which is below the 0.01 criterion value of 9.210. Thus the three-variable model fits—the discrepancy between model and actual data is not statistically significant at the 0.01 alpha level we have arbitrarily chosen for this example.

The interpretation is a natural extension of previous argument. Satisfactory fit (as in our example) implies that all higher-order effects (here, the four-variable interaction) are zero; significant discrepancy implies that not all higher-order effects are zero.

The procedure can be applied to models of progressively higher order, provided that the cross-tabulation has enough variables. Remember that to test an X-level hypothesis (that is, to rule out $X + 1$ level and higher effects) one must have at least $X + 1$ variables in the cross-tabulation.

We shall not continue for two reasons. First the rationale for the scheme should now be clear. Second our example will no longer be useful since we have only four variables. Note further that even if we had more variables, there is no point in continuing with the data in the example. Of mathematical necessity, if a model at level X fits, all higher-order models must also fit. In sum we continue to test increasingly higher-order models until we obtain fit or run out of variables.

Mixed Models and Testing Specific Effects

Assume for purposes of explanation that we have tested progressively complex models and have finally obtained fit with an L-variable (L for level) model. In the Schwartz data, for example, we fitted the three-variable ($L = 3$) model after failing with the equal-probability, single-variable, and two-variable hypotheses.

What do we know? We know two things. First we need no effects more complex than level L to describe the cell frequencies. Second we need at least one L-level effect. The first result follows from the success

---

[1] The remaining degrees of freedom are associated with the lone four-variable relationship $(E - 1)(R - 1)(J - 1)(T - 1) = 2 * 1 * 1 * 1 = 2$.

in fit at level L, the second from the previous failure to fit at level $L - 1$. But we may not need all possible L-level effects. In the Schwartz data, for example, our model included four distinct three-variable effects: (E,R,J) (E,R,T) (E,J,T), and (R,J,T). But it could be that only one of them is nonzero (or that two or three or all four of them are nonzero).

Invoking the principle of scientific parsimony, we say that the analyst's aim is to find the least complex set of effects that are necessary and sufficient to account for the data.

Knowing that a model with all possible L-level effects is sufficient, we turn to the question of whether all of them are necessary. This leads us to the construction of mixed models with effects of differing levels. I do not know of any algorithm that provides the best way to find a good mixed model and I do not know whether there is always a unique solution—a single model that meets the criteria—but the following common-sense steps provide one approach.

As a first step, try a series of models with just one L-level effect. In the Schwartz data, for example, we might try a model with only one three-variable effect, for example (education, region, jobs). But taken literally the model (E,R,J) says to allow an interaction effect for the three items but to set the other three relationships (ET), (RT), and (JT) to zero. We have no warrant for such an excision. Rather, when testing to see whether we can fit a model containing only the single interaction (E,R,J) we have to supplement that effect with all possible lower-order effects. Putting it a little more abstractly, here is step 1: begin by testing all possible models with a single L-level effect and all $L - 1$ level effects not subsumed in it. Following the rule we would add two-variable effects for (ET), (RT), and (JT), but we would not build in two-variable effects for (ER), (EJ), and (RJ) since they are subsumed in (E,R,J).

Table 13 gives the results of step 1. The bottom half of Table 13 gives good news. Three of the new models fail and one fits. We can describe the data in our table by the model (ER) (RJ) (RT) (EJT) as well as the model (ERJ) (ERT) (EJT) (RJT). Which is more parsimonious? Goodman does not discuss the matter but the following are suggested as rules: The level of parsimony of a model is the highest-order effect present; among models at the same level L, those with fewer L-level effects are more parsimonious; among models with the same number of L-level effects, the one with fewer $L - 1$ level effects is more parsimonious; and so on. Our new model is more parsimonious from the second of these rules. These results came out neatly but such an event is not inevitable. Thus more steps.

Step 2: if only one model constructed in step 1 fits, go to step 3.

TABLE 13
Some Mixed Models for Schwartz Data

Effects								Chi Square	DF	Criterion[a]
ER	EJ	ET	RJ	RT	JT	ERJ	ERT	EJT	RJT			
					Previous Results					2798.49	23	40.289*
(E)	(R)	(J)	(T)							823.53	18	34.805*
(ER)	(EJ)	(ET)	(RJ)							31.35	9	21.666*
										6.91	2	9.210
		(ET)		(RT)	(JT)	(ERJ)	(ERT)	(EJT)	(RJT)	28.52	7	18.475*
	(EJ)		(RJ)	(RT)	(JT)	(ERJ)	(ERT)			27.97	7	18.475*
(ER)			(RJ)					(EJT)		16.4	7	18.475
(ER)	(EJ)	(ET)							(RJT)	27.5	8	20.090*

[a] Value of chi square for significance at the 0.01 level for the number of degrees of freedom. Asterisks indicate significant values in data.

If none of the models in step 1 fits, try models with one more L-level effect in each and return to step 1. If two or more fit, go to step 3 and analyze each.

Step 3: next we ask whether the model can be further reduced. Steps 1 and 2 establish the minimum number of L-level effects that must be present in the final model, but we have learned nothing yet about the $L - 1$ or still lower-level effects. It is possible that we could fit an even simpler model that deletes one or more lower-level effects. To test for possible deletions we next build a series of models containing the necessary L-level effects but removing the $L - 1$ effects one at a time. In our Schwartz example this amounts to three models each containing (E,J,T) and two out of the trio (ER) (RJ) (RT).

Table 14 gives the results when we drop particular two-variable effects in our example. None of the three models fits, as the chi squares each exceed the criterion value for the 0.01 level. And that is the end of our hunt for a satisfactory model. We now know that the model (ER) (RJ) (RT) (EJT) fits the data, and that no less complex model does.

TABLE 14
Mixed Models for Schwartz Data Deleting
Two-Variable Effects One at a Time

	Model			Chi Square	DF	Criterion[a]
	(RJ)	(RT)	(EJT)	25.53	9	21.666*
(ER)	(RJ)		(EJT)	58.50	8	20.090*
(ER)		(RT)	(EJT)	148.07	8	20.090*

[a] Value of chi square for significance at the 0.01 level for the number of degrees of freedom. Asterisks indicate significant values in data.

In other situations, of course, one or more of the new models might fit the data. If so, one should continue the process of simplification through models deleting more than one $L - 1$ level effect or those deleting $L - 2$ and successively lower-level effects.

To summarize: in step 3, test simplified models by deleting $L - 1$ and lower-level effects while maintaining the L-level effects determined in step 2.[2] The process continues until all simpler effects have either been eliminated or shown to be necessary to achieve fit.

At the end of step 3—which might involve a more extensive sequence of model-testing than in our lucky example—one has a model

[2] We do not test models deleting L-level effects since—under the assumption at the beginning of this section—the model denying any L-level effects failed to fit.

(or possibly more than one model) that meets the parsimony criterion. It is the least complex set of effects that are necessary and sufficient to fit the raw data. More effects are not necessary because the model fits; any simpler model with fewer effects is not sufficient since we tried all of them and they failed to fit.

The final step in the analysis is to test the significance of individual effects. The model as a whole is significant in the sense explained above, but it does not follow that each part standing alone is significant. From the logic of the whole enterprise one may expect that almost all the component effects are individually significant, but it is worthwhile to make the tests to nail the point down.

To test the significance of a particular effect, one attempts to fit a model containing "everything else." A significant failure is equivalent to rejecting the null hypothesis that the effect is nil. A model excluding one specific effect may be constructed as follows. First list all $V - 1$ level effects, where V is the number of variables. For example, with four variables list all the three-variable effects. Next delete any that include (or are) the effect in question. For example, if the effect in question is (AC) then the third-order effect (ABC) would be deleted. (This is why the V-level effect is not listed; it includes all other effects.) Then check whether lower-level effects included in the one in question are included in the results of step 2 above. If not, add them.

Let us find a model to test the significance of (ER) in the Schwartz example. Since there are four variables, $V - 1 = 3$ and we first list all the three-variable effects: (EJT), (RJT), (ERT), and (ERJ). Second we delete (ERT) and (ERJ) since they include the pair ER. This leaves (EJT) and (RJT) as our model. Third we see that the lower-level components of ER—E and R—appear in (EJT) and (RJT). Thus we test the model (EJT) (RJT).

Table 15 gives the results for the four effects in our final model for the Schwartz data. All four effects are statistically significant at the 0.01 level. In each case the model that allows all other effects save the one in question has a more than chance discrepancy when compared with the raw data.

Step 4 in the all-purpose plan of analysis is to test the significance of the individual effects in the final model. What if one or more effects are not significant? Such an outcome may seem contradictory since all effects have been shown to be significant in steps 1 or 3. The difference is that the tested models are not exactly the same. Consider the effect (ER). In the top line of Table 14 we concluded that it was significant because the model (RJ) (RT) (EJT) failed; in the top line of Table 15, we concluded that it was significant because the model (EJT) (RJT) failed.

TABLE 15
Test for Specific Effects in the Model (ER) (RJ) (RT) (EJT)

Effect Tested	Model		Chi Square	DF	Criterion[a]
(ER)	(EJT)	(RJT)	21.94	8	20.090*
(RJ)	(ERT)	(EJT)	146.25	6	16.812*
(RT)	(ERJ)	(EJT)	54.65	6	16.812*
(EJT) (ERJ) (ERT)	(RJT)		20.55	4	13.277*

[a] Value of chi square for significance at the 0.01 level for the number of degrees of freedom. Asterisks indicate significant values in data.

Although similar, the two models are not identical. The Table 15 model allows the interaction (RJT); in Table 14 it is set to zero (for good reasons, of course). Since the models are not identical, their conclusions do not have to be identical.

Generally the results of the two forms of significance-testing should be close because the logic of the system guarantees that the two models will be quite similar. In the (ER) example in the previous paragraph, the only difference between (RJ) (RT) (EJT) and (RJT) (EJT) is that the latter permits the interaction (RJT). We know that (RJT) is not a strong effect since the next-to-last line of Table 13 tells us that we can fit the data without it. Thus any play between the two results is because one model allows an effect so small that it is not required to obtain fit.

In sum it is quite unlikely that the two significance tests disagree sharply, but it is quite possible that effects that achieve significance in steps 1 or 3 may turn out to be borderline when specific tests are made.

Substantive Conclusions

At last we are ready to state the substantive conclusions of this investigation. The following propositions are necessary and sufficient to account for the cell frequencies in Table 8. First there is a significant partial association between education and region, controlling for time and jobs, that is essentially similar in magnitude within each control condition. Second there is a statistically significant partial association between region and jobs, controlling for time and education, that is essentially similar in magnitude within each control condition. Third there is a statistically significant partial association between region and time, controlling for education and jobs, that is essentially similar in magnitude within each control condition. And fourth there is a statistically significant interaction involving the three variables education, jobs, and time, such that the degree of association for any two varies with the level of the third. This pattern is essentially similar in each region. The sign and degree of the effects remain to be seen and must be stated before the results can be interpreted (this is discussed in the next section), but these four propositions are an English translation of the conclusions in this part of the analysis.

DISCUSSION

Here I shall discuss the uses and limitations of the system. The uses may be divided into the intellectual and the practical; the limitations into the intrinsic and the extrinsic.

From a purely intellectual point of view, the major utility of the system is that it is a system. Starting with the seemingly trivial concept of odds ratio, it builds a consistent and flexible language for talking about almost any aspect of contingency tables. It is thus possible to see how such concepts as marginal skews, associations, partial associations, interactions, independence, and specification fit together. I believe that anyone who masters the vocabulary and concepts will find a deeper understanding of the logic and properties of contingency tables.

Practically speaking, the system gives us an important general tool and a number of useful specific tests. At the general level, the search for a final model, if successful, gives the analyst a clear and concise statement of what is going on in his contingency tables. With more than two or three variables, it is easy to thrash around endlessly running this-that-and-the-other concatenation of statistics. A final model cuts through all of this and tells us what is there and what is not there. Consider, for example, how a hypothetical final model such as (AB) (CDE) (F) neatly summarizes the dozens of possible relationships in the 64 or more cells of a six-variable table.

Turning to specific practical applications, the system provides at least three significance tests that are not commonly known or used by research workers. First it provides a test for the significance of a partial association, regardless of the number of categories or level of measurement in the associated variables or control items. The question of whether the partial vanishes when such-and-such is controlled is a strategic one in much social research, and the system gives us a significance test for it. Second the system gives us a general test for the significance of interactions and specifications. Goodman's test for a significant difference in Q when the control variable has two levels (Goodman, 1965, p. 291) is well known (Davis, 1971, p. 100), but we can now extend the test to a control variable with more than two categories or to a combination of control variables. Third the fit or failure to fit of the single-variable model provides a simple answer to the question, "Is *anything* going on?" Particularly when working with small samples, an investigator can save time and money by making this test before trying specific hypotheses.

Shifting to the limitations of the system, we shall consider one limitation intrinsic to this particular approach and others that stem from the extrinsic properties of the general problem. The only limitation intrinsic to the system of which I am aware is the possibility of an ambiguous result. I strongly suspect, but cannot prove, that it is possible to fail in the attempt to find a final model. The problem seems to occur in a set of data with a large number of effects of borderline strength. I suspect, for example, that in a set of data with many borderline associations, it could happen that the single-variable model would not fit but that no particular association would be strong enough that its deletion would produce lack of fit for a final model. Putting the same idea another way, the failure of a general model such as the single-variable or the two-variable model means "it is not the case that nothing is going on," which is not quite the same as saying "something definite is going on." In a strict sense the failure is in the empirical data, not in the system; but analysts should be alert to the possibility that there may be no clearcut answer to the problem of finding an unambiguous final model.

Other limitations arise not from the logic of this system itself but from familiar problems in any multivariate significance-testing enterprise. First one should remember that in any analysis all relationships are partials. Any effect has the implicit phrase "all other variables held constant." In practice the investigator—especially if he is working in the tradition of causal models—may wish to control different variables at different stages in his analysis. For example we noted earlier that it seemed awkward to control for jobs when examining the correlation between education and region. This problem is not serious; it is always possible to collapse a multivariate table into a smaller one and carry out the analysis with the collapsed variable(s) ignored. However, it means that the analysis is not self-contained. One needs further assumptions to carry out multivariate analysis. One such set of assumptions is given in Davis (1971, chap. 5 and 6). Goodman does not treat this issue in his early publications, but he does address it in an unpublished paper that has arrived too recently for discussion here (Goodman, 1972c).

Second one should not forget the elementary principle that significance tests are sensitive to sample size as well as to effect magnitudes. When working with extremely large samples, even the most trivial effect can be significant, and the analyst may end up with a model that includes a number of significant higher-order interactions maddening to interpret but trivial in magnitude. One should always remember that unless the data have odds ratios of exactly 1.000, there is always some number by which the frequencies could each be multiplied to obtain significance. Conversely the analyst working with small samples obtains significance only for very large effects.

Third there is the perpetual problem that when generalizing beyond the sample in hand, the chi square test assumes that the cases are a simple random sample (SRS). This is seldom or never the case with social science data. The Schwartz data, for example, come from multistage cluster samples that probably have quota features in the final stage. Since all the tests used in the most sophisticated journals also assume simple random sample, this problem is not unique to the Goodman system.

Fourth, significance tests need to be supplemented by descriptive statistics that convey the magnitude and, when appropriate, the direction of the relationship. There are many possibilities—percentage tables, multivariate Qs and gammas (Davis, 1971), the new measures proposed in Goodman's recent papers but not discussed here, or the odds ratios themselves. Since the odds ratios may be unfamiliar, I shall describe the Schwartz data in terms of odds ratios to show how they look.

Our final model is (ER) (RJ) (RT) (EJT), which was translated into English at the end of the previous section. We take each of the four English conclusions in turn.

The first association, between education and region (ER), is interpreted as saying that there is some association between education and region and that it does not vary significantly in magnitude across the control conditions formed by cross-tabulating jobs and time. Since education is a trichotomy, we need to examine $(3)(2)(2)(1)/4$, or three odds ratios, according to Equation (3). Table 16 gives the results.

The results turn out to be a little complicated—which may be useful for our purposes, as they illustrate a number of issues that arise in interpreting the results in the Goodman system. We begin with the odds ratio

$$\begin{array}{cc} \text{High} & \text{South} \\ E & R \\ \text{Grade} & \text{Other} \end{array}$$

and note that all four conditional figures are less than 1.000 (0.641, 0.767, 0.871, and 0.772) with a weighted average of 0.767. The weighted average of the odds ratios, a useful summary statistic, is obtained by multiplying each conditional odds ratio by its case base (the sum of the four cells involved), summing these products, and dividing the sum by

TABLE 16
Odds Ratios for Education and Region

Control Conditions		High E Grade	South R Other	College E Grade	South R Other	College E High	South R Other
Time	Jobs						
1963	As good	0.641		0.570		0.890	
			(775)[a]		(475)		(792)
	Other	0.767		2.426		3.161	
			(192)		(127)		(109)
1946	As good	0.871		1.231		1.412	
			(866)		(609)		(749)
	Other	0.772		1.089		1.410	
			(1108)		(705)		(671)
Weighted average[b]		0.767		1.094		1.315	
Zero order		0.712		0.775		1.410	

[a] Total cases in the fourfold subtable.
[b] See text for description.

the total for the constituent case bases. The purpose of all this is to give those odds ratios based on more cases a greater contribution to the overall average. This says that for the two education levels (high school and grade school) Southerners are less likely than others to be high school graduates. (An odds ratio less than 1.000 may be thought of as a negative association if the categories on top of the letters are assigned to the higher values of ordinal or dichotomous variables.) The value of 0.712 in the bottom line tells us the value in the zero-order table for education and region.

Shifting to the middle column, we see a weighted average value of 1.094 and what appears to be considerable fluctuation from condition to condition. Since the two-variable hypothesis (ER) fits the data, however, we do not consider these variations as more than chance. (Note: it is possible that if we had run only the two education levels, college versus grade school, a significant interaction—failure of the two-variable hypothesis—might have occurred. Our significance test applies to the total set of 12 conditional odds ratios in Table 16, not necessarily to a particular subgrouping. Those familiar with analysis of variance will see an analogy between this property and the ANOVA property that significance for a given effect does not mean that particular pairs of means are significantly different.) The zero-order correlation is negative (0.775 is less than 1.000), whereas most of the conditionals are positive with an average of 1.329. This is a familiar property of multivariate analysis and can be interpreted as meaning that when time and jobs are controlled, the association reverses sign. Among persons similar in time and jobs, Southerners are relatively more often college graduates and others are more often grade school graduates.

The pattern for college versus high school is as follows: both the zero-order and conditional associations tend to be positive with a weighted average of 1.315 for the conditionals. Controlling for time and jobs, Southerners are relatively better educated in terms of college versus high school.

As mentioned in the previous section, one would not generally control for an item such as racial attitudes when analyzing the relationship between region and education, and the results here are both complex and somewhat artificial. But for didactic purposes we can summarize the interpretation as follows: when time and attitudes toward jobs are controlled, Southerners tend to be less educated in terms of high school graduation versus grade school only, and better educated in terms of college versus high school or grade school.

The second effect (RJ) tells us to look at the association between region and jobs within time and education groups, as in Table 17. This one is a lot simpler. In each of the six conditions the odds ratio is less than 1.000 with a weighted average of 0.379. Within time and education levels, Southerners are less likely to endorse job equality.

The third effect (RT), a partial association between region and time, controlling education and jobs, is another finding that would probably not be run in actual research work and I shall not report the figures here.

Finally we turn to the three-variable effect (EJT). It says that the three variables have an interaction effect that is about the same in each region. One may interpret it using the formulation that the correlation between two of the items varies according to the level of the third.

TABLE 17
Odds Ratios for Region and Jobs

Time	Education	South R Other	As Good J Other	Time, Education (N)
1946	Grade		0.296	934
	High school		0.334	1040
	College		0.335	380
1963	Grade		0.665	324
	High school		0.555	623
	College		0.156	278
Weighted average			0.379	
Zero order			0.445	

The choice of the specifying variable is not dictated by anything in the Goodman system. One could try: the correlation between education and time varies with category of jobs; the correlation between time and jobs varies with education level; the correlation between education and jobs varies with time. I chose the second version because it is intuitively agreeable and also because a nondichotomous variable is easier to handle as a condition than as one of the correlated items. Table 18 presents the results.

TABLE 18
Association between Time (1946–1963) and Jobs (as good, other) within Education Level and Region

Education Level	South	(N)	Other	(N)	Weighted Average
College	4.770		10.222		8.880
		(162)		(496)	
High school	10.352		6.237		7.187
		(384)		(1279)	
Grade school	6.392		2.848		3.899
		(373)		(885)	

All the odds ratios are positive. Attitudes toward jobs became more favorable from 1946 to 1963 in all education and region groups. Looking at the weighted averages it seems that change has been greater in the better-educated groups. The odds ratios increase with educational attainment. This is clearly the case among the others, but the college-educated Southerners do not quite fit the pattern. However—and here we see one of the advantages of the Goodman system—if the college-South combination was really out of line, the result would be a four-variable interaction; but this was rejected during significance-testing. A more reasonable interpretation is that this group is small (162 cases in contrast to 496 for college-other) and the discrepancy is explainable by chance fluctuations. Thus our summary: job attitudes became more favorable from 1946 to 1963 in both regional groups, especially among the better-educated.

APPENDIX: ITERATION TECHNIQUE

Three-or-more-variable models permitting effects of level 2 or higher must be constructed by iteration (successive approximations). Here I explain how to carry out the operation, following Goodman (1970, p. 237, Equation 3.8). Readers interested in the history and rationale for the procedure will find a number of useful references in Goodman's

article. My approach is purely descriptive and gives no rationale or interpretation. The technique has eight steps:
1. List the effects to be permitted in some arbitrary order, for example AB, CDE, FG.
2. For trial number zero, enter the value 1.00 in each cell of the $ABCDEFG$ table.
3. Find the frequencies for the collapsed table involving only the first effect by summing the appropriate frequencies in step 2. (If the first effect is AB, we build the zero-order, two-variable table A by B; if the first effect is CDE, we build the three-variable table C by D by E.)
4. Calculate weights for the next trial. For each cell of the subtable in step 3:

$$\frac{\text{Actual frequency in raw data}}{\text{Frequency in most recent trial}} = \text{Weight}$$

5. Next trial. Multiply each cell frequency in step 2 (or previous trial) by the appropriate weight from step 4. (For example, if AB was the first effect, every cell that is $A+\ B-$ in the larger table $ABCDEFG$ in the previous trial would be multiplied by the weight calculated for the $A+\ B-$ cell in step 4.)
6. Find the next effect in the list of step 1 (for example, after doing AB do CDE).

TABLE 19
Raw Data for Iteration of $(JR)\ (JE)\ (RE)$
$(N = 3579)$

(a) Jobs by Region by Education

Jobs	Grade		High School		College	
	South	Other	South	Other	South	Other
As good	123	459	190	849	97	405
Other	250	426	194	430	65	91

(b) Jobs by Region

Jobs	South	Other
As good	410	1713
Other	509	947

(c) Jobs by Education

Jobs	Grade	High School	College
As good	582	1039	502
Other	676	624	156

(d) Region by Education

Region	Grade	High School	College
South	373	384	162
Other	885	1279	496

7. Go through steps 3 to 5 substituting the effect in step 6 for first effect.
8. When all effects in the list in step 1 have been used, compare the raw data tables for the effects with those produced by the last iteration. If each cell agrees to within one or two decimals, stop. If not, repeat the cycle starting at step 3 with the first effect in the list.

The technique can be illustrated with three of the variables in our Schwartz data, J (jobs), R (region), and E (education), and the two-variable model (JR) (JE) (RE). Table 19 gives the necessary raw data calculations.

The following figures are numbered according to the steps in the iteration scheme described in Table 19 and are presented with minimal text. By working back and forth from the description to the examples the reader should be able to see how it all works.

Step 1. JR, JE, RE

		Grade		High School		College	
Step 2.		South	Other	South	Other	South	Other
	As good	1	1	1	1	1	1
	Other	1	1	1	1	1	1

Step 3.

	South	Other
As good	3	3
Other	3	3

Step 4.

	South	Other
As good	$410/3 = 136.7$	$1713/3 = 571.0$
Other	$509/3 = 169.7$	$947/3 = 315.7$

Step 5.

	Grade		High School		College	
	South	Other	South	Other	South	Other
As good	1×136.7 $=136.7$	1×571.0 $=571.0$	1×136.7 $=136.7$	1×571.0 $=571.0$	1×136.7 $=136.7$	1×571.0 $=571.0$
Other	1×169.7 $=169.7$	1×315.7 $=315.7$	1×169.7 $=169.7$	1×315.7 $=315.7$	1×169.7 $=169.7$	1×315.7 $=315.7$

Step 6. JE

Step 3 (second trial).

	Grade	High School	College
As good	707.7	707.7	707.7
Other	485.4	485.4	485.4

Step 4 (second trial).

	Grade	High School	College
As good	$582/707.7 = 0.822$	$1039/707.7 = 1.468$	$502/707.7 = 0.709$
Other	$676/485.4 = 1.393$	$624/485.4 = 1.286$	$156/485.4 = 0.321$

TABLE 20
Iterated and Raw Data Values for Region and Education

Region	Cell Education	0	1	2	3	4	5	6	Raw Data
South	Grade school	2	306.4	348.8	372.9	372.5	371.8	372.9	373
	High school	2	306.4	418.9	384.1	384.2	385.1	383.9	384
	College	2	306.4	151.4	162.0	162.3	162.0	162.0	162
Other	Grade school	2	886.7	909.2	884.6	885.0	886.1	885.2	885
	High school	2	886.7	1244.2	1279.1	1279.0	1278.0	1279.2	1279
	College	2	886.7	506.1	496.0	495.8	496.0	496.0	496

(Trial columns: 1–6)

Step 5 (second trial).

	Grade		High School	
	South	Other	South	Other
As good	136.7 × 0.822 = 112.4	571.0 × 0.822 = 469.4	136.7 × 1.468 = 200.7	571.0 × 1.468 = 838.2
Other	169.7 × 1.393 = 236.4	315.7 × 1.393 = 439.8	169.7 × 1.286 = 218.2	315.7 × 1.286 = 406.0

	College	
	South	Other
As good	136.7 × 0.709 = 96.9	571.0 × 0.709 = 404.8
Other	169.7 × 0.321 = 54.5	315.7 × 0.321 = 101.3

Step 6 (second trial). RE
Step 3 (third trial).

	Grade	High School	College
South	348.8	418.9	151.4
Other	909.2	1244.2	506.1

And so on. The work continued through two complete cycles, giving six trials. Table 20 shows how the figures converge rapidly on the raw data for one of the three effects, region and education.

REFERENCES

DAVIS, J. A.
    1971 *Elementary Survey Analysis*. Englewood Cliffs, N.J.: Prentice-Hall.

GOODMAN, L. A.
    1965 "On the multivariate analysis of three dichotomous variables." *American Journal of Sociology* 71:290–301.
    1970 "The multivariate analysis of qualitative data: Interactions among multiple classifications." *Journal of the American Statistical Association* 65:226–256.
    1971 "The analysis of multidimensional contingency tables: Stepwise procedures and direct estimation methods for building models for multiple classifications." *Technometrics* 13:33–61.
    1972a "A modified multiple regression approach to the analysis of dichotomous variables." *American Sociological Review* 37:28–46.
    1972b "A general model for the analysis of surveys." *American Journal of Sociology* 77:1035–1086.
    1972c "Causal analysis of panel study data and other kinds of survey data." (memorandum)

SCHWARTZ, M. A.
    1967 *Trends in White Attitudes Toward Negroes*. University of Chicago, NORC Report No. 119.

9

QUESTIONS ABOUT ATTITUDE SURVEY QUESTIONS

Howard Schuman
UNIVERSITY OF MICHIGAN

Otis Dudley Duncan
UNIVERSITY OF ARIZONA

Both data and time for this analysis have been drawn from projects supported by the National Institute of Mental Health and the National Science Foundation (to Schuman) and the Russell Sage Foundation (to Duncan).

Survey investigators are aware that there are many ways to word the same question and that these various wordings can produce different response distributions. Stouffer (1955) notes that "even slight variations in the wording of a question can produce variations in response, just as is the case with questions used by the Census to ascertain whether a person is in the labor market and seeking work. In this book we have tried to pin a finding not upon one question alone but upon a variety of questions." More recently Davis (1971) provides specific warning: "You should always be suspicious of single-variable results.... It is well known that the distribution of answers on attitude and opinion questions will vary by 15 or 20 percent with apparently slight changes in question wording, even though both versions may provide valid orderings."

Despite these cautions, inexperienced survey investigators, and on occasion those of us who claim some experience, are tempted to interpret survey items as having clearer and more absolute meaning than they possess. We do not argue here that all interpretations of item content are misguided, but only that the path from item results to substantive content is more tortuous than first appears.

This chapter provides several illustrations of the hazards of inferences from closed attitude survey questions. It begins with familiar phenomena not dissimilar to those noted elsewhere (as in Payne, 1951) and proceeds to examples of less frequently recognized problems and to more elaborate analysis. Our illustrations are not always precise: they sometimes involve comparisons of data from two different surveys taken at slightly different points in time. In each instance we feel some confidence that it is question wording that is the primary independent variable; nevertheless more strictly experimental work is needed—and is now being planned—to rule out confounding effects of short-term attitude change, real population differences, and variations among survey organizations.

As an example of the basic problem, here are two questions that were asked at about the same point in 1969 concerning the president's plans for withdrawal of troops from Vietnam.

The Gallup Poll (June 1969): "President Nixon has ordered the withdrawal of 25,000 United States troops from Vietnam in the next three months. How do you feel about this—do you think troops should be withdrawn at a faster rate or slower rate?" ("Same as now" not presented, but accepted if volunteered.) Responses: Faster, 42 percent; same as now, 29; slower, 16; no opinion, 13.

The Harris Poll (September–October 1969): "In general, do you feel the pace at which the president is withdrawing troops is too fast, too slow, or about right?" Responses: Too slow, 28 percent; about right, 49; too fast, 6; no opinion, 18.

On the reasonable assumption in this case that most of the difference in distributions results from variations in choice and wording (rather than sampling error, differences in organizations, or the slight shift in time), we see that different conclusions about public sentiment on this issue would be drawn depending on which question is cited. In particular, support for the president seems to vary from 29 to 49 percent between the two questions, corresponding to whether such a possibility was directly presented to respondents or simply allowed as a spontaneous reply.[1]

The solution to this problem advocated by Davis and other experienced survey investigators is to ignore single-variable attitudinal results and concentrate on relationships. The assumption seems to be that single-variable distributions vary for reasons that are artifactual, frivolous, or even quite meaningless, but that the orderings of respondents on items—and therefore associations among items—are largely immune to this problem. Stouffer's recommendation is to use "a variety of questions," a stance that generally, though not inevitably, leads to the construction of multiitem scales. Both these recommendations have obvious merit, but for several reasons neither is completely satisfactory. Four such reasons are discussed here.

Actual Practice. The fact is that survey reports do frequently draw conclusions on the basis of single-item marginals. This is most obvious in the case of commercial polls, where item distributions are often the main focus of attention. We are told by Gallup or Harris that x percent of the public supports gun control, was against admission of China to the U.N., opposes legalized abortion, favors legalized marijuana, and so forth. Social science reports are more likely to concentrate on relationships, but few studies of a new area can resist giving some attention to what are essentially item marginals. Thus the classic volume by Stouffer quoted earlier does draw some conclusions about the extent to which freedom of speech was perceived by the general American public as endangered in the mid-1950s; the discussion is not entirely confined to differences among educational levels, age categories, and the like. Moreover newspaper and other public reports of current social science research tend to stress these absolute findings. Given this widespread propensity to interpret item distributions as meaningful, it is important that we have as complete an understanding as possible of the problems associated with single-variable results.

Meaningful Variations in Question Marginals. As already noted, many survey investigators advocate ignoring marginal results, and the

---

[1] The Gallup data are from the *Gallup Opinion Index* (July 1969, p. 12), and the Harris data are from the *Harris Survey Yearbook of Public Opinion* (1971, p. 500). The Gallup data are reported for persons 21 and over, and we have adjusted the Harris data to the same age range by removing the effects of those 16 to 20. Exact Ns are not given; however, the Gallup national sample is reported to be about 1500 and the Harris sample 1600 but reduced to 1392 when those under 21 are removed. On these bases we calculated the likelihood-ratio chi square for the 2 $\times$ 4 table: $\chi^2 = 196.5$, DF $= 3$, $P < 0.001$.

one concrete example thus far given does suggest that such findings may tell us more about question wording than about respondents. But sometimes this is decidedly not the case, because item marginals can be substantively meaningful and important when they are compared one to another. In the area of racial attitudes, Levine (1971) reviews national poll data showing that most whites are willing to accept a small proportion of blacks into their neighborhoods but are opposed to open-housing laws and probably also to the movement of large numbers of blacks into their neighborhoods. These are obviously not mere variations in the wording of a single "housing question," but quite distinct social issues that could generate real and important differences in attitude. It can certainly be argued that these are indeed different questions, but just such differences are often ignored when one or two (or even four or five) items are selected from a larger set for inclusion in a final survey questionnaire.

A clear example of what is involved here is provided in a report (Schuman, 1972) showing that marginals vary depending on whether a value is stated in isolation or is opposed by another value. The main example concerns a story about racial discrimination, followed by several questions about the respondent's willingness to discriminate. The story and distributions for 640 metropolitan Detroit whites to two of the questions are as follows. "Suppose a good Negro engineer applied for a job as an engineering executive. The personnel director explained to him: 'Personally I'd never given your race a thought, but the two men you have to work with most closely—the plant manager and the chief engineer—both have strong feelings about Negroes. I *can* offer you a job as a regular engineer but *not* at the executive level, because any serious friction at the top could ruin the organization.'"

"Was it all right for the personnel director in this case to refuse to hire the Negro engineer as an executive in order to avoid friction with the other employees?" Yes, 39.1 percent; no, 56.4; other, D.K., N.A., 4.5. "In general, do you think employers should hire men for top management without paying any attention to whether they are white or Negro?" Yes, 84.5 percent; no, 12.3; other, D.K., N.A., 3.1.

Nondiscrimination as such is agreed to in principle by some 85 percent of the white metroplitan Detroit population, but when the principle is opposed to the harmony and economic well-being of the firm, support for it drops to 50 percent. This is not a result of sampling fluctuations; the same findings were obtained in an earlier survey, and similar findings are reported by Williams (1964) and in somewhat different form by Westie (1965). Nor is there evidence that respondents were tricked by one question rather than another. To be sure, the first question is a bit awkward in wording, but analysis by education does not suggest that misunderstanding was a serious problem.

The correct interpretation is probably that the first percentage is an estimate of adherence to the general value of nondiscrimination when it is stated abstractly; the second percentage is an estimate of adherence to that value when respondents must choose between it and another specific value or goal with which it conflicts. Both percentages are doubtless influenced also by other tangential features of wording, but this basic difference is very likely the key one. Since it is a quite meaningful conceptual difference and leads to a major shift in the percentage indicating support for nondiscrimination, we are dealing with a type of variation in question wording that is both interpretable and important. Our basic estimate of attitudinal support for nondiscrimination in employment seems to vary systematically with the way the question is asked.

Associations. We now turn from the neglected importance of marginal distributions to the claim that orderings and associations are invariant in the face of changes in question wording. There are in fact few demonstrations that this assumption is generally true. The following example, neither contrived nor the result of special searching, may exemplify a more common experience than is recognized. Questions on black control of community schools were asked of blacks in two surveys conducted in early 1968.[2] Version A: "Some people say that there should be Negro principals in schools with mostly Negro students because Negroes should have the most say in running inner-city schools." Would you agree with that or not? Agree, 43.1 percent; not agree, 56.9; $N = 427$. Version B: "Suppose there is a public school that is attended mostly by Negro children—do you think the principal should be a Negro, a white person, or that his race should not make any difference?" Negro, 12 percent; no difference, 87; white, 1; $N = 146$.

Both questions are aimed at exactly the same point, and although the differences in wording are substantial, they are not more marked here than for many survey questionnaires. We are already prepared by our earlier review for the sharp difference in marginals shown by the two questions: Are exclusively black principals in black schools supported by

---

[2] The first was the 1968 Detroit Area Study; the second was the 1968 study of "Racial Attitudes in Fifteen American Cities," reported initially in Campbell and Schuman (1968). Only data for Detroit are used here, except where noted, and in other ways the two survey samples have been made almost exactly comparable. Although the survey dates differ by some three months, other analysis indicates that this does not account for the variations discussed later in this chapter.

TABLE 1
Percentage Advocating Black Principals Only, by Education and Age[a]

Education	Version A (Detroit)	N	Version B (Detroit)	N	Version B (14 cities)	N
0–8	50.0	103	11.7	39	15.0	485
9–11	46.9	127	13.2	51	16.0	591
12	40.0	118	11.3	38	16.6	537
13	29.6	80	11.8	17	18.1	286
Age						
21–29	42.7	68	26.2	13	19.0	422
30–39	47.9	112	13.8	36	17.8	543
40–49	35.0	119	13.2	40	14.6	464
50–59	44.2	75	8.0	38	12.0	277
60–69	53.2	49	10.0	21	16.2	193

[a] These samples consist of black heads of household and wives, 21 to 69 years old, interviewed by black interviewers. Weighting has been used to achieve comparability between versions A and B, but unweighted Ns are shown and are used in statistical tests.

12 percent or by 43 percent of the Detroit black population?[3] The difference is presumably due partly to the strong agree-disagree format of version A, which encourages an agreeing response not different from that involved in F-scale and anomie items in the general population (Carr, 1971; Jackman, 1973), and partly to the additional reason or double-barreled aspect offered in connection with the agree response in version A ("because Negroes should have the most say in running inner-city schools"). We cannot disentangle these and possibly other factors that are operating here, but the 31 percent difference serves again as a warning of the considerable effect that question wording can have on single-variable distributions. Davis, as quoted earlier, spoke of a 15 or 20 percent wording effect, but here as in our other examples the magnitude of the effect is well beyond that level.

But marginal differences are not our main concern here. Let us pose the more usual survey inquiry about the correlates of such responses. Table 1 presents associations within each sample between the key responses and education and age. Version A of the question shows a positive relation to education ($\chi^2 = 9.46$, DF = 3, $P < 0.05$) and no apparent relation to age; version B shows a possibly negative (but non-significant) relation to age and little if any to education. A three-variable

[3] Equating "Negro" in version B to "agree" in version A, and both "no difference" and "white" to "not agree," the difference is highly significant: $\chi^2 = 49.6$, DF = 1, $P < 0.001$).

analysis has not been pursued but, knowing that age and education are negatively correlated, this would be a natural next step. The point here is that our conclusions about correlates on this issue are affected by the wording in which it is expressed.

A more rigorous test of the difference between versions A and B would involve a demonstration that the associations between response and education (or age) are significantly different in the two versions. Using Goodman's procedure (1970, 1972) for testing for interaction among three variables, we do not find significant three-way effects for Detroit alone. However, the Detroit sample for version B is very small. Since this version was asked in 14 other cities as well, and the differences between version B associations for Detroit and for the combined 14 other cities do not approach significance ($\chi^2 < 1.0$ for both education and age), we may plausibly substitute the much larger 14-city sample in the case of version B. When this is done, the interaction between version, response, and education is significant ($\chi^2 = 10.4$, DF $= 3$, $P < 0.02$), although the parallel test for age is not ($\chi^2 = 4.4$, DF $= 4$). Thus for education we find not only that an investigator would draw different conclusions depending on which question he happened to use, but that even the use of both versions simultaneously would not resolve the issue. Nor is it entirely clear which is the more valid conclusion, although most investigators would probably argue for the more rational forced-choice item (version B) rather than the agree-disagree format. The latter, however, continues to occur regularly in sociological surveys.

The problem here is apparently not restricted to "agreeing response set" in the usual sense, as becomes clear when we compare in Table 2 the association of education to the two Vietnam questions discussed earlier. The Gallup question, which did not explicitly present the alternative "present rate of withdrawal" to respondents, shows a modest trend for that alternative to be offered spontaneously more frequently by persons with more education. The Harris question, on the contrary, reveals an even sharper trend in the opposite direction: less-educated respondents are especially likely to choose the "present rate" alternative. Moreover the Harris question shows a positive relation between education and advocacy of faster withdrawal, whereas there is practically no relation at all in the parallel Gallup comparison. The three-way interaction involving question form, response, and education is significant for the total distributions shown in Table 2 ($\chi^2 = 35.4$, DF $= 6$, $P < 0.001$), as well as for the simpler distributions that result if the "no opinion" category is removed and the "faster" and "slower" categories collapsed in opposition to "present rate" ($\chi^2 = 29.2$, DF $= 2$, $P < 0.001$).

Thus quite opposite conclusions must be drawn from the two

TABLE 2
Percentage Distributions on Withdrawal from Vietnam Questions,
by Education: Gallup and Harris Polls[a]

	Advocates Faster Withdrawal	Advocates Slower Withdrawal	Advocates Present Rate[b]	No Opinion	Total %	N[c]
Gallup						
College (13 and over)	42	16	31	11	100	300
High school (9–12)	42	16	30	12	100	765
Grade school (0–8)	41	19	24	16	100	435
						1500
Harris[d]						
College (13 and over)	36	4	42	18	100	320
High school (9–12)	27	7	51	15	100	816
Grade school (0–8)	18	5	61	16	100	468
						1604

[a] See text for wording of Gallup and Harris questions. Responses to the two questions have been equated and relabeled here in terms of intended meaning; for example, "faster" for Gallup question and "too slow" for Harris question are both considered "advocates faster withdrawal."

[b] This alternative is explicitly presented to respondents in the Harris question but not in the Gallup question.

[c] Ns have been calculated by applying Harris's report of the percentage distribution by education (*Harris Survey Yearbook of Public Opinion*, 1971, p. 512) to both the Gallup and Harris general sample Ns. The Harris data here are for persons 16 and over, the Gallup data for persons 21 and over.

[d] This Harris distribution includes 208 persons 16 to 20 years old; the Gallup distribution does not. Harris separately reports that the 16 to 20 age category responds as follows: 33 percent for faster withdrawal, 5 percent for slower withdrawal, 55 percent for present rate, and 7 percent no opinion. Since most persons in this age category must be located in the high school education row and almost all the rest in the college row, it is highly probable that their removal would not alter the Harris distribution to any important extent.

questions as to the association between education and this facet of attitudes toward the Vietnam War. To simplify, the Gallup question indicates that education was little related in 1969 to impatience over withdrawal from Vietnam, whereas the Harris question indicates that support for the president's position on this important issue was inversely related to education. It is easy to speculate on the reason for this striking interaction. Very likely less-educated persons are more severely constrained by the question frame of reference, though whether this is due primarily to cognitive limitations or to passivity in the interview situation is not clear.

Even less certain is which, if either, of these questions reveals the more valid picture. Are the less educated "misled" by the explicit statement of an alternative that is tied to the majesty of presidential decision? Or does such an explicit statement "allow" them simply to express true opinions that are hidden when they are forced to choose between "too fast" and "too slow"? The former position suggests that the problem is agreeing response set in a new guise, where the asserter is really the president and the agreeing response appears as one of several multiple choices. The latter suggests that the dichotomous forced-choice question fails to reveal the substantial body of opinion eager or at least willing to go along with presidential policy. We are as yet far from being able to solve this problem, but we do know that for the two pairs of survey items dealt with here—and no doubt for others in the sociological literature—one's conclusions about the most basic background correlates of an attitude vary decisively with item wording and format.

Variations in Attitude Items in Change Studies. Our final example, presented in somewhat greater detail, has features in common with the previous cases. It has special interest, however, in view of the growing use of surveys to produce social indicators. This use typically involves investigation of the association between responses and time (Davis, 1972). A significant association between one item and time means that the marginal distribution for that item has changed. If, however, different versions of the item are used at different times, the comparison is compromised.

In the 1971 survey conducted by the Detroit Area Study (DAS) we carried out a small experiment relating to this point. One of the items in the 1956 DAS that we wished to replicate was a somewhat lengthy and (we feared) potentially ambiguous question involving four response alternatives (see Table 3). We thought that the sense of the question would be retained if only the second and third alternatives were presented. The substitution of the revised for the original question was made only in half the 1971 interviews (form B), however, so that we could test their equivalence. Our hypothesis, recorded before the fact, read: "When the four original alternatives are collapsed appropriately into two, the two questions will not differ significantly in results." Forms A and B were each adminstered to approximately half the respondents, the form to be used in each interview being randomly predesignated.

The data in Table 3 clearly refute our hypothesis, and it is easy to see that the consequences would have been serious if we had used the form B version throughout the 1971 survey. First, if we had assumed

TABLE 3
Percentage Distributions of Responses to Question on Willingness to Change
How Country Is Run: 1956 and 1971 Detroit Area Study

Response[a]	1956	1971A	1971B
(1) Rarely	2.1	1.6	...
(2) Cautious	48.9	42.5	63.2
(3) Free	36.6	31.7	36.8
(4) Constantly	12.4	24.1	...
Total %	100.0	99.9	100.0
N	757	924	927
Unclassified	40	12	18

[a] Question wording: People feel differently about making changes in the way our country is run. (Show Card) [In order to keep America great,] which of these (four/two) statements do you think is best?
1. We should rarely, if ever, make changes in the way our country is run.
2. We should be very cautious of making changes in the way our country is run.
3. We should feel free to make changes in the way our country is run.
4. We must constantly make changes in the way our country is run.
(Wording in brackets was used only in 1956. Only statements 2 and 3, renumbered 1 and 2, were supplied in the 1971 form B interview.)

equivalence of form B to collapsed form A, the direction, as well as the magnitude, of change would have been erroneously estimated. Second, if one chose to interpret the marginals as indicating where the majority opinion lies, he would reach contrary conclusions from (collapsed) form A and form B. The former suggests a small liberal majority (responses 3 and 4), whereas form B indicates a substantial conservative majority. Third, all the change between 1956 and 1971A can be shown to involve the contrast of response 4 with the remaining three responses, whereas the latter did not undergo changes in popularity relative to each other. The (likelihood-ratio) chi square statistic for the first three responses by 1956 versus 1971A is $\chi^2 = 0.1$, DF $= 2$, $P > 0.5$, not significant. For the aggregate of the first three rows versus response 4 by 1956 versus 1971A we have $\chi^2 = 38.5$, DF $= 1$, $P < 0.001$. For the entire 4×2 table, the overall value is the sum of these, $\chi^2 = 38.6$, DF $= 3$, $P < 0.001$. (We are here applying the procedure outlined by Goodman, 1968, pp. 1102–1103, 1117, and 1122–1123 for partitioning of contingency tables.) Fourth, the presence of alternatives 1 and 4 alters the relative attractiveness of responses 2 and 3. This is seen by constructing the 2×2 table, responses 2 versus 3 by 1971A versus 1971B: $\chi^2 = 5.8$, DF $= 1$, $P < 0.025$.

Thus we cannot be sure what change, if any, would have been registered if the form B version had been used in both years. This uncertainty speaks against the possibility of substituting form B for form A in future surveys, even though the 1971 survey has provided a splice, since we have no reliable way to estimate what the change would have been between 1956 and 1971 with that version of the question. If such a substitution were seen as highly desirable, the splice should involve at least one more year in which both questions are used. It would be especially helpful if both versions were asked of the same respondents, perhaps in the main survey and a slightly later reinterview.

A serendipitous result of our experiment is the demonstration, which follows, that the four response categories of the form A version (in the order shown in Table 3) do not lie on a single dimension, as (we presume) the investigators who devised them for the 1956 study thought. Suppose that the four responses did lie on a single dimension which was used by all respondents, even though the distances separating the responses are not necessarily the same for everyone. That is, we are considering the postulate that all respondents order the four responses in the same way, in that they agree as to which responses mean more or less willingness to see changes made. If we now consider the hypothetical experiment of having each respondent rank the responses in order of their proximity to his own view, then it is an elementary deduction from unfolding theory (Coombs, 1964, pp. 83–87) that only eight possible preference rankings, those shown in the stub of Table 4, are logically possible out of the 4! = 24 different ways in which the four responses

TABLE 4

Permissible Rankings of Response Alternatives (on Hypothesis of Unidimensionality) to Question on Willingness to Change How Country is Run, Related to Marginal Distributions Obtained in 1971 Detroit Area Study

Ranking of Four Response Alternatives[a]	Form B Response		Form A Response[a] (first choice)
	2 (cautious) Preferred to 3 (free)	3 (free) Preferred to 2 (cautious)	
1 2 3 4		0	1.6 (1)
2 1 3 4		0	⎫
2 3 1 4		0	⎬ 42.6 (2)
2 3 4 1		0	⎭
3 2 1 4	0		⎫
3 2 4 1	0		⎬ 31.7 (3)
3 4 2 1	0		⎭
4 3 2 1	0		24.1 (4)
Total %	63.2	36.8	100.0

[a] See Table 3 for identification of response alternatives.

could be ranked. We suggest that in our two forms portions of the hypothetical ranking experiment were actually performed. In form A the respondent, in effect, designated his first choice among the four alternatives. In form B he told us whether the preference ranking was one in which response 2, "cautious," was or was not preferred to response 3, "free." Thus we have estimated marginal distributions for Table 3; and, by hypothesis, four of its eight cells must have null frequencies. We see that the remaining cells cannot be filled consistently with the given marginals. We are led to reject the postulate that responses 1, 2, 3, and 4 are interpreted as lying on a single dimension in that order by all respondents. Interestingly, the design of our experiment, given the results, is not such that we can similarly reject the hypothesis that a single dimension is defined by the ordering 1, 2, 4, 3. In that case the permissible rankings would not be the same as those listed in Table 3.

If the foregoing argument seems strained, we can consider other evidence that forms A and B really involve different questions, not just innocuous variation in wording. Table 5 shows response distributions by political party identification. Looking first at the four individual panels of the table, we note that they do not produce the same association of

TABLE 5
Percentage Distributions of Responses to Question on Willingness to Change How Country Is Run, by Political Party Identification: 1956 and 1971 Detroit Area Study

Year, Form, and Political Party	Response[a]					
	(1) Rarely	(2) Cautious	(3) Free	(4) Constantly	Total %	N
1956						
Republican	2.0	47.0	37.0	14.0	100.0	200
Democrat	2.1	49.0	38.1	10.9	100.1	431
Independent	1.1	51.1	31.1	16.7	100.0	90
1971A						
Republican	1.3	53.4	25.8	19.5	100.0	159
Democrat	2.2	42.4	32.6	22.8	100.0	509
Independent	0.4	36.0	33.0	30.6	100.0	242
1971A Collapsed						
Republican	...	54.7	45.3	...	100.0	159
Democrat	...	44.6	55.4	...	100.0	509
Independent	...	36.4	63.6	...	100.0	242
1971B						
Republican	...	69.1	30.9	...	100.0	162
Democrat	...	60.9	39.1	...	100.0	481
Independent	...	65.5	34.5	...	100.0	264

[a] See Table 3 for complete wording.

party with response. In 1956 there is no significant association; for the 3×4 table, $\chi^2 = 4.1$, DF = 6, $P = 0.67$. Nor can we find a significant association by considering partitionings of the response categories. For 1971A, we find $\chi^2 = 18.6$, DF = 6, $P < 0.005$. Considering responses 1 and 2 alone we have $\chi^2 = 3.5$, DF = 2, $P > 0.1$; and considering responses 3 and 4 alone we have $\chi^2 = 1.9$, DF = 2, $P > 0.25$ so that the relationship does not pertain to either of these contrasts. On the other hand, for responses 1 and 2 combined versus 3 and 4 combined, by party, we have $\chi^2 = 13.2$, DF = 2, $P < 0.005$. So it is this contrast, the very one that would be retained in seeking comparability with form B, that almost entirely accounts for the association of party with response in the 1971A data. Yet when we come to 1971B that association fails to appear; for party by the two response categories we have $\chi^2 = 4.1$, DF = 2, $P > 0.1$. We note, moreover, that the apparent relationship of party to response in 1971B is not the same as in 1971A collapsed. Thus we are led to consider a three-way problem, using methods proposed by Goodman (1970, 1972) for analyzing multiway contingency tables. We have three parties by two responses by two forms (1971A versus 1971B). A model that fits all three sets of two-way marginals (party by response; party by form; response by form) yields $\chi^2 = 6.5$, DF = 2, $P < 0.05$. The hypothesis considered here is that of zero three-factor interaction (Goodman, 1970, p. 233); the outcome, of course, is that we can reject this hypothesis with confidence. Substantively the nonzero three-way interaction means that 1971A and 1971B cannot be considered to come from the same population as far as the relationship of party to response is concerned. It should be noted that the model considered is one that takes into account the marginal differences in response between the two forms. Thus it simply is not true, if we credit these results, that the two questions give the same results, marginal differences aside.

A similar interaction is observed in Table 6, where the question on willingness to change is related to one asking whether American families should be required to own flags. When form A responses are collapsed it appears that conservative respondents are more likely to endorse compulsory flag ownership than are liberal respondents. But the direction of the relationship is reversed on form B. For the three-way problem, form by response to change question by response to flag question, the model fitting all three sets of two-way marginals yields $\chi^2 = 7.0$, DF = 1, $P = 0.008$. Hence there is a highly significant three-factor interaction, which implies that the association between the two questions is not the same on form B as it is on form A.

It should not be assumed that interactions of this type occur in relating the two forms of the question to all other questions and respond-

TABLE 6
Response to Question on Requiring Flag Ownership by Response to Question on Willingness to Change, by Form: 1971 Detroit Area Study

Response to Question on Willingness to Change[a]	Percentage[b] Agreeing That "Every American Family Should Be Required by Law to Own a Flag"		
	1971A	1971A Collapsed	1971B
(1) Rarely	26.7 (15)	...	...
(2) Cautious	19.9 (382)	20.2 (397)	17.6 (574)
(3) Free	13.4 (283)	12.7 (502)	19.5 (333)
(4) Constantly	11.9 (219)	...	...
All responses	16.0 (899)	16.0 (899)	18.3 (907)

[a] See Table 3 for complete wording.
[b] Base excludes unclassifiable responses and nonresponses.

ent characteristics. Indeed, for most of the variables we have examined, such interactions do not appear. Table 7 provides an example in which the two forms do produce the same estimate of a relationship, despite the marked difference in marginals. With 1971A collapsed we may consider the three-way problem, form by color by response. When we fit all sets of two-way marginals we find $\chi^2 = 0.7$, DF = 1, $P = 0.41$, so that there is no evidence for three-way interaction. Substantively the relationship of response to color is the same on both forms, despite the difference in marginals; or (equivalently) the relationship of response to form is the same for black and white respondents, despite the effect of form on the marginal distributions and the difference in marginals by color. It should be noted, however, that for blacks and whites separately, as for the aggregate of all respondents, the entirety of the change between 1956 and 1971A is accounted for by the increased popularity of the fourth response relative to the other three, while there is no detectable shift in their popularity relative to each other. It is true that with the response distribution collapsed to match form B we would have detected change between 1956 and 1971A for both blacks and whites. However, we cannot be sure that such change would have been registered if the form B question had actually been asked in 1956.

Analysis of responses by education suggests that certain nuances of the form A question are missed in the form B version. The last panel in Table 8 shows that the form B version produces no response variation

TABLE 7
Percentage Distributions of Responses to Question on Willingness
to Change How Country Is Run, by Color of Respondent:
1956 and 1971 Detroit Area Study

Color and Response[a]	1956	1971A	1971A Collapsed	1971B
Black				
(1) Rarely	1.5	2.4	...	...
(2) Cautious	44.7	33.0	35.4	50.5
(3) Free	43.2	41.0	64.6	49.5
(4) Constantly	10.6	23.6	...	...
Total %	100.0	100.0	100.0	100.0
N	132	212	212	190
White				
(1) Rarely	2.2	1.4	...	...
(2) Cautious	49.8	45.4	46.8	66.5
(3) Free	35.2	28.9	53.2	33.5
(4) Constantly	12.8	24.3	...	...
Total %	100.0	100.0	100.0	100.0
N	625	712	712	737

[a] See Table 3 for complete wording.

by education. (A preliminary analysis established that subdivisions of the three broad education categories produced no reliable differences in response on either form or for either year.) By contrast the form A results suggest a mild relationship of response to education. That relationship is not, however, highly reliable. For the two (collapsed) response categories by three education levels, we find $\chi^2 = 4.1$, DF = 3, $P > 0.1$. Combining high school and college, to be contrasted with elementary, we obtain $\chi^2 = 3.8$, DF = 2, $P = 0.053$. The residual, due to the contrast of high school with college, is $\chi^2 = 0.3$, DF = 1, $P > 0.50$. The data do suggest, therefore, that elementary-level respondents are slightly more conservative than those with more advanced schooling, an effect that is completely lost in form B. We are warned not to stress this result too strongly, however, by the outcome of a three-way analysis. With two responses by two forms by three education levels, when we fit all three sets of two-way marginals we obtain a satisfactory fit. Indeed a model that fits only the two-way marginals for form by response and the one-way marginals for education (thus ignoring any effect of education on response) fits the data quite acceptably: $\chi^2 = 5.9$, DF = 6, $P = 0.43$.

Thus we cannot show conclusively that forms A and B produce different associations of education with response. What we can show,

TABLE 8
Percentage Distributions of Responses to Question on Willingness
to Change How Country Is Run, by Educational Attainment
of Respondent: 1956 and 1971 Detroit Area Study

Year, Form, and Response[a]	Educational Attainment		
	Elementary	High School	College
1956			
(1) Rarely	4.3	1.1	1.7
(2) Cautious	55.3	48.8	38.1
(3) Free	34.6	35.8	42.4
(4) Constantly	5.8	14.2	17.8
Total %	100.0	99.9	100.0
N	208	430	118
1971A			
(1) Rarely	6.1	0.6	1.1
(2) Cautious	45.8	43.0	40.3
(3) Free	35.9	31.4	30.4
(4) Constantly	12.2	25.0	28.2
Total %	100.0	100.0	100.0
N	131	512	280
1971A Collapsed			
(1) and (2)	51.9	43.6	41.4
(3) and (4)	48.1	56.4	58.6
Total %	100.0	100.0	100.0
N	131	512	280
1971B			
(2) Cautious	63.0	63.4	63.4
(3) Free	37.0	36.6	36.6
Total %	100.0	100.0	100.0
N	135	535	254

[a] See Table 3 for complete wording.

however, is that for both 1956 and 1971A the salient contrasts are those involving responses 1 and 4, so that the form A version of the question does produce variation that is lost in form B. We proceed by partitioning the table for each year in the manner presented in Table 9. The same configuration of results emerges for the two years. High school and college respondents are more likely than elementary respondents to select response 4 over all others. Elementary respondents are more likely to choose response 1 disproportionately to their choices of response 2 than are high school and college respondents. These two contrasts, each with

TABLE 9
Partitioning of Chi Square Tests of the Associations between Education
and Response Shown in Table 8

Year and Partitioning	χ^2	DF	P
1956			
(i) Four response × three education categories (total)	24.7	6	<0.001
(ii) Responses (1 + 2 + 3) vs. (4) × elem. vs. (HS and college)	13.4	1	<0.001
(iii) (1) vs. (2) × elem. vs. (HS + college)	4.1	1	<0.05
(iv) Remainder	7.2	4	>0.1
1971A			
(i) Four response × three education categories (total)	27.4	6	<0.001
(ii) Responses (1 + 2 + 3) vs. (4) × elem. vs. (HS and college)	13.5	1	<0.001
(iii) (1) vs. (2) × elem. vs. (HS and college)	12.3	1	<0.001
(iv) Remainder	1.6	4	>0.75

a single degree of freedom, account for all the reliable association present in the table for either year, since the remainder χ^2 is not significant.

What we have shown, then, is that the form A question with its four alternatives produces results not obtained with form B and its two responses and that, in some instances, relationships as well as marginal distributions are not the same for the two forms. We have not, however, shown that form A is a superior question (except in the sense that it provides comparability with the earlier survey). Indeed, since our results suggest that more than one dimension differentiates the four responses, the question may actually be hopelessly ambiguous. Although we can estimate change in the response distribution elicited by the question, we remain unsure of the meaning of that change. A tentative suggestion is that the two responses in form B differentiate respondents who feel comfortable with the prospect of change and those who feel uncomfortable, whereas responses 4 and 1 in form A distinguish between those who acknowledge the realistic necessity for change and those unable or unwilling to do so. If two such facets of willingness to change are indeed distinguishable empirically (even though they might be correlated), then mixing them up in a single question can only create confusion.

Our example here has been an unusual one in which wording was deliberately altered in order to test for the persistence in meaningfulness of a presumed simple dimension. It is evident, however, that similar problems could well occur with some of the pairs of items discussed earlier. Version A of the "black principal" question was repeated in 1971, along with a number of other items from the 1968 Detroit Area Study. Although some of the items showed significant differences between those two time points, the "principals" item did not. However, it is possible that version B would have shown such indication of change in marginals or that the two versions would have shown different changes over time in such correlates as education. Clearly much careful work needs to be done on item variability in social indicator studies. Indeed the recent emphasis on studying social change through replication (Duncan, 1969) makes salient problems of item wording that have been treated as of only minor importance in the past.

Multiitem Approaches. Stouffer's recommendation, it will be recalled, was to use multiple items to measure a particular construct, and this suggestion is endorsed by most social scientists with exposure to scaling. The nature and cost of surveys probably makes such advice unrealistic for many variables (it is common to construct a scale for one or two focal dependent variables but not for all), but even if we consider the matter apart from practical constraints, this solution is far from complete. Cumulating items adds to the reliability of whatever they measure in common—often an extremely useful step—but the operation cannot produce something not already in the individual items. If one of the "school principal" questions referred to earlier is the model for other questions on, say, black separatism, then that question effect is also cumulated. Even the more idiosyncratic effects of individual items are dealt with in a haphazard way in scale construction, since their final contribution depends on an averaging process that is often unplanned and unrecognized. Thus the creation of scales does not free an investigator from format and wording effects of items. There is a good deal more to be said for the analysis of a set of items one by one, thereby replicating a main finding across the multiple indicators of the construct involved. Of course the value of this approach depends, from our present standpoint, on whether type, not only content, of question is varied systematically.

Conclusions. We have presented examples of substantial variations in findings due to question wording. Our aim has been the modest one of reminding ourselves and other sociologists of the formidable measurement problems inherent in attitude survey research. Little attempt has been made here to systematize these effects or to distinguish between, say, agreeing response set and other less easily conceptualized wording problems. That important task remains to be done, but for the moment it may be useful to avoid narrowing our focus to exclusive concern with a single, traditionally defined methodological problem such as response set. Future work will need to cast a wider net with regard to question wording and indeed might well attempt to include within a single theoretical framework problems of interviewer bias (Hyman,

1954; Schuman and Converse, 1971) on the one hand, and problems of the consistency and stability of mass attitudes (Converse, 1964, 1970) on the other.

It does appear that the administration of attitude survey questionnaires has two broad and inevitable features that are easily forgotten when investigators set out to operationalize theoretical constructs.

First, the public responds to questions, not to constructs, and public attitudes may not even be well represented by the constructs that sociologists frequently start from. Individual respondents often see differences between questions that investigators regard as essentially similar. Given in addition the vagueness of construct definition and inadequacies of scaling in much sociological survey research, it is likely that we are often measuring phenomena quite different from our intention.

Second, interviewing, like any social interaction, involves influence, whether intended or not. This is more than a matter of status differences between interviewer and respondent or interviewer effects more generally, because it also involves the substantive argument inherent in any question wording. Public attitudes are seldom so well crystalized that they fail to be affected by the strength and content with which particular questions and their alternatives are worded.

Both these points emphasize the extreme importance of individual question construction in attitude studies and of the need to understand better the types and magnitudes of wording effects in typical large-scale survey investigations.

REFERENCES

CAMPBELL, A. AND SCHUMAN, H.
    1968   *Racial Attitudes in Fifteen American Cities.* Ann Arbor, Mich.: Institute for Social Research.

CARR, L. G.
    1971   "The Srole items and acquiescence." *American Sociological Review* 36:287–293.

CONVERSE, P. E.
    1964   "The nature of belief systems in mass publics." Pp. 206–261 in D. E. Apter (Ed.), *Ideology and Discontent.* New York: Free Press.
    1970   "Attitudes and non-attitudes: Continuation of a dialogue." Pp. 168–189 in E. R. Tufte (Ed.), *The Quantitative Analysis of Social Problems.* Reading, Mass.: Addison-Wesley.

COOMBS, C. H.
    1964   *A Theory of Data.* New York: Wiley.

DAVIS, J. A.
    1971   *Elementary Survey Analysis.* Englewood Cliffs, N.J.: Prentice-Hall.

1972 "Survey replication, the log linear model, and theories of social change." Paper presented to the Russell Sage Foundation Conference on Social Indicator Models.

DUNCAN, O. D.
1969 *Toward Social Reporting: Next Steps.* New York: Russell Sage Foundation.

GALLUP OPINION INDEX
1969 Report No. 49, July. Princeton, N.J.: Gallup International, Inc.

GOODMAN, L. A.
1969 "The analysis of cross-classified data: Independence, quasi-independence, and interactions in contingency tables with or without missing entries." *Journal of the American Statistical Association* 63:1091–1131.
1970 "The multivariate analysis of qualitative data: Interactions among multiple classifications." *Journal of the American Statistical Association* 65:226–256.
1972 "A general model for the analysis of surveys." *American Journal of Sociology* 77:1035–1086.

HARRIS SURVEY YEARBOOK OF PUBLIC OPINION
1971 New York: Louis Harris and Associates.

HYMAN, H.
1954 *Interviewing in Social Research.* Chicago: University of Chicago Press.

JACKMAN, M. R.
1973 "Education and prejudice or education and response-set?" *American Sociological Review* 30:327–339.

LEVINE, R. A.
1971 "The silent majority: Neither simple nor simple-minded." *Public Opinion Quarterly* 35:571–577.

PAYNE, S. L.
1951 *The Art of Asking Questions.* Princeton, N.J.: Princeton University Press.

SCHUMAN, H.
1972 "Attitudes vs. actions *versus* attitudes vs. attitudes." *Public Opinion Quarterly* 36:347–354.

SCHUMAN, H. AND CONVERSE, J. M.
1971 "The effects of black and white interviewers on black responses." *Public Opinion Quarterly* 35:44–68.

STOUFFER, S. A.
1955 *Communism, Conformity, and Civil Liberties.* Garden City, N.Y.: Doubleday.

WESTIE, F. R.
1965 "The American dilemma: An empirical test." *American Sociological Review* 30:527–538.

WILLIAMS, R. M., JR.
1964 *Strangers Next Door.* Englewood Cliffs, N.J.: Prentice-Hall.

10

PROBLEMS OF STATISTICAL ESTIMATION AND CAUSAL INFERENCE IN TIME-SERIES REGRESSION MODELS

Douglas A. Hibbs, Jr.
MASSACHUSETTS INSTITUTE OF TECHNOLOGY

I am grateful to Arthur Goldberger and Robert Hall for comments on an earlier draft, to Franklin Fisher for stimulating discussions on many of the topics treated, to Samuel Popkin and Lawrence McCray for valuable editorial suggestions, and to Raisa Deber, Robert Eccles, and Takashi Inoguchi for research assistance. A timely grant from the office of Provost Walter Rosenblith covered production expenses.

Thus far in the development of quantitative social research there are relatively few examples of dynamic, time-series models of sociopolitical processes. Cross-sectional analyses are predominant in the literature. However, sociologists and political scientists are increasingly likely to utilize time-series data in their empirical research as the advantages of the historical-dynamic perspective become more widely appreciated, and the scope and quality of longitudinal data improve. Hence it may be useful at this point to survey the problems of statistical estimation and causal inference in the time-series context. This chapter focuses on the implications of employing the classical linear regression model in the presence of autocorrelated disturbances—a common situation in time-series analysis that has important consequences for estimation and inference.

The first section of the essay reviews the classic linear regression model, which is among the most widely applied tools of quantitative social science. The following section examines the consequences of time-dependent disturbances and develops the theoretical solution—generalized least squares (GLS). Next some empirically common and mathematically tractable time-dependence models are considered, namely, autoregressive and moving-average processes. This is followed by a discussion of how the observed residuals can be analyzed to determine the process generating the disturbance interdependence, and an evaluation of what modifications in the original equation and estimation procedure are therefore appropriate. Finally these issues are considered in the context of truly dynamic models, that is, models that incorporate lagged endogenous variables on the right-hand side of the equation.

CLASSICAL LINEAR REGRESSION MODEL

Before dealing with the principal topics of this chapter, it is useful to review some of the key features of the classical linear regression model, which has become a familiar analytic tool for most quantitative social scientists. In the classical model we have[1]

$$Y = XB + U \qquad (1)$$

$$E(U) = 0 \qquad (2)$$

$$E(UU') = \sigma_u^2 I \qquad (3)$$

$$X \text{ is fixed and has rank } (K + 1) < T \qquad (4)$$

where Y is a $T \times 1$ vector of observations on the dependent or endogenous variable; X is a $T \times (1 + K)$ matrix of observations on the K independent or exogenous variables and the intercept vector (of 1s); B is a

---

[1] The results to follow could be shown without great difficulty to hold for the case of stochastic regressors distributed independently of U. To keep the exposition simple, I have retained the classical assumption of fixed X. Readers familiar with these well-known derivations are encouraged to pass over this section, perhaps after glancing at the key results.

$(1 + K) \times 1$ vector of coefficients to be estimated; U is a $T \times 1$ vector of disturbances; and E denotes the "expected value of," such that $E(U) = \Sigma u_t \cdot \text{prob}(u_t) = \text{mean of } U$.

The first assumption of the classical linear regression model specifies that each observation on the endogenous variable Y can be expressed as a linear function of the exogenous variables X plus the disturbance U. In the more familiar scalar notation this is expressed simply as $Y_t = \beta_0 + \sum_k \beta_k X_{tk} + u_t$. The second property of the model implies that the disturbances have no systematic components and therefore each has zero expectation. The third assumption says that the expected value of u_t^2 is σ_u^2 for all t (constant variance-homoscedasticity) and that the covariance of u_t with $u_{t \pm \theta}$ is zero whenever $\theta \neq 0$ (no autocorrelation). The final property of the classical model specifies that the X_{tk} are fixed in repeated sampling, uncorrelated with any omitted variables, and thus independent of the disturbances u_t.

Given sample data on Y and X and the prior (theoretical) assumptions of Equations (1) to (4), the researcher seeks to estimate the model

$$Y = X\hat{B} + \hat{U} \tag{5}$$

such that the sum of the squared errors $\hat{U}'\hat{U}$ is minimized. Since by definition $\hat{U}$ is expressed

$$\hat{U} = (Y - X\hat{B}) \tag{6}$$

ordinary least-squares estimation involves minimizing:

$$\begin{aligned}\hat{U}'\hat{U} &= (Y - X\hat{B})'(Y - X\hat{B}) \\ &= Y'Y - Y'X\hat{B} - (X\hat{B})'Y + (X\hat{B})'X\hat{B} \\ &= Y'Y - 2\hat{B}'X'Y + \hat{B}'X'X\hat{B}\end{aligned} \tag{7}$$

Solving for the parameters $\hat{B}$ so that $\hat{U}'\hat{U}$ is minimized requires differentiating Equation (7) with respect to $\hat{B}$:

$$\begin{aligned}\partial \hat{U}'\hat{U}/\partial \hat{B} &= 0 - 2X'Y + 2X'X\hat{B} \\ &= -X'Y + X'X\hat{B}\end{aligned} \tag{8}$$

By setting Equation (8) equal to zero and rearranging terms to isolate $\hat{B}$, we obtain the ordinary least-squares (OLS) estimator:

$$\begin{aligned}-X'Y + X'X\hat{B} &= 0 \\ X'X\hat{B} &= X'Y \\ (X'X)^{-1}X'X\hat{B} &= (X'X)^{-1}X'Y \\ \hat{B} &= (X'X)^{-1}X'Y\end{aligned} \tag{9}$$

In the case of simple bivariate regression the OLS estimator in Equation (9) has the familiar algebraic expression:

$$\hat{\beta} = \frac{\sum_t (X_t - \bar{X})(Y_t - \bar{Y})}{\sum_t (X_t - \bar{X})^2} \qquad (10)$$

A few additional preliminary results need to be established by way of background to the main issues that follow. First it must be demonstrated that the OLS estimator $\hat{B}$ is unbiased; that is, on the average it hits the target parameter(s) B.[2] This is easily shown by substituting the expression for Y in Equation (1) into the expression for $\hat{B}$ in Equation (9):

$$\begin{aligned}\hat{B} &= (X'X)^{-1}X'(XB + U) \\ &= (X'X)^{-1}X'XB + (X'X)^{-1}X'U \\ &= B + (X'X)^{-1}X'U\end{aligned} \qquad (11)$$

The unbiasedness of $\hat{B}$ is proved by taking the expected value of Equation (11):

$$\begin{aligned}E(\hat{B}) &= B + E[(X'X)^{-1}X'U] \\ &= B + [(X'X)^{-1}X'E(U)] \quad \text{by Eq. (4)} \\ E(\hat{B}) &= B \quad \text{by Eq. (2)}\end{aligned} \qquad (12)$$

Finally the variance of $\hat{B}$ in the classical model must be generated because great parts of the ensuing discussion evaluate the precision and significance of parameter estimates when disturbances are autocorrelated. The variance-covariance matrix of the OLS estimator is defined as

$$\text{var}(\hat{B}) = E[(\hat{B} - B)(\hat{B} - B)'] \qquad (13)$$

It is convenient to use the expression for $\hat{B}$ in Equation (11) and to rewrite Equation (13) as

$$\begin{aligned}\text{var}(\hat{B}) &= E[B + (X'X)^{-1}X'U - B][B + (X'X)^{-1}X'U - B]' \\ &= E[(X'X)^{-1}X'U][(X'X)^{-1}X'U]' \\ &= E[(X'X)^{-1}X'U\, U'X(X'X)^{-1}] \\ &= [(X'X)^{-1}X'E(UU')\, X(X'X)^{-1}] \quad \text{by Eq. (4)} \\ &= (X'X)^{-1}X'(\sigma_u^2 I)X(X'X)^{-1} \quad \text{by Eq. (3)} \\ \text{var}(\hat{B}) &= \sigma_u^2 (X'X)^{-1} \quad \text{(since } \sigma_u^2 \text{ is a scalar quantity and the identity matrix may be suppressed)}\end{aligned} \qquad (14)$$

In the more familiar bivariate case, the variance of the OLS estimator may be expressed:

$$\text{var}(\hat{\beta}) = \sigma_u^2 / \sum_t (X_t - \bar{X})^2 \qquad (15)$$

---

[2] More formally, an estimator is unbiased if $E(\hat{B}) = B$.

It is important to remember that least-squares regression computer programs (implicitly) assume the classical model of Equations (1) to (4) and hence routinely output the estimate of B in Equation (9), whose variance is given by (the diagonal elements of) Equation (14). The sample estimates of these equations generate the t-statistic commonly used to evaluate the precision and significance of individual regression coefficients:

$$t = \hat{B}/\sqrt{\text{var}(\hat{B})} \tag{16}$$

AUTOCORRELATED DISTURBANCES AND GENERALIZED LEAST-SQUARES ESTIMATION

The Consequences of Autocorrelation

What are the consequences of serially dependent disturbances for statistical estimation, hypothesis-testing, and causal inference? The classical model is clearly no longer appropriate. In particular, assumption (3) must be revised as follows:

$$E(UU') = \sigma_u^2 \Omega \tag{17}$$

where Ω is a $T \times T$, symmetric, positive definite matrix.

The Ω specification in the revised, generalized linear regression model allows for both heteroscedasticity (nonconstant diagonal elements) and autocorrelation (nonzero off-diagonal elements). However, we are principally concerned with problems of time-series estimation and inference, and heteroscedasticity is commonly a cross-sectional problem. For our purposes, then, the Ω matrix is considered to have 1s in the diagonal and autocorrelation parameters in the off-diagonal cells. Hence in scalar notation Equation (17) implies:

$$\begin{aligned} E(u_t u_{t \pm \theta}) &= \sigma_u^2 & \text{for } \theta = 0 \text{ (homoscedasticity)} \\ &= \gamma_\theta & \text{for } \theta \neq 0 \text{ (autocovariance)} \end{aligned} \tag{18}$$

where γ_θ is the lag θ autocovariance.

Perhaps the first point to be made concerning the impact of autocorrelated disturbances is that OLS estimates remain unbiased. This important result is worth showing explicitly. Recall from Equation (11) that the OLS estimator of B may be expressed:

$$\hat{B} = B + (X'X)^{-1}X'U \tag{19}$$

Since in the revised, autocorrelation model X remains fixed or $E(X'U)$ remains zero, the OLS estimator still has expectation B:

$$\begin{aligned} E(\hat{B}) &= B + E[(X'X)^{-1}X'U] \\ &= B + [(X'X)^{-1}X'E(U)] \\ E(\hat{B}) &= B \end{aligned} \tag{20}$$

Hence it is possible to estimate a regression model in the conventional (OLS) manner without danger of bias even if the disturbances are serially correlated.[3]

However, the variance of $\hat{B}$ in the presence of autocorrelated disturbances is no longer that of the classical model in Equation (14), but is

$$\begin{aligned}
\operatorname{var}(\hat{B}) &= E[(\hat{B} - B)(\hat{B} - B)'] \quad \text{[see Eq. (14)]} \\
&= E[(X'X)^{-1}X'(UU')X(X'X)^{-1}] \\
&= E[(X'X)^{-1}X'(\sigma_u^2\Omega)X(X'X)^{-1}] \quad \text{by Eq. (17)} \\
\operatorname{var}(\hat{B}) &= \sigma_u^2(X'X)^{-1}X'\Omega X(X'X)^{-1}
\end{aligned} \quad (21)$$

Thus, when disturbances are interdependent, which frequently is true in time-series models, OLS regression yields biased estimates of the coefficient variances. Since the bias is generally negative, the estimated variances and standard errors understate, perhaps very seriously, the true variances and standard errors.[4] This produces inflated t-ratios, a false sense of confidence in the precision of the parameter estimates, and often leads to spurious attributions of significance to independent variables. Moreover the OLS estimate of the disturbance variance σ_u^2 is also biased, and since the bias is typically negative, R^2 as well as t- and F-statistics tend to be exaggerated.

Again this result is straightforwardly demonstrated. Note that the true disturbances are never observed directly but must be derived from the fitted model and hence are "filtered" through the Xs. Thus the residuals $\hat{u}_t$ are generated:

$$\begin{aligned}
\hat{U} &= Y - X\hat{B} \\
&= Y - X(X'X)^{-1}X'Y \quad \text{by Eq. (9)} \\
&= (XB + U) - X(X'X)^{-1}X'(XB + U) \quad \text{by Eq. (1)} \\
&= (XB + U) - X(X'X)^{-1}X'XB - X(X'X)^{-1}X'U \\
&= (XB + U) - XB - X(X'X)^{-1}X'U \\
&= U - X(X'X)^{-1}X'U \\
&= [I_T - X(X'X)^{-1}X']U \\
&= MU
\end{aligned} \quad (22)$$

where $M = [I_T - X(X'X)^{-1}X']$.

Equation (22) establishes that the residuals of the classic model are a linear function of the unknown disturbances. The sum of the

---

[3] As we shall see later in this chapter, this result does not obtain in dynamic models where lagged endogenous variables ($Y_{t-\theta}$) appear on the right-hand side of the equation, because then the assumption that regressors and disturbances are uncorrelated is no longer tenable.

[4] The sign and magnitude of the bias hinge on the mechanism generating the serial dependence and on the autocorrelation of the Xs. I return to this later in this chapter.

squared residuals—the quantity minimized by least-squares regression—can therefore be expressed:

$$\begin{aligned}\hat{U}'\hat{U} &= U'M'MU \\ &= U'M^2U \\ &= U'MU \quad \text{(since } M \text{ is symmetric and idempotent)}^5 \\ &= U'[I_T - X(X'X)^{-1}X']U \quad \text{by Eq. (22)}\end{aligned} \quad (23)$$

The expected value of Equation (23) yields the classical estimator of the disturbance sum of squares in terms of the true disturbance variance σ_u^2:

$$\begin{aligned}E(\hat{U}'\hat{U}) &= E(U'MU) \\ &= E \operatorname{tr}(U'MU) \quad \text{(since } U'MU \text{ is scalar and therefore equal to its trace)} \\ &= E \operatorname{tr}(MUU') \quad \text{(since tr } AB = \operatorname{tr} BA) \\ &= \sigma_u^2 \operatorname{tr} M \\ &= \sigma_u^2 \operatorname{tr}[I_T - X(X'X)^{-1}X'] \quad \text{by Eqs. (22) and (23)} \\ &= \sigma_u^2 \operatorname{tr}(I_T) - \operatorname{tr}[(X'X)(X'X)^{-1}] \\ &= \sigma_u^2 \operatorname{tr}(I_T) - \operatorname{tr}(I_{K+1}) \\ &= \sigma_u^2(T - K - 1)\end{aligned} \quad (24)$$

where K denotes the number of exogenous variables and tr denotes trace—the sum of the diagonal elements of a matrix. Thus an unbiased sample estimate of the disturbance variance in the classical case is given by

$$\hat{\sigma}_u^2 = \hat{U}'\hat{U}/(T - K - 1) \quad (25)$$

In scalar algebra this is expressed as

$$\hat{\sigma}_u^2 = \sum_t \hat{u}_t^2/(T - K - 1) \quad (26)$$

When the disturbances are autocorrelated, however, the expectation of $\hat{U}'\hat{U}$ is no longer $\sigma_u^2 \operatorname{tr} M$, but rather

$$\begin{aligned}E(\hat{U}'\hat{U}) &= \operatorname{tr}(MUU') \quad \text{by Eq. (24)} \\ &= \sigma_u^2 \operatorname{tr}(M\Omega) \quad \text{by Eq. (17)} \\ &= \sigma_u^2 \operatorname{tr}[\Omega - X(X'X)^{-1}X'\Omega] \\ &= \sigma_u^2 \operatorname{tr} \Omega - \operatorname{tr}(X'X)^{-1}X'\Omega X \\ &= \sigma_u^2 T - \operatorname{tr}[(X'X)^{-1}X'\Omega X] \quad \text{by the specification in Eq. (17) that } \Omega \text{ is } T \times T \text{ with 1s in the diagonal}\end{aligned} \quad (27)$$

---

[5] A symmetric matrix is a square matrix that is not changed by transposition, such that $M' = M$ and $m_{ij} = m_{ji}; i \neq j; ij = 1, 2, \ldots, T$. A symmetric, idempotent matrix is one that is not changed upon multiplication by itself; that is, $M' = M$ and $M^2 = M$. It is easily verified that M in (22) and (23) is symmetric and idempotent by transposing and by squaring it.

Hence the classical OLS estimator of the disturbance variance is biased to the extent that $\text{tr}[(X'X)^{-1}X'\Omega X]$ differs from $\text{tr}[(X'X)^{-1}X'X]$. Furthermore this bias is negative (toward zero) whenever positive autocorrelation predominates in regressors and disturbances,[6] which is generally the case for socioeconomic and political time series.

This result has two implications that are of interest here. First the $\text{var}(\hat{B})$ is biased not only because $(X'X)^{-1}X'\Omega X(X'X)^{-1} \neq (X'X)^{-1}$ [see (14) and (21)], but also because $E(\hat{\sigma}_u^2) \neq \sigma_u^2$. More importantly, this means that if an equation is estimated via ordinary least squares when regressors and disturbances are (positively) autocorrelated, the researcher will obtain a spurious underestimate of the error variance and an inflation of the R^2. The model will appear to provide a much better fit to the empirical data than is actually the case.[7]

Nevertheless OLS regression in the presence of serially correlated disturbances is not necessarily disastrous—especially when the functional form of a model is not in question because of well-established theory, prior empirical results, and so on. After all, the parameter estimates are unbiased. More problematic and more typical, however, is the situation where the researcher analyzes many equations in the process of evaluating competing hypotheses and equally plausible alternative functional forms. Given the characteristic collinearity of independent variables in such studies, the erroneous selection of variables or entire equations because of differential bias in t- and F-statistics can seriously impair the causal inference-model building process. In time-series analyses of this sort, it is clear that autocorrelation is no longer a comparatively minor problem of estimation precision: if the sequential development of complex, multivariate models is grounded on biased and unreliable decision rules, errors of inference may cumulate and far exceed those that arise in a single analysis of a single equation.

The Theory of Generalized Least Squares

If the researcher has prior information about Ω, that is, knowledge of the mechanism generating the disturbance time dependence,[8] the difficulties outlined above can be avoided by applying the known Ω matrix to Equations (21) and (24). However, the sampling variances of estimates secured in this way are needlessly large compared with those

---

[6] See Goldberger (1964, chap. 5.4) and Malinvaud (1970, chap 13.4).

[7] Since time-series models typically have high R^2's in any case, most of the literature focuses on coefficient variances and t-statistics rather than on R^2's and (overall) F-statistics.

[8] How such information can be obtained empirically from the observed residuals is taken up later in this chapter.

rendered by Aitken's generalized least squares (GLS).[9] Consider again the generalized linear regression model:

$$Y = XB + U \qquad (28)$$

$$E(U) = 0 \qquad (29)$$

$$E(UU') = \sigma_u^2 \Omega \qquad (30)$$

$$X \text{ is fixed and has rank } (K + 1) < T \qquad (31)$$

where all terms are as previously defined.

Aitken's generalization of the Gauss-Markov least-squares theorem established that the best linear unbiased estimator of the true parameter vector B in the model of Equations (28) to (31) is the GLS estimator $\hat{B}^*$:

$$\hat{B}^* = (X'\Omega^{-1}X)^{-1}X'\Omega^{-1}Y \qquad (32)$$

It is readily shown that $\hat{B}^*$ is unbiased:
$$\begin{aligned}
E(\hat{B}^*) &= E[(X'\Omega^{-1}X)^{-1}X'\Omega^{-1}(XB + U)] \\
&= E[(X'\Omega^{-1}X)^{-1}X'\Omega^{-1}XB + (X'\Omega^{-1}X)^{-1}X'\Omega^{-1}U] \qquad (33) \\
&= B + E[(X'\Omega^{-1}X)^{-1}X'\Omega^{-1}U] \\
&= B + [(X'\Omega^{-1}X)^{-1}X'\Omega^{-1}E(U)] \qquad \text{(since } X \text{ and } \Omega \text{ are fixed)} \\
E(\hat{B}^*) &= B
\end{aligned}$$

Aitken demonstrated that the GLS estimator has minimum variance in the class of linear unbiased estimators. The variance of $\hat{B}^*$ is given by

$$\begin{aligned}
\text{var}(\hat{B}^*) &= E[(\hat{B}^* - B)(\hat{B}^* - B)'] \\
&= E\{[B + (X'\Omega^{-1}X)^{-1}X'\Omega^{-1}U - B][B + (X'\Omega^{-1}X)^{-1}X'\Omega^{-1}U - B]'\} \\
&\qquad\qquad\qquad\qquad\qquad\qquad\qquad\qquad\qquad \text{by Eq.(33)} \\
&= E[(X'\Omega^{-1}X)^{-1}X'\Omega^{-1}(UU')\Omega^{-1}X(X'\Omega^{-1}X)^{-1}] \qquad (34) \\
&= [(X'\Omega^{-1}X)^{-1}X'\Omega^{-1}\sigma_u^2\Omega\Omega^{-1}X(X'\Omega^{-1}X)^{-1}] \qquad \text{by Eq. (30)} \\
&= \sigma_u^2(X'\Omega^{-1}X)^{-1}
\end{aligned}$$

Unlike the classical OLS estimator, generalized least squares yields an unbiased estimate of the error variance σ_u^2 when disturbances are autocorrelated. This is demonstrated by operations analogous to Equations (22) to (25). The residuals in the generalized model, $\hat{u}_t^*$, are defined:

[9] Aitken (1935).

$$\begin{aligned}
\hat{U}^* &= Y - X\hat{B}^* \\
&= Y - X(X'\Omega^{-1}X)^{-1}X'\Omega^{-1}Y \quad \text{by Eq. (32)} \\
&= (XB + U) - X(X'\Omega^{-1}X)^{-1}X'\Omega^{-1}(XB + U) \quad \text{by Eq. (28)} \\
&= (XB + U) - X(X'\Omega^{-1}X)^{-1}X'\Omega^{-1}XB - X(X'\Omega^{-1}X)^{-1}X'\Omega^{-1}U \\
&= XB + U - XB - X(X'\Omega^{-1}X)^{-1}X'\Omega^{-1}U \quad (35) \\
&= U - X(X'\Omega^{-1}X)^{-1}X'\Omega^{-1}U \\
&= [I_T - X(X'\Omega^{-1}X)^{-1}X'\Omega^{-1}]U \\
&= M^*U
\end{aligned}$$

where $M^* = [I_T - X(X'\Omega^{-1}X)^{-1}X'\Omega^{-1}]$.

It can be shown that GLS minimizes a quadratic form in the residual vector $\hat{U}^*$ with Ω^{-1} as matrix; that is,

$$\begin{aligned}
(Y - X\hat{B}^*)'\Omega^{-1}(Y - X\hat{B}^*) &= \hat{U}^{*'}\Omega^{-1}\hat{U}^* \\
&= (M^*U)'\Omega^{-1}(M^*U) \quad \text{by Eq. (35)} \\
&= U'M^{*'}\Omega^{-1}M^*U \quad (36)
\end{aligned}$$

is minimized.[10] Direct calculation shows that $M^{*'}\Omega^{-1}M^* = \Omega^{-1}M^*$. It follows that the expected value of the sum of squared residuals from (Eq. 36) gives the GLS estimator of the disturbance sum of squares:

$$\begin{aligned}
E(\hat{U}^{*'}\Omega^{-1}\hat{U}^*) &= E(U'\Omega^{-1}M^*U) \\
&= E\operatorname{tr}(U'\Omega^{-1}M^*U) \quad \text{(since } U'\Omega^{-1}M^*U \text{ is scalar and} \\
&\qquad\qquad\qquad\qquad\qquad \text{therefore equal to its trace)} \\
&= E\operatorname{tr}(M^*UU'\Omega^{-1}) \quad \text{(since tr } AB = \operatorname{tr} BA\text{)} \\
&= \operatorname{tr}(M^*\sigma_u^2\Omega\Omega^{-1}) \quad \text{by Eq. (30)} \\
&= \sigma_u^2 \operatorname{tr} M^* \\
&= \sigma_u^2 \operatorname{tr}[I_T - X(X'\Omega^{-1}X)^{-1}X'\Omega^{-1}] \quad \text{by Eq. (35)} \\
&= \sigma_u^2 \operatorname{tr}(I_T) - \operatorname{tr}[(X'\Omega^{-1}X)^{-1}X'\Omega^{-1}X] \\
&= \sigma_u^2 \operatorname{tr}(I_T) - \operatorname{tr}(I_{K+1}) \\
&= \sigma_u^2(T - K - 1)
\end{aligned} \quad (37)$$

Hence the unbiased GLS estimate of the disturbance variance is obtained by

$$\sigma_u^2 = \hat{U}^{*'}\Omega^{-1}\hat{U}^*/(T - K - 1) \quad (38)$$

The results in this section establish that generalized least squares provides what is in theory the optimum solution to the problems created by autocorrelated disturbances. However, GLS presumes prior knowledge of the disturbance variance-covariance matrix Ω, and of course this is not in general available. It is important, therefore, to consider some common mechanisms that generate serial dependence in the disturbances of regression models so that the character of Ω can more readily be deduced from sample data.

[10] See Theil (1971, p. 239ff.).

SOME MODELS FOR TIME-DEPENDENT DISTURBANCES

We noted above that to employ GLS and thereby secure efficient, linear, unbiased estimates of B and $\text{var}(\hat{B})$ in models with serially correlated errors, the investigator must have information about the variance-covariance matrix Ω. However, it is not possible to determine the $[T \times (T + 1)]/2$ distinct elements of Ω in a "barefoot," empirical fashion. Therefore it is necessary to ascertain (from the residuals of preliminary OLS regressions) the process generating the time-dependence and thereby to characterize Ω in terms of a smaller number of parameters. This section considers—again at the theoretical level—some of the most typical processes: autoregressive and moving-average models. The following section then explores how the observed residuals can be "squeezed" to reveal the dependence process that is operative in a particular regression model in order that sample estimation of Ω can be undertaken.

First-Order Autoregressive Processes

The time-dependence model that has by far received the most attention in the econometric literature is the first-order autoregressive process [AR(1)].[11] Here each disturbance u_t depends only on its own previous value (the Markov property) and a random, "white noise" component. The basic model is as follows:

$$Y_t = \beta_0 + \sum_k \beta_k X_{tk} + u_t \quad \text{(equation to be estimated)} \quad (39)$$

$$u_t = \phi_1 u_{t-1} + v_t \quad \text{(disturbance time-dependence process)} \quad (40)$$

$$-1 < \phi_1 < 1 \quad \text{(stationarity condition)}^{12} \quad (41)$$

[11] Virtually all econometrics texts, and most experimental studies, focus on this model. An important exception is the literature on distributed lags, which I treat briefly later on. The attention given the AR(1) process probably stems from its mathematical-statistical tractability or perhaps from a widespread assumption that AR(1) disturbance processes prevail empirically. However, since alternative models are seldom entertained, the empirical regularity of AR(1) remains an open question. Apparently it is also widely believed in the econometric world that reliance on a "truncated" GLS estimator, that is, applying AR(1) even though a higher-order process may be operative, is superior to OLS in any case. This would seem to be false prima facie by simply staring at the Ω matrices that correspond to alternative time-dependence models. More convincing is a recent study by Engle (1973) which demonstrates that OLS dominates truncated GLS in some important cases. More analytic (and experimental) work along these lines is surely needed.

[12] Stationarity implies that the u_t vary about a fixed mean (in this case zero) with variance and autocovariances independent of time.

$$E(u_t) = E(\nu_t) = E(u_{t-\theta}\nu_t) = 0 \qquad \theta > 0$$
$$E(\nu_t\nu_{t\pm\theta}) = \sigma_\nu^2 \qquad\qquad\qquad \theta = 0 \Bigg\} \text{ for all } t \qquad (42)$$
$$\phantom{E(\nu_t\nu_{t\pm\theta})} = 0 \qquad\qquad\qquad \theta \neq 0$$

The variance of u_t in the AR(1) process is derived as follows:

$$\begin{aligned}\sigma_u^2 &= E(u_t^2) \\ &= E[(\phi_1 u_{t-1} + \nu_t)(\phi_1 u_{t-1} + \nu_t)] \\ &= \phi_1^2 E(u_{t-1}^2) + 2\phi_1 E(u_{t-1}\nu_t) + E(\nu_t^2)\end{aligned} \qquad (43)$$

By assumption (41) that the u_t follow a stationary stochastic process and therefore have identical variance for all t, and by assumption (42) that the lagged u_t are independent of the random ν_t components, the result in Eq. (43) becomes

$$\begin{aligned}\sigma_u^2 &= \phi_1^2 \sigma_u^2 + \sigma_\nu^2 \\ \sigma_u^2 - \phi_1^2 \sigma_u^2 &= \sigma_\nu^2 \\ \sigma_u^2(1 - \phi_1^2) &= \sigma_\nu^2 \\ \sigma_u^2 &= \sigma_\nu^2/(1 - \phi_1^2) = \gamma_0\end{aligned} \qquad (44)$$

where γ_0 denotes the variance of u. The autocovariance and autocorrelation function for the AR(1) model (denoted γ_θ and ρ_θ respectively) are similarly generated. Autocovariances are derived by multiplying through the expression for u_t [Eq. (40)] by lag $u_{t-\theta}$ and taking expectations. Hence the autocovariance of u_t and u_{t-1} is obtained:

$$\begin{aligned}\gamma_1 &= E[u_{t-1}(\phi_1 u_{t-1} + \nu_t)] \\ &= \phi_1 E(u_{t-1}^2) + E(u_{t-1}\nu_t) \\ &= \phi_1 \sigma_u^2 \qquad \text{by Eqs. (41) and (42)}\end{aligned} \qquad (45)$$

Parallel operations give the autocovariance of u_t and u_{t-2}:

$$\begin{aligned}\gamma_2 &= E[u_{t-2}(\phi_1 u_{t-1} + \nu_t)] \\ &= \phi_1 E(u_{t-2}u_{t-1}) + E(u_{t-2}\nu_t) \\ &= \phi_1 E(u_{t-2}u_{t-1}) \qquad \text{by Eq. (42)} \\ &= \phi_1 \gamma_1 \qquad\qquad\;\; \text{by Eq. (41)} \\ &= \phi_1^2 \sigma_u^2 \qquad\qquad \text{by Eq. (45)}\end{aligned} \qquad (46)$$

Successive operations of the same sort would show the general autocovariance function for a first-order autoregressive model to be

$$\begin{aligned}\gamma_\theta &= \phi_1^{|\theta|} \sigma_u^2 \\ &= \phi_1^{|\theta|} \gamma_0\end{aligned} \qquad (47)$$

It is now easy to derive the general autocorrelation function for

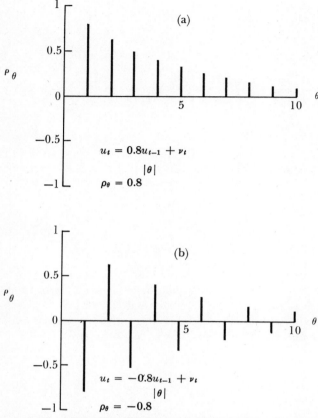

Figure 1. Theoretical Correlograms for AR(1) Disturbance Processes.

AR(1) processes. The (auto)correlation of u_t and $u_{t\pm\theta}$ is conventionally defined:

$$\rho_\theta = \frac{\text{cov}(u_t u_{t\pm\theta})}{\sqrt{\text{var } u_t}\sqrt{\text{var } u_{t\pm\theta}}} = \rho_{-\theta} \qquad (48)$$
$$= \gamma_\theta/\sigma_u^2 = \gamma_\theta/\gamma_0 \qquad \text{by Eq. (41)}$$

It now follows directly from Equation (47) that the lag autocorrelation function of the u_t is[13]

$$\rho_\theta = \phi_1^{|\theta|} \qquad (49)$$

[13] Note that in the AR(1) model the autoregressive parameter ϕ_1 equals the lag 1 autocorrelation coefficient ρ_1. Hence the autocorrelation function is sometimes written $\rho_\theta = \rho_1^{|\theta|}$. It is also easily verified that $\rho_\theta = \rho_{-\theta}$ and that $\gamma_\theta = \gamma_{-\theta}$.

Equation (49) is an important result because it describes (theoretically) the autocorrelation function when the disturbance is in fact generated by a first-order autoregressive mechanism. The correlograms in Figure 1, where θ (time lags) form the abscissa and ρ_θ (autocorrelation coefficients) form the ordinate, illustrate the AR(1) autocorrelation function for two hypothetical cases. Notice that when there is positive autoregression ($\phi_1 > 0$) the ρ_θ damp off smoothly and exponentially, whereas negative autoregression ($\phi_1 < 0$) produces oscillatory, exponential decay of successive ρ_θ. As we shall see in the next section, correlogram analysis plays a central role in identifying the time-dependence process characterizing the disturbances of a particular regression model.[14]

Before considering several other dependence processes to be introduced in this section, it is useful to pursue two diversions that build on the foregoing results and motivate (somewhat belatedly) the rather abstract discussion of autocorrelated disturbances and GLS estimation developed previously.

The Consequences of First-Order Autoregression

Simple regression models in which the disturbance and regressor follow a stationary, first-order autoregressive process have been thoroughly investigated by econometricians,[15] and it is worth relating some of the results to the theoretical material presented earlier. Consider, then, a bivariate regression model where both regressor and disturbance are stationary stochastic AR(1) processes:

$$y_t = \beta x_t + u_t \tag{50}$$

$$u_t = \phi_1 u_{t-1} + \nu_t \tag{51}$$

$$x_t = \lambda x_{t-1} + \omega_t \tag{52}$$

$$-1 < \phi_1 < 1 \tag{53}$$
$$-1 < \lambda < 1$$

where all variables are mean deviates.

Equation (21) established that the variance of the parameter vector $\hat{B}$ when disturbances are interdependent is

$$\text{var}(\hat{B}) = \sigma_u^2 (X'X)^{-1} X'\Omega X (X'X)^{-1} \tag{54}$$

---

[14] The topics developed here and in following sections by covariance analysis in the time domain may also be approached via spectral analysis in the frequency domain. See Dhrymes (1970, chap. 9–12), Durbin (1969), Fishman (1969), Granger (1964), Hannan (1960, 1970), Jenkins (1961), and Jenkins and Watts (1968).

[15] See especially Rao and Griliches (1969).

In the simple example of Equations (50) to (53) this general formula is closely approximated in large samples by[16]

$$\text{var}(\hat{\beta}) = \frac{\sigma_u^2}{\sum_t (x_t^2)} \left[\frac{1 + \phi_1 \lambda}{1 - \phi_1 \lambda}\right] \quad (55)$$

Ordinary least squares, however, routinely produces an estimate of the variance of $\hat{B}$ equal to

$$\text{var}(\hat{B}) = \hat{\sigma}_u^2 (X'X)^{-1} \quad [\text{see Eq. (15)}] \quad (56)$$

In the bivariate regression model, the OLS estimate of Equation (56) becomes

$$\text{var}(\hat{\beta}) = \hat{\sigma}_u^2 / \left[\sum_t (x_t^2)\right] \quad (57)$$

Comparison of the OLS estimate in Equation (57) to the true variance in Equation (55) shows clearly that the conjunction of positive or negative autocorrelation in regressor and disturbance (both are typically positive) produces a serious underestimation of var($\hat{\beta}$). For example, if $\phi_1 = \lambda = 0.8$ the bracketed ratio in Equation (55) would be

$$\frac{1 + 0.64}{1 - 0.64} = 4.56 \quad (58)$$

Hence OLS would underestimate the true variance of $\hat{\beta}$ by 456 percent and inflate the t-ratio by more than 200 percent.[17] It is easy to see, therefore, how one might erroneously conclude that a variable exerts significant causal influence if the model in question suffers from serially correlated errors and is estimated by ordinary least squares.

GLS as OLS after Transformation

This second diversion develops the specific matrix operations for the AR(1) model that are implied by the general expressions presented previously, and also illustrates how GLS estimation can be undertaken by OLS after simple transformation of variables.

Recall that our attention is confined to equations in which dis-

---

[16] Rao and Griliches (1969, appendix, eq. 1).

[17] Actually the inflation factor is even greater because $\hat{\sigma}_u^2$ underestimates the true error variance σ_u^2 [see Eqs. (24) and (27)]. However, this component of the bias becomes less significant as sample size gets large. Malinvaud (1970, p. 522) presents a table showing the bias factor for various combinations of ϕ_1 and λ that includes the contribution of $\hat{\sigma}_u^2$. Notice that when the independent variable is not autocorrelated the bias is small even if ϕ_1 is large.

turbances are serially correlated but not heteroscedastic. Hence:

$$E(UU') = \sigma_u^2 \Omega \tag{59}$$

such that $E(u_t u_{t\pm\theta}) = \sigma_u^2 \quad \theta = 0$
$\phantom{such that E(u_t u_{t\pm\theta})} = \gamma_\theta \quad \theta \neq 0$

Previously the autocorrelation function of the u_t in the AR(1) model was shown to be

$$\rho_\theta = \phi_1^{|\theta|} \qquad \text{[see Eq. (49)]} \tag{60}$$

The matrix expression for the disturbance interdependence represented by Eq. (59) therefore takes the form:

$$E(UU') = \sigma_u^2 \begin{bmatrix} 1 & \phi_1 & \phi_1^2 & \phi_1^3 & \cdot & \cdot & \cdot & \phi_1^{T-1} \\ \phi_1 & 1 & \phi_1 & \phi_1^2 & \cdot & \cdot & \cdot & \phi_1^{T-2} \\ \phi_1^2 & \phi_1 & 1 & \phi_1 & \cdot & \cdot & \cdot & \phi_1^{T-3} \\ \cdot & & & & & & & \cdot \\ \cdot & & & & & & & \cdot \\ \cdot & & & & & & & \cdot \\ \phi_1^{T-1} & \phi_1^{T-2} & \phi_1^{T-3} & \phi_1^{T-4} & \cdot & \cdot & \cdot & 1 \end{bmatrix} \tag{61}$$

$$(T \times T)$$

Equation (60) specifies the character of the matrix Ω; however, GLS estimation requires Ω^{-1}. Recall:

$$\hat{B}^* = (X'\Omega^{-1}X)^{-1}X'\Omega^{-1}Y \qquad \text{[see Eq. (32)]} \tag{62}$$

and $\quad \text{var}(\hat{B}^*) = \sigma_u^2 (X'\Omega^{-1}X)^{-1} \qquad \text{[see Eq. (34)]} \tag{63}$

It is readily verified that Ω^{-1} is

$$\Omega^{-1} = 1/(1-\phi_1^2) \begin{bmatrix} 1 & -\phi_1 & 0 & \cdot & \cdot & \cdot & 0 & 0 \\ -\phi_1 & 1+\phi_1^2 & -\phi_1 & \cdot & \cdot & \cdot & 0 & 0 \\ 0 & -\phi_1 & 1+\phi_1^2 & \cdot & \cdot & \cdot & 0 & 0 \\ \cdot & & & & & & & \cdot \\ \cdot & & & & & & & \cdot \\ \cdot & & & & & & & \cdot \\ 0 & 0 & 0 & \cdot & \cdot & \cdot & 1+\phi_1^2 & -\phi_1 \\ 0 & 0 & 0 & \cdot & \cdot & \cdot & -\phi_1 & 1 \end{bmatrix} \tag{64}$$

$$(T \times T)$$

The minimum-variance, linear-unbiased GLS estimates of B and $\text{var}(\hat{B})$ can now be secured by inserting Ω^{-1} into Eqs. (62) and (63). However, this is rather cumbersome for the nonprogramer who does not have access to a computer package that performs matrix operations. It is in practice more convenient, therefore, to find a nonsingular transformation matrix, say A, such that:

$$A'A = \Omega^{-1}$$
$$A\Omega A' = I \qquad (65)$$

GLS estimation may then be achieved by applying OLS to the original model after premultiplication by A.[18] That is, if the equation to be estimated is premultiplied by A, such that $AY = AXB + AU$, then OLS applied to the transformed variables—$Y^* = AY$, $X^* = AX$, and $U^* = AU$—is equivalent to GLS.

Consider the case of the OLS estimator of B in the transformed data:

$$\begin{aligned}\hat{B}_{\text{OLS}} &= (X^{*\prime}X^*)^{-1}X^{*\prime}Y^* \qquad [\text{see Eq. (9)}] \\ &= [(AX)'AX]^{-1}(AX)'AY \\ &= [X'(A'A)X]^{-1}X'(A'A)Y \\ &= (X'\Omega^{-1}X)^{-1}X'\Omega^{-1}Y = \hat{B}^*_{\text{GLS}} \qquad \text{by Eq. (65)}\end{aligned} \qquad (66)$$

The equivalence can easily be shown to hold for $\text{var}(\hat{B})$ as well. Thus OLS regression of the transformed observations Y^* and X^* amounts to GLS. The disturbances of the transformed model now of course satisfy the classical assumptions:

$$\begin{aligned}E(U^*U^{*\prime}) &= E(AUU'A') \\ &= A\sigma_u^2\Omega A' \\ &= \sigma_u^2 A\Omega A' \\ &= \sigma_u^2 I \qquad \text{by Eq. (65)}\end{aligned} \qquad (67)$$

If the disturbance autocorrelation is generated by a first-order autoregressive process and Ω is therefore characterized by Eq. (61), the transformation matrix A is well known to be[19]

$$A = 1/\sqrt{1-\phi_1^2} \begin{bmatrix} \sqrt{1-\phi_1^2} & 0 & 0 & \cdot & \cdot & \cdot & 0 & 0 \\ -\phi_1 & 1 & 0 & \cdot & \cdot & \cdot & 0 & 0 \\ 0 & -\phi_1 & 1 & \cdot & \cdot & \cdot & 0 & 0 \\ & & & \cdot & & & & \\ & & & \cdot & & & & \\ & & & \cdot & & & & \\ 0 & 0 & 0 & \cdot & \cdot & \cdot & 1 & 0 \\ 0 & 0 & 0 & \cdot & \cdot & \cdot & -\phi_1 & 1 \end{bmatrix} \qquad (68)$$

$(T \times T)$

[18] A theorem in matrix algebra ensures that a matrix A with the properties of (65) exists for positive definite Ω. See Hadley (1961, chap. 7).

[19] See Theil (1971, p. 253).

Execution of the matrix multiplications $Y^* = AY$ and $X^* = AX$ confirms that the transformed variables are constructed as follows:[20]

$$\begin{aligned}
Y_1^* &= \sqrt{1 - \phi_1^2}\, Y_1 & t &= 1 \\
Y_t^* &= Y_t - \phi_1 Y_{t-1} & t &= 2 \ldots T \\
X_{k1}^* &= \sqrt{1 - \phi_1^2}\, X_{k1} & t &= 1; k = 1 \ldots K \\
X_{kt}^* &= X_{kt} - \phi_1 X_{kt-1} & t &= 2 \ldots T; k = 1 \ldots K
\end{aligned} \tag{69}$$

When Y_t^* is regressed on the X_{kt}^* it is clear from Equation (67) that the errors also are (implicitly) transformed:

$$u_t^* = u_t - \phi_1 u_{t-1} \qquad t = 2 \ldots T \tag{70}$$

Since the u_t are assumed to follow an AR(1) mechanism it is apparent that the errors of the revised model are

$$\begin{aligned}
u_t^* &= \phi_1 u_{t-1} + v_t - \phi_1 u_{t-1} \\
u_t^* &= v_t
\end{aligned} \tag{71}$$

Recall that the v_t are independent random variables and so the revised model satisfies the classical assumptions.[21] Therefore ordinary least-squares regression performed on the transformed variables Y_t^* and X_{tk}^* is equivalent to generalized least squares and yields minimum-variance, linear-unbiased estimates of B and $\mathrm{var}(\hat{B})$.

Second- and Higher-Order Autoregressive Processes

Although AR(1) processes have received the most attention in the literature, there is no reason to expect a priori that autocorrelation of disturbances in time-series regression models will be generated by such a simple, albeit appealing, mechanism. It is probably accurate to say,

---

[20] The scalar $1/\sqrt{1 - \phi_1^2}$ affects all elements of the transformed disturbance variance-covariance matrix equally and is therefore disregarded.

[21] Notice that this means the residual variance of the transformed model estimates σ_v^2 rather than σ_u^2. If we retained the scalar $1/\sqrt{1 - \phi_1^2}$ when applying the transformation matrix A to the raw data, then an estimate of σ_u^2 would be secured. That is,

$$\begin{aligned}
u_t^* &= \phi_1 u_{t-1} + v_t - \phi_1 u_{t-1}/\sqrt{1 - \phi_1^2} \\
u_t^* &= v_t/\sqrt{1 - \phi_1^2}
\end{aligned}$$

which has variance $\sigma_{u_t^*}^2 = \sigma_{v_t}^2/(1 - \phi_1^2) = \sigma_u^2$ [see Eq. (44)]. Since GLS computer algorithms typically disregard such scalars the estimates of error variance and regression standard error are not comparable to the corresponding OLS statistics (see the empirical examples in the following sections). An informed discussion of the problems with commonly used GLS goodness-of-fit statistics is provided by Buse (1973). I am grateful to G. Markus for raising this issue.

however, that autoregressive processes of order higher than two are relatively uncommon—unless the data have cyclical or seasonal variability, in which case appropriate dummy variables should appear in the model.

Consider, then, a regression model where the disturbance follows a second-order autoregressive scheme (AR(2)] such that u_t depends on u_{t-1}, u_{t-2} and a random perturbation:

$$Y_t = \beta_0 + \sum_k \beta_k X_{tk} + u_t \quad \text{(equation to be estimated)} \tag{72}$$

$$u_t = \phi_1 u_{t-1} + \phi_2 u_{t-2} + \nu_t \quad \text{(disturbance time-dependence process)} \tag{73}$$

$$\left.\begin{array}{l} \phi_2 + \phi_1 < 1 \\ \phi_2 - \phi_1 < 1 \\ -1 < \phi_2 < 1 \end{array}\right\} \text{(stationarity conditions)} \tag{74}$$

$$\left.\begin{array}{l} E(u_t) = E(\nu_t) = E(u_{t-\theta}\nu_t) = 0 \quad \theta > 0 \\ E(\nu_t \nu_{t\pm\theta}) = \sigma_\nu^2 \qquad\qquad\qquad\quad \theta = 0 \\ \qquad\quad\; = 0 \qquad\qquad\qquad\qquad \theta \neq 0 \end{array}\right\} \text{for all } t \tag{75}$$

The variance of u_t in the AR(2) model is conveniently derived as follows:

$$\begin{aligned} \sigma_u^2 &= E(u_t)^2 \\ &= E[u_t(\phi_1 u_{t-1} + \phi_2 u_{t-2} + \nu_t)] \quad \text{by Eq. (73)} \\ &= \phi_1 \gamma_1 + \phi_2 \gamma_2 + \sigma_\nu^2 \quad \text{(since the only part of } u_t \text{ correlated with } \nu_t \text{ is the current perturbation } \nu_t) \end{aligned} \tag{76}$$

Dividing Eq. (76) by σ_u^2 allows the variance of the process to be expressed in terms of ϕs, ρs, and σ_ν^2:

$$\begin{aligned} \sigma_u^2/\sigma_u^2 &= \phi_1 \rho_1 + \phi_2 \rho_2 + \sigma_\nu^2/\sigma_u^2 \quad \text{by Eq. (48)} \\ 1 - \phi_1 \rho_1 - \phi_2 \rho_2 &= \sigma_\nu^2/\sigma_u^2 \\ \sigma_u^2 &= \sigma_\nu^2/(1 - \phi_1 \rho_1 - \phi_2 \rho_2) = \gamma_0 \end{aligned} \tag{77}$$

The autocovariance and autocorrelation functions are generated analogously by multiplying the equation for u_t through by $u_{t\pm\theta}$ and taking expectations. Accordingly the autocovariance of u_t and u_{t-1} is

$$\begin{aligned} \gamma_1 &= E[u_{t-1}(\phi_1 u_{t-1} + \phi_2 u_{t-2} + \nu_t)] \\ &= \phi_1 E(u_{t-1}^2) + \phi_2 E(u_{t-1} u_{t-2}) + E(u_{t-1}\nu_t) \\ &= \phi_1 \sigma_u^2 + \phi_2 \gamma_1 \quad \text{by Eqs. (74) and (75)} \end{aligned} \tag{78}$$

Similarly the autocovariance of u_t and u_{t-2} is derived:

$$\begin{aligned} \gamma_2 &= E[u_{t-2}(\phi_1 u_{t-1} + \phi_2 u_{t-2} + \nu_t)] \\ &= \phi_1 E(u_{t-2} u_{t-1}) + \phi_2 E(u_{t-2}^2) + E(u_{t-2}\nu_t) \\ &= \phi_1 \gamma_1 + \phi_2 \sigma_u^2 \quad \text{by Eqs. (74) and (75)} \end{aligned} \tag{79}$$

Recalling that γ_0 denotes σ_u^2, successive operations would show the autocovariance function of the second-order autoregressive process to be

$$\gamma_\theta = \phi_1\gamma_{\theta-1} + \phi_2\gamma_{\theta-2} \quad \theta > 0 \tag{80}$$

The autocorrelation function for this model follows straightforwardly. Recall that ρ_θ is defined as follows:

$$\rho_\theta = \gamma_\theta/\sigma_u^2 = \gamma_\theta/\gamma_0 \tag{81}$$

Hence we need only divide the autocovariance function in Eq. (80) by γ_0 to obtain the AR(2) autocorrelation function:

$$\begin{aligned}\rho_\theta &= (\phi_1\gamma_{\theta-1} + \phi_2\gamma_{\theta-2})/\gamma_0 \\ \rho_\theta &= \phi_1\rho_{\theta-1} + \phi_2\rho_{\theta-2} \quad \theta > 0\end{aligned} \tag{82}$$

Again our interest centers primarily on the autocorrelation function[22] because it specifies the behavior of the ρ_θ when the disturbances in a particular equation do indeed follow an AR(2) process. Figure 2 depicts hypothetical correlograms for various combinations of the parameters ϕ_1 and ϕ_2. Note how these correlograms contrast with the autocorrelation functions of AR(1) processes illustrated in Figure 1.

Autoregressive processes of order greater than two are likely to be less common empirically, but are worth introducing briefly. The essentials involve minor extensions of previous results. Here the disturbance is generated by a pth-order autoregressive scheme:

$$u_t = \phi_1 u_{t-1} + \phi_2 u_{t-2} + \cdots + \phi_p u_{t-p} + \nu_t \tag{83}$$

The variance of u_t is easily shown to be

$$\sigma_u^2 = \frac{\sigma_\nu^2}{1 - \rho_1\phi_1 - \rho_2\phi_2 - \cdots - \rho_p\phi_p} \tag{84}$$

The autocovariance function is

$$\gamma_\theta = \phi_1\gamma_{\theta-1} + \phi_2\gamma_{\theta-2} + \cdots + \phi_p\gamma_{\theta-p} \quad \theta > 0 \tag{85}$$

Finally the autocorrelation function of a pth-order autoregressive model is given by

$$\rho_\theta = \phi_1\rho_{\theta-1} + \phi_2\rho_{\theta-2} + \cdots + \phi_p\rho_{\theta-p} \quad \theta > 0 \tag{86}$$

These general expressions, and in particular Eq. (86), can be used to deduce the empirical behavior of disturbances generated by an auto-

---

[22] Note that Eq. (82) yields $\phi_1\rho_0 + \phi_2\rho_{-1}$ as the expression for ρ_1. Since $\rho_0 = 1$ and $\rho_{-\theta} = \rho_\theta$, this becomes $\rho_1 = \phi_1 + \phi_2\rho_1$. Hence ρ_1, the starting point of the AR(2) autocorrelation function, may be written as: $\rho_1 = \phi_1/(1 - \phi_2)$.

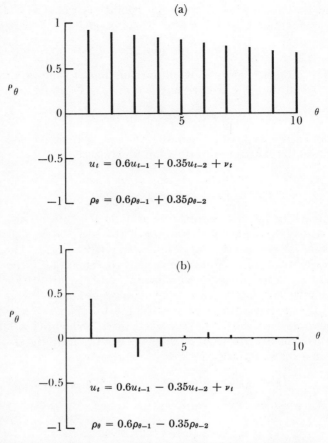

Figure 2. Theoretical Correlograms for AR(2) Disturbance Processes.

regressive process of any order. We pursue this further after considering moving average models.

First-Order Moving Average Processes

An alternative class of models for time-dependent disturbances is provided by moving average processes. In contrast to autoregressive models, disturbances generated by moving-average schemes depend only on a moving linear combination of random variables v_t with coefficients $(1, -\phi_1, \ldots, -\phi_p)$. Hence a random shock v_t enters the system at time t and disturbs the equilibrium level of u_t for $(p+1)$ periods before dissipation. The autocorrelation functions and correlograms produced by moving-average processes therefore differ sharply from those of autoregressive models.

In the first-order moving-average process [MA(1)] we have

$$Y_t = \beta_0 + \sum_k \beta_k X_{tk} + u_t \quad \text{(equation to be estimated)} \tag{87}$$

$$u_t = \nu_t - \phi_1 \nu_{t-1} \quad \text{(disturbance time-dependence process)} \tag{88}$$

$$-1 < \phi_1 < 1 \quad \text{(invertibility condition)}[23] \tag{89}$$

$$\begin{aligned} E(u_t) = E(\nu_t) = E(u_{t-\theta}\nu_t) &= 0 \\ E(\nu_t \nu_{t \pm \theta}) = \sigma_\nu^2 \quad \theta = 0 \quad \theta > 0 & \\ = 0 \quad \theta \neq 0 & \end{aligned} \bigg\} \text{for all } t \tag{90}$$

The variance of the first-order moving-average model may be derived as follows:

$$\begin{aligned} \sigma_u^2 &= E(u_t^2) \\ &= E[(\nu_t - \phi_1 \nu_{t-1})(\nu_t - \phi_1 \nu_{t-1})] \\ &= E(\nu_t^2) - 2\phi_1 E(\nu_{t-1}\nu_t) + \phi_1^2 E(\nu_{t-1}^2) \\ &= \sigma_\nu^2 + \phi_1^2 \sigma_\nu^2 \quad \text{by Eq. (90)} \\ \sigma_u^2 &= \sigma_\nu^2(1 + \phi_1^2) = \gamma_0 \end{aligned} \tag{91}$$

The MA(1) autocovariance function is similarly generated. Thus the autocovariance of u_t and u_{t-1} is

$$\begin{aligned} \gamma_1 &= E(u_t u_{t-1}) \\ &= E[(\nu_t - \phi_1 \nu_{t-1})(\nu_{t-1} - \phi_1 \nu_{t-2})] \\ &= E(\nu_t \nu_{t-1}) - \phi_1 E(\nu_t \nu_{t-2}) - \phi_1 E(\nu_{t-1}^2) + \phi_1^2 E(\nu_{t-1}\nu_{t-2}) \\ &= -\phi_1 \sigma_\nu^2 \quad \text{by Eq. (90)} \end{aligned} \tag{92}$$

Parallel operations yield autocovariances of greater lag. For example, γ_2 is obtained:

$$\begin{aligned} \gamma_2 &= E(u_t u_{t-2}) \\ &= E[(\nu_t - \phi_1 \nu_{t-1})(\nu_{t-2} - \phi_1 \nu_{t-3})] \\ &= E(\nu_t \nu_{t-2}) - \phi_1 E(\nu_t \nu_{t-3}) - \phi_1 E(\nu_{t-1}\nu_{t-2}) + \phi_1^2 E(\nu_{t-1}\nu_{t-3}) \\ &= 0 \quad \text{by Eq. (90)} \end{aligned} \tag{93}$$

It should now be apparent that in first-order moving-average processes all autocovariances beyond lag 1 are zero. Thus the general autocovariance function for the MA(1) model is written:

$$\begin{aligned} \gamma_\theta &= -\phi_1 \sigma_\nu^2 \quad \theta = \pm 1 \\ &= 0 \quad |\theta| > 1 \end{aligned} \tag{94}$$

[23] The invertibility conditions for moving-average processes parallel the stationarity conditions of autoregressive models by defining the admissible region for the parameters ϕ_1. See Box and Jenkins (1970, chap. 3.3).

Obviously the autocorrelation function of the MA(1) process, defined by $\rho_\theta = \gamma_\theta/\gamma_0$, shares the same property. Thus

$$\rho_1 = \frac{\gamma_1}{\gamma_0} = \frac{-\phi_1 \sigma_\nu^2}{(1+\phi_1^2)\sigma_\nu^2} = \frac{-\phi_1}{(1+\phi_1^2)}$$

and successive lag ρ_θ are zero. Therefore the general autocorrelation functron is expressed:

$$\begin{aligned}\rho_\theta &= -\phi_1/(1+\phi_1^2) & \theta &= \pm 1 \\ &= 0 & |\theta| &> 1\end{aligned} \quad (95)$$

The results in Eqs. (94) and (95) establish that the autocovariances and autocorrelations of the first-order moving-average process have a cutoff after lag 1. This produces a correlogram (see Figure 3) that is readily distinguished from the dampoff of the AR(1) correlogram

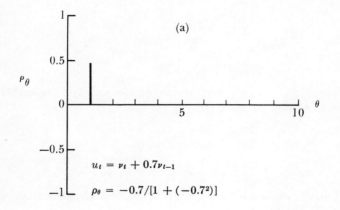

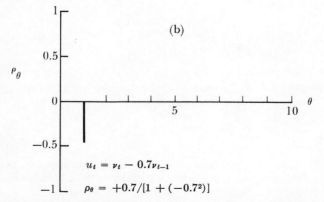

Figure 3. Theoretical correlograms for MA(1) disturbance processes.

(Figure 1)[24] and the decay pattern of AR(2)–AR(p) correlograms (Figure 2).

Second- and Higher-Order Moving-Average Processes

This discussion of second- and higher-order moving-average processes is brief since the essential results follow straightforwardly from those developed above. Consider, then, a regression model where the disturbance follows a second-order moving-average scheme [MA(2)]:

$$Y_t = \beta_0 + \sum_k \beta_k X_{tk} + u_t \quad \text{(equation to be estimated)} \quad (96)$$

$$u_t = \nu_t - \phi_1 \nu_{t-1} - \phi_2 \nu_{t-2} \quad \text{(disturbance time-dependence process)} \quad (97)$$

$$\begin{aligned}\phi_2 + \phi_1 &< 1 \\ \phi_2 - \phi_1 &< 1 \quad \text{(invertibility conditions)} \\ -1 &< \phi_2 < 1\end{aligned} \quad (98)$$

$$\left.\begin{aligned}E(u_t) &= u_{t-\theta}\nu_t = 0 \\ E(\nu_t \nu_{t\pm\theta}) &= \sigma_\nu^2 \quad &\theta > 0 \\ &= 0 \quad &\theta \neq 0\end{aligned}\right\} \text{for all } t \quad (99)$$

The variance of the MA(2) model is

$$\begin{aligned}\sigma_u^2 &= E(u_t^2) \\ &= E[(\nu_t - \phi_1\nu_{t-1} - \phi_2\nu_{t-2})(\nu_t - \phi_1\nu_{t-1} - \phi_2\nu_{t-2})] \\ &= E(\nu_t^2) - 2\phi_1 E(\nu_t\nu_{t-1}) - 2\phi_2 E(\nu_t\nu_{t-2}) \\ &\quad + 2\phi_1\phi_2 E(\nu_{t-1}\nu_{t-2}) + \phi_1^2 E(\nu_{t-1}^2) \\ &\quad + \phi_2^2 E(\nu_{t-2}^2) \\ &= \sigma_\nu^2 + \phi_1^2\sigma_\nu^2 + \phi_2^2\sigma_\nu^2 \quad \text{by Eq. (99)} \\ \sigma_u^2 &= \sigma_\nu^2(1 + \phi_1^2 + \phi_2^2) = \gamma_0\end{aligned} \quad (100)$$

[24] Similarly the MA(1) Ω matrix contrasts sharply with that of the AR(1) model [see Eq. (61)]:

$$E(UU') = \sigma_u^2 \begin{bmatrix} 1 & \dfrac{-\phi_1}{1+\phi_1^2} & 0 & \cdots & 0 \\ \dfrac{-\phi_1}{1+\phi_1^2} & 1 & \dfrac{-\phi_1}{1+\phi_1^2} & \cdots & 0 \\ \cdot & & & & \cdot \\ \cdot & & & & \cdot \\ \cdot & & & & \cdot \\ 0 & 0 & 0 & \cdots & 1 \end{bmatrix}$$

$$(T \times T)$$

The autocovariance function is derived analogously:

$$\begin{aligned}
\gamma_1 &= E(u_t u_{t-1}) \\
&= E[(\nu_t - \phi_1 \nu_{t-1} - \phi_2 \nu_{t-2})(\nu_{t-1} - \phi_1 \nu_{t-2} - \phi_2 \nu_{t-3})] \\
&= E(\nu_t \nu_{t-1}) - \phi_1 E(\nu_t \nu_{t-2}) - \phi_2 E(\nu_t \nu_{t-3}) \\
&\quad - \phi_1 E(\nu_{t-1}^2) + \phi_1^2 E(\nu_{t-1} \nu_{t-2}) \\
&\quad + \phi_1 \phi_2 E(\nu_{t-1} \nu_{t-3}) - \phi_2 E(\nu_{t-2} \nu_{t-1}) \\
&\quad + \phi_1 \phi_2 E(\nu_{t-2}^2) + \phi_2^2 E(\nu_{t-2} \nu_{t-3}) \\
&= (-\phi_1 + \phi_1 \phi_2) \sigma_\nu^2 \quad \text{by Eq. (99)}
\end{aligned} \quad (101)$$

$$\begin{aligned}
\gamma_2 &= E(u_t u_{t-2}) \\
&= E[(\nu_t - \phi_1 \nu_{t-1} - \phi_2 \nu_{t-2})(\nu_{t-2} - \phi_1 \nu_{t-3} - \phi_2 \nu_{t-4})] \\
&= E(\nu_t \nu_{t-2}) - \phi_1 E(\nu_t \nu_{t-3}) - \phi_2 E(\nu_t \nu_{t-4}) \\
&\quad - \phi_1 E(\nu_{t-1} \nu_{t-2}) + \phi_1^2 E(\nu_{t-1} \nu_{t-3}) + \phi_1 \phi_2 E(\nu_{t-1} \nu_{t-4}) \\
&\quad - \phi_2 E(\nu_{t-2}^2) + \phi_2 \phi_1 E(\nu_{t-2} \nu_{t-3}) + \phi_2^2 E(\nu_{t-2} \nu_{t-4}) \\
&= -\phi_2 \sigma_\nu^2 \quad \text{by Eq. (99)}
\end{aligned} \quad (102)$$

$$\begin{aligned}
\gamma_3 &= E(u_t u_{t-3}) \\
&= E[(\nu_t - \phi_1 \nu_{t-1} - \phi_2 \nu_{t-2})(\nu_{t-3} - \phi_1 \nu_{t-4} - \phi_2 \nu_{t-5})] \\
&= E(\nu_t \nu_{t-3}) - \phi_1 E(\nu_t \nu_{t-4}) - \phi_2 E(\nu_t \nu_{t-5}) \\
&\quad - \phi_1 E(\nu_{t-1} \nu_{t-3}) + \phi_1^2 E(\nu_{t-1} \nu_{t-4}) + \phi_1 \phi_2 E(\nu_{t-1} \nu_{t-5}) \\
&\quad - \phi_2 E(\nu_{t-2} \nu_{t-3}) + \phi_2 \phi_1 E(\nu_{t-2} \nu_{t-4}) + \phi_2^2 E(\nu_{t-2} \nu_{t-5}) \\
&= 0 \quad \text{by Eq. (99)}
\end{aligned} \quad (103)$$

In generalized notation, the autocovariance function for the second-order moving-average process is therefore:

$$\begin{aligned}
\gamma_\theta &= (-\phi_\theta + \phi_1 \phi_{\theta+1}) \sigma_\nu^2 \quad \theta = \pm 1, 2 \\
&= 0 \quad \theta > \pm 2
\end{aligned} \quad (104)$$

Since $\rho_\theta = \gamma_\theta / \gamma_0$, the general autocorrelation function for the MA(2) mechanism follows directly:

$$\begin{aligned}
\rho_\theta &= \frac{(-\phi_\theta + \phi_1 \phi_{\theta+1}) \sigma_\nu^2}{(1 + \phi_1^2 + \phi_2^2) \sigma_\nu^2} \quad \theta = \pm 1, 2 \\
\rho_\theta &= \frac{-\phi_\theta + \phi_1 \phi_{\theta+1}}{1 + \phi_1^2 + \phi_2^2} \quad \theta = \pm 1, 2 \\
&= 0 \quad |\theta| > 2
\end{aligned} \quad (105)$$

Hence in the second-order moving-average process the autocovariance and autocorrelation functions are zero after lag 2. The corresponding correlograms (see Figure 4) are therefore easily differentiated from those of autoregressive processes and lower (or higher) order moving-average processes. Moreover, moving-average models of higher order [MA(p)] have analogous properties; that is, autocovariances and autocorrelations exhibit a cutoff beyond lag p.

PROBLEMS OF STATISTICAL ESTIMATION AND CAUSAL INFERENCE

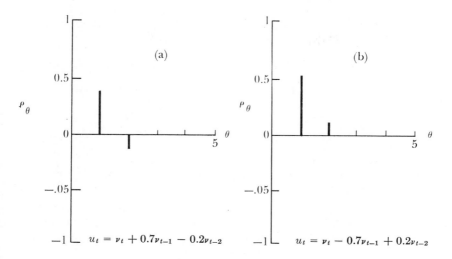

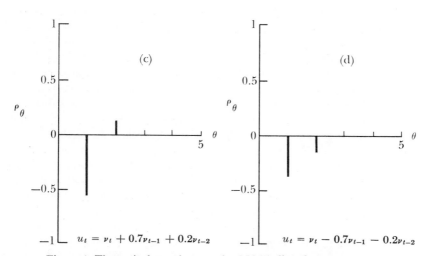

Figure 4. Theoretical correlograms for MA(2) disturbance processes.

Briefly, in the pth-order moving-average process we have

$$u_t = v_t - \phi_1 v_{t-1} - \phi_2 v_{t-2} - \cdots - \phi_p v_{t-p} \tag{106}$$

The u_t in this model have variance

$$\sigma_u^2 = \sigma_v^2(1 + \phi_1^2 + \phi_2^2 + \cdots + \phi_p^2) = \gamma_0 \tag{107}$$

and autocovariance

$$\gamma_\theta = (-\phi_\theta + \phi_1\phi_{\theta+1} + \phi_2\phi_{\theta+2} + \cdots + \phi_{p-\theta}\phi_p)\sigma_\nu^2 \quad \theta = \pm 1, 2, \ldots, p$$
$$= 0 \quad |\theta| > p \quad (108)$$

Finally, and most importantly, the autocorrelation function of the $\mathrm{MA}(p)$ process is

$$\rho_\theta = \frac{-\phi_\theta + \phi_1\phi_{\theta+1} + \cdots + \phi_{p-\theta}\phi_p}{1 + \phi_1^2 + \cdots + \phi_p^2} \quad \theta = \pm 1, 2, \ldots, p$$
$$= 0 \quad |\theta| > p \quad (109)$$

Like higher-order autoregressive models, moving-average processes of order greater than two are likely to be rare in practice, although just how rare is essentially an empirical question.

INFORMATION ABOUT Ω: CORRELOGRAM ANALYSIS AND PSEUDO-GENERALIZED LEAST SQUARES ESTIMATION

Previous results established that generalized least squares is the optimum method to estimate regression models with autocorrelated disturbances. However, GLS requires knowledge of the disturbance variance-covariance matrix Ω whose $[T \times (T+1)]/2$ distinct elements can be ascertained only if the disturbance interdependence is generated by a known process. This issue led to our examination of some empirically common, mathematically tractable models for time-dependent disturbances. After deriving the variance, autocovariance, and autocorrelation functions of these models, we indicated that correlogram analysis is an effective way to deduce the time-dependence process characterizing the disturbances of a particular regression equation. Hence, given an equation that (the researcher suspects) suffers from serially correlated errors, the magnitude and the form of the interdependence can be determined by undertaking a preliminary OLS regression, retrieving the residuals, and generating the empirical correlogram. The empirical correlogram should then be compared to the theoretical correlograms of potentially appropriate models $[\mathrm{AR}(p), \mathrm{MA}(p)]$ so that an informed specification of a process can be made. The corresponding Ω, Ω^{-1} matrices and/or the appropriate transformation matrix (earlier denoted A) are then straightforwardly estimated and (pseudo) GLS estimates secured.

Theoretical and Empirical Correlograms

The efficacy of the procedure outlined above hinges in large part on the comparison of empirical to theoretical correlograms, which in practice determines the time-dependence process that is chosen. Consider first autoregressive processes. Recall that the general autocorrelation function is given by

$$\rho_\theta = \phi_1 \rho_{\theta-1} + \phi_2 \rho_{\theta-2} + \cdots + \phi_p \rho_{\theta-p} \qquad \theta > 0 \qquad [\text{see Eq. (86)}] \qquad (110)$$

Hence in the AR(1) case, where $u_t = \phi_1 u_{t-1} + \nu_t$, we have

$$\rho_\theta = \phi_1 \rho_{\theta-1} \qquad (111)$$

Since $\rho_1 = \phi_1$ in this process, Equation (111) may be written

$$\rho_\theta = \phi_1^{|\theta|} \qquad [\text{see Eq. (49)}] \qquad (112)$$

For AR(2) models, where $u_t = \phi_1 u_{t-1} + \phi_2 u_{t-2} + \nu_t$, the autocorrela- function is

$$\rho_\theta = \phi_1 \rho_{\theta-1} + \phi_2 \rho_{\theta-2} \qquad [\text{see Eq. (82)}] \qquad (113)$$

Let ρ_θ^* denote the theoretical autocorrelations and $\hat{\rho}_\theta$ denote the corresponding empirical autocorrelations. In the context of a particular regression equation the ρ_θ^* for the AR(1) model are therefore obtained by regressing $\hat{u}_t$ on $\hat{u}_{t-1}$ (OLS residuals) to secure a sample estimate of ϕ_1, and then calculating iteratively $\rho_2^*, \rho_3^*, \ldots, \rho_\theta^*$:

$$\rho_\theta^* = \hat{\phi}_1^{|\theta|} \qquad (114)$$

The ρ_θ^* of the AR(2) process are obtained analogously. First secure sample estimates of ϕ_1 and ϕ_2 from the OLS residuals by regressing $\hat{u}_t$ on $\hat{u}_{t-1}$ and $\hat{u}_{t-2}$. The ρ_θ^* are then generated recursively:

$$\rho_\theta^* = \hat{\phi}_1 \rho_{\theta-1}^* + \hat{\phi}_2 \rho_{\theta-2}^* \qquad (115)$$

where $\rho_1^* = \hat{\phi}_1/(1 - \hat{\phi}_2)$ (see footnote 22). Similar operations yield the theoretical autocorrelations for higher-order autoregressive models. The ρ_θ^* derived by this procedure are theoretical in the sense that empirical-sample data are used only to estimate the parameters of $\phi_1 \ldots \phi_p$. Thereafter the ρ_θ^* are determined entirely by the (theoretical) autocorrelation function of the time-dependence process being considered.

Derivation of the theoretical autocorrelations for moving-average processes are more problematic. Recall that the general MA(p) autocorrelation function is

$$\rho_\theta = \frac{-\phi_\theta + \phi_1 \phi_{\theta+1} + \cdots + \phi_{p-\theta}\phi_p}{1 + \phi_1^2 + \phi_2^2 + \cdots + \phi_p^2} \qquad \theta = \pm 1, 2, \ldots, p$$
$$= 0 \qquad\qquad\qquad\qquad\qquad |\theta| > p \qquad (116)$$

Unlike the situation in the analysis of autoregressive models, the parameters ϕ_p of moving-average processes cannot be estimated by direct least squares from the OLS residuals $\hat{u}_t$. Nor can they be derived linearly from the empirical $\hat{\rho}_\theta$ (except in the simplest case where $p = 1$). Hence the theoretical ρ_θ^* are not readily generated prior to selection of a model. We do know, however, that the theoretical autocorrelation function exhibits a cutoff where $\theta > p$ (see Figures 3 and 4), so moving-average schemes generally can be identified from the empirical correlogram without formal comparison to the theoretical autocorrelation function.[25]

The empirical autocorrelations are of course obtained simply by computing successive $\hat{\rho}_\theta$ from the OLS residuals $\hat{u}_t$. That is, $\hat{\rho}_1$ equals the correlation of $\hat{u}_t$ and $\hat{u}_{t-1}$; $\hat{\rho}_2$ equals the correlation of $\hat{u}_t$ and $\hat{u}_{t-2}$; and so on. However, the observed residuals do not perfectly reflect the theoretical disturbances, and therefore one cannot expect perfect congruence between the empirical correlogram and that of the underlying theoretical process. Residuals, and hence empirical autocorrelations, are "noisy," and the noise tends to predominate as the lag increases and the true ρ_θ cutoff or dampoff. As Box and Jenkins put it: "Moderately large estimated autocorrelations can occur after the theoretical autocorrelation function has damped out, and apparent ripples and trends can occur in the estimated [empirical] function which have no basis in the theoretical function. In employing the estimated autocorrelation function as a tool for identification [model selection], it is usually possible to be fairly sure about broad characteristics, but more subtle indications may or may not represent real effects, and two or more related models may need to be entertained and investigated further at the estimation and diagnostic checking stages of model building."[26] We must anticipate, therefore, less than perfect correspondence between empirical and theoretical autocorrelations, and as a practical rule should compute and analyze no more than $T/5$ or $T/4$ $\hat{\rho}_\theta$ (where T = sample size).

Since the noise in the empirical autocorrelations prevails as θ increases, it is useful when comparing empirical to theoretical correlograms to know whether large lag $\hat{\rho}_\theta$ are effectively zero. Following Bartlett (1946) the standard deviation of large lag $\hat{\rho}_\theta$ is closely approximated by

$$\hat{\sigma}_{\hat{\rho}_\theta} = 1/T^{1/2} [1 + 2(\hat{\rho}_1^2 + \hat{\rho}_2^2 + \cdots + \hat{\rho}_p^2)]^{1/2} \qquad \theta > p \qquad (117)$$

where p is the lag beyond which the process is deemed to have "died out."

For moderate sample sizes, R. L. Anderson (1942) has shown that the distribution of $\hat{\rho}_\theta$, whose corresponding population value is zero, is very nearly normal. Hence the researcher can determine whether the

---

[25] It is sometimes difficult, however, to distinguish moving-average processes from autoregressive models that damp off quickly. See Hannan (1960, pp. 41ff.) and the ensuing discussion in this chapter.

[26] Box and Jenkins (1970, p. 177).

empirical autocorrelation function or correlogram has in fact damped off or cut off in the fashion predicted by the theoretical process being entertained by calculating the test statistic $\hat{\rho}_\theta/\hat{\sigma}_{\hat{\rho}_\theta}$, which is distributed approximately as a unit normal deviate. The hypothesis that $\hat{\rho}_\theta = 0 (\theta > p)$ is then evaluated in the conventional manner.

In addition the partial autocorrelation function may be examined. Let $\rho_{t\theta}$ denote the partial correlation between u_t and $u_{t+\theta}$ holding $u_{t+1} \ldots u_{t+\theta-1}$ fixed. If the disturbances follow an autoregressive process of order p, the partial autocorrelations (as well as the partial coefficients ϕ_p) will be nonzero for $\theta \leq p$ and zero for $\theta > p$. Hence the partial autocorrelations of a pth-order autoregressive process exhibit a cutoff beyond lag p. Quenouille (1949) has established that the $\hat{\rho}_{t\theta}$ estimated in the sample are approximately independently distributed for $\theta > p$ and have standard error: $\hat{\sigma}_{\hat{\rho}_{t\theta}} \approx 1/\sqrt{T}$. Thus the test statistic $\hat{\rho}_{t\theta}/\hat{\sigma}_{\hat{\rho}_{t\theta}}$, which is distributed as a unit normal deviate, can be used to evaluate the hypothesis that $\hat{\rho}_{t\theta} = 0$ $(\theta > p)$ and thereby aid in identifying the order of an autoregressive process (or the presence of a moving-average process) in the OLS residuals.[27]

The partial autocorrelation functions of moving-average processes are complicated and so do not lend themselves to precise evaluation in the sample. However, unlike the partial autocorrelations of autoregressive models that cut off after lag p, the partial autocorrelations of disturbances generated by a moving-average process tail off or damp off in a manner analogous to the (nonpartial) autocorrelation function of AR(p) mechanisms (see Figures 1 and 2). Hence we have an important duality that facilitates the choice of a model for time-dependent disturbances: pth-order moving-average processes have autocorrelation functions that are zero after lag p, and partial autocorrelation functions that are infinite in extent and dominated by damped exponentials and/or damped sine waves. Conversely, pth-order autoregressive processes have autocorrelation functions that are infinite in extent and consist of mixed damped exponentials and/or damped sine waves, and have partial autocorrelation functions that are zero after lag p.[28]

[27] The tests given here and in (117), however, are designed for observed variables u_t rather than residuals $\hat{u}_t$, which are computed after least-squares fitting. Hence they should be undertaken with caution and only aid in detecting the order of the process. Exact tests for specific autoregressive models are provided by Durbin and Watson (1950, 1951) and Wallis (1972). Also see footnote 34.

[28] This duality extends to other features of MA and AR processes as well. See Box and Jenkins (1970, chap. 3). Also relevant to this section are T. W. Anderson (1971, chap. 5 and 6), Kendall and Stuart (1968, chap. 47 to 50), and especially Rudra (1952).

The $\hat{\rho}_\theta$ are not only noisy but are negatively biased (in small samples) as well.[29] The negative bias poses no great difficulty when comparing empirical correlograms to the various theoretical alternatives, since the ρ_θ^* are generated with empirically derived $\hat{\phi}_p$ as starting points. Hence the sample bias of $\hat{\rho}_\theta$ should not distort identification or choice of the time-dependence model. It does become troublesome, however, when undertaking sample-based (pseudo) GLS estimation.

Pseudo-GLS Estimation

The purpose of identifying the time-dependence process followed by the disturbances is, of course, to secure GLS estimates of B, var(B), and so on. Previous sections have developed the logic of GLS generally (and theoretically) and have outlined the specifics for the AR(1) case. The point to be emphasized here is that once the dependence process has been ascertained the investigator still must rely on sample estimates of the parameters ϕ_p and can therefore derive only estimates of the variance-covariance matrix Ω, its inverse Ω^{-1}, and the transformation matrix A. Since $\hat{\phi}_p$ and $\hat{\rho}_\theta$ are biased in the sample (the magnitude of the bias depending on ρ_p, T, and the autocorrelation of the exogenous variables), $\hat{\Omega}$, $\hat{\Omega}^{-1}$, and $\hat{A}$ are biased as well. Hence we use the denotation *pseudo-GLS* when ϕ_θ, ρ_θ, Ω, and A are not known exactly.

For autoregressive processes, psudo-GLS can be achieved by OLS after transformation—and therefore without access to specialized computer programs—according to the procedures previously outlined in the context of the AR(1) model.[30] To secure small-sample regression coefficient estimates that are substantially better than those produced by OLS, however, it is important to have accurate estimates of the ϕ_p. Rao and Griliches have evaluated the merits of competing estimators of ϕ_1

---

[29] See Kendall (1954), Kendall and Stuart (1968, chap. 48.3), and Marriott and Pope (1954).

[30] For higher-order autoregressive models the appropriate transformations are

$$Y_1^* = \sqrt{1 - \phi_1^2 - \phi_2^2 - \cdots - \phi_p^2}\, Y_1 \qquad t = 1$$
$$Y_t^* = Y_t - \phi_1 Y_{t-1} - \phi_2 Y_{t-2} - \cdots - \phi_p Y_{t-p} \qquad t = 2\ldots T$$
$$X_{k_1}^* = \sqrt{1 - \phi_1^2 - \phi_2^2 - \cdots - \phi_p^2}\, X_1 \qquad t = 1; k = 1\ldots K$$
$$X_{kt}^* = X_{kt} - \phi_1 X_{kt-1} - \phi_2 X_{kt-2} - \cdots - \phi_p X_{kt-p} \qquad t = 2\ldots T, k = 1\ldots K$$

Notice that when GLS is undertaken in this way the intercept does not estimate β_0 but: $\beta_0(1 - \phi_1 - \phi_2 - \cdots - \phi_p)$.

Direct matrix solutions are also feasible. The appropriate Ω^{-1} matrices are given by Wise (1955, p. 155).

in the AR(1) process,[31] and Malinvaud suggests some small-sample corrections for bias.[32] In AR(2) models the estimates

$$\hat{\phi}_1 = \frac{\hat{\rho}_1(1 - \hat{\rho}_2)}{1 - \hat{\rho}_1^2}$$

and

$$\hat{\phi}_2 = \frac{\hat{\rho}_2 - \hat{\rho}_1^2}{1 - \hat{\rho}_1^2}$$

approximate fully efficient maximum-likelihood estimates and are therefore preferred to those obtained from OLS residual regressions.[33] Ideally the investigator will have access to maximum-likelihood computer programs that yield the best possible estimates of the ϕ_p and proceed directly to GLS, making transformation of variables unnecessary.

Specialized (nonlinear) programs are necessary in any case to estimate the ϕ_p of moving-average models since, as we noted previously, they are nonlinear functions of the $\hat{\rho}_\theta$. Thus, moving-average processes require rather complex operations and are not easily handled unless ap-

---

[31] Rao and Griliches (1969). The Monte Carlo experiments ($T = 20$) reported in this study suggest that when the disturbance is generated by an AR(1) process and $|\phi_1| \geq 0.3$, pseudo-GLS offers a considerable improvement over OLS. I find this a more appealing rule of thumb than the conventional Durbin-Watson test. See Durbin and Watson (1950, 1951). Since time-series-oriented, least-squares computer programs routinely report the Durbin-Watson d statistic it is perhaps useful to point out that an estimate of ρ_1 is easily deduced from it. Recall that

$$\hat{\rho}_1 = \frac{\hat{\gamma}_1}{\hat{\gamma}_0} = \frac{\text{cov}(\hat{u}_t\, \hat{u}_{t-1})}{\text{var } \hat{u}_t}$$

The Durbin-Watson d is computed:

$$d = \frac{\sum_t (\hat{u}_t - \hat{u}_{t-1})^2}{\sum_t \hat{u}_t^2}$$

Expanding the previous equation gives

$$d = \frac{\sum_t \hat{u}_t^2 - 2\sum_t \hat{u}_t\, \hat{u}_{t-1} + \sum_t \hat{u}_{t-1}^2}{\sum_t \hat{u}_t^2}$$

$$d \simeq 1 - 2\hat{\rho}_1 + 1$$
$$d \simeq 2 - 2\hat{\rho}_1$$

Hence $\hat{\rho}_1$ can be deduced as follows: $\hat{\rho}_1 \simeq 1 - d/2$

[32] Malinvaud (1970, chap. 13.4).
[33] See Box and Jenkins (1970, chap. 6.3).

propriate computer algorithms are available.³⁴ However, it is clear that if care is taken in specifying the form of Ω (time-dependence process), and if theoretical as well as experimental results are utilized to minimize bias in the ϕ_p, pseudo-GLS is not only asymptotically efficient but also dominates OLS in small samples, as Rao and Griliches (1969) have shown.

An empirical example is surely overdue.

Presidential Popularity from Truman to Johnson

A recent, imaginative study of presidential popularity from Truman to Johnson by John Mueller provides a useful benchmark for an illustration of some of the theoretical points developed in previous sections.³⁵ Mueller was interested in developing a model to explain the temporal decline in the percentage of the public approving the way an incumbent is handling his job as president—a phenomenon of considerable interest for which there are some 299 data points (via the Gallup Poll) from the beginning of the Truman administration in 1945 to the end of the Johnson administration in January 1969.

Mueller presents six equations that are based on prior theory and the preliminary analysis of literally hundreds of regression models. There is of course no way to determine how Mueller's use of conventional significance tests in the presence of autocorrelation might have affected this massive process of causal inference and model reformulation. However, each of the reported equations suffers from serious serial correlation, and undoubtedly this was also true of the unreported models examined by Mueller in preparing the published results.³⁶

Let us reexamine Mueller's final model (his Equation 6) in some detail. Briefly this model specifies the dependent variable—the percent-

---

³⁴ Box and Jenkins (1970) present the appropriate algorithms and provide charts that allow one to read off estimates of the ϕ_p given values of the empirical $\hat{\rho}_\theta$. See chap. 7 and part V. It is also worth noting that after specification of Ω and estimation via pseudo-GLS, the transformed errors $\hat{\nu}_t$ should of course behave as a white-noise process. Therefore autocorrelations of the $\hat{\nu}_t$ might be inspected to ensure that the set of GLS residuals are indeed serially independent. Moreover, specification errors in the functional form linking Y_t to the X_{kt} can often be detected by evaluating the cross-correlations of $\hat{\nu}_t$ and $X_{kt-\theta}$. See Box and Jenkins (1970, chap. 11), Box and Pierce (1970), Pierce (1971a, 1971b, 1972).

³⁵ Mueller (1970). See also Mueller (1973, chap. 9).

³⁶ Mueller refers to the autocorrelation problem throughout his study and notes that the Durbin-Watson statistic [which presumes an AR(1) process] is highly significant for each equation. Although this tells us nothing about the form of the disturbance time-dependence model it does indicate that $\hat{\rho}_1$ in each equation was sizable. See footnote 31.

age of the public approving the way the incumbent is handling his job as president (% Approve)—to be a linear function of:
1. A "rally round the flag" variable (Rally)—the length of time, in years, since the last rally point. Rally points include the start of each presidential term and all international events deemed dramatic enough to give a sudden boost to the president's popularity rating.
2. An "economic slump" variable (Ecoslump)—the unemployment rate at the time the incumbent's term began subtracted from the rate at the time of the poll, but set equal to zero whenever the unemployment rate was lower at the time of the survey than it had been at the start of the incumbent's present term. (A slumping economy is expected to harm a president's popularity, but an improving economy is not anticipated to help his rating.)
3. "Dummy" or binary variables for each presidential term, which are designed to permit a term-by-term comparison of the personal, idiosyncratic appeal (or lack thereof) of individual presidents (HST1, HST2; IKE1, IKE2; JFK1; LBJ1, LBJ2).
4. A "coalition of minorities" (Mincoals) variable, term-by-term (HST1 * Mincoals, HST2 * Mincoals, ..., LBJ2 * Mincoals)— the length of time, in years, since the incumbent was inaugurated or reelected, multiplied by the appropriate presidential term, dummy variable. It allows for the progressive alienation of former supporters at a rate (slope) that varies across individual terms.
5. "War" dummy variables designed to capture the (presumably negative) impact on presidential popularity of the Korean and Vietnamese adventures (Warkorea, Warviet).

Mueller's final equation to explain presidential popularity is therefore expressed as follows:

$$\begin{aligned}\% \text{ Approve} = {}& \beta_0 + \beta_1 \text{ Rally} + \beta_2 \text{ Ecoslump} + \beta_3 \text{ HST2} \\ & + \beta_4 \text{ IKE1} + \beta_5 \text{ IKE2} + \beta_6 \text{ JFK1} \\ & + \beta_7 \text{ LBJ1} + \beta_8 \text{ LBJ2} + \beta_9 \text{ HST1} * \text{Mincoals} \\ & + \beta_{10} \text{ HST2} * \text{Mincoals} + \beta_{11} \text{ IKE1} * \text{Mincoals} \\ & + \beta_{12} \text{ IKE2} * \text{Mincoals} + \beta_{13} \text{ JFK1} * \text{Mincoals} \\ & + \beta_{14} \text{ LBJ1} * \text{Mincoals} + \beta_{15} \text{ LBJ2} * \text{Mincoals} \\ & + \beta_{16} \text{ Warkorea} + \beta_{17} \text{ Warviet} + u_t \end{aligned} \quad (118)$$

The theoretical rationale of the model is summarized by Mueller as follows: It is anticipated (1) that each president will experience in each

TABLE 1
OLS Estimates for Equation (118)

Independent Variable	Parameter Estimate	Standard Error	t-Statistic
Intercept (HST1)	72.38	2.49	29.02
Rally	−6.17	1.03	−5.96
Ecoslump	−3.72	0.64	−5.79
HST2	−12.42	3.53	−3.52
IKE1	−2.41	2.98	−0.81
IKE2	−4.35	2.90	−1.50
JFK1	7.18	3.10	2.31
LBJ1	4.02	3.89	1.03
LBJ2	−1.06	3.21	−0.33
HST1*Mincoals	−8.92	1.33	−6.70
HST2*Mincoals	−2.82	1.35	−2.09
IKE1*Mincoals	2.58	0.81	3.18
IKE2*Mincoals	0.22	0.62	0.35
JFK1*Mincoals	−4.75	1.15	−4.13
LBJ1*Mincoals	2.53	8.43	0.30
LBJ2*Mincoals	−8.13	0.79	−10.33
Warkorea	−18.20	3.39	−5.37
Warviet	−0.01	2.77	−0.00

$R^2 = 0.859$ Regression standard error = 5.73 $F = 100.9$; $DF = 17{,}281$

term a general decline of popularity; (2) that this decline will be interrupted from time to time by temporary upsurges associated with international crises and similar events; (3) that the decline will be accelerated in direct relation to increases in unemployment rates over those prevailing when the president began his term, but that improvement in unemployment rates will not affect his popularity one way or the other; and (4) that the president will experience an additional loss of popularity if a war is underway.

The OLS results for Eq. (118) are reported in Table 1.[37] The residuals of this equation were retrieved and subjected to correlogram analysis in order to deduce the form, as well as initial estimates of the coefficients, of the disturbance time-dependence process. A first-order autoregressive process clearly provides the best fit to the empirical autocorrelations, although, as Figure 5 indicates, the empirical function

---

[37] The data for this analysis were kindly made available to me by Professor Mueller. The OLS estimates in Table 1 differ slightly from those reported in the published article because they are based on Mueller's revised sample of 299 observations versus 292 used in the original study). The OLS estimates do, however, correspond perfectly to Mueller's own revised results, which appear in Mueller (1973, chap. 9).

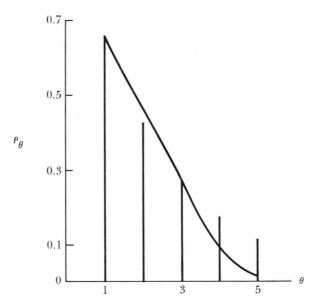

Figure 5. Empirical and theoretical correlograms for Equation (118). Curved line plots empirical autocorrelations; bar lines plot theoretical autocorrelations.

(curved line) damps off a bit more quickly than the theoretical function (bar lines). Note that the estimate of ϕ_1 used to generate the theoretical correlogram (0.650) was secured by regressing $\hat{u}_t$ on $\hat{u}_{t-1}$. The empirical autocorrelations were of course obtained simply by computing successive $\hat{\rho}_\theta$ from the OLS residuals ($\hat{u}_t$) of Eq. (118). The partial autocorrelation function also corresponded to the AR(1) pattern—that is, all $\hat{\rho}_{t\theta}$ were effectively zero.

Having established that an AR(1) process characterizes the disturbance time dependence, and having secured an initial guess of ϕ_1, Eq. (118) was reestimated by generalized least squares.[38] The GLS results appear in Table 2.

What difference does this reanalysis of Mueller's final model make? The GLS estimates should not lead to causal inferences that differ radically from those of Mueller, since we have not attempted a complete replication of his large-scale investigation but have confined

---

[38] The TROLL/1 econometric system was used to estimate the model. See Eisner (1972). 0.650 was provided as the initial guess of ϕ_1, which converged to the (maximum-likelihood) value of 0.823. Note that the opinion sample points are not uniformly equidistant, and so the estimate of ϕ_1 is somewhat, but not significantly, weakened. See Kendall and Stuart (1968, chap. 49.22).

TABLE 2
GLS Estimates for Equation (118)

Independent Variable	Parameter Estimate	Standard Error	t-Statistic
Intercept (HST1)	84.63	6.55	12.93
Rally	−4.92	1.14	−4.31
Ecoslump	−1.68	1.17	−1.45
HST2	−31.12	9.50	−3.28
IKE1	−20.58	7.98	−2.58
IKE2	−14.25	7.92	−1.80
JFK1	−10.22	8.19	−1.25
LBJ1	−4.52	8.89	−0.51
LBJ2	−17.71	8.22	−2.15
HST1*Mincoals	−17.02	3.01	−5.65
HST2*Mincoals	−6.18	2.45	−2.52
IKE1*Mincoals	2.81	2.15	1.31
IKE2*Mincoals	−1.15	1.80	−0.64
JFK1*Mincoals	−3.13	2.91	−1.08
LBJ1*Mincoals	−9.09	14.16	−0.64
LBJ2*Mincoals	−7.76	2.15	−3.61
Warkorea	2.49	4.37	0.57
Warviet	4.84	4.15	1.17

$R^2 = 0.551^a$ Regression standard error = 4.10^a $F = 20.3^a$; $DF = 17{,}281$

^a These GLS statistics should not be compared to the corresponding OLS statistics because they are based on the transformed disturbances AU. See the previous discussion in this chapter, especially footnote 21. Let us apply the relevant expression in footnote 21 to get some idea of the OLS understatement of the regression standard error $\sqrt{\hat{\sigma}_u^2}$ or average error of prediction in Equation (118). We have $\hat{\sigma}_u^2 = \hat{\sigma}_\nu^2/1 - \hat{\phi}_1^2$ (see footnote 21). Noting that $\sqrt{\hat{\sigma}_\nu^2} = 4.1$ (Table 2) and $\hat{\phi}_1 = 0.823$ (footnote 38), we may derive an estimate of the true OLS residual variance and regression standard error: $\hat{\sigma}_u^2 = (4.1)^2/1 - (0.823)^2 = 52.5$. The true OLS regression standard error $\sqrt{\hat{\sigma}_u^2}$ is therefore 7.25, which is considerably understated by the estimate 5.73 reported in Table 1.

the example to a single analysis of a single equation (see the previous discussion). However, the GLS estimates do indicate that substantively nontrivial modifications of Mueller's conclusions are in order. Moreover, even where the thrust of Mueller's inferences need not be altered, the exact GLS parameter values are surely more reliable than the OLS estimates whose true variances are needlessly large [see Equations (21) and (27)].

The first important difference between the GLS and OLS results involves the Ecoslump variable. The GLS estimates for this variable in Table 2 demonstrate that the significance attributed to Ecoslump in the OLS analysis is a spurious artifact of autocorrelation. Hence the rate of unemployment (as transformed by Mueller) exhibits neither a statistically significant nor a theoretically important influence on presidential popularity.

The results for the presidential term dummy variables also differ markedly across estimation methods. Here the most dramatic lack of correspondence shows up in the parameter values rather than in the standard errors or t-statistics. The GLS estimate of 84.6 percent for the starting point of Truman's first-term popularity rating (HST1)—which as the null case in the dummy variable formulation is given by the intercept term—provides a much better fit to the empirical data than does the OLS estimate of 72.4 percent.[39] Indeed Mueller's analysis of the OLS residuals led him to make special note of the poor performance of the model in accounting for Truman's extremely high initial popularity in the aftermath of Roosevelt's death. Naturally the remaining term dummies, which are interpreted as deviations from the Truman starting point, have correspondingly larger absolute values. The Truman Mincoals or rate of alienation slopes (HST1 * Mincoals, HST2 * Mincoals) are also larger (negative) in the GLS results. Again the GLS estimates outperform the OLS results in capturing the dynamics of the enormous decline in Truman's popularity—especially during the first few years of his incumbency.

Finally the GLS results indicate that Mueller's inferences concerning the influence of undeclared war should be modified. The OLS estimates suggest that the Korean expedition had a dramatic negative impact on Truman's popularity, whereas the involvement in Vietnam had no independent effect on the mass public's approval of LBJ. Mueller attributes this rather disconcerting outcome to the collinearity of the Mincoals variables and the war dummies—and to the fact that Korea became "Truman's War" in a way that Vietnam never became "Johnson's War." The GLS parameter estimates and t-statistics demonstrate that the latter explanation is unnecessary and erroneous. Neither war dummy coefficient is sizable, significant, or even has the anticipated sign. A more plausible interpretation is that Mincoals variables have absorbed the antiwar effect along with other alienating factors in both cases.

INTERDEPENDENT DISTURBANCES AND DYNAMIC FORMULATIONS

Lagged Endogenous Variables and Autocorrelated Disturbances

Thus far our examination of statistical estimation and causal inference in regression equations with serially correlated disturbances has

[39] Time plots of the popularity data are provided by Mueller (1973, pp. 198–201).

been confined to static models—that is, independent variables have been exclusively exogenous and time has not appeared in an essential way. Although OLS estimation of such regression models gives rise to a number of statistical pathologies and frequently leads to erroneous causal inferences, we have seen that the coefficient estimates remain unbiased. This no longer obtains in truly dynamic models, which incorporate lagged endogenous variables on the right-hand side,[40] because it is well known that the conjunction of lagged $y_{t-\theta}$ and autocorrelated disturbances produces biased and inconsistent estimates.[41] Hence, even if the researcher has an infinite number of empirical observations at his disposal, the OLS estimates do not converge to the true parameter values.

The point is readily demonstrated for some simple cases. Consider the following bivariate equation where both regressor and disturbance follow a stationary, stochastic first-order autoregressive process:[42]

$$y_t = \beta y_{t-1} + u_t \quad \text{(equation to be estimated)} \quad (119)$$

where y_t is a mean deviate.

$$u_t = \phi_1 u_{t-1} + \nu_t \quad \text{(disturbance time-dependence process)} \quad (120)$$

$$\left.\begin{array}{l} -1 < \beta < 1 \\ -1 < \phi_1 < 1 \end{array}\right\} \text{(stationarity conditions)} \quad (121)$$

$$E(u_t) = E(\nu_t) = E(u_{t-\theta}\nu_t) = E(y_{t-\theta}\nu_t) = 0 \} \text{for } \theta > 0 \text{ and all } t \quad (122)$$

If we lag Equation (119) one period and multiply through by ϕ_1 we obtain

$$\phi_1 y_{t-1} = \phi_1 \beta y_{t-2} + \phi_1 u_{t-1} \quad (123)$$

This yields a useful expression for the autoregressive component of the disturbance in the original model—$\phi_1 u_{t-1}$:

$$\phi_1 u_{t-1} = \phi_1 y_{t-1} - \phi_1 \beta y_{t-2} \quad (124)$$

Hence the original model [Equation (119)] may be written

$$\begin{aligned} y_t &= \beta y_{t-1} + \phi_1 u_{t-1} + \nu_t \\ &= \beta y_{t-1} + \phi_1 y_{t-1} - \phi_1 \beta y_{t-2} + \nu_t \\ &= (\beta + \phi_1) y_{t-1} - \phi_1 \beta y_{t-2} + \nu_t \end{aligned} \quad (125)$$

---

[40] For an especially good treatment of the theoretical differences between static and dynamic models in the econometric context see Christ (1966).

[41] A consistent estimator is defined: plim $\hat{\beta} = \beta$, where plim denotes "in the probability limit." An alternative but not identical formulation is "consistency in mean square": $E(\hat{\beta} - \beta)^2 \to 0$ as $N \to \infty$. Hence a consistent estimator is one whose bias and variance converge to zero as sample size becomes infinite.

[42] An exhaustive treatment of this case is provided by Griliches (1961).

It is now obvious that application of ordinary least squares to the equation as initially specified is equivalent to the classic omitted-variables situation in which the coefficient estimate of the included variable y_{t-1} picks up some influence of the excluded variable y_{t-2}.

More precisely, it is well known that if the "true" equation takes the form

$$y_t = \beta_1 x_{1t} + \beta_2 x_{2t} + \cdots + \beta_k x_{kt} + u_t$$

and the investigator mistakenly omits variables and estimates some subset of the true function, then, in the probability limit, the OLS estimates of the included parameters will be

$$\text{plim } \hat{\beta}_k = \beta_k + \sum_j \beta_j * b_{jk} \tag{126}$$

where β_k denotes the true parameter of the kth included variable; β_j denotes the true parameter of the jth omitted variable; b_{jk} denotes partial coefficients from the (multivariate) auxiliary regressions of each omitted variable on all included variables; and * denotes multiplication.[43]

In the example at hand, we have $(\beta + \phi_1)$ as the true coefficient of the included variable y_{t-1}, and $-\phi_1 \beta$ as the true coefficient of the omitted variable y_{t-2} [see Equation (125)]. The OLS estimate of β in the original model will therefore be

$$\begin{aligned}
\text{plim } \hat{\beta} &= (\beta + \phi_1) + [-\phi_1\beta * \text{plim } b_{y_{t-2},\, y_{t-1}}] \\
\text{plim } \hat{\beta} &= (\beta + \phi_1) + [-\phi_1\beta * \text{plim } \hat{\beta}] \\
&\quad \text{by the stationarity assumption of} \\
&\quad \text{Eq. (121)} \\
\text{plim } \hat{\beta} + (\phi_1\beta * \text{plim } \hat{\beta}) &= (\beta + \phi_1) \\
\text{plim } \hat{\beta}(1 + \phi_1\beta) &= (\beta + \phi_1) \\
\text{plim } \hat{\beta} &= (\beta + \phi_1)/(1 + \phi_1\beta)
\end{aligned} \tag{127}$$

It is clear, therefore, that ordinary least squares renders inconsistent parameter estimates for dynamic models with temporally dependent

---

[43] A matrix demonstration easily proves this result. If the "truth" is $Y = X_1 B_1 + X_2 B_2 + U$, and the estimated model is $Y = X_1 B_1$, then the OLS estimates in the misspecified equation are given by $\hat{B}_1 = (X_1'X_1)^{-1} X_1'Y$ [see Eq. (9)]. Substituting in for Y yields $\hat{B}_1 = (X_1'X_1)^{-1} (X_1 X_1) B_1 + (X_1'X_1)^{-1} (X_1'X_2) B_2 + (X_1'X_1)^{-1} X_1'U$. In the probability limit this becomes plim $\hat{B}_1 = B_1 + [AB_2]$, where $A = (X_1'X_1)^{-1} X_1'X_2$ and the bracketed expression gives the asymptotic bias. For further analysis along these lines see Griliches (1957) and Theil (1957). We focus exclusively on asymptotic properties in this section because all estimators of dynamic models exhibit small-sample bias. Only consistency or asymptotic unbiasedness can be preserved by the estimation methods to be introduced shortly.

disturbances. In simple autoregressive models of the sort in Equations (119) to (122), the asymptotic bias is

$$\text{plim } (\hat{\beta} - \beta) = \frac{\phi_1(1 - \beta^2)}{(1 + \phi_1\beta)}$$

and hence is positive (overestimating the impact of y_{t-1}) whenever ϕ_1 is positive.[44] As a result the causal influence attributed to lagged $y_{t-\theta}$ in autoregressive equations is commonly exaggerated.

Moreover the OLS residuals no longer accurately reflect the true underlying disturbances. This, of course, follows directly from the fact that the lagged $y_{t-\theta}$ have a tendency to absorb the systematic component of the disturbances. Hence the previous procedures cannot be used to ascertain the structure of the disturbance time dependence since the residual estimates of ϕ_p and ρ_θ as well as the Durbin-Watson statistic will be biased, even in unlimited samples.[45] In contrast to the comparatively minor, small-sample bias in the models of the previous section, the asymptotic bias of $\hat{\phi}_1$ in autoregressive models can be severe, especially when ϕ_1 is large and β is small. Specifically, for the model in Equations (119) to (122) it is easily shown that[46]

$$\text{plim } \hat{\phi}_1 = \frac{\beta\phi_1(\beta + \phi_1)}{(1 + \beta\phi_1)} \tag{128}$$

so that the asymptotic bias is

$$\text{plim } (\hat{\phi}_1 - \phi_1) = \frac{-\phi_1(1 - \beta^2)}{(1 + \phi_1\beta)} \tag{129}$$

Thus the bias in $\hat{\phi}_1$ is equal in size but opposite in sign to that of the regression coefficient estimate $\hat{\beta}$, and so conventional tests applied to the OLS residuals underestimate the true magnitude of the serial correlation.

The bivariate autoregressive model of Eq. (119) is useful for

---

[44] This result is derived as follows. Asymptotic bias is defined as $\text{plim}(\hat{\beta} - \beta)$ and we know $\text{plim } \hat{\beta}$ to be $(\beta + \phi_1)/(1 + \phi_1\beta)$. Thus $\text{plim}(\hat{\beta} - \beta) = [(\beta + \phi_1)/(1 + \phi_1\beta)] - \beta = [(\beta + \phi_1) - \beta(1 + \phi_1\beta)]/(1 + \phi_1\beta) = (\beta + \phi_1 - \beta - \phi_1\beta^2)/(1 + \phi_1\beta) = [\phi_1(1 - \beta^2)]/(1 + \phi_1\beta)$.

An alternative way to derive the result in Equation (127) is to notice that y_t is an AR(2) process with $\phi_1 = (\beta + \phi_1)$ and $\phi_2 = (-\phi_1\beta)$. Since β is by definition the first-order autocorrelation coefficient ρ_1, it follows that $\beta = \rho_1 = \phi_1/(1 - \phi_2) = (\beta + \phi_1)/(1 + \phi_1\beta)$ (see footnote 22). However, the omitted-variables approach we have taken here will be useful when considering more complex formulations later on.

[45] See Nerlove and Wallis (1966) on the inappropriateness of the Durbin-Watson statistic in dynamic models. Durbin (1970) has developed an autocorrelation test statistic designed especially for such situations.

[46] See Malinvaud (1970, chap. 14.5).

illustrating some basic results, but applied problems are rarely so simple. In practice, dynamic models usually incorporate one or more exogenous variables which, as Malinvaud's Monte Carlo experiments have shown, reduce (but do not eliminate) OLS bias.[47] Equations (130) to (133) provide a more realistic example, where, for ease of exposition, we again assume that the disturbance follows an AR(1) process:

$$y_t = \beta y_{t-1} + \gamma x_t + u_t \quad \text{(equation to be estimated)} \quad (130)$$

where all variables are mean deviates and x_t is an exogenous variable independent of u_t.

$$u_t = \phi_1 u_{t-1} + v_t \quad \text{(disturbance time-dependence process)} \quad (131)$$

$$\left.\begin{array}{l} -1 < \beta < 1 \\ -1 < \phi_1 < 1 \end{array}\right\} \quad \text{(stationarity conditions)} \quad (132)$$

$$\left.\begin{array}{l} E(u_t) = E(v_t) = E(u_{t-\theta}v_t) \\ = E(y_{t-\theta}v_t) = 0 \end{array}\right\} \text{for } \theta > 0 \text{ and all } t \quad (133)$$

Equation (130) might have included additional lagged $y_{t-\theta}$ and contemporaneous or lagged x_{kt} without fundamentally affecting the results that follow. Note that we assume x_t to be a genuine exogenous variable independent of u_t, but of course this is not true of y_{t-1}, which is necessarily linked to u_t via the serial dependence.

Performing operations analogous to Eqs. (123) to (125) generates the following expression for the systematic component of the disturbances:

$$\phi_1 u_{t-1} = \phi_1 y_{t-1} - \phi_1 \beta y_{t-2} - \phi_1 \gamma x_{t-1} \quad (134)$$

Combining Eqs. (130) and (131) of the original model and substituting (134) for $\phi_1 u_{t-1}$ allows the equation for y_t to be rewritten as

$$\begin{aligned} y_t &= \beta y_{t-1} + \gamma x_t + \phi_1 y_{t-1} \\ &\quad - \phi_1 \beta y_{t-2} - \phi_1 \gamma x_{t-1} + v_t \\ y_t &= (\beta + \phi_1) y_{t-1} + \gamma x_t - \phi_1 \beta y_{t-2} \\ &\quad - \phi_1 \gamma x_{t-1} + v_t \end{aligned} \quad (135)$$

Again it is apparent that the dynamic equation in (130), whose disturbance follows the mechanism in (131), may be transformed into a more tractable omitted-variables problem. Hence we have $(\beta + \phi_1)$ and γ as the "true" coefficients of the included variables y_{t-1} and x_t, and $-\phi_1\beta$ and $-\phi_1\gamma$ as the "true" parameters of the omitted variables y_{t-2} and x_{t-1}. It follows straightforwardly from Eq. (126) that OLS ap-

[47] Malinvaud (1961).

plied to the original equation does not consistently estimate β and γ, but rather:

$$\text{plim } \hat{\beta} = (\beta + \phi_1) + [-\phi_1\beta * b_{y_{t-2},\, y_{t-1}\cdot x_t} \\ - \phi_1\gamma * b_{x_{t-1},\, y_{t-1}\cdot x_t}] \tag{136}$$

$$\text{plim } \hat{\gamma} = \gamma + [-\phi_1\beta * b_{y_{t-2},\, x_t\cdot y_{t-1}} \\ - \phi_1\gamma * b_{x_{t-1},\, x_t\cdot y_{t-1}}] \tag{137}$$

where ϕ_1 plus the bracketed expression in (136) is the asymptotic bias of $\hat{\beta}$; the bracketed expression in (137) is the asymptotic bias of $\hat{\gamma}$; and $*$ denotes multiplication.

These results admit a variety of possibilities, but clearly the most common is an overestimate of β (the coefficient of y_{t-1}) and an underestimate of γ (the coefficient of x_t).[48] Therefore OLS estimation of dynamic models with autocorrelated disturbances typically produces upwardly biased coefficients for the lagged $y_{t-\theta}$ and downwardly biased (toward zero) coefficients for the exogenous x_{kt}. Since the lagged dependent variables tend to dominate the outcomes of such equations (partially) at the expense of exogenous influences, this leads to erroneous inferences about the importance of the dynamic terms. Finally the essentials of the results developed for simple autoregressive models concerning the asymptotic bias in $\hat{\phi}_1$ and $\hat{\rho}_1$ obtain here as well. OLS residuals cannot therefore be used to determine the structure or the magnitude of the disturbance time dependence.

So far we have shown that the parameters secured from OLS estimation of models with lagged endogenous variables and serially correlated disturbances do not accurately assess the true magnitude of causal influences. Moreover correlogram and related analyses are no longer feasible, and so pseudo-GLS estimation cannot be undertaken in the usual way. This brings us to an examination of estimation methods that are appropriate to the problem.

Estimation Methods for Dynamic Models with Serially Correlated Errors

If the structure as well as the parameters of the disturbance time-dependence process are known a priori, then the special estimation pro-

---

[48] Note, however, that β is inflated less here than in the pure autoregressive model of Eq. (119). If $\phi_1 < 0$, that is, if the disturbances are negatively autocorrelated, then the consequences are just the opposite: underestimation of β and overestimation of γ. However, negative serial correlation is rare except in certain types of transformed, distributed lag models. See Griliches (1961, 1967) and Wallis (1969). It should also be pointed out that these basic results apply to cross-section based models that incorporate lagged endogenous variables, although in such situations it is not possible to determine the structure of the disturbance autocorrelation.

cedures developed in what follows need not be considered—one may proceed directly with generalized least squares. It is obvious, however, that such knowledge is rarely, if ever, available in practice, and so we are left with two realistic situations that regularly arise in applied research.

First consider the case where the form but not the parameter values of the interdependence process is known.[49] Suppose, for example, we have a model of the sort in Eq. (138) whose disturbance can be assumed to follow a first-order autoregressive process.

$$y_t = \beta y_{t-1} + \gamma x_t + u_t \tag{138}$$

$$u_t = \phi_1 u_{t-1} + \nu_t \tag{139}$$

It was demonstrated earlier [see (135)] that the y_t in this model satisfy the revised equation:

$$y_t = (\beta + \phi_1)y_{t-1} + \gamma x_t - \phi_1 \beta y_{t-2} \\ -\phi_1 \gamma x_{t-1} + \nu_t \tag{140}$$

Since the disturbance term ν_t of the revised model is serially uncorrelated, Eq. (140) has all the desirable properties for least-squares estimation. Two methods are available to derive the parameters (β, γ) and ϕ_1. The first involves simultaneous estimation of the coefficients (subject to the nonlinear constraints) via an appropriate nonlinear regression program.[50] Convergence to the true parameter values, or indeed to any values at all, is of course not guaranteed but is probable if the investigator provides good starting guesses for the iterative search procedure employed by most nonlinear algorithms. For example in Eq. (140) starting guesses in the range $0 < \phi_1 < 1$ and $0 < \beta < 1$ (that of γ would depend on the substantive context) would surely make convergence to the true parameter values more likely than relying entirely on the default options of the available nonlinear program. Although simultaneous, nonlinear, iterative, and related search techniques are con-

[49] Typically such information is based on prior theory. See, for example, Davis, Dempster, and Wildavsky's second model for congressional budgeting behavior (1966). Perhaps the best-known example of a theoretically defined process derives from distributed lag models in economics. The most common formulation is $y_t = \alpha \sum_{\theta=0}^{\infty} \lambda^\theta x_{t-\theta} + u_t$, where $|\lambda| < 1$ and u_t is white noise. Subtracting λy_{t-1} produces the estimating equation: $y_t = \alpha x_t + \lambda y_{t-1} + u_t - \lambda u_t$, where the disturbance now follows an MA(1) process. An enormous econometric literature deals with the specification and estimation of such models. The former is surveyed by Griliches (1967) and the latter is reviewed by Aigner (1971). A comprehensive treatment on both counts is provided by Dhrymes (1971). The estimation techniques developed by Box and Jenkins (1970), although largely ignored in economics (Aigner excepted), are also relevant here.

[50] For example, see Marquardt (1963).

ceptually complex and computationally expensive, the limited experimental evidence indicates that such methods perform very well even in small samples.[51]

A second way to estimate the coefficients of Eq. (140), and hence indirectly those of Eq. (138), is by direct application of OLS. Thus the estimating equation is

$$y_t = \alpha_1 y_{t-1} + \alpha_2 x_t + \alpha_3 y_{t-2} \\ + \alpha_4 x_{t-1} + \nu_t \quad (141)$$

Since we know that $\alpha_1 = (\beta + \phi_1)$, $\alpha_2 = \gamma$, $\alpha_3 = -\phi_1\beta$, and $\alpha_4 = -\phi_1\gamma$, the parameter estimates of interest are readily deduced as follows:

$$\hat{\phi}_1 = -(\hat{\alpha}_4/\hat{\alpha}_2) = -(-\hat{\phi}_1\hat{\gamma}/\hat{\gamma}) \\ \hat{\beta} = (\hat{\alpha}_1 - \hat{\phi}_1) = (\beta + \phi_1) - \phi_1 \quad (142) \\ \hat{\gamma} = \hat{\alpha}_2$$

Alternatively we might retain only the estimate of the AR(1) parameter ϕ_1 from Eq. (142) to generate $\hat{\Omega}$, $\hat{\Omega}^{-1}$, or the transformation matrix $\hat{A}$, and then reestimate the original model via pseudo-GLS. This should yield somewhat sharper estimates of β and γ.

The principal limitation of the procedures developed above is the requirement of prior knowledge of the form of the interdependence. The desirable properties of GLS are not in general preserved if the time-dependence process is incorrectly specified—indeed, the investigator who proceeds on the basis of a misspecified process may do more damage than good. For example, a study by Robert Engle (1973) demonstrates that even in the low-order autoregressive world, OLS can be vastly superior to GLS when Ω is truncated. In particular, Engle shows in the context of a simple model with one exogenous regressor that if the true disturbance is AR(2) and the process is mistakenly assumed to be AR(1), OLS may dominate GLS.

Since prior knowledge about the structure of the disturbance time dependence is not typically available for models of interest to sociologists and political scientists, it is probably more useful to examine the case in which neither the form nor the coefficients of the interdependence process are known in advance. Consider, then, a model of the sort in Eq. (143), where the u_t are autocorrelated but the mechanism producing the serial dependence is not known a priori.

$$y_t = \beta y_{t-1} + \sum_k \gamma_k x_{kt} + u_t \quad (143)$$

What is required to obtain consistent and efficient estimates of the parameters in Eq. (143)? Consistency alone may be secured by using

[51] See Dhyrmes (1971, appendix), Morrison (1970), and Sargent (1968).

a two-stage instrumental variables (IV) procedure which parallels the two-stage least-squares solution to the simultaneous equations problem. In the first stage the systematic part of the lagged endogenous variable is created by regressing y_{t-1} on the exogenous, instrumental variables x_{kt} and x_{kt-1}. That is, we perform the regression:

$$y_{t-1} = \sum_k \alpha_k x_{kt} + \sum_k \delta_k x_{kt-1} + \eta_{t-1} \qquad (144)$$

Hence the systematic part of y_{t-1}, designated as $\hat{y}_{t-1}$, is

$$\hat{y}_{t-1} = y_{t-1} - \hat{\eta}_{t-1} = \sum_k \hat{\alpha}_k x_{kt} + \sum_k \hat{\delta}_k x_{kt-1} \qquad (145)$$

Consistent estimates of the parameters of the original model are now straightforwardly obtained by replacing y_{t-1} with its "purified" counterpart $\hat{y}_{t-1}$ in a second-stage OLS regression:[52]

$$y_t = \beta \hat{y}_{t-1} + \sum_k \gamma_k x_{kt} + \omega_t \qquad (146)$$

where $\omega_t = u_t + \hat{\beta}\hat{\eta}_{t-1}$.

All variables are now asymptotically uncorrelated with the composite disturbance ω_t. This is assured because the current and lagged x_{kt} are uncorrelated in the probability limit with the u_t by assumption, and are uncorrelated in the sample with the $\hat{\eta}_{t-1}$ by construction. Since $\hat{y}_{t-1}$ is created from a linear combination of the x_{kt}, it too is asymptotically uncorrelated with the composite disturbance ω_t. Hence the two-stage IV method of Eqs. (145) and (146) is robust against all forms of serial dependence and renders consistent estimates of β and γ_k.[53] However, IV estimation may produce a considerable loss of precision, and although it is generally superior to OLS in large samples, the small-sample evidence has not been encouraging.[54]

---

[52] Equivalently one may proceed with classic IV estimation and use $\hat{y}_{t-1}$ as an instrument instead of actually replacing y_{t-1} with it. The estimating equation would then be $\hat{B} = (z'x)^{-1} z'y$, where $\hat{B} = (\hat{\beta}, \hat{\gamma}_k)$; $z = (\hat{y}_{t-1}, x_{kt})$; and $x = (y_{t-1}, x_{kt})$. See Liviatan (1963). These procedures are easily adapted to the general case of m lagged endogeneous variables as long as there are sufficient instrumental variables available—a condition known as the *identification problem* in the simultaneous equations literature. See Fisher (1966, 1970) and Hibbs (1973).

[53] Provided that $\hat{y}_{t-1}$ and x_{kt} are not connected by linear identities; that is, the current x_{kt} and the lagged x_{kt-1} must not be connected by nonstochastic, linear, first-order difference equations. Also, note that Eq. (146) does not yield appropriate estimates of R^2, σ_u, and so on. These are derived by using the consistent estimates of β and γ_k from Eq. (146) in conjunction with the original data and model to generate goodness of fit and error variance statistics. See Eq. (147).

[54] See Malinvaud (1961), Morrison (1970), Sargent (1968), and Wallis (1967).

It is therefore advantageous to utilize, but extend further, the IV procedure in order to secure more efficient pseudo-GLS estimates. This is undertaken as follows. First use the consistent estimates of β and γ_k from the second-stage IV regression of Eq. (146) in conjunction with the original data and model to form estimates of the original disturbances u_t. That is, calculate $\hat{u}_t$:

$$\hat{u}_t = y_t - \left[\hat{\beta} y_{t-1} + \sum_k \hat{\gamma}_k x_{kt}\right] \tag{147}$$

Unlike the $\hat{u}_t$ obtained from direct OLS analysis of the initial model, the residuals derived from (147) are deduced from consistent parameter estimates applied to the original data. Accordingly they may be subjected to autocorrelation-correlogram analysis in order to determine the structure [AR(p), MA(p)] and coefficients ϕ_p of the disturbance time-dependence process via the procedures described previously.[55]

It is now easy to secure consistent pseudo-GLS estimates of (β, γ_k) and $\text{var}(\hat{\beta}, \hat{\gamma}_k)$:

$$\hat{B}^* = (X'\hat{\Omega}^{-1}X)^{-1}X'\hat{\Omega}^{-1}Y \tag{148}$$

or alternatively

$$\hat{B}^* = (X^{*\prime}X^*)^{-1}X^{*\prime}Y^*$$
$$\text{var}(\hat{B}^*) = \sigma_u^2(X'\hat{\Omega}^{-1}X)^{-1} \tag{149}$$

or alternatively

$$\text{var}(\hat{B}^*) = \sigma_u^2(X^{*\prime}X^*)^{-1}$$

where X denotes a matrix of right-hand side variables (Y_{t-1}, X_t); X^* denotes a matrix of transformed right-hand side variables (AY_{t-1}, AX_t); Y^* denotes a vector for the transformed dependent variable AY_t; and $\hat{B}^*$ denotes a vector of GLS estimates $(\hat{\beta}^*, \hat{\gamma}^*)$.

The existing Monte Carlo evidence, based on artificial samples of 50 observations, demonstrates that the IV-GLS method outperforms OLS and IV alone for models such as Eq. (143), whose disturbance is first-order autoregressive.[56] There is no reason to believe that IV-GLS performs less well in situations where the form of the process is not assumed in advance, although this surely deserves further investigation.[57] At this point a substantive example is clearly in order.

---

[55] If correlogram analysis indicates that a moving average process is operative, then nonlinear estimation of the ϕ_p is necessary when $p > 1$. The ϕ_p estimates should also be corrected for small-sample bias before undertaking GLS. See my discussion and footnotes 31–34 for the particulars.

[56] See Wallis (1967).

[57] Two points should be added here. First, although the IV-GLS method is based on a consistent estimate of Ω and therefore yields consistent parameter estimates, the latter are not asymptotically efficient (unlike the case considered

Dynamics of Pre-World War I Arms Races

As an example of the issues surrounding the estimation of dynamic equations with autocorrelated disturbances, in which both the structure and the coefficients of the time-dependence process must be deduced from sample data, we reevaluate the British arms expenditures equation from Choucri and North's research on the causes of World War I.[58] Choucri and North's work is an impressive effort to model the most important dynamic interrelationships among the six great powers (Great Britain, Italy, France, Germany, Austria-Hungary, and Russia) that ultimately led to the outbreak of World War I. Naturally arms expenditures play a central role in the model.

In their single-equation analyses, Choucri and North specify Great Britain's defense expenditures during the 1871–1914 period (GB-Mil$_t$) to be a linear function of:

1. Defense expenditures during the previous year (GB-Mil$_{t-1}$) —the dynamic term representing the independent influence of bureaucratic-organizational momentum.
2. The sum of the previous year's defense expenditures of non-allied, competitor nations in the six-power system (Adversary-Mil$_{t-1}$)—which incorporates the arms-race, adversary-stimulation effect.
3. A scaled variable that measures the peak intensity of hostile interactions over spheres of influence (Clash$_t$)—a term scored from 1 to 30 that includes such interactions as disputes over patterns of influence in client states and confrontations over control of colonial territory between Britain and the other great powers.
4. The size of Britain's colonial area, log transformed (ln Col-area$_t$)—which is designed to capture the defense imperative of territorial-colonial expansion.
5. A variable representing the multiplicative effect of population,

---

previously where only exogenous variables appear on the right-hand side). Second, Maddala (1971) has shown analytically that if the disturbance is autoregressive it pays to iterate Eq. (148), which amounts to an iterative solution of the relevant maximum-likelihood equations. However, if the disturbance follows an MA process defined by the model in footnote 49, then Hannan's (1965) two-step GLS procedure [which uses $\hat{Y}_{t-1}$ instead of Y_{t-1} in the right-hand side of (148)] amounts to an iterative solution of the maximum-likelihood equations. What these asymptotic results imply for the small-sample properties of the estimators remains to be definitively resolved.

[58] See Choucri and North (1972a, 1972b). The data for this example were kindly supplied by Professor Choucri.

or internal demands, and iron and steel production, or industrial capabilities and resources (Pop * Capabilities$_t$)—a measure of the domestic pressure for external expansion that is hypothesized to be a joint function of population size and level of technological-industrial capabilities.

The Choucri-North model for British arms expenditure during the 44 years preceding the onset of World War I can therefore be expressed as follows:

$$\begin{aligned}\widehat{\text{GB-Mil\$}}_t = {}& \beta_0 + \beta_1 \text{ GB-Mil\$}_{t-1} \\ & + \beta_2 \text{ Adversary-Mil\$}_{t-1} + \beta_3 \text{ Clash}_t \\ & + \beta_4 \ln \text{Colarea}_t + \beta_5 \text{ Pop * Capabilities}_t \\ & + u_t \end{aligned} \quad (150)$$

Table 3 reports the OLS estimates for Eq. (150). Unless great parts of previous sections are in error, these results should exaggerate the influence of the lagged endogenous variable GB-Mil\$$_{t-1}$, and understate the impact of most of the exogenous causal factors—assuming, of course, that the disturbances are autocorrelated.

Since neither the form nor the parameters of the disturbance time-dependence process are known, an IV-GLS procedure is appropriate. Thus we first create the systematic part of GB-Mil\$$_{t-1}$ to obtain consistent estimates of the regression coefficients, which can then be applied to the original data and model to yield estimates of the true disturbances. The relevant IV equation is

$$\begin{aligned}\text{GB-Mil\$}_{t-1} = {}& \hat{\alpha}_0 + \hat{\alpha}_1 \text{ Adversary-Mil\$}_{t-1} + \hat{\alpha}_2 \text{ Adversary-Mil\$}_{t-2} \\ & + \hat{\alpha}_3 \text{ Clash}_t + \hat{\alpha}_4 \text{ Clash}_{t-1} + \hat{\alpha}_5 \ln \text{Colarea}_t \\ & + \hat{\alpha}_6 \ln \text{Colarea}_{t-1} + \hat{\alpha}_7 \text{ Pop * Capabilities}_t \\ & + \hat{\alpha}_8 \text{ Pop * Capabilities}_{t-1} \end{aligned} \quad (151)$$

Consistent estimates of the regression coefficients in the original model are now secured by estimating the second-stage equation:

TABLE 3
OLS Estimates for Equation (150)

Independent Variable	Parameter Estimate	Standard Error	t-Statistic
Intercept	$-3.61E + 6$	$1.11E + 6$	-3.26
GB-Mil\$$_{t-1}$	0.55	0.10	5.73
Adversary-Mil\$$_{t-1}$	0.10	0.03	4.01
Clash$_t$	-915.03	959.07	-0.95
ln Colarea$_t$	$4.08E + 5$	$1.24E + 5$	3.28
Pop*Capabilities$_t$	$-2.28E - 4$	$7.17E - 5$	-3.18

$R^2 = 0.900$ Regression standard error $= 4.37E + 4$ $F = 68.6$; $DF = 5{,}38$

$$\begin{aligned}\text{GB-Mil\$}_t = {} & \beta_0 + \beta_1 \widehat{\text{GB-Mil\$}}_{t-1} \\ & + \beta_2 \text{ Adversary-Mil\$}_{t-1} + \beta_3 \text{ Clash}_t \\ & + \beta_4 \ln \text{Colarea}_t + \beta_5 \text{ Pop} * \text{Capabilities}_t \\ & + \omega_t\end{aligned} \quad (152)$$

Finally we use the coefficients of Eq. (152) in conjunction with the original data to form estimates of the disturbances u_t:

$$\begin{aligned}\hat{u}_t = {} & \text{GB-Mil\$}_t - [\hat{\beta}_0 + \hat{\beta}_1 \text{ GB-Mil\$}_{t-1} \\ & + \hat{\beta}_2 \text{ Adversary-Mil\$}_{t-1} + \hat{\beta}_3 \text{ Clash}_t \\ & + \hat{\beta}_4 \ln \text{Colarea}_t + \hat{\beta}_5 \text{ Pop} * \text{Capabilities}_t]\end{aligned} \quad (153)$$

The disturbance estimates of Eq. (153), unlike those of the OLS results in Table 1, can legitimately be analyzed to determine the structure and coefficients of the time-dependence process. Figure 6 depicts

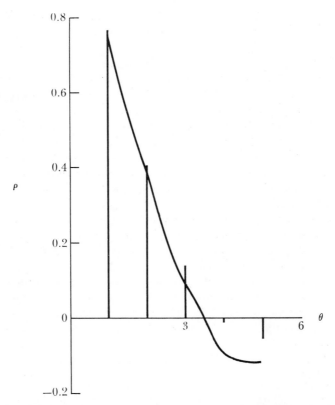

Figure 6. Empirical and theoretical correlograms for Equation (150). Curved line plots empirical autocorrelations; bar lines plot theoretical autocorrelations.

TABLE 4
GLS Estimates for Equation (150)

Independent Variable	Parameter Estimate	Standard Error	t-Statistic
Intercept	$-5.50E+6$	$1.74E+6$	-3.15
GB-Mil\$$_{t-1}$	0.31	0.14	2.29
Adversary-Mil\$$_{t-1}$	0.08	0.03	2.84
Clash$_t$	-274.34	709.48	-0.39
ln Colarea$_t$	$6.20E+5$	$1.94E+5$	3.19
Pop*Capabilities$_t$	$-2.51E-4$	$1.12E-4$	-2.24

$R^2 = 0.593^a$ Regression standard error $= 3.81E+4^a$ $F = 11.07^a$; $DF = 5{,}38$

[a] These GLS statistics should not be compared to the corresponding OLS statistics because they are based on the transformed disturbances AU. See the previous discussion, especially footnote 21.

the empirical (curved line) and theoretical (bar lines) correlograms of the best-fitting model—a second-order autoregressive process with coefficients $\phi_1 = 1.0$ and $\phi_2 = -0.362$.

It is now possible to undertake pseudo-GLS estimation of the initial Choucri-North model for pre-World War I British military expenditures. Table 4 displays the results, which contrast sharply with the biased and inconsistent OLS estimates in Table 3. As one would expect from the statistical theory developed in previous sections, the most important difference involves the coefficient of lagged military expenditures—it decreases in size by about 44 percent. This vitiates considerably Choucri and North's conclusion that the single most important factor affecting the current defense budget is the level of the budget at the previous time period. The bureaucratic-organizational or incrementalist effect is simply not predominant.[59] For example, the standardized regression coefficient or path coefficient of GB-Mil\$$_{t-1}$ (not reported here) exceeds that of all other variables in the OLS results but drops to third place in the GLS results.

Finally the coefficient estimates of the exogenous, independent variables also conform to statistical theory, being on the whole larger in the GLS outcomes than in the OLS results. Specifically the parameter of Adversary-Mil\$$_{t-1}$ is a bit smaller;[60] the parameter of Clash$_t$ remains

---

[59] I suspect that a great many incrementalist theories—which posit the previous year's expenditure or behavior as having a prevailing influence on the current year's outcome—would fare rather poorly when properly estimated.

[60] Although the military expenditure of adversary nations was specified in the early Choucri-North work as exogenous, and has been so treated in the replication here, it is clear from the arms race literature that Adversary-Mil\$ is

insignificant; and the coefficients of ln Colarea$_t$ and Pop * Capabilities$_t$ are significantly larger. Therefore it appears that OLS produced an inflated estimate of the causal influence of lagged expenditures while understating the impact of colonial expansion and internal population-resource pressure.[61]

CONCLUDING REMARKS

I have argued that to proceed with OLS regression in the presence of serially correlated disturbances can seriously impair the statistical estimation-causal inference process. At a minimum OLS produces inflated t, F, and goodness-of-fit statistics and can lead to spurious attribution of significance to independent variables and to exaggerated claims about the success of a model in explaining the phenomena being investigated. In large-scale studies, where a great many equations are estimated sequentially in order to develop final functional forms, initial errors of inference may be compounded—because if the process of model formulation and causal inference is cumulative, then so may be the ultimate impact of mistaken inferences made along the way.

The consequences for estimation of dynamic models, which incorporate lagged endogenous variables on the right-hand side, are even more discouraging. Here consistency—the minimal property of any estimator—is not ensured. Hence neither the absolute nor the relative values of the causal parameters can be taken seriously.

Ideally the causes of autocorrelated disturbances should be included explicitly in an equation, thereby obviating the necessity of pursuing rather complicated estimation techniques designed to deal with the problem. However, this would require that the investigator identify the systematic errors of measurement, the serially correlated minor influences omitted from the model, and other subtle errors in functional form that can produce interdependent disturbances. This simply is not feasible for most models confronted in applied social research, and so we shall have to live with the difficulties of parameter estimation via alternatives to OLS regression.

---

really endogenous. Hence the GLS results that give smaller coefficients and t-statistics for Adversary-Mil\$$_{t-1}$ as well as for GB-Mil\$$_{t-1}$ (and for that matter for Clash$_t$) are entirely compatible with the statistical theory developed above. Choucri and North's current reformulation of the model takes these points fully into account.

[61] Note, however, that the substantial impact of the Pop*Capabilities variable is opposite in sign to that anticipated by the Choucri-North theory in both the OLS and GLS results.

Finally, all the problems surveyed in this chapter apply to multi-equation models as well. Recursive causal systems pose no special difficulty in the sense that the techniques outlined earlier can be straightforwardly employed.[62] Simultaneous equations formulations, however, present additional complications that cannot be developed here without extending this essay far beyond its present length, and in any case have yet to be resolved completely.[63]

REFERENCES

AIGNER, D. J.
- 1971 "A compendium on estimation of the autoregressive-moving average Model from time series data." *International Economic Review* 12 (October).

AITKEN, A. C.
- 1935 "On least squares and linear combination of observations." *Proceedings of the Royal Society of Edinburgh* 55.

AMEMIYA, T.
- 1966 "Specification analysis in the estimation of parameters of a simultaneous equation model with autoregressive residuals." *Econometrica* 34 (April).

ANDERSON, R. L.
- 1942 "Distribution of the serial correlation coefficient." *Annals of Mathematical Statistics* 13.

ANDERSON, T. W.
- 1971 *The Statistical Analysis of Time Series*. New York: Wiley.

BARTLETT, M. S.
- 1946 "On the theoretical specification of sampling properties of autocorrelated time series." *Journal of Royal Statistical Society*, Series B, 8.

BOX, G. E. P. AND JENKINS, G. M.
- 1970 *Time Series Analysis: Forecasting and Control*. San Francisco: Holden-Day.

BOX, G. E. P. AND PIERCE, D. A.
- 1970 "Distribution of residual autocorrelations in autoregressive-integrated moving average time series models." *Journal of the American Statistical Association* 65 (December).

---

[62] Recall that such systems require causal influences to flow hierarchically or unidirectionally (the matrix of endogenous-variable coefficients is triangular) and also require disturbances to be uncorrelated across equations (the cross-equation disturbance variance-covariance matrix must be diagonal). If a lagged endogenous variable appears in such a model and disturbances are autocorrelated, the latter assumption of recursive models must break down and the techniques presented in the last section become appropriate. Otherwise the procedures developed in earlier sections are servicable.

[63] See Amemiya (1966), Fair (1970), and Sargan (1961).

BUSE, A.
  1973 "Goodness of fit in generalized least squares estimation." *The American Statistician* 27 (June).
CHOUCRI, N. AND NORTH, R. C.
  1972a "Causes of World War I: A quantitative analysis of longer-range dynamics." In K. J. Gantzel, G. Kress, and V. Rittberger (Eds.), *Grossmachtrivalität und Weltkrieg: Sozialwissenschaftliche Studien zum Ausbruch des Ersten Weltkrieges und Historikerkommentare*. Gutersloh: Bertelsmann Universitätsverlag.
  1972b "Dynamics of international conflict: Some policy implications of population, resources, and technology." *World Politics* 24, Supplement.
CHRIST, C. F.
  1966 *Econometric Models and Methods*. New York: Wiley.
COCHRANE, D. AND ORCUTT, G. H.
  1949 "Application of least squares regression to relationships containing auto-correlated error terms." *Journal of the American Statistical Association* 44 (March).
DAVIS, O. A., DEMPSTER, M. A. H. AND WILDAVSKY, A.
  1966 "On the process of budgeting: An empirical study of congressional appropriation." In Tullock (Ed.), *Papers on Non-Market Decision Making*. Charlottesville: University of Virginia Press.
DHRYMES, P. J.
  1970 *Econometrics: Statistical Foundations and Applications*. New York: Harper & Row.
  1971 *Distributed Lags: Problems of Estimation and Formulation*. San Francisco: Holden-Day.
DURBIN, J.
  1969 "Tests for serial correlation in regression analysis based on the periodogram of least-squares residuals." *Biometrika* 56 (March).
  1970 "Testing for serial correlation in least-squares regression when some of the regressors are lagged dependent variables." *Econometrica* 38 (May).
DURBIN, J. AND WATSON, G. S.
  1950 "Testing for serial correlation in least squares regression I." *Biometrika* 37 (December).
  1951 "Testing for serial correlation in least squares regression II." *Biometrika* 38 (June).
EISNER, M.
  1972 "TROLL/1: An interactive computer system for econometric research." *Annals of Economic and Social Measurement* 1 (January).
ENGLE, R. F.
  1973 "Specification of the disturbance for efficient estimation." *Econometrica*, forthcoming.
FAIR, R. C.
  1970 "The estimation of simultaneous equation models with lagged

endogenous variables and first order serially correlated errors." *Econometrica* 38 (May).

FISHER, F. M.
1966 *The Identification Problem in Econometrics.* New York: McGraw-Hill.
1970 "Simultaneous equations estimation: The state of the art." *I.D.A. Economic Papers* (July).

FISHMAN, G. S.
1969 *Spectral Methods in Econometrics.* Cambridge, Mass.: Harvard University Press.

GOLDBERGER, A. S.
1964 *Econometric Theory.* New York: Wiley.

GRANGER, C. W. J. AND HATANAKA, M.
1964 *Spectral Analysis of Economic Time Series.* Princeton: Princeton University Press.

GRILICHES, Z.
1957 "Specification bias in estimates of production functions." *Journal of Farm Economics* 39 (February).
1961 "A note on serial correlation bias in estimates of distributed lags." *Econometrica* 29 (January).
1967 "Distributed lags: A survey." *Econometrica* 35 (January).

HADLEY, G.
1961 *Linear Algebra.* Reading, Mass.: Addison-Wesley.

HANNAN, E. J.
1960 *Time Series Analysis.* London: Methuen.
1965 "The estimation of relationships involving distributed lags." *Econometrica* 33 (January).
1970 *Multiple Time Series.* New York: Wiley.

HIBBS, D. A.
1973 "Estimation and identification of multiequation causal models." Appendix 3 in *Mass Political Violence: A Cross-National Causal Analysis.* New York: Wiley.

JENKINS, G. M.
1961 "General considerations in the analysis of spectra." *Technometrics* 3 (May).

JENKINS, G. M. AND WATTS, D. G.
1968 *Spectral Analysis and Its Applications.* San Francisco: Holden-Day.

KENDALL, M. G.
1954 "Note on bias in the estimation of autocorrelation." *Biometrika* 41.

KENDALL, M. G. AND STUART, A.
1968 *Design and Analysis, and Time Series.* Vol. 3 of *The Advanced Theory of Statistics.* New York: Hafner.

LIVIATAN, N.
1963 "Consistent estimation of distributed lags." *International Economic Review* 4.

MADDALA, G. S.
1971 "Generalized least squares with an estimated variance covariance matrix." *Econometrica* 39 (January).

MALINVAUD, E.
  1961 "Estimation et prevision dans les modeles economiques autoregressifs." *Revue de l'Institut International de Statistique* 29.
  1970 *Statistical Methods of Econometrics.* (2nd ed.) London: North-Holland.
MARQUARDT, D. W.
  1963 "An algorithm for least squares estimation of non-linear parameters." *Journal of the Society of Industrial Applied Mathematics* 11 (June).
MARRIOTT, F. H. C. AND POPE, J. A.
  1954 "Bias in the estimation of autocorrelations." *Biometrika* 41.
MORRISON, J. L.
  1970 "Small sample properties of selected distributed lag estimators." *International Economic Review* 11 (February).
MUELLER, J. E.
  1970 "Presidential popularity from Truman to Johnson." *American Political Science Review* 64 (March).
  1973 *War, Presidents and Public Opinion.* New York: Wiley.
NERLOVE, M. AND WALLIS, K. F.
  1966 "Uses of the Durbin-Watson statistic in inappropriate situations." *Econometrica* 34 (January).
ORCUTT, G. H. AND WINOKUR, H. S., JR.
  1969 "First order autoregression: Inference, estimation, and prediction." *Econometrica* 37.
PIERCE, D. A.
  1971a "Distribution of residual autocorrelations in the regression model with autoregressive-moving average errors." *Journal of the Royal Statistical Society*, Series B, 33.
  1971b "Least squares estimation in the regression model with autoregressive-moving average errors." *Biometrika* 58 (August).
  1972 "Least squares estimation in dynamic-disturbance time series models." *Biometrika* 59 (April).
QUENOUILLE, M. H.
  1949 "Approximate tests of correlation in time-series." *Journal of the Royal Statistical Society*, Series B, 11.
RAO, P. AND GRILICHES, Z.
  1969 "Small sample properties of several two-stage regression methods in the context of auto-correlated errors." *Journal of the American Statistical Association* 64 (March).
RUDRA, A.
  1952 "Discrimination in time-series analysis." *Biometrica* 39.
SARGAN, J. D.
  1961 "The maximum likelihood estimation of economic relationships with auto-regressive residuals." *Econometrica* 29 (July).
SARGENT, T. J.
  1968 "Some evidence on the small sample properties of distributed lag estimators in the presence of autocorrelated disturbances." *Review of Economics and Statistics* 50 (February).

THEIL, H.
1957 "Specification errors and the estimation of economic relationships." *Revue de l'Institut International de Statistique* 25.
1971 *Principles of Econometrics.* New York: Wiley.

WALLIS, K. F.
1967 "Lagged dependent variables and serially correlated errors: A reappraisal of three-pass least squares." *Review of Economics and Statistics* 44 (November).
1969 "Some recent developments in applied econometrics: Dynamic models and simultaneous equation systems." *Journal of Economic Literature* 7 (September).
1972 "Testing for fourth order autocorrelation in quarterly regression equations." *Econometrica* 40 (July).

WISE, J.
1955 "The autocorrelation function and the spectral density function." *Biometrika* 42, Part 1 and 2 (June).

11

SPECTRAL ANALYSIS AND THE STUDY OF SOCIAL CHANGE

Thomas F. Mayer
UNIVERSITY OF COLORADO

William Ray Arney
UNIVERSITY OF COLORADO

This research has been supported by a grant from the National Science Foundation (Spectral Theory and the Analysis of Social Change, Grant No. GS-31913, principal investigator Thomas F. Mayer). The assistance of the National Science Foundation is gratefully acknowledged.

Can rigorous quantitative methods be used to study historically significant processes of social change? If such a possibility exists it must surely involve the statistical analysis of time-series data. For many important social processes, highly aggregated time series are virtually the only quantitative indicators presently available. Fundamentally, any quantitative record of social change is a time series of sorts.

What is a time series, and what is time-series analysis? According to T. W. Anderson (1971, p. 1): "A time series is a sequence of observations, usually ordered in time, although in some cases the ordering may be according to another dimension. The feature of time-series analysis which distinguishes it from other statistical analysis is the explicit recognition of the importance of the order in which the observations are made. While in many problems the observations are statistically independent, in time series successive observations may be dependent, and the dependence may depend on the positions in the sequence."

Stated slightly differently, a time series is a sequence of values assumed by some variable. The main objectives of time-series analysis are to establish the principal characteristics of a time series, to determine the nature of the system assumed to be generating a time series, to forecast future values of a series, and to specify the relationships between different time series.

TIME SERIES AND SOCIAL CHANGE

Students of social change have long considered such issues as the causation of change, the consequences of change, the relationship between different processes of change, and the future directions of social change. Time-series analysis may be able to elucidate these issues. The relevance of time-series analysis depends of course on the availability of empirical time series that bear upon the change process of interest.

Some areas of vital interest to the student of social change are totally devoid of pertinent time-series data, but this is not always the case. In the fields of education, the family, migration, minority studies, politics, population, stratification, and urbanization an ample supply of time-series data exists. True, the quality of these time series often leaves much to be desired, but something is usually better than nothing, and if time-series analysis proves to be a fruitful approach to the study of social change much can be done to improve and extend the present data collection system.

Often in the past sociologists interested in the rigorous analysis of social change have despaired over the absence of suitable data. The essential import of time-series analysis is to mitigate such despair since available time series provide data that can in principle sustain a highly quantitative approach to the study of social change.

This chapter attempts to explain and illustrate spectral analysis, a specific variety of time-series analysis that has been widely used in economics, engineering, and other fields. Our hope is to make a relatively complicated subject intelligible to sociologists with some mathematical aptitude, and to help these sociologists identify the conditions under which a spectral approach might prove useful.

PURPOSE OF SPECTRAL ANALYSIS

Modern spectral analysis is a post-World War II development deriving largely from the work of Wiener (1949), Bartlett (1966), and Blackman and Tukey (1958). The founders of spectral analysis were mainly concerned with problems arising in the area of communications engineering, but they soon recognized that the spectral method had a very broad range of application.

Spectral analysis could be described as the result of applying Fourier methods to the statistical analysis of time series. Spectral analysis uses Fourier methods to represent a time series—or more precisely some salient features of a time series—in a different way. This new representation emphasizes aspects of the series otherwise remaining obscure, establishes relations between different points of the series, and provides a springboard for inferences about the nature of the theoretical system generating the series (Fishman, 1969, p. v).

Spectral analysis has at least six capabilities that should be of interest to sociologists: variance decomposition, cyclic analysis, lag estimation, model identification, input-output analysis, and linear system concatenation. In this section we discuss briefly and heuristically each of these capabilities in hopes of motivating the reader to read further. In the section that follows we outline the mathematical concepts necessary for a deeper comprehension of these six capabilities.

Spectral analysis regards a time series as a combination of periodic functions each having a similar mathematical form. Spectral methods distribute the variation manifested by a time series among these constituent periodic functions. This process is sometimes referred to as the *decomposition of variance according to frequency*. A spectral variance decomposition reveals the relative weight of the repetitive tendencies inherent in the empirical time series.[1]

Cyclic analysis flows directly out of variance decomposition. Sometimes it is necessary to specify a social cycle of some kind on the

---

[1] A qualification is necessary here. For purposes of simplicity we speak about decomposition of the variance manifested by a time series. Actually spectral analysis treats an empirical time series as a specific realization of an underlying stochastic process. It is this underlying stochastic process rather than the empirical time series that is of real interest. Consequently spectral analysis aims at decomposing the variance associated with the underlying process, and the empirical series becomes merely the vehicle for accomplishing this end.

basis of a time series that partly reveals and partly obscures this cycle. Spectral analysis makes it possible to identify the most prominent cycle latent in an empirical time series. Not only can spectral methods specify the form of the latent cycle, but they can also indicate the proportion of the overall time-series variance attributable to this cycle. Moreover spectral methods can identify the most prominent cycles satisfying certain a priori constraints. Cyclic analysis has figured prominently in the uses of spectral methods in economics; however, this application is probably less important for sociologists.

Lag estimation refers to the analysis of causation both within a single time series and between different time series. The causal impact of one variable on another is not always instantaneous. Often causation operates only after a certain delay, and equally often causal impact is distributed over a number of time intervals (as opposed to exhausting itself at a single point in time). If relevant time series exist, spectral analysis makes it possible to estimate the lag or delay in the causal relationship between variables. It also makes possible estimation of the way in which causation is distributed over time, plus an educated guess as to which variable is causally prior and which variable is causally subsequent. If one conceives a variable as self-generating or autocausal—that is, if one regards earlier values of the variable as causally related to subsequent values—spectral methods will specify the distribution of causal lag within a single time series.

A social scientist might want to construct a formal model relating several variables as they interact over time. But is it possible to determine what kind of model is most appropriate for the particular variables under consideration? Spectral analysis is extremely useful as a tool for preliminary model identification. It enables the investigator to use the available time-series data to identify which of all linear system models appear most promising.[2] In addition spectral methods can estimate the parameters of the linear system models thus identified.

Input-output analysis refers to investigations of the way in which a system processes inputs to generate outputs. Often the purpose of such an investigation is to decide the kind of input best suited to produce a desired output holding the system constant, or else to choose the system most appropriate for generating a desired output from a given input.[3] Spectral methods are extremely useful in performing input-output analysis, especially for designing optimal systems or optimal system inputs.

[2] A linear system model is a model that can be represented by a system of linear algebraic equations, linear difference equations, linear differential equations, linear integral equations, or any combination thereof.

[3] In the literature on spectral analysis, what we here refer to as input-output analysis is often called *frequency response analysis*.

The reader is probably skeptical as to whether input-output analysis is germane to sociological problems. A little reflection, however, suggests that many social processes can be cast into an input-output framework. Consider, for example, the process of higher education, where the input might be high school graduates of various backgrounds and abilities, the system might be construed as the institutional characteristics of the university, and the output might be college graduates with sundry specializations and competencies. As another example, consider the process of marriage formation and dissolution. Here pairs of men and women would be the input, the family might be the system, and levels of personal satisfaction (or dissatisfaction) and marital stability (or instability) could be the output. Given precise formulation of the input-output system and availability of pertinent time-series data, spectral analysis might advance our understanding of these well-established sociological questions.

Sometimes people pass through several systems in succession. For example, a professional career might be conceptualized as successive passage through secondary education, higher education, military, and several levels of employment. We might wish to infer the net effect of these systems on the basis of information about each separate system. If social systems can be formalized as systems that are linear in the mathematical sense, then spectral analysis accomplishes an enormous simplification in determining the net effect of passage through these systems. This is what we earlier called the use of spectral analysis for concatenating linear systems. Moreover the same mathematical methods enable decomposition of a complex linear system into simple linear components.

In reviewing the capabilities of spectral analysis, brevity (sometimes brevity to the point of obscurity) has been unavoidable. We have also been speculative and vague about concrete applications of spectral methods to sociology. Within the space of a single chapter we cannot hope to illustrate all the applications suggested above, but we will endeavor to illustrate some of these applications with considerable detail. Hopefully these examples (together with the remainder of our exposition) will illuminate both the scope and the limitations of spectral analysis in social science.

BASIC CONCEPTS

The starting point of spectral analysis is the concept of a stochastic process that may be understood as a probabilistic process developing through time. More formally a stochastic process may be defined as follows:

Definition 1 (Stochastic Process): A stochastic process is an ordered collection of random variables $\{X_t\}$.

Just as one can speak of a sample value of a single random variable, one can also speak about a sample value of a stochastic process, sometimes called a realization of the process. A realization of a stochastic process is nothing more than a set of sample values, one for each of the random variables defining the process (taking into consideration the interdependencies among these variables).

Stochastic processes provide an essential link between empirical data and spectral analysis. An empirical phenomenon which unfolds over time is conceptualized as a stochastic process. The empirical time series generated by this phenomenon is interpreted as a realization of the underlying stochastic process. The major point of univariate spectral analysis is to use an empirical time series to learn something about the underlying stochastic process.

A simple stochastic process that occurs repeatedly in spectral analysis is called the purely random process or discrete white noise:

Definition 2 (Discrete White Noise): Let $\{Z_t, t = \ldots, -1, 0, +1, \ldots\}$ be a discrete collection of identically distributed and mutually independent random variables. The stochastic process defined by this collection of random variables is called discrete white noise.

Discrete white noise functions as a building block for constructing more complicated processes and also as a means of testing the adequacy of fit between a model and an observed time series.[4]

One of the most important characteristics of a stochastic process is its autocovariance function, which measures the strength of the linear relationship between the random variables that constitute the process. More precisely:

Definition 3 (Autocovariance Function): Let $\{X_t\}$ be a stochastic process. The autocovariance function of this process $\gamma_{xx}(u,v)$ is defined as

$$\gamma_{xx}(u,v) = E[X_u \cdot X_v] - E[X_u]E[X_v] \quad (1)$$

where $E[Z]$ denotes the expected value of Z.[5]

The autocovariance function is useful not only for the information

---

[4] Continuous white noise is another stochastic process that frequently occurs in spectral analysis. The definition of continuous white noise is somewhat more complicated than that of its discrete counterpart. Since we shall be concerned mainly with discrete time series we can safely confine attention to discrete white noise.

[5] The estimate of the autovariance function of series $\{x_t\}$ used in this chapter is $\gamma_{xx}(p) = 1/(n-p) \sum_{q=1}^{n-p} (x_q - \bar{x})(x_{p+q} - \bar{x})$, where n is the number of points in series $\{x_t\}$.

it provides about a stochastic process, but also as a means of classifying stochastic processes. An important class of processes is covariance stationary processes.

Definition 4 (Covariance Stationary Process): A stochastic process $\{X_t\}$ is called covariance stationary if its autocovariance function $\gamma_{xx}(u,v)$ depends only on the difference $v - u$ and not on the particular values of u and v.

If we write the autocovariance function of a covariance stationary process $\{X_t\}$ in the form $\gamma_{xx}(t, t + u)$, the following notational simplification is justified:

$$\gamma_{xx}(t, t + u) = \gamma_{xx}(u) \tag{2}$$

We shall make extensive use of this simplification.

Spectral analysis focuses almost exclusively on covariance stationary processes. This is largely because a single realization of such a process can be used to make statistically valid inferences about the nature of the process itself. If an empirical time series is generated by a covariance stationary process, we can use the time series to make plausible statements about the underlying process. If the empirical series arises from a process that is not covariance stationary, very little can be said about the process on the basis of the series.

An important example of a covariance stationary process is the linear process, which is derived from white noise:

Definition 5 (Discrete Linear Process): Let $\{Z_t\}$ be discrete white noise and let $E[Z_t] = 0$ for all t. A process $\{X_t\}$ defined as

$$X_t - \mu = \sum_{i=0}^{\infty} a_i Z_{t-i} \tag{3}$$

where the a_i are constants is called a discrete linear process. The autocovariance function of a discrete linear process is

$$\gamma_{xx}(u) = \sigma_z^2 \sum_{i=0}^{\infty} a_i a_{i+u} \tag{4}$$

where σ_z^2 is the common variance of the Z_t variables (that is, σ_z^2 is the variance of each Z_t variable).

Suppose we have two stochastic processes. One meaningful indicator of the relationship between these processes is the cross-covariance function:

Definition 6 (Cross-Covariance Function): Let $\{X_t\}$ and $\{Y_t\}$ be two stochastic processes. The cross-covariance function $\gamma_{xy}(u,v)$ is defined as

$$\gamma_{xy}(u,v) = E[X_u \cdot Y_v] - E[X_u]E[Y_v] \tag{5}$$

The cross-covariance function measures the strength of a linear relationship between two processes at any pair of time points. If processes $\{X_t\}$ and $\{Y_t\}$ are both covariance stationary, their cross-covariance function $\gamma_{xy}(u,v)$ depends only on the difference $v - u$ and we may write

$$\gamma_{xy}(t, t + u) = \gamma_{xy}(u) \tag{6}$$

Autocovariance and cross-covariance functions are extermely important for problems of prediction. Suppose we have two covariance stationary processes $\{X_t\}$ and $\{Y_t\}$ and wish to construct the best linear predictor for process $\{Y_t\}$ based on process $\{X_t\}$. We want, that is, to find a set of constants h_i such that the function

$$\sum_{i=0}^{\infty} h_i X_{t-i} \qquad t = \ldots, -1, 0, +1, \ldots \tag{7}$$

provides the best possible estimate of Y_t.[6] The theoretical basis for a method of selecting constants h_i is given by the Wiener-Hopf theorem:

Theorem 1 (Wiener-Hopf Theorem)[7]: Let $\{X_t\}$ and $\{Y_t\}$ be covariance stationary processes. Let the constants h_i define a linear predictor based on $\{X_t\}$ that minimizes the mean square error between its predictions and the values of the variables in process $\{Y_t\}$. The constants h_i must satisfy the following equation:

$$\gamma_{xy}(u) = \sum_{i=0}^{\infty} h_i \gamma_{xx}(u - i) \tag{8}$$

The Wiener-Hopf theorem is a crucial result for spectral analysis.

So far we have discussed general concepts of time-series analysis, and not those that are peculiar to spectral theory. To explain such concepts as power spectrum and cross-spectrum, we must say a word about Fourier analysis. At considerable risk of oversimplification we can say that the main point of Fourier analysis is to represent functions or series as sums of periodic functions. The main problem of Fourier analysis concerns how such a representation can be accomplished.

Suppose we have a finite series $s_{-n}, \ldots, s_0, \ldots, s_{n-1}$ containing exactly $N = 2n$ terms. According to Fourier analysis, this series can be represented by the following sum of sines and cosines:

$$s_i = A_0 + 2\sum_{k=1}^{n-1} A_k \cos(2\pi i k/N) + A_n \cos(\pi i) + 2\sum_{k=1}^{n-1} B_k \sin(2\pi i k/N) \tag{9}$$
$$i = -n, \ldots, 0, \ldots, n-1$$

[6] For the sake of notational simplicity, we are ignoring constants that would correct for the means of variables X_t and Y_t. This simplification does not affect the essential argument given if the text.

[7] Actually this is only the discrete version of the Wiener-Hopf theorem.

where
$$A_k = 1/N \sum_{i=-n}^{n-1} s_i \cos(2\pi i k/N) \qquad k = 0, \ldots, n \qquad (10)$$

and
$$B_k = 1/N \sum_{i=-n}^{n-1} s_i \sin(2\pi i k/N) \qquad (11)$$

Although sines and cosines have clear intuitive content, it is frequently more convenient to work with the complex exponential function e^{jx}, $j^2 = -1$, defined as

$$e^{jx} = \cos(x) + j \sin(x) \qquad (12)$$

Suppose we want to represent an infinite series $\ldots, s_i, \ldots$. Using the complex exponential function, we have

$$s_i = \int_{-\frac{1}{2}}^{\frac{1}{2}} S(f) e^{j2\pi i f} df \qquad (13)$$

and
$$S(f) = \sum_{i=-\infty}^{\infty} s_i e^{-j2\pi i f} \qquad -\frac{1}{2} \leq f \leq \frac{1}{2} \qquad (14)$$

The function $S(f)$ is called the Fourier transform of the series s_i.

One might think the proper way of proceeding would be to find a Fourier representation of a time series. According to the spectral model, however, a time series is merely a particular realization of an underlying stochastic process. A single process has many different realizations, and the Fourier representation of any single realization is not particularly informative. Of much more interest is the Fourier representation of the autocovariance function. This leads us directly to the power spectrum concept.

Definition 7 (Power Spectrum): Let $\{X_t\}$ be a covariance stationary stochastic process with autocovariance function $\gamma_{xx}(u)$. The power spectrum $\Gamma_{xx}(f)$ of process $\{X_t\}$ is the Fourier transform of the autocovariance function. That is,

$$\Gamma_{xx}(f) = \sum_{u=-\infty}^{\infty} \gamma_{xx}(u) e^{-j2\pi u f} \qquad -\frac{1}{2} \leq f \leq \frac{1}{2}; j^2 = -1 \qquad (15)$$

The power spectrum $\Gamma_{xx}(f)$ is nonnegative for all values $-\frac{1}{2} \leq f \leq \frac{1}{2}$. Moreover it is possible to recover the autocovariance function from the power spectrum using this formula:

$$\gamma_{xx}(u) = \int_{-\frac{1}{2}}^{\frac{1}{2}} \Gamma_{xx}(f) e^{j2\pi u f} df \qquad (16)$$

Thus no information is lost in moving from the autocovariance function to the power spectrum or vice versa.

The last expression may provide some insight into the real meaning of the power spectrum concept. The independent variable f of the power spectrum $\Gamma_{xx}(f)$ indicates frequencies of the complex exponential periodic functions $e^{j2\pi uf}$ that are used to represent the autocovariance function $\gamma_{xx}(u)$. The power spectrum specifies the importance or weight of each frequency in the Fourier representation of the autocovariance function. It thereby suggests the strength of various periodic tendencies in the covariance stationary process, which presumably generates an observed time series. The autocovariance function is sometimes called the *time domain representation* and the power spectrum the *frequency domain representation* of a covariance stationary stochastic process.

If we set u equal to zero in (16), the following equality results:

$$\sigma_x^2 = \int_{-\frac{1}{2}}^{\frac{1}{2}} \Gamma_{xx}(f) df \qquad (17)$$

where σ_x^2 equals the common variance of all random variables that constitute the covariance stationary process $\{X_t\}$. According to (17) the power spectrum provides a decomposition of the variance of process $\{X_t\}$ with respect to frequency.

Just as the autocovariance function leads to the power spectrum, the cross-covariance function leads to another important concept of spectral analysis called the cross-spectrum:

Definition 8 (Cross-spectrum): Let $\{X_t\}$ and $\{Y_t\}$ be discrete covariance stationary processes having cross-covariance function $\gamma_{xy}(u)$. The cross-spectrum $\Gamma_{xy}(f)$ of processes $\{X_t\}$ and $\{Y_t\}$ is the Fourier transform of the cross-covariance function. That is,

$$\Gamma_{xy}(f) = \sum_{u=-\infty}^{\infty} \gamma_{xy}(u) e^{-j2\pi uf} \qquad -\tfrac{1}{2} \leq f \leq \tfrac{1}{2}\,;\, j^2 = -1 \qquad (18)$$

As in the case of the power spectrum, it is possible to recover the cross-covariance function from the cross-spectrum using an inversion formula completely analogous to (16):

$$\gamma_{xy}(u) = \int_{-\frac{1}{2}}^{\frac{1}{2}} \Gamma_{xy}(f) e^{j2\pi uf} df \qquad (19)$$

The cross-spectrum expresses the relationship between two covariance stationary processes in frequency terms. Specifically the cross-spectrum expresses the strength of periodic components at each frequency level that are common to both processes. The power spectrum is always a real-valued function, but the cross-spectrum is often complex-valued.

The cross-spectrum gives rise to spectra of several different types that are useful for investigating various aspects of the relationship between a pair of covariance stationary processes.

Definition 9 (Cospectrum and Quadrature Spectrum): Let $\Gamma_{xy}(f)$ be the cross-spectrum between two covariance stationary processes $\{X_t\}$ and $\{Y_t\}$. Represent $\Gamma_{xy}(f)$ in terms of its real and imaginary parts as follows:

$$\Gamma_{xy}(f) = L_{xy}(f) - jQ_{xy}(f) \qquad (20)$$

where $j^2 = -1$, and both $L_{xy}(f)$ and $Q_{xy}(f)$ are real-valued. The function $L_{xy}(f)$ is called the cospectrum of $\{X_t\}$ and $\{Y_t\}$; the function $Q_{xy}(f)$ is called the quadrature spectrum of these processes. The cospectrum measures the symmetric component of the relationship between processes $\{X_t\}$ and $\{Y_t\}$ at each frequency, whereas the quadrature spectrum measures the asymmetric component of this relationship.[8]

Another way of representing the cross-spectrum is called phase-amplitude representation.

Definition 10 (Phase Spectrum and Cross-amplitude Spectrum): Let $\Gamma_{xy}(f)$ be the cross-spectrum between two covariance stationary processes $\{X_t\}$ and $\{Y_t\}$. It is always possible to write $\Gamma_{xy}(f)$ in the following complex exponential form, which is called the phase-amplitude representation:

$$\Gamma_{xy}(f) = \alpha_{xy}(f) e^{j\varphi_{xy}(f)} \qquad (21)$$

where $j^2 = -1$, and both $\alpha_{xy}(f)$ and $\varphi_{xy}(f)$ are real-valued functions. The function $\varphi_{xy}(f)$ is called the phase spectrum of $\{X_t\}$ and $\{Y_t\}$; the function $\alpha_{xy}(f)$ is called the cross-amplitude spectrum of these processes.

The phase spectrum $\varphi_{xy}(f)$ indicates whether the periodic component of process $\{X_t\}$ at frequency f leads or lags behind the periodic component of the same frequency of process $\{Y_t\}$, and by how much. The cross-amplitude spectrum $\alpha_{xy}(f)$ measures the degree of association between the amplitude of the periodic component at frequency f of process $\{X_t\}$ and the amplitude of the periodic component at the same frequency of process $\{Y_t\}$.

The relationships between the cospectrum and quadrature spectrum on the one hand, and the phase spectrum and cross-amplitude spectrum on the other, are given by the following expressions:

$$\alpha_{xy}(f) = \sqrt{L_{xy}^2(f) + Q_{xy}^2(f)} \qquad (22)$$

$$\varphi_{xy}(f) = \arctan - \frac{Q_{xy}(f)}{L_{xy}(f)} \qquad (23)$$

---

[8] The cross-covariance function can be represented as the sum of an even function and an odd function. The cospectrum is the Fourier transform of the even function in this sum; the quadrature spectrum is the Fourier transform of the odd function.

One further type of spectrum is frequently used:

Definition 11 (Squared Coherency Spectrum): Let $\{X_t\}$ and $\{Y_t\}$ be covariance stationary processes having power spectra $\Gamma_{xx}(f)$ and $\Gamma_{yy}(f)$ respectively. Let $\Gamma_{xy}(f)$ be the cross-spectrum of these processes. The squared coherency spectrum $\kappa_{xy}^2(f)$ is defined as follows:

$$\begin{aligned}\kappa_{xy}^2(f) &= |\Gamma_{xy}(f)|^2/\Gamma_{xx}(f)\,\Gamma_{yy}(f) \\ &= \alpha_{xy}^2(f)/\Gamma_{xx}(f)\,\Gamma_{yy}(f)\end{aligned} \quad (24)$$

The squared coherency spectrum is essentially a normalized version of the cross-amplitude spectrum. It is analogous to a correlation coefficient between two processes defined at each frequency f. The squared coherency spectrum remains unchanged when the two processes generating it are subjected to a wide variety of operations.

The practical value of spectral analysis is closely connected with the use of spectral concepts for the investigation of time-invariant linear systems. From a mathematical point of view a system is a set of relationships between input functions and output functions. A system is completely characterized when the nature of the dependence between input and output functions is known. A system is time-invariant when a time displacement in the input functions produces a similar time displacement in the output functions. Definition 12 states this idea in more precise terms:

Definition 12 (Time-invariant System): Consider a system for which input function $f(t)$ generates output function $g(t)$. This system is called time-invariant if input function $f(t + t_0)$ generates output function $g(t + t_0)$ for all values of t_0.

A system is linear if a linear combination of input functions produces the same linear combination of corresponding output functions.

Definition 13 (Linear System): Consider a system for which input function $f_i(t)$ produces output function $g_i(t)$. This system is called linear if input $f(t) = af_1(t) + bf_2(t)$ produces output $g(t) = ag_1(t) + bg_2(t)$.

Time-invariant linear systems are frequently characterized by systems of linear algebraic equations, linear difference equations, linear differential equations, linear integral equations, or combinations thereof.

A discrete time-invariant linear system is a time-invariant linear system for which the input and output functions are discrete time series. Such a system can be characterized in a number of standardized ways. One standardized method of characterization is through the impulse response function.

Definition 14 (Discrete Impulse Response Function): Consider a discrete time-invariant linear system having input series $\{x_k\}$ and output series $\{y_k\}$. It is always possible to write the relationship between input and output in the following form:

$$y_k = \sum_{i=0}^{\infty} h_i x_{k-i} \qquad (25)$$

where $h_0, h_1, \ldots$ are constants. The collection of these constants $\{h_i\}$ is called the impulse response function of the discrete time-invariant linear system.

There is a one-to-one relationship between time-invariant linear systems and impulse response functions. Each impulse response function corresponds to a unique time-invariant linear system, and each such system corresponds to a unique impulse response function.

A second way of characterizing a time-invariant linear system is through its frequency response function.

Definition 15 (Discrete Frequency Response Function): Consider a discrete time-invariant linear system having impulse response function $\{h_i\}$. The frequency response function of the system $H(f)$ is simply the Fourier transform of the impulse response function. That is,

$$H(f) = \sum_{i=0}^{\infty} h_i e^{-j2\pi i f} \qquad -\tfrac{1}{2} \leq f \leq \tfrac{1}{2} \, ; j^2 = -1 \qquad (26)$$

As in the case of impulse functions, there is a one-to-one relationship between frequency response functions and time-invariant linear systems.

Suppose we have a discrete time-invariant linear system with input series $\{x_k\}$, output series $\{y_k\}$, and impulse response function $\{h_i\}$. The relationship between these entities is given in (25). Let $H(f)$ be the frequency response function of the system, and let $X(f)$ and $Y(f)$ be the Fourier transforms of $\{x_k\}$ and $\{y_k\}$ respectively. thus

$$X(f) = \sum_{k=0}^{\infty} x_k e^{-j2\pi k f} \qquad (27)$$

and
$$Y(f) = \sum_{k=0}^{\infty} y_k e^{-j2\pi k f} \qquad (28)$$

The following relationship holds:

$$Y(f) = H(f) \cdot X(f) \qquad (29)$$

Expression (29) is sometimes referred to as the representation of the time-invariant linear system in the frequency domain, whereas expression (25) is its representation in the time domain. Note that the frequency domain representation of the system involves simple multiplication only. This extreme simplification helps explain the value of Fourier analysis for investigating linear systems. As we shall soon see, it also helps explain the utility of spectral analysis.

So far we have dealt with linear systems only in their deterministic aspects. It is also possible to conceive of linear systems in which the input is a stochastic process and the output is another stochastic process. Two stochastic processes connected in this way are said to be linearly related. Generally we may define linearly related stochastic processes as follows:

Definition 16 (Discrete Linearly Related Stochastic Processes): Let $\{X_t\}$ and $\{Y_t\}$ be discrete covariance stationary stochastic processes that are related like this:

$$Y_t = \sum_{i=0}^{\infty} h_i X_{t-i} + Z_t \qquad (30)$$

where $h_0, h_1, \ldots$ are constants and $\{Z_t\}$ is discrete white noise. The two processes $\{X_t\}$ and $\{Y_t\}$ are said to be linearly related. Moreover the collection of constants $\{h_i\}$ is called the impulse response function of the linearly related processes. Finally the Fourier transform $H(f)$ of this impulse response function is called the frequency response function of the linearly related processes.

Suppose $\{X_t\}$ and $\{Y_t\}$ are linearly related processes with impulse response function $\{h_i\}$. Let $\gamma_{xx}(u)$ be the autocovariance function of process $\{X_t\}$ and let $\gamma_{xy}(u)$ be the cross-covariance function for the two processes. Then

$$\gamma_{xy}(u) = \sum_{i=0}^{\infty} h_i \gamma_{xx}(u - i) \qquad (31)$$

Note that the specific properties of the white-noise process included in (30) have no effect on the above relationship between the covariance functions. This relationship depends entirely on the impulse response function. Note also that (31) and (8) are identical. If two processes are linearly related, their impulse response function defines the best linear predictor of one on the basis of the other. Moreover, to determine the best linear predictor of one process on the basis of another, one assumes that they are linearly related and calculates an impulse response function on this basis.

Let us carry this example one step further. Let $\Gamma_{xx}(f)$ be the power spectrum of process $\{X_t\}$, let $\Gamma_{xy}(f)$ be the cross-spectrum of the two linearly related processes, and let $H(f)$ be their frequency response function. Then

$$\Gamma_{xy}(f) = H(f)\Gamma_{xx}(f) \qquad (32)$$

or

$$H(f) = \Gamma_{xy}(f)/\Gamma_{xx}(f) \qquad (33)$$

Clearly spectral functions provide a convenient way of specifying the linear system that connects two linearly related processes. The Wiener-Hopf theorem in conjunction with (13) and (33) shows that spectral methods enable estimation of the best linear predictor of one process on the basis of another. The estimation of linear models constitutes an extremely important use of spectral analysis.

The reader who has followed the exposition to this point should have a fairly good idea about the central ideas of spectral analysis. Further discussion would take us within the realm of multivariate spectral analysis. The symbolism entailed in multivariate spectral analysis is considerably more intricate than the symbolism used for univariate analysis, but the basic notions are similar. Some aspects of multivariate spectral analysis receive brief consideration in subsequent sections that focus on practical applications of spectral methods. Readers who wish to learn more about spectral analysis should consult the books by Anderson (1971), Fishman (1969), Granger and Hatanaka (1964), Hannan (1970), and Jenkins and Watts (1968).

PRACTICAL ASPECTS

The application of spectral analysis raises problems not discussed in our review of basic concepts. We now consider four of these problems: the problem of filtering time-series data, the problem of aligning different time series, the problem of smoothing spectral estimates, and the problem of testing time-series models.

The results of spectral analysis rest heavily on the assumption of covariance stationary processes. When considering the application of spectral analysis to a specific time series we must immediately ask whether the series in question is a realization of a covariance stationary process.

There are several ways of deciding whether a time series may be regarded as a realization of a covariance stationary process. A series generated by a nonstationary process is likely to show monotonic trends or regular oscillatory behavior.[9] The power spectrum of such a series may well concentrate most of its power in a very narrow frequency range typically at very low frequencies.

If these criteria suggest that a time series may emanate from a nonstationary process, direct application of spectral methods can result in serious misinterpretations. Before applying spectral methods it is

[9] Monotonic trending and regular oscillatory behavior are frequently but not inevitably associated with nonstationary processes. Some stationary processes exhibit characteristics of these kinds.

necessary to transform the original time series to create a new series that displays neither strong monotonic trends nor regular oscillatory behavior, and whose spectrum does not concentrate the bulk of its power in a narrow frequency range. This new series may be regarded as the stationary component of the original series, and the procedure by which it is obtained is called filtering.

The most common method transforming a time series is called digital filtering. If $\{x_t\}$ is the original and $\{x_t^*\}$ the transformed time series, a digital filter has the following form:

$$x_t^* = \sum_{i=-\infty}^{\infty} h_i x_{t-i} \qquad (34)$$

where the h_i are constants chosen so as to eleminate the nonstationary components of the original time series $\{x_t\}$.

Although methods of selecting an appropriate digital filter can be quite complicated, two extremely simple digital filters are often adequate for social and economic time series.[10] The first-difference filter has the form

$$x_t^* = x_t - x_{t-1} \qquad (35)$$

and is useful for eliminating monotonic trends in a time series. The second-difference filter may be written as follows:

$$x_t^* = x_t - 2x_{t-1} + x_{t-2} \qquad (36)$$

It is simply the result of applying the first-difference filter twice, and functions to eliminate regular oscillatory components.

The substantive meaning of filtering is briefly discussed in the section *Problems of Spectral Analysis*. Filtering, we should mention here, removes much information contained in the original series. Subsequent explanation pertains only to information that remains after the filtering operation. Some readers may feel that the requirement of covariance stationarity and the filtering necessary to achieve it invalidate the use of spectral methods for analyzing long-term social change. This is not our view.

Difference filters are in some ways the discrete analogs of derivatives, the first-difference filter corresponding to the first derivative, the second-difference filter corresponding to the second derivative, and so on. No one would argue that casting information in terms of derivatives

[10] For additional information about filtering, the reader should consult Morrison (1969).

eliminates the possibility of studying processes of change. The parallel argument with respect to finite differences is hardly more plausible.

Strictly speaking, filtering removes, but does not eliminate, information. Knowing the nature of the filter we can generally reconstruct the original series using the filtered series plus information about the initial values of the original. Such reconstructability is particularly relevant to parametric uses of spectral analysis.

Sometimes it is possible to partition an apparently nonstationary time series into the sum of a baseline series and a stationary series. Typically the baseline series would be a simple function of time (perhaps a polynomial function) with parameters estimated via well-known least-squares methods. The stationary series, which represents deviations from the baseline series, is usually more interesting but less smooth. Naturally it can be analyzed using spectral methods. The results of such analysis help uncover the dynamics by which an empirical process departs from an elementary model of social change.

After a time series has been filtered, it should be inspected to determine whether the desired results have been achieved. This is most easily done by examining the power spectrum of the transformed time series, which should not contain large, narrow peaks (that is, an excessive concentration of power in a narrow frequency range).

A second aspect of applied spectral analysis is called *alignment* or time coordination of different time series. Suppose we have one dependent or output time series and several independent or input time series. Alignment shifts the time variables, indexing the various input time series so that the largest absolute value of each cross-covariance function between the output (dependent) series and each input (independent) series occurs at zero lags (that is, when the abscissa of the cross-covariance function equals zero). The necessity for alignment arises from statistical considerations. Unless input series are aligned with the output series, estimates of spectral parameters suffer from considerable bias. Alignment, it should be noted, leaves the cross-amplitude spectrum unchanged but induces a shift in the phase spectrum.[11]

Another problem encountered in applying spectral theory concerns the shape and stability of estimates of the various spectral concepts. If, for example, one estimates a power spectrum from an empirical time series using formula (15), the result is likely to be extremely jagged in appearance thus obscuring the main theoretical properties of the power

---

[11] The reader who wishes further discussion of alignment can consult Jenkins and Watts (1968, pp. 399–404).

spectrum. Moreover the variance associated with an estimate of this kind is disturbingly high. These considerations suggest the use of smoothing procedures to reduce the variance of the spectral estimate and to emphasize its main properties.

The principal instruments of smoothing in spectral analysis are functions $W(f)$ called spectral windows. Suppose $C_{xx}(f)$ is the power spectrum estimated directly from an empirical time series, whereas $\bar{C}_{xx}(f)$ is an estimate that has been smoothed using the spectral window $W(f)$. Then the following relationship holds:

$$\bar{C}_{xx}(f) = \int_{-\infty}^{\infty} W(g) C_{xx}(f-g) dg \qquad (37)$$

In practice the smoothing operation is carried out somewhat differently than this result suggests, but the preceding equation expresses the essential logic of smoothing.

A general definition of spectral window functions may clarify matters:

Definition 17 (Spectral Window): A spectral window is a function $W(f)$ satisfying the following two conditions: $\int_{-\infty}^{\infty} W(f) = 1$; $W(f) = W(-f)$ (symmetry).

A frequently used spectral window is the Parzen window $W_p(f)$, defined as

$$W_p(f) = \tfrac{3}{4} M \left[\frac{\sin(\pi f M/2)}{\pi f M/2} \right]^4 \qquad -\infty \leq f \leq \infty \qquad (38)$$

where M equals the number of lags for which the autocovariance function has been calculated. Considerable energy has gone into determining precisely which spectral window is best suited for which purpose. Other important spectral windows include the rectangular window, the Bartlett window, the Tukey-Hanning window, and the Tukey-Hamming window.[12]

Another problem of application concerns testing models constructed via spectral analysis. Since the perspective of spectral analysis views time series as a particular realization of an underlying stochastic process, an adequate model need not achieve an exact fit. What is important is that the discrepancy between the model and the empirical time series have a strictly random character. In other words, the residual time series defined by the discrepancies between the model and the empirical series should appear as a realization of a purely random process or what in Definition 2 we called white noise.

---

[12] General discussions of spectral windows appear in Jenkins and Watts (1968, pp. 239–257), Anderson (1971, pp. 506–518), and Neave (1972, pp. 152–158).

The power spectrum of white noise is entirely flat. In fact, if σ_z^2 is the common variance of the random variables included in the discrete white-noise process $\{Z_t\}$ in which the observations are assumed to be separated by a time unit of 1, then[13]

$$\Gamma_{zz}(f) = \sigma_z^2 \tag{39}$$

The preferred test of a time-series model involves determining whether the residual series corresponding to the model has a reasonably flat power spectrum.

The preferred testing method is feasible only if the residual spectrum can be estimated at a large number of frequencies. When this is not the case more conventional (and less subtle) testing procedures must be used. For example, the proportion of the variance in the empirical time series explained by the model may function as an evaluation criterion. This is actually the criterion most often used in the analysis that follows.

The squared coherency spectrum makes possible a nonparametric approach to model-testing. As mentioned in the discussion following Definition 11 the squared coherency spectrum in the frequency domain is comparable to a correlation coefficient in regression analysis. It measures the degree of association between two processes at each frequency f. For each frequency it indicates the degree of success that a model of one process based on another can expect to have.

The squared coherency spectrum illuminates which aspects (defined in frequency terms) of a bivariate model are likely to be successful and which are not. For example, large coherence at low frequencies would indicate that the model probably would have greater success predicting long-term trends than rapid fluctuations in the dependent series.

BIVARIATE SPECTRAL ANALYSIS

The most elementary variety of spectral analysis involves only a single time series. Such univariate spectral analysis attempts to establish

[13] Readers already familiar with spectral analysis may look askance at this result. Some authors derive a slightly different power spectrum for white noise. Fishman (1969, p. 40), for example, gives the power spectrum of white noise as $\sigma_z^2/2\pi$. This divergence does not, however, reflect substantive disagreement. It arises from slightly differing definitions of the Fourier transform. The basic nature of the argument is in no way affected by these variations, but they can lead to minor differences on particular results. By applying Definition 7 to the autocovariance function of white noise $\gamma_{zz}(u) = \begin{cases} \sigma_z^2 & \text{if } u = 0 \\ 0 & \text{if } u \neq 0 \end{cases}$, the reader can easily derive (39).

relationships between past and future values of a time series. This endeavor is by no means devoid of interest for the social sciences; however, we anticipate that the relationship between two or more time series will prove to be of greater interest. Hence we move directly to considering the relationship between two time series, that is, bivariate spectral analysis.

The basic logic of bivariate spectral analysis is rather simple. We are given two empirical time series $\{x_t\}$ and $\{y_t\}$ and for one reason or another decide to treat $\{x_t\}$ as the independent and $\{y_t\}$ as the dependent series. After appropriate filtering we regard the transformed series as realizations of underlying covariance stationary stochastic processes $\{X_t\}$ and $\{Y_t\}$. Let us assume that $\{X_t\}$ and $\{Y_t\}$ are linearly related stochastic processes, which means they are related as in Equation (30). We view the immediate task of bivariate spectral analysis to be twofold: the estimation of the impulse response function $\{h_i\}$ and assistance in deciding about the overall propriety of the linear model.

Our first step is to estimate the autocovariance and cross covariance functions for the given time series: $k_{xx}(u)$, $k_{yy}(u)$, and $k_{xy}(u)$ respectively. This estimation may be accomplished by straightforward extensions of the formulas defining these concepts. The Wiener-Hopf theorem (Theorem 1) implies that the impulse response function estimate $\{\hat{h}_i\}$ which minimizes the mean square error must satisfy the equation

$$k_{xy}(u) = \sum_{i=0}^{m} \hat{h}_i k_{xx}(u - i) \qquad (40)$$

where m equals the number of lags for which the covariance functions have been calculated.

Next we calculate the power spectra and cross-spectrum of the given time series and smooth these estimates using appropriate spectral windows. The analog of Equation (32) is

$$\bar{C}_{xy}(f) = \hat{H}(f)\bar{C}_{xx}(f) \qquad (41)$$

where $\bar{C}_{xx}(f)$ is the smoothed, estimated power spectrum, $\bar{C}_{xy}(f)$ is the smoothed, estimated cross-spectrum, and $\hat{H}(f)$ is an estimate of the frequency response function. Note that (41) is the equation that would result from taking Fourier transforms and smoothing both sides of Equation (40). Thus an optimal estimate of the frequency response function may be obtained from

$$\hat{H}(f) = \bar{C}_{xy}(f)/\bar{C}_{xx}(f) \qquad (42)$$

which is the direct analog of (33).

Finally we obtain an estimate of the impulse response function by taking the inverse Fourier transform of the estimated frequency response function. That is,

$$\hat{h}_i = \int_{-\frac{1}{2}}^{\frac{1}{2}} \hat{H}(f) e^{j2\pi i f} df \qquad i = 0, \ldots, m \qquad (43)$$

Let us illustrate bivariate spectral analysis with a hypothetical example. Suppose we have two linearly related stochastic processes $\{X_t\}$ and $\{Y_t\}$ whose relationship is defined as follows:

$$Y_t = 0.5X_t + 0.75X_{t-1} - 0.6X_{t-3} + Z_t \qquad (44)$$

where Z_t are random terms with mean zero and variance 0.5. Using (44) we generated a pair of time series $\{x_t\}$ and $\{y_t\}$ each with 100 terms. These hypothetical time series were analyzed according to the scheme given above. The frequency response function estimated on the basis of eight lags in the autocovariance and cross-covariance functions appears in Table 1. The impulse response function calculated on the basis of the estimated frequency response function is given in Table 2. Note the close agreement between theoretical and estimated impulse response functions.

Having vindicated the basic procedure by means of a hypothetical example, let us apply spectral methods to real data. Specifically let us consider the relationship between mortality and fertility rates in the United States between 1919 and 1967. Our basic time series are deaths per 1000 persons (residing in the death registration area prior to 1933) symbolized $\{d_t\}$ and births per 1000 women aged 15 to 44 years symbolized $\{f_t\}$.[14]

Before computing spectra of any kind we must filter the mortality and fertility time series to achieve approximate stationarity. A first-difference filter was applied to the mortality series:

$$d_t^* = 10[d_t - d_{t-1}] \qquad (45)$$

The factor of 10 is added to increase the spectral estimates and thus to reduce computational error. The fertility series was processed with a second-difference filter:

$$f_t^* = f_t - 2f_{t-1} + f_{t-2} \qquad (46)$$

Our next step is to align the filtered fertility and filtered mortality series so that the cross-covariance function attains its maximum at zero

---

[14] These two time series and those used in the multivariate model were taken from the U.S. Department of Commerce (1960, 1965) and various issues of the *Statistical Abstract of the United States*. The urbanization series is actually a non-farm population series constructed from the U.S. Department of Agriculture's annual estimates of the farm population.

TABLE 1
Estimated Frequency Response Function for the Single-input Hypothetical Model (100 terms)[a]

Frequency (f)	$\hat{H}(f)$
0.0000	0.691
0.0625	$0.910 + 0.230j$
0.1250	$1.425 - 0.230j$
0.1875	$1.155 - 0.988j$
0.2500	$0.611 - 1.261j$
0.3125	$-0.270 - 1.010j$
0.3750	$-0.385 - 0.074j$
0.4375	$0.113 + 0.228j$
0.5000	0.295

[a] Only the positive half of the frequency response function is shown since $H(-f)$ equals the complex conjugate of $H(f)$. $j^2 = -1$.

TABLE 2
Theoretical and Estimated Impulse Response Function for the Single-input Hypothetical Example (100 terms)

i	Theoretical h_i	Estimated $\hat{h}_i$
0	0.5000	0.5068
1	0.7500	0.7387
2	0	0.0148
3	−0.6000	−0.5412
4	0	0.0105
5	0	−0.0268
6	0	−0.0486
7	0	0.0489
8	0	0.0295

lag. We shall treat mortality as the independent and fertility as the dependent series. Thus alignment entails a transformation of the time variable indexing the mortality series. Equation (47) gives the specific alignment transformation:

$$d_t^{**} = d_{t-4}^{*} \tag{47}$$

Table 3 reveals that the spectra of the transformed series have relatively low power at low frequencies, suggesting that the condition of stationarity is approximated in both series. Table 3 also gives the cross-amplitude spectrum between the filtered, aligned mortality and the filtered fertility series, and the squared coherency spectrum. Note the concentration of power in the higher frequencies of the cross-amplitude spectrum and the large coherence at the same frequencies.

Using the techniques discussed above, and treating mortality as the independent and fertility as the dependent series, let us compute the

TABLE 3
Power Spectra, Cross-amplitude Spectrum, and Squared Coherency Spectrum for Filtered and Aligned Mortality Series and Filtered Fertility Series (43 terms)[a]

Frequency (f)	Power Spectrum of Filtered and Aligned Mortality Series (d^{**})	Power Spectrum of Filtered Fertility Series (f^*)	Cross-amplitude Spectrum of Transformed Mortality and Fertility Series	Squared Coherency Spectrum of Transformed Mortality and Fertility Series
0.0000	0.634	0.347	0.208	0.196
0.0625	1.568	0.387	0.262	0.113
0.1250	2.820	3.751	1.047	0.104
0.1875	3.105	14.633	1.442	0.046
0.2500	5.065	19.228	4.143	0.176
0.3125	9.500	12.448	3.898	0.128
0.3750	9.394	8.575	5.114	0.324
0.4375	5.693	7.069	4.809	0.575
0.5000	6.337	6.129	5.639	0.816

[a] Spectral estimates were smoothed using the Tukey-Hamming window (see Neave, 1972, p. 154).

TABLE 4
Estimated Frequency Response Function for Bivariate Spectral Analysis with Fertility as the Dependent and Mortality as the Independent Series[a]

Frequency (f)	$\hat{H}(f)$
0.0000	0.5854
0.0625	$-0.0382 + 0.1251j$
0.1250	$-0.1534 - 0.3366j$
0.1875	$-0.0699 + 0.8433j$
0.2500	$-0.4147 - 1.9041j$
0.3125	$0.1422 - 0.4533j$
0.3750	$0.6844 + 0.2514j$
0.4375	$0.1803 - 0.7378j$
0.5000	0.7323

[a] Only the positive half of the frequency response function is shown since $H(-f)$ equals the complex conjugate of $H(f)$. $j^2 = -1$.

frequency response function and the impulse response function. Tables 4 and 5 display these functions. The impulse response function has several fairly substantial negative components, which is consistent with the concentration of power in higher frequencies observed in the cross-amplitude function.

How well can we project fertility on the basis of mortality using the estimated impulse response function? From the squared coherency spectrum in Table 3 we would expect a model to explain a large amount

TABLE 5
Estimated Impulse Response Function Relating the Filtered and Unaligned Mortality Series to the Fertility Series

i	$\hat{h}_i$
0	0.0322
1	0.0980
2	0.0116
3	0.0728
4	−0.1866
5	0.5056
6	−0.1476
7	−0.3224
8	−0.0215

of the rapid fluctuations in the fertility series, a moderate amount of fluctuations of a slightly lower frequency, and very little about long-term trends in the data. (Note that the filtering procedure has removed most of the long-term trend and that there thus remains little to be explained at the lower frequencies.) The linear predictor implied by the impulse response function is

$$f_t^* = \sum_{i=0}^{8} \hat{h}_i d_{t-i}^* \qquad (48)$$

The fertility projection based on this formula is plotted against the filtered fertility series in Figure 1.

Visual inspection of Figure 1 suggests that agreement between the projected and the observed series is reasonably close, but a more rigorous comparison is necessary. Let us examine the residual series defined by the differences between the observed and the projected series. If the process generating mortality were indeed linearly related to the process generating fertility, then the residual series should approximate white noise. Were this true, the spectrum of the residual series (or, more appropriately, the residual spectrum) would be flat or nearly so.

Figure 2 presents the residual spectrum[15] along with the spectrum

---

[15] Assume that a system has a single-covariance stationary, dependent process $\{Y_t\}$ and q covariance stationary, independent processes $\{X_{1,t}\}$, $\{X_{2,t}\}$, ..., $\{X_{q,t}\}$. The spectrum of $\{Y_t\}$ is $\Gamma_{yy}(f)$ and the cross-spectra between each independent process and the dependent process are $\Gamma_{yx_i}(f)$, $i = 1, 2, ..., q$. Furthermore the partial frequency response functions (see Definition 18) $H_{yx_1}(f)$, $H_{yx_2}(f)$, ..., $H_{yx_q}(f)$ are known. Now the spectrum of the residuals of the system characterized in such a way is

$$\Gamma_{zz}(f) = \Gamma_{yy}(f) - \sum_{i=1}^{q} H_{yx_i}(f) \Gamma_{yx_i}(f) \qquad 0 \leq f \leq \tfrac{1}{2}$$

In the bivariate case where a system has a single independent and a single dependent process the residual spectrum is $\Gamma_{zz}(f) = \Gamma_{yy}(f) - H_{yx}(f) \Gamma_{yx}(f)$, $0 \leq f \leq \tfrac{1}{2}$.

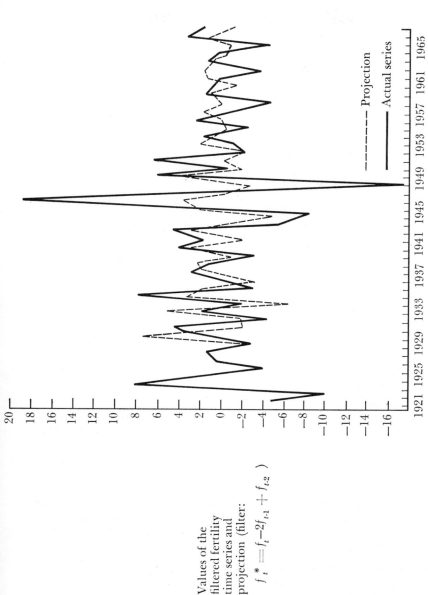

Figure 1. Plots of filtered fertility time series and fertility projected on the basis of the filtered and aligned mortality series. The first eight values of fertility were not projected because the first eight terms of the mortality series were used to initiate the projection.

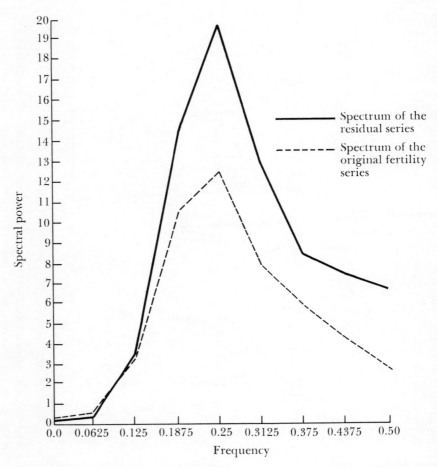

Figure 2. Power spectra of the filtered fertility series and the residual series based on the projection of fertility from mortality.

of the original filtered fertility series. The residual spectrum is certainly not flat, indicating that the fertility process cannot be predicted with a great deal of reliability through a linear relationship with mortality. Nevertheless some flattening has been accomplished; the residual spectrum contains a substantially smaller peak than does the original fertility spectrum. Comparing fertility series suggests that the mortality process explains about 35 percent of the variance in fertility via a linear relationship. Also, note that expectations about the frequency-specific explanatory power of the model which were obtained from our interpretation of the squared coherency spectrum are confirmed.

Several other things can be learned by comparison of the residual and the original fertility spectra. If the residual spectrum were exactly proportional to the fertility spectrum at all frequencies, the impact of mortality on fertility would be tantamount to a change in the scale of the fertility variable. Examination of Equation (15) should convince the reader of this. However, the relationship between the fertility and residual spectra is not one of exact proportionality. The peaks of the two spectra do occur at the same frequency, but as frequency increases, the power of the residual spectrum constitutes a progressively smaller fraction of the fertility spectrum power. Mortality, this suggests, explains more about the short-range than the long-range fluctuations in fertility. Together the invariant position of the spectral peak and the unaltered shape of the power spectrum (that is, unaltered between the fertility spectrum and the residual spectrum) imply that the overall character of the fertility process is not attributable to a linear relationship with mortality.

Before leaving bivariate spectral analysis let us examine the substantive meaning of the impulse response function presented in Table 5. Using this impulse response function, which is already corrected for alignment, we shall calculate a relationship between the original (unfiltered) mortality and fertility time series. This is accomplished by substituting the filtering equations (45) and (46) into the impulse response function. The following relationship results:

$$f_t = (2f_{t-1} - f_{t-2}) + (0.3d_t + 0.7d_{t-1} - 0.9d_{t-2} \\ + 0.6d_{t-3} - 2.6d_{t-4} + 7.0d_{t-5} - 6.6d_{t-6} \\ + 4.7d_{t-7} - 3.4d_{t-8} + 0.2d_{t-9}) \quad (49)$$

What substantive conclusions does this formal relationship suggest? There appears to be a feedback mechanism operating with respect to fertility. This mechanism affects the present fertility rate in the direction of continuing the trend manifest between the previous two time periods. Insofar as this feedback meahanism holds sway, it generates a stable rate of change in fertility.

In very general terms, the effect of mortality is to alter the fertility from what it would be if only the feedback mechanism were operative. The use of a first-difference filter requires that the sum of the positive coefficients of mortality terms in (49) equal the sum of the negative coefficients. Thus we cannot determine whether the net effect of mortality on fertility is positive or negative. However, the presence of both positive and negative terms suggests that cscillations originating in the mortality series may appear in even more pronounced form in the fertility series. Conversely a constant mortality rate, irrespective of level, exerts no net influence on fertility. Generally the principal impact of mortality on fertility occurs only after a lag of five, six, and seven years.

MULTIVARIATE SPECTRAL ANALYSIS

For our purposes multivariate spectral analysis can be distinguished from its bivariate counterpart by the number of independent or input processes involved. Bivariate spectral analysis considers one dependent (or output) process and one independent (or input) process. Multivariate spectral analysis, on the other hand, deals with one dependent but many independent processes.

As a point of departure, let us define *multivariate linearly related stochastic processes:*

Definition 18 (*Discrete Multivariate Linearly Related Stochastic Processes*): Let $\{X_{1,t}\}$, $\{X_{2,t}\}$, ..., $\{X_{q,t}\}$, and $\{Y_t\}$ be discrete covariance stationary processes that are related as follows:

$$Y_t = \sum_{i=1}^{q}\left[\sum_{j=0}^{\infty} h_{ij}X_{i,t-j}\right] + Z_t \qquad (50)$$

where the h_{ij} are constants and $\{Z_t\}$ is discrete white noise. Process $\{Y_t\}$ is said to be linearly dependent on processes $\{X_{1,t}\}$, ..., $\{X_{q,t}\}$. More simply, processes $\{X_{1,t}\}$, ..., $\{X_{q,t}\}$ and $\{Y_t\}$ are said to be multivariate linearly related stochastic processes. The collections $\{h_{1,j}\}$, ..., $\{h_{q,j}\}$ are called partial impulse response functions; the Fourier transforms of these functions $H_1(f)$, ..., $H_q(f)$ are called the partial frequency response functions of the multivariate linearly related stochastic processes.

The cross-covariance functions for multivariate linearly related stochastic processes may be written thusly:

$$\gamma_{X_k Y}(u) = \sum_{i=1}^{q}\sum_{j=0}^{\infty} h_{ij}\gamma_{X_k X_i}(u-j) \qquad k = 1, \ldots, q \qquad (51)$$

Taking the Fourier transform of both sides of (51) establishes the following relationships between spectra:

$$\Gamma_{X_k Y}(f) = \sum_{i=1}^{q} \Gamma_{X_k X_i}(f) H_i(f) \qquad k = 1, \ldots, q \ ; \ -\tfrac{1}{2} \leq f \leq \tfrac{1}{2} \qquad (52)$$

It is convenient to write these relationships in matrix notation:

$$G_{XY}(f) = G_{XX}(f)E(f) \qquad -\tfrac{1}{2} \leq f \leq \tfrac{1}{2} \qquad (53)$$

where

$$G_{XY}(f) = \begin{bmatrix} \Gamma_{X_1Y}(f) \\ \cdot \\ \cdot \\ \cdot \\ \Gamma_{X_qY}(f) \end{bmatrix} \quad G_{XX}(f) = \begin{bmatrix} \Gamma_{X_1X_1}(f) & \cdot & \cdot & \cdot & \Gamma_{X_1X_q}(f) \\ \cdot \\ \cdot \\ \cdot \\ \Gamma_{X_qX_1}(f) & \cdot & \cdot & \cdot & \Gamma_{X_qX_q}(f) \end{bmatrix}$$

$$E(f) = \begin{bmatrix} H_1(f) \\ \cdot \\ \cdot \\ \cdot \\ H_q(f) \end{bmatrix}$$

If the inverse $G_{XX}^{-1}(f)$ exists, (53) can be rewritten as

$$E(f) = G_{XX}^{-1}(f) \, G_{XY}(f) \quad -\tfrac{1}{2} \leq f \leq \tfrac{1}{2} \quad (54)$$

This provides an expression for the matrix of partial frequency response functions in terms of cross-spectral matrices. The partial impulse response functions may be obtained by taking the inverse Fourier transform of the partial frequency response functions. Formula (54) furnishes the rationale undergirding many calculations of applied multivariate spectral analysis.

To obtain a nonparametric indication of the propriety of a model the squared multiple coherency spectrum may be used:

Definition 19 (Squared Multiple Coherency Spectrum): Let $\{Y_t\}$, $\{X_{1,t}\}, \{X_{2,t}\}, \ldots, \{X_{q,t}\}$ be covariance stationary processes with $\{Y_t\}$ linearly related to all the $\{X_{i,t}\}$, $i = 1, 2, \ldots, q$ as in (50). Let $H_{yx_i}(f)$ be the partial frequency response function between $\{Y_t\}$ and $\{X_{i,t}\}$, $i = 1, 2, \ldots, q$ and $\Gamma_{yx_i}(f)$ be the cross-spectrum between $\{Y_t\}$ and $\{X_{i,t}\}$. The squared multiple coherency spectrum is defined as follows:

$$\kappa^2_{yx_1x_2\cdots x_q} = \sum_{i=1}^{q} H_{yx_i}(f)\Gamma_{yx_i}(f)/\Gamma_{yy}(f) \quad (55)$$

The squared multiple coherency spectrum is the multivariate counterpart of the squared coherency spectrum defined in Definition 11. It is similar to a multiple correlation coefficient in regression analysis in that it measures the association at each frequency between the dependent process and all the independent processes on the basis of a linear model. Strictly speaking, the squared multiple coherency measures the proportion of the spectrum of the dependent process explicable by the independent processes. Also, note the relationship between the residual spectrum (see footnote 15) and the squared multiple coherency spectrum.

The residual spectrum in a multiple-input model is

$$\Gamma_{zz}(f) = \Gamma_{yy}(f)[1 - \kappa^2_{yx_1x_2...x_q}(f)] \tag{56}$$

Let us illustrate multivariate spectral analysis with a hypothetical example that involves three covariance stationary-input processes $\{X_{1,t}\}$, $\{X_{2,t}\}$, and $\{X_{3,t}\}$ and one output process $\{Y_t\}$ related by the following equation:

$$Y_t = 0.3X_{1,t} - 0.5X_{1,t-1} - 0.4X_{1,t-2} + 0.25X_{2,t-1} - 0.75X_{2,t-3} \\ + 0.99X_{3,t} - 0.1X_{3,t-2} - 0.6X_{3,t-3} + Z_t \tag{57}$$

where $\{Z_t\}$ is a white-noise process in which each constituent variable Z_t has mean zero and variance 0.5.

Four hundred data points were generated using the model specified by Equation (57) and analyzed according to the procedures outlined above. The estimated partial frequency response functions are presented in Table 6; the estimated partial impulse response functions appear in Table 7. As the reader will observe, close agreement exists between theoretical and estimated impulse response functions. However, 400 data points were necessary to achieve the fit reported in Table 7. When fewer data points were used, agreement between theoretical and estimated partial impulse response functions was not particularly impressive. We discuss the implications of this fact in a subsequent section.

We now turn to a real empirical application of multivariate spectral analysis. Specifically we consider the relationship between fertility on the one hand and mortality, unemployment, and urbanization on the

TABLE 6
Estimated Partial Frequency Response Functions
for the Three-input Hypothetical Example

Frequency (f)	Partial Frequency Response Functions[a]		
	$H_1(f)$	$H_2(f)$	$H_3(f)$
0.0000	−0.540	0.395	0.266
0.0625	−0.398 + 0.472j	−0.202 + 0.516j	0.742 + 0.599j
0.1250	−0.136 + 0.807j	0.659 + 0.094j	1.437 + 0.494j
0.1875	0.355 + 0.775j	0.764 − 0.424j	1.572 − 0.143j
0.2500	0.654 + 0.428j	0.004 − 0.979j	1.127 − 0.569j
0.3125	0.791 + 0.152j	−0.767 − 0.507j	0.518 − 0.202j
0.3750	0.661 + 0.015j	−0.607 + 0.279j	0.546 + 0.302j
0.4375	0.411 + 0.091j	0.164 + 0.595j	1.145 + 0.432j
0.5000	0.298	0.448	1.474

[a] Only the positive part of the frequency response function is shown. $H(-f)$ is equal to the complex conjugate of $H(f)$.

TABLE 7
Partial Impulse Response Functions for the Three-input
Hypothetical Example ($N = 400$)

Partial Impulse Response Functions

	$h_{1,j}$		$h_{2,j}$		$h_{3,j}$	
j	Theoretical	Estimated	Theoretical	Estimated	Theoretical	Estimated
0	0.300	0.277	0	0.005	0.990	0.995
1	−0.500	−0.498	0.250	0.234	0	−0.001
2	−0.400	−0.385	0	0.022	−0.100	−0.094
3	0	−0.010	−0.750	−0.688	−0.600	−0.573
4	0	0.031	0	0.017	0	−0.012
5	0	0.005	0	0.012	0	−0.007
6	0	0.013	0	−0.018	0	−0.010
7	0	−0.016	0	−0.007	0	−0.011
8	0	−0.013	0	0.016	0	0.000

other. Fertility and mortality are measured as before; the indicators of unemployment and urbanization are the percentage of the population classified as unemployed and the percentage of the population living in urban areas respectively. All four time series pertain to the United States during the period from 1919 to 1967.

The mortality and fertility series were filtered in the manner indicated by Equations (45) and (46). The unemployment and urbanization time series were both subjected to first-difference filters:

Unemployment: $\quad u_t^* = u_t - u_{t-1}$ \hfill (58)

Urbanization: $\quad v_t^* = v_t - v_{t-1}$ \hfill (59)

The power spectra of the filtered fertility and mortality series appear in Table 3; the spectra of the filtered unemployment and urbanization series are given in Table 8 together with the squared multiple coherency spectrum for the multiple-input model of fertility. The estimates of the squared multiple coherency spectrum indicate that a model of fertility based on unemployment, urbanization, and mortality should leave few unexplained long-term trends and rapid fluctuations. However, we expect a large proportion of the variation caused by fluctuations of moderate frequency to remain unexplained. This information, together with the knowledge that most of the long-term trends in the data have been removed by filtering, suggests that a linear prediction of fertility in terms of mortality, urbanization, and unemployment will be most successful in explaining rapid fluctuations in the filtered fertility series.

Our next step is to align the unemployment and urbanization series with the fertility series [Equation (47) aligns mortality with fertil-

TABLE 8
Power Spectra for Filtered and Aligned Unemployment and Urbanization Time Series and Squared Multiple Coherency for the Multiple-input Model of Fertility[a]

Frequency (f)	Power Spectrum of Filtered and Aligned Unemployment Series	Power Spectrum of Filtered and Aligned Urbanization Series	Squared Multiple Coherency Spectrum
0.0000	109.372	0.139	0.974
0.0625	126.687	0.140	0.301
0.1250	130.830	0.150	0.832
0.1875	78.174	0.119	0.634
0.2500	39.874	0.059	0.994
0.3125	45.071	0.041	0.201
0.3750	43.101	0.045	0.882
0.4375	26.048	0.029	0.884
0.5000	20.789	0.015	0.994

[a] Spectral estimates were smoothed using the Tukey-Hamming window.

ity]. Examination of the cross-covariance functions suggests the following alignment equations:

Unemployment: $\quad u_t^{**} = u_{t-1}^{*}$ \hfill (60)

Urbanization: $\quad v_t^{**} = v_{t-4}^{*}$ \hfill (61)

We can now apply the methods of multivariate spectral analysis outlined at the beginning of this section to the filtered and aligned time series. Power spectra and cross-spectra were calculated using autocovariance and cross-covariance functions computed up to eight lags. Partial frequency response functions were then estimated using Equation (54), and these estimates are reported in Table 9. Partial impulse response functions were calculated by taking the inverse Fourier transform of these partial frequency response functions. Estimates of the partial impulse response functions appear in Table 10. The partial impulse response functions, it should be emphasized, are calculated for the filtered and aligned series, not the original series.

A difficulty encountered in multiple spectral analysis concerns the number of partial impulse response function terms to be included in the projection model. One might think that the more partial impulse response function terms included the better the projection, but this is not the case. Each term of a partial impulse response function includes a certain redundancy, both with respect to previous terms of the same function and with respect to terms of other partial impulse response functions. Thus inclusion of additional terms may actually impair the

TABLE 9
Partial Frequency Response Functions for Three-input Models of Fertility[a]

Frequency (f)	Partial Frequency Response Functions Input Series		
	Mortality (d_t^{**})	Unemployment (u_t^{**})	Urbanization (v_t^{**})
0.0000	1.235	−0.060	1.223
0.0625	−0.017 − 0.203j	0.027 − 0.032j	0.297 + 1.001j
0.1250	−0.001 + 0.274j	0.048 − 0.013j	−2.094 + 1.562j
0.1875	−1.375 − 0.677j	0.411 − 0.081j	−0.720 − 1.724j
0.2500	0.333 − 1.010j	−0.094 + 0.033j	−15.583 − 8.548j
0.3125	−0.451 − 0.531j	0.046 − 0.182j	−1.428 − 6.019j
0.3750	−0.693 − 0.491j	−0.167 − 0.138j	−6.492 − 4.296j
0.4375	−1.706 + 0.023j	−0.100 − 0.180j	7.544 − 6.130j
0.5000	−0.936	0.182	−3.094

[a] $j^2 = -1$.

TABLE 10
Partial Impulse response Functions for Three-input Models of Fertility

Lags (k)	Partial Impulse Response Functions (h_{ik}) Input Series		
	Mortality (d_t^{**})	Unemployment (u_t^{**})	Urbanization (v_t^{**})
0	−0.4706	0.0288	−3.2317
1	0.6414	0.0860	1.9914
2	−0.0768	−0.0650	1.5449
3	0.1176	−0.0406	−0.3994
4	0.1572	0.0048	−1.3519
5	−0.0428	−0.0039	0.6135
6	0.0968	0.0600	0.0967
7	0.0491	0.0031	1.5983
8	0.4178	−0.0672	−3.0336

effectiveness of a projection model. Choosing the number of partial impulse response function terms to be included in a model is a matter of considerable subtlety.

One method of selecting terms is based on inspection of the various cross-covariance functions. Consider the cross-covariance function between fertility and mortality. If the absolute value of this function declines sharply after three lags, we include four terms of the partial impulse response function corresponding to mortality. In this way we can select the number of terms included from each partial impulse response function. A projection model was constructed on this basis. This model contained two terms from the mortality partial impulse response function, four terms from the unemployment impulse response function, and six terms from the urbanization function. Fertility was projected on this basis and the projection is compared with the empirical data in Figure 3.

A second projection model was determined by a computer search procedure using variance explained as the criterion variable. The model selected in this manner was identical to the first model with respect to the mortality and unemployment inputs, but it included only one term (as opposed to six terms) of the urbanization partial impulse response function. A graphic presentation of the results of applying this impulse response function appears in Figure 4.

The residual series corresponding to each projection model was analyzed. The spectra of the residual series are presented graphically in Figure 5. Again our expectations about the success of the models are confirmed. We see that although reduction of the peak at moderate frequencies did occur there remains a large proportion of the variance to be explained at those frequencies. Also we see that the greatest proportion of explained frequency-specific variation occurred at high frequencies as expected. The first model accounts for about 46 percent of the original variance whereas the second model explains about 51 percent of this variance. In neither model does the residual spectrum even remotely resemble the spectrum of white noise, and in some respects the residual series corresponding to the second model deviates further from white noise than does the residual series corresponding to the first model. Evidently mortality, unemployment, and urbanization do not explain all systematic changes in fertility.

Using the second projection model we can obtain a relationship between the original (that is, unfiltered and nonaligned) fertility time series on the one hand, and the original mortality, unemployment, and urbanization series on the other. As in the case of bivariate spectral analysis, this involves first substituting the filtering equations (45), (46), (58), and (59) in the equations for the second projection model and then correcting for alignment using expressions (47), (60), and (61). The resulting relationship may be written as follows:

$$\begin{aligned} f_t = {} & (2f_{t-1} - f_{t-2}) \\ & + (-4.7d_{t-4} + 1.1d_{t-5} - 6.4d_{t-6}) \\ & + (0.03u_{t-1} + 0.06u_{t-2} - 0.16u_{t-3} + 0.03u_{t-4} + 0.04u_{t-5}) \\ & + (-3.23v_{t-4} + 3.23v_{t-5}) \end{aligned} \quad (62)$$

The fertility feedback mechanism discussed in the previous section is evident again in the preceding equation. The influence of unemployment on fertility apparently occurs somewhat sooner and is distributed over a longer time span than are influences of mortality or urbanization. This multivariate model assigns approximately the same

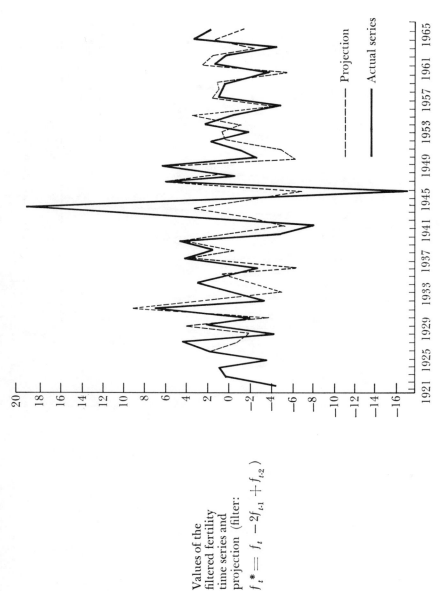

Values of the filtered fertility time series and projection (filter: $f_t^* = f_t - 2f_{t-1} + f_{t-2}$)

------- Projection
———— Actual series

Figure 3. Plots of the filtered fertility time series and fertility projected on the basis of mortality, unemployment, and urbanization (first projection model).

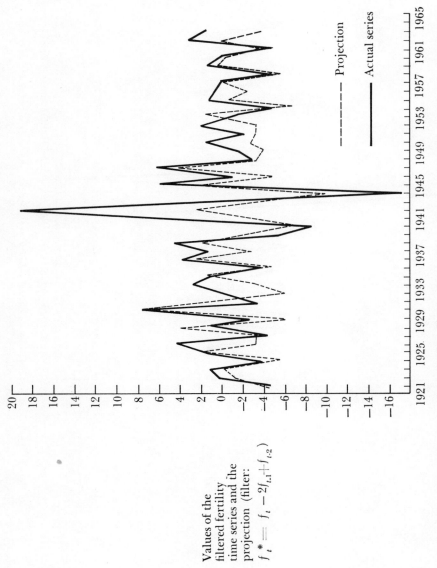

Figure 4. Plots of the filtered fertility time series and fertility projected on the basis of the mortality, unemployment, and urbanization series (second projection model).

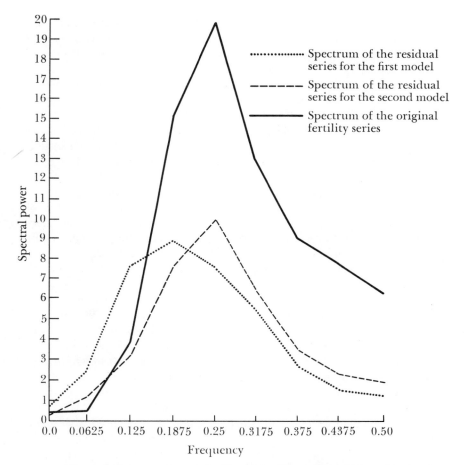

Figure 5. Power spectra of the filtered fertility series and the residual series based on two projections of fertility from mortality, unemployment, and urbanization series.

lag to the influence of mortality on fertility as did the bivariate model discussed earlier. Finally we might note that oscillatory tendencies in the mortality, unemployment, and urbanization series are likely to reappear in the fertility series.

PROBLEMS

Data Adequacy and Data Availability

Spectral analysis requires long time series. Granger and Hatanaka (1964, p. 61) recommend against attempting spectral analysis unless a time series contains at least 100 points. Jenkins and Watts (1968, pp. 285–286) suggest that the length of a series required for spectral analysis depends on the properties of the spectral window used for smoothing and also on the fineness of detail in the power spectrum that the investigator hopes to discriminate. For any available spectral window, and to achieve even moderate discrimination, the Jenkins-Watts criterion requires rather lengthy time series (usually in excess of 100 points).

Recall that the empirical time series analyzed in previous sections contained fewer than 100 points and would probably be judged insufficient by both the Granger-Hatanaka and the Jenkins-Watts standards. Nonetheless our efforts may be defended on grounds that our interest focused on the characteristics of linear systems and not on the properties of spectra per se. Small inaccuracies in spectral estimates are often of minor consequence in estimating the parameters of linear systems. However, extreme caution is imperative when drawing conclusions from the relatively short time series typically available to sociologists.

Some insight regarding the effect of series length on parameter estimation may be derived from more detailed examination of the hypothetical three-input example. Table 11 compares the theoretical parameters with estimates obtained from series of lengths 60, 100, 200, and 400. The partial impulse response function estimates improve with each increase in the length of the input series, but the most decisive improvement occurs when the input series change from length 60 to length 100. The extent of improvement decreases with each successive increment. This result indicates that prohibitively long time series are not always necessary to obtain reasonable parameter estimates.

Insufficient length is not the only difficulty associated with sociological time series. Often a time series has several missing data points. Sometimes the length of the time interval separating adjacent data points shifts. Even more troublesome, the definition of a time series may shift in midstream while the name remains constant. For many years, United States unemployment figures were obtained by subtracting the number of employed persons from the total labor force. Currently, however, unemployment is defined by a list of complex criteria.

These problems of data adequacy exist and cannot be ignored. Though frequently irksome these difficulties are rarely insuperable and certainly should not obscure the resources of sociologically relevant time series presently available in government archives and elsewhere. These time series provide a valuable, and until now underutilized, repository of information about the processes of social stability and change. Perhaps spectral analysis and other related techniques will help social scientists derive greater benefit from this information.

TABLE 11
Partial Impulse Response Functions for the Three-input Hypothetical Example Using Inputs of Length 60, 100, 200, and 400

(a) Partial Impulse Response Functions (h_{1j}) for Input Variable One

j	Theoretical	Estimated $N = 60$	$N = 100$	$N = 200$	$N = 400$
0	0.300	0.222	0.214	0.238	0.277
1	−0.500	−0.150	−0.416	−0.518	−0.498
2	−0.400	−0.632	−0.404	−0.359	−0.385
3	0	0.162	−0.042	0.010	−0.010
4	0	0.038	0.010	0.062	0.031
5	0	0.163	−0.008	0.077	0.005
6	0	−0.134	0.079	0.076	0.013
7	0	0.223	−0.043	−0.028	−0.016

(b) Partial Impulse Response Functions (h_{2j}) for Input Variable Two

j	Theoretical	Estimated $N = 60$	$N = 100$	$N = 200$	$N = 400$
0	0	0.222	−0.116	0.018	0.005
1	0.250	0.370	0.205	0.216	0.234
2	0	0.072	0.022	0.018	0.022
3	−0.750	−0.101	−0.703	−0.667	−0.688
4	0	−0.140	0.018	0.041	0.017
5	0	0.124	0.017	0.046	0.012
6	0	0.123	−0.091	0.012	−0.018
7	0	0.280	0.023	0.010	−0.007

(c) Partial Impulse Response Functions (h_{3j}) for Input Variable Three

j	Theoretical	Estimated $N = 60$	$N = 100$	$N = 200$	$N = 400$
0	0.990	1.066	1.017	0.976	0.995
1	0	−0.202	0.021	−0.016	−0.001
2	−0.100	−0.255	−0.107	−0.095	−0.094
3	−0.600	−0.577	−0.583	−0.589	−0.573
4	0	0.077	0.037	−0.023	−0.012
5	0	−0.168	0.060	−0.003	−0.007
6	0	0.011	−0.005	−0.015	−0.010
7	0	−0.081	−0.039	−0.009	−0.011

Confidence Intervals for Parameter Estimates

How much confidence can be placed in the impulse response function estimates obtained via spectral methods? Confidence intervals can be established for a number of spectral concepts including the power spectrum, but we have not been able to discover a viable method for setting confidence intervals around estimates of the impulse response function. As a consequence we can say very little about the stability or the fidelity of our impulse response function estimates.

Our work with hypothetical examples suggests that the time-series length required to achieve a given level of estimation accuracy increases sharply as the complexity of the system increases. In other words a three-input model requires longer series to attain a fixed degree of estimation accuracy than does a one-input model. A method of estimating the series length required to achieve a certain level of accuracy (that is, a specified confidence interval width) given system structure would be extremely useful, but is not presently available.

Model Identification

In general terms the problem of model identification involves the selection of an appropriate time-series model. This broad interpretation of the identification problem embraces issues that we cannot discuss here. We shall consider only a limited aspect of the general identification problem: the number of impulse response function terms to be included in a time-series model.

Increasing the number of impulse response function terms included in a model does not always increase the accuracy of the model. This phenomenon was illustrated by the three-input fertility model presented in the previous section. Although the causes of this effect remain somewhat obscure, we do know that it arises because different input series are not entirely independent. As a consequence of the dependency between different input series, various periodic components of the output series can be attributed to alternative sources. This introduces certain redundancies within the partial impulse response functions, and these in turn generate the paradox of decreasing accuracy even while the number of impulse response function terms is increasing.

Exactly which terms of the impulse response function should be included in a time-series model? When dealing with the three-input fertility model we used two ad hoc methods to answer this question. One method was based on inspection of the partial cross-covariance functions; the other used a computer search procedure. Neither method is theoretically satisfying, and neither method ensures that the set of terms included is optimal.

An analytic procedure for selecting an optimal set of impulse response function terms would significantly enhance the effectiveness of multivariate spectral analysis. If the number of terms to be included can be determined, the parameter estimates obtained via spectral methods can be improved by using standard least-squares methods (Jenkins and Watts, 1968, pp. 426–429).

Filtering

A number of questions are associated with filtering time-series data to meet the assumptions of spectral analysis. Is a filter adequate to produce the necessary covariance stationarity? How can an optimum, or even a satisfactory, filter be chosen? What information is sacrificed as a consequence of filtering and how serious is the loss?

Nonstationary elements in a time series typically manifest themselves by contributing to the low-frequency power of the series spectrum. Thus an important test of filter adequacy is potency in reducing spectral power at low frequencies. But how is it possible to select a filter that reduces low-frequency power? In this chapter we have confined ourselves to simple first- and second-difference filters; however, these filters are often inadequate.

Three different approaches seem plausible: autoregressive filtering, joint filtering, and theoretical filtering. Autoregressive filtering involves the construction of an autoregressive (that is, autocausal) model for a time series that fails to satisfy the covariance stationary criterion. Subsequently this autoregressive model is used as a filter. Practical methods for building autoregressive models are fairly well known; however, these methods themselves rest on the covariance stationarity assumption, which casts serious doubt on the properties of the resulting filter. Moreover autoregressive filtering eliminates much information in the unfiltered time series. It can also seriously efface relationships between different time series.

Joint filtering means either the application of an identical filter to process several different time series, or the use of one series to filter another. The advantage of this method lies in its capacity to preserve relationships between different time series. Its disadvantages reside in the paucity of techniques for selecting appropriate joint filters.

Theoretical filtering depends on the availability of a prior formal theory applicable to the time-series data in question. This theory is then constituted as a filter (that is, the theory is allowed to explain as much of the various time series as it can) and spectral analysis proceeds with the residual data (those which the theory cannot explain). Under these conditions the objective of spectral analysis becomes modification and improvement of the theory. Theoretical filtering possesses indubitable conceptual merits but encounters serious practical difficulties. Rarely in social science does the requisite quantitative theory exist. Even when it does, there are few compelling reasons to believe that the residual series will be covariance stationary.

Filtering unquestionably eliminates information, but the severity of the loss depends largely on the objective of inquiry. If interest focuses on aspects of a process that give rise to high-frequency spectral components, or on relationships between time series that remain relatively stable during the process of change, then filtering will not induce serious analytic distortions. Even when this is not the case, however, it is usually possible to compensate for the filtering operation when synthesizing a theoretical model. Exactly this was done in setting up Equations (49) and (62). Ultimately it may prove possible to select filters that accomplish the necessary covariance stationarity but leave intact time-series features of special interest. Let us take this opportunity to reiterate the advantages of spectral methods over other forms of time-series analysis. Spectral functions such as the power spectrum, cross-spectrum, and squared coherency spectrum give an overall perspective on the evolution of time series and on the relationship between different time series as this relationship unfolds over time. Spectral functions isolate different aspects of time series that can then receive separate consideration. Moreover they suggest the kinds of time-series models that may be appropriate.

Could this same information be conveyed by concepts, such as the auto- and cross-covariance functions, which may be more intuitively meaningful to sociologists? Spectral functions have important statistical advantages over covariance functions for reasons that have been well expressed by Jenkins and Watts (1968, pp. 5–7): "The autocorrelation function [and by implication the autocovariance function] is sometimes difficult to interpret because neighboring values can be highly correlated. This means that the sample autocorrelation function may be distorted visually. . . . In the analysis of a finite length of record the spectrum is often preferable to the autocovariance function . . . estimates of the spectrum at neighboring frequencies are approximately independent, and hence the interpretation of the sample spectrum is usually easier than that of the sample autocovariance function."

Spectral methods also have significant advantages over parametric techniques with regard to model-building, especially during the exploratory phase. Spectral analysis requires no prior assumption about the number of impulse response function terms to be included in a time-series model. Suppose spectral methods are used to identify an initial model that is then modified by the addition of new terms. The parameters of the initial model remain unaffected by the new terms that have been added, a property which vastly simplifies the process of model construction.

FUTURE DIRECTIONS

Our objective in this chapter has been to outline the basic ideas of spectral analysis and to indicate how these ideas might be applied to certain problems arising in the realm of social science. In this concluding section we briefly discuss some promising avenues for future research.

System Determination

We have treated calculation of an impulse response function as the endpoint of spectral analysis, but this need not be the case. As mentioned earlier, there exists a one-to-one correspondence between impulse response functions and time-invariant linear systems. The nature of a linear system may become far more apparent if the system is represented by something other than its impulse or frequency response function. For example, a more revealing representation might be a set of linear differential equations.

By *system determination* we mean the translation of the impulse response function into a more intuitively meaningful representational form. This involves a good deal more than simply constructing a "transformational dictionary." It also entails counteracting the distortions wrought by the manner in which specific time series are constructed. Some series are constructed by aggregating data over time intervals of specified length. Other series are generated by sampling an empirical process at regular periods. Still other series are constructed so as to render an essentially continuous process discrete. The method of series construction exercises a definite influence on the character of the estimated impulse response function. When determining the linear system representation most suitable to an underlying empirical process, careful consideration must be given to this influence.

To summarize, a significant line of future research may endeavor to express time-series models not merely in impulse response function terms, but in forms that are more intuitively and substantively meaningful and that consider the method of time-series construction.

Simultaneous Projection

Spectral theory suggests some new approaches to projecting social trends. Specifically it suggests the notion of simultaneous projection. Rather than projecting trends one at a time, this concept recommends projecting several trends simultaneously, and in such a way that certain relationships between the projected trends are maintained. This approach seems likely to yield more realistic results than previous projection techniques.

Although the basic idea of simultaneous projection is fairly clear, the concrete procedures involved are by no means fully developed. Which relationships between trends should be held constant? Under what conditions is it possible to satisfy the requirements of different relationships? If simultaneous projection results in overdetermination of a particular trend, how can conflicting claims be systematically reconciled?

These problems and others like them must be solved before simultaneous projection becomes a practical reality. Nevertheless the development of improved projection methods constitutes a promising sphere for the application of spectral analysis.

Feedback Analysis

Throughout this chapter we have made a sharp distinction between input (independent) time series and output (dependent) time series. Actually, however, a rigid demarcation between dependent and independent series is not very plausible. Usually variables in a system are mutually dependent on one another. We say that feedback occurs in a system if a variable exerts an indirect effect on itself through the agency of its effect on another variable. Feedback may have a corrective effect that functions essentially to stabilize a time series, or it may have a disequilibrating influence.

There has already been some research dealing with feedback mechanisms, but the results to date are fairly sparse and provide little instruction about how to construct feedback models in the time domain.[16] Intuition strongly suggests that feedback mechanisms are of decisive importance in many social processes and merit further investigation. Moreover spectral methods appear to furnish a promising way of approaching the analysis of feedback. We expect the study of feedback mechanisms to receive substantial attention from persons interested in applying spectral analysis to social science.

Anticipation Effects

It is mathematically possible to construct a system in which the output at time t depends on inputs occurring at times later than t. Such systems have usually been dismissed as mathematical oddities lacking any empirical relevance, and it is certainly difficult to imagine how future values of one time series could influence present values of another series. However, it is not particularly difficult to understand how anticipations regarding future values of a time series can affect present values of another series (or for that matter of the same time series). Certainly people often anticipate the future and adjust their behavior accordingly. In fact most policy decisions derive from anticipation of future events. Fishman (1969, pp. 170–172) provides an example of how to include an anticipation of future values of an independent variable in a distributed lag model.

[16] Granger and Hatanaka (1964, pp. 109–126) and Fishman (1969, pp. 72–73) mainly discuss the spectral properties of feedback mechanisms. For a suggestion on how to estimate feedback effects in a time domain model see Akaike (1967, pp. 81–107).

A useful application of spectral theory in sociology would be to investigate the effect of anticipation (which might be called *intuitive projection*) of a system's output on itself. This might be done as follows. First one constructs simple projection formulas that presumably indicate the dominant anticipations regarding future values of important input series. These formulas are then used to project future values of the relevant input series, and the projected values are introduced as new inputs. A natural extension of this basic idea would entail comparing the implications of different anticipation methods (that is, intuitive projection formulas).

Nonlinear Models

The construction of nonlinear models provides yet another field for the application of spectral theory. Two different lines of attack suggest themselves. One approach involves the use of higher-order spectra, that is, of Fourier transforms of higher-order moment functions. This approach entails formidable mathematical complexity, and its results to date have not been especially impressive. According to E. J. Hannan (1970, p. 91): "Uses of higher-order spectra in data analysis have been very few so far and none appear to have involved anything beyond the bispectrum.... Experience in the classical part of statistics suggests that these concepts will be of limited use and will be replaced, rather, by the consideration of special models when the need for them appears to arise."

The second approach, certainly less elegant but perhaps more practical than the first, seeks essentially to linearize the nonlinearity. Suppose one starts with the input series $\{x_{1_t}\}, \ldots, \{x_{n_t}\}$. To develop a nonlinear model one introduces selected series of the form $[x_{1_t}^{k_1}] \ldots [x_{n_t}^{k_n}]$, where $k_1, \ldots, k_n$ are nonnegative integers, as new input series and proceeds as before. The linear model constructed with regard to the supplemental set of input series is actually a nonlinear model with respect to the original input series set.

Recursive Spectral Analysis

Recursive spectral analysis aims at constructing more finely grained causal models than the usual multivariate spectral analysis. Recursive spectral analysis has quite a bit in common with recursive regression techniques such as path analysis. Its basic logic rests on an elaboration of the distinction between input and output series. Rather than classifying all series as input or output, we now have series that are input with respect to some series and output with respect to others. Moreover all time series can be put into a recursive order: that is, an order in which no series is input for any series that occurs earlier in the order, and every series is either input or output for at least one other series in the order. The recursive order is easily expressed by means of a causal diagram similar to those used in path analysis.

Recursive spectral analysis makes possible a partition of causation between direct effects and various orders of indirect effects. The partition effected here is much more elaborate than that accomplished via path analysis since it is a partition of causation distributed over time. In other words, recursive spectral analysis partitions not just one measure of aggregate effect (such as the correlation coefficient), but also the effect transmitted at each conceivable time lag.

At the present time spectral analysis may fairly be regarded as an approach which *might* prove useful in the study of social change. Whether this potentiality blossoms or remains dormant depends largely upon the direction and success of future research. Two general research directions are essential for the maturation of spectral analysis as a viable sociological method. Research in one direction aims at eliminating the barriers to the application of spectral analysis to the sort of time series data typically available to sociologists. Research in the second direction strives to extend the kinds of models that can be constructed through spectral analysis.

Much of the research in both of these directions will inevitably be of a highly technical nature. Much will be carried out by mathematicians rather than sociologists. However, the concern that sociologists express for the rigorous study of social change in general, and for spectral analysis in particular, can exert an important influence on the problems that mathematicians regard as worthwhile. Thus sociologists may be able to expedite the emergence of spectral analysis as a practical tool for studying social change even when they are not responsible for its most powerful results.

REFERENCES

AKAIKE, H.
    1967 "Some problems of the cross-spectral method." Pp. 81–107 in B. Harris (Ed.), *Spectral Analysis of Time Series*. New York: Wiley.

ANDERSON, T. W.
    1971 *The Statistical Analysis of Time Series*. New York: Wiley.

BARTLETT, M. S.
    1966 *An Introduction to Stochastic Processes with Special Reference to Methods and Applications*. Cambridge: Cambridge University Press.

BLACKMAN, R. B. AND TUKEY, J. W.
    1958 *The Measurement of Power Spectra from the Point of View of Communications Engineering*. New York: Dover.

DUNCAN, O. D.
  1966 "Path analysis: Sociological examples." *American Journal of Sociology* 72:2–7.
FISHMAN, G. S.
  1969 *Spectral Methods in Econometrics*. Cambridge, Mass.: Harvard University Press.
GRANGER, C. W. J. AND HATANAKA, M.
  1964 *Spectral Analysis of Economic Time Series*. Princeton, N.J.: Princeton University Press.
HANNAN, E. J.
  1970 *Multiple Time Series*. New York: Wiley.
JENKINS, G. M. AND WATTS, D. G.
  1968 *Spectral Analysis and Its Applications*. San Francisco: Holden-Day.
MORRISON, N.
  1969 *Introduction to Sequential Smoothing and Prediction*. New York: McGraw-Hill.
NEAVE, H. R.
  1972 "Comparison of lag window generators." *Journal of the American Statistical Association* 67:152–158.
U.S. DEPARTMENT OF COMMERCE
     Statistical Abstract of the United States. Washington, D.C.: Government Printing Office.
  1960 *Historical Statistics of the United States: Colonial Times to 1957*. Washington, D.C.: Government Printing Office.
  1965 *Historical Statistics of the United States: Continuation to 1962 and Revisions*. Washington, D.C.: Government Printing Office.
WIENER, N.
  1949 *The Extrapolation, Interpolation, and Smoothing of Stationary Time Series with Engineering Applications*. New York: Wiley.

12

SOCIAL MOBILITY MODELS FOR HETEROGENEOUS POPULATIONS

Burton Singer
COLUMBIA UNIVERSITY AND PRINCETON UNIVERSITY

Seymour Spilerman
UNIVERSITY OF WISCONSIN

The work reported here was supported by grants N00014-67-A-0151-0017 at Princeton University, NSF-GP-31505X at Columbia University, and by the Russell Sage Foundation and the University of Wisconsin—Madison's Institute for Research on Poverty. The institute's funds were provided by the Office of Economic Opportunity pursuant to the Economic Opportunity Act of 1964. We wish to thank Neil Henry and I: Richard Savage for their comments on an earlier draft.

1. INTRODUCTION

There is an extensive and diverse literature on the application of discrete-state Markov models to social processes. This formal structure has been an important analytic device in the study of occupational and industrial mobility (Matras, 1960; Hodge, 1966; Blumen, Kogan, and McCarthy, 1955), income dynamics (Smith and Cain, 1967; McCall, 1971), and geographic migration (Rogers, 1966; Tarver and Gurley, 1965; Brown, 1970). The key features of a problem that suggest the use of Markov models as a baseline or for projection are (a) a specified list of system states which may be occupations, industries, income categories, or geographic regions; (b) the availability of repeated observations on population movements among the states; and (c) an interest in the dynamics of the transition process.

In applications of Markov models it is frequently assumed (often implicitly) that the population can be considered to be homogeneous and is therefore representable by a single Markov process. However, where investigators have obtained data at several time points so that n-step matrices could be observed and compared with the Markov predictions—that is, checking the validity of $\hat{P}(n) = [\hat{P}(1)]^n$—it has often been found that the projections deviate from the observed values in a characteristic manner. Blumen, Kogan, and McCarthy (1955) were the first to suggest that the tendency of the Markov model to underpredict the main diagonal entries of an observed matrix can be attributed, in many research contexts, to population heterogeneity.

Blumen, Kogan, and McCarthy introduced the *mover-stayer* model to contend with this phenomenon. They postulated the presence of two types of persons: movers, who transfer according to a single Markov chain; and stayers, who remain permanently rooted in their origin states. Using this extremely restrictive form of the notion of heterogeneity, they constructed a simple mathematical model for the evolution of the total population and devised estimation procedures for its parameters. Recent work on extending the Markov framework to incorporate population heterogeneity in a more flexible manner has proceeded in two directions. The difference between them derives from the particular strategy adopted to accommodate heterogeneity; what they share in common is an assumption that the individual-level process can be considered Markovian.

In one approach (McFarland, 1970; Spilerman, 1972a) each person is assumed to move according to a Markov chain, but follows a transition matrix that is unique to him. Population heterogeneity is therefore attributed to individual differences in the tendency to select particular destination states at a move. In the second approach (Ginsberg, 1971; Spilerman, 1972b) heterogeneity is accommodated by permitting individual differences in the rate at which transition events occur. At each transition, however, it is assumed that a single matrix common to all persons governs choice of destination. Thus in this formulation, the burden of explaining heterogeneity is cast entirely upon variations in the rate of movement.

With regard to the utility of these extensions,[1] each provides a suitable framework for analyzing certain processes. Investigations into job mobility (Palmer, 1954, p. 50) and geographic migration (Taeuber, Chiazze, and Haenszel, 1968) have concluded that substantial individual differences exist in rate of movement. The second formulation would be appropriate for studying these processes and forecasting changes in their state distributions. In contrast there are social phenomena for which population heterogeneity is primarily a consequence of individual differences in the probability of making particular transitions. Intergenerational occupational mobility is the most apparent instance; indeed the very notion of different rates of movement seems inappropriate so that all population heterogeneity would have to arise from individual proclivities for certain transitions. A more detailed comparison of these complementary perspectives is presented in Spilerman (1972a).

In this chapter we present a unified framework in which to view the models mentioned above as well as more intricate social mobility models. The essence of our conceptual apparatus involves a formal distinction between the individual-level or microscopic process, which is usually unobserved, and the population-level or macroscopic process. An individual is identified by a collection of rates that describe the average times he stays in particular states before moving, or by a stochastic matrix whose entries can be interpreted as propensities to favor transitions to certain states. It is also conceivable that an individual can be classified by specifying *both* a matrix of rates of movement and a stochastic matrix listing probabilities of making particular transitions when a move occurs.

From a description of individual-level behavior and a specification of the form that heterogeneity takes, we show how the population-level process can be constituted. From a data analysis perspective, however, our situation is usually the reverse; we generally lack sufficient information to identify the individual-level process. Instead a researcher is constrained to sample the population at a few points in time and obtain counts of the number of persons making particular transitions, as well as other statistics concerning the population-level process. From these observations we wish to infer the parameters of the unobserved, individual-level process. One reason for recovering these parameters is that they can be used to reject a model by showing the implied, individual-level

[1] We assume that the reader is familiar with the four papers cited in the preceding paragraph and with the rudiments of discrete- and continuous-time Markov processes.

description to be unrealistic for the problem at hand. Another reason is that they provide the basic ingredients for making statements about future trends in the population.

Our program is first to describe a class of Markov and semi-Markov processes which will serve as models for the evolution of individual behavior. In addition the ideas involved in identification of nondirectly observable parameters are illustrated by examples with the simplest Markov chain models (section 2). In section 3 we again proceed via a sequence of examples to show how the above mentioned population processes can be described mathematically. The basic mathematical structures characterizing the observable macroscopic-level processes are mixtures of Markov and semi-Markov models. This notion is explained from the point of view of weighted averages of stochastic processes and from the alternative perspective of observable histories.

Finally we present some examples in section 4 of an "inverse problem" where gross macroscopic-level information is used to obtain partial, and in a few instances complete, information about the mechanics of the individual-level process. This aspect of our study involves an independent mathematical development which will be presented elsewhere in a joint paper by the authors. Our purpose here is simply to illustrate the ideas involved and communicate their relevance for the study of social mobility.

2. MARKOV CHAINS: TRANSITION PROBABILITIES

2.1. Discrete-time Processes

The simplest mathematical caricature that we shall employ to describe the evolution of an individual (or a homogeneous population) is a discrete-time Markov chain. This stochastic process $\{X(k), k = 1, 2, 3, \ldots\}$ should be viewed as detailing state transitions by an individual, where the system states might be geographic regions, occupations, industries, or income categories, depending on the particular substantive problem. Probability statements about the process are governed by the analytical recipe

$$\text{prob}[X(k+n) = j \,|\, X(k) = i] = m_{ij}^{(n)}$$

for $k = 0, 1, 2, \ldots$, and $n = 0, 1, 2, \ldots$. The element $m_{ij}^{(n)}$ is the (i,j) entry in the stochastic matrix M^n (n-fold matrix multiplication of M). M is itself a stochastic matrix and describes single transitions by an individual; its (i,j) entry m_{ij} has the interpretation, "probability of moving from state i to state j in one step."

The typical empirical setting in which mobility data are gathered does not allow the matrix M to be estimated directly from the movements of an individual. An investigator usually observes the locations of many persons at a few time points $n_0 = 0, n_1, n_2, \ldots$, and estimates stochastic matrices $\hat{P}(n_1), \hat{P}(n_2), \ldots$, where the (i,j) entry in $\hat{P}(n_k)$ denotes[2] the proportion of individuals from among those in state i at time n_0 who are in state j at time n_k.

One assumption which is frequently made is that the population is homogeneous in its movements. This permits the matrix $\hat{P}(n_k)$, estimated from the observed locations of the population at times n_0 and n_k, to be associated with the evolution of a single individual. We also make this assumption in the present section. A second specification that is often adopted is to identify the smallest observational time interval (n_0,n_1) with the unit interval of the process. Thus we might define $M = \hat{P}(n_1)$, in which case, if $n_k = hn_1$ for some integer h, we have

$$P(n_k) = \hat{P}(n_1)^h = M^h$$

This identification is commonly used when a discrete-time mathematical model is desired for a process evolving continuously in time but having no natural unit time interval which can be associated with it. On the other hand, when a discrete sequence of times can be identified as spaced at substantively meaningful intervals, it sometimes happens that the unit time interval is smaller than the minimum observation interval. That is, while we observe a population at times n_0 and n_1, the unit interval of the process could be $(n_0,[1/h]n_1)$ for some integer $h > 1$. A problem of this sort might arise if we collected data on respondent's occupation ($n_1 = 2$) and grandfather's occupation ($n_0 = 0$), but neglected to obtain information on father's occupation. Given the observed $\hat{P}(2)$ matrix we might inquire into whether it can be represented in the form $\hat{P}(2) = M^2$ for some stochastic matrix M. A question of this very nature was posed by R. W. Hodge (1966) in an inquiry into the extent of inheritance of occupational status beyond a single generation.

The problem of deciding whether a particular observed matrix $\hat{P}(n)$ may be represented in the form $\hat{P}(n) = M^n$ for some stochastic matrix M is the simplest version of what we shall refer to as the *embeddability problem*. This is equivalent to asking whether or not the observed data are compatible with a discrete-time Markov model. If the answer to this question is affirmative, we require a procedure for recovering the one-step transition matrix M. This is a statement of the *inverse problem*.

---

[2] The symbol ^ over a stochastic matrix means that it should be thought of as a quantity estimated directly from data; matrices without this symbol should be viewed as obtained from a mathematical model.

In the present context it entails tabulating the nth roots of $\hat{P}(n)$ in order to determine all transition matrices M that are compatible with our observations.

To illustrate these ideas in a simple mathematical setting suppose we are in a substantive situation which allows observations to be made only at times $n_0 = 0$ and $n_1 = 3$, and that we estimate the stochastic matrix

$$\hat{P}(3) = \begin{pmatrix} 1/3 & 2/3 \\ 2/3 & 1/3 \end{pmatrix} \tag{1}$$

Computing cube roots of this matrix we find that

$$[\hat{P}(3)]^{1/3} = \begin{pmatrix} \frac{1}{2}[1 - 1/\sqrt[3]{3}] & \frac{1}{2}[1 + 1/\sqrt[3]{3}] \\ \frac{1}{2}[1 + 1/\sqrt[3]{3}] & \frac{1}{2}[1 - 1/\sqrt[3]{3}] \end{pmatrix} = M \tag{2}$$

is the unique stochastic matrix which is a cube root of $\hat{P}(3)$. Thus the empirically determined matrix $\hat{P}(3)$ is embeddable in a discrete-time Markov chain with one-step transition matrix M given by Equation (3).

In general we shall be able to ascertain embeddability without having to compute the nth roots of $\hat{P}(n)$ (see section 4). If the matrix is found to be embeddable in a discrete-time Markov process, we should be able to identify at least one stochastic matrix M such that $\hat{P}(n) = M^n$. In the preceding example the inverse problem reduced to calculating all cube roots of $\hat{P}(3)$ which are stochastic matrices. An explicit analytical recipe for calculating the roots of an arbitrary stochastic matrix is described in the appendix to this chapter.

If the natural time scale of the problem is such that the matrix (1) corresponds to observations at times $n = 0$ and $n = 2$, then the process is incompatible with a discrete-time Markov chain theory.[3] This is because Equation (1) has no square roots which are stochastic matrices; thus the observations in this new time scale cannot be represented in the form $\hat{P}(2) = M^2$, and the process is not embeddable in a discrete-time Markov chain structure.

A further illustration of the complexity of inverse problems can be seen from the following mathematical example. Suppose you initially take observations at times $n = 0$ and $n = 2$ and estimate

$$\hat{P}(2) = \begin{pmatrix} 1 & 0 & 0 \\ 0 & 1 & 0 \\ 0 & 0 & 1 \end{pmatrix}$$

---

[3] Incompatibility with a discrete-time Markov chain implies incompatibility with a continuous-time Markov structure. The converse is not true.

On the surface it might appear as though you are observing a population in which there is no mobility between states. However, $\hat{P}(2)$ has four distinct square roots, all of which are stochastic matrices:

$$\sqrt{\hat{P}(2)} = \begin{cases} \begin{pmatrix} 1 & 0 & 0 \\ 0 & 1 & 0 \\ 0 & 0 & 1 \end{pmatrix} \\ \begin{pmatrix} 0 & 0 & 1 \\ 0 & 1 & 0 \\ 1 & 0 & 0 \end{pmatrix} \\ \begin{pmatrix} 0 & 1 & 0 \\ 1 & 0 & 0 \\ 0 & 0 & 1 \end{pmatrix} \\ \begin{pmatrix} 1 & 0 & 0 \\ 0 & 0 & 1 \\ 0 & 1 & 0 \end{pmatrix} \end{cases}$$

Each square root has a different substantive interpretation, and only the first of these (the identity matrix) corresponds to no mobility. The second matrix in the preceding list corresponds to a situation in which individuals starting in either state 1 or state 3 cycle back and forth between these states while an individual starting in state 2 never moves. The third matrix may be identified with a population in which individuals either cycle back and forth between states 1 and 2 or remain stationary in state 3, etc. Discrimination between alternatives may be either on substantive grounds or on the basis of a further set of observations.

If additional observations are possible, they should be taken at one of the times 3, 5, 7, ..., etc., and *not* at an even time period. In particular, if $\hat{P}(2)$ is the identity and a Markov model adequately describes the process then the pair of matrices $[\hat{P}(2), \hat{P}(3)]$ must be one of the following distinct sets:

$$S_1: \begin{pmatrix} 1 & 0 & 0 \\ 0 & 1 & 0 \\ 0 & 0 & 1 \end{pmatrix}, \begin{pmatrix} 1 & 0 & 0 \\ 0 & 1 & 0 \\ 0 & 0 & 1 \end{pmatrix} \quad S_3: \begin{pmatrix} 1 & 0 & 0 \\ 0 & 1 & 0 \\ 0 & 0 & 1 \end{pmatrix}, \begin{pmatrix} 0 & 1 & 0 \\ 1 & 0 & 0 \\ 0 & 0 & 1 \end{pmatrix}$$

$$S_2: \begin{pmatrix} 1 & 0 & 0 \\ 0 & 1 & 0 \\ 0 & 0 & 1 \end{pmatrix}, \begin{pmatrix} 0 & 0 & 1 \\ 0 & 1 & 0 \\ 1 & 0 & 0 \end{pmatrix} \quad S_4: \left(\begin{pmatrix} 1 & 0 & 0 \\ 0 & 1 & 0 \\ 0 & 0 & 1 \end{pmatrix}, \begin{pmatrix} 1 & 0 & 0 \\ 0 & 0 & 1 \\ 0 & 1 & 0 \end{pmatrix} \right)$$

while the pair $[\hat{P}(2), \hat{P}(4)]$ must be

$$S_5: \begin{pmatrix} 1 & 0 & 0 \\ 0 & 1 & 0 \\ 0 & 0 & 1 \end{pmatrix}, \begin{pmatrix} 1 & 0 & 0 \\ 0 & 1 & 0 \\ 0 & 0 & 1 \end{pmatrix}$$

The set S_1 is compatible with a unique Markov chain model with

$$M = \begin{pmatrix} 1 & 0 & 0 \\ 0 & 1 & 0 \\ 0 & 0 & 1 \end{pmatrix}$$

Similarly S_2 is only compatible with

$$M = \begin{pmatrix} 0 & 0 & 1 \\ 0 & 1 & 0 \\ 1 & 0 & 0 \end{pmatrix},$$

while S_3 and S_4 are only compatible, respectively, with

$$M = \begin{pmatrix} 0 & 1 & 0 \\ 1 & 0 & 0 \\ 0 & 0 & 1 \end{pmatrix}, \quad \text{and} \quad M = \begin{pmatrix} 1 & 0 & 0 \\ 0 & 0 & 1 \\ 0 & 1 & 0 \end{pmatrix}$$

On the other hand S_5 is consistent with all four models, *indicating that it is often desirable to take observations at time points which are not evenly spaced if you want to discriminate between substantively distinct stochastic models all compatible with data from a few periods.*

A further point is that if $[\hat{P}(2), \hat{P}(3)]$ with $\hat{P}(2)$ equal to the identity deviates from all of the four sets S_1, S_2, S_3, S_4 then the data are not consistent with a discrete-time Markov structure. You can also rule out a Markov model by obtaining empirical matrices $[\hat{P}(2), \hat{P}(4)]$ with $\hat{P}(2)$ equal to the identity but $\hat{P}(4)$ being a stochastic matrix not equal to the identity. These examples illustrate the importance of not regarding compatibility of observations with a particular model during a small number of time periods as strong evidence for validity of the model as a description of the underlying process. Nevertheless examination of alternative solutions of the inverse problem based on observations at a few time points can be a useful exploratory tool for calling attention to possibly unsuspected mobility mechanisms M and for suggesting more realistic models.

2.2. Continuous-time Processes

The natural time scale for many mobility processes is not a discrete sequence of intervals such as generations or decades, but a continuum of time points. In particular, geographic migration (Brown, 1970; Spilerman, 1972b) and occupational mobility (Blumen, Kogan, and McCarthy, 1955) can be viewed more realistically as processes in which state changes occur at random time points, and probabilities of moves between particular states are governed by Markov transition matrices. Several extensions of this formulation which are appropriate for heterogeneous environments appear in section 3. In the present discussion we establish a framework for the extensions by indicating three alternative descriptions of continuous-time Markov chains; the level of generality and substantive utility of each is delineated.

I. Q-Matrices. Consider a stochastic process with a finite number of states whose transition probabilities are governed by the system of ordinary differential equations

$$dP(t)/dt = QP(t), \qquad P(0) = I \qquad (3)$$

where Q is an $r \times r$ matrix whose entries satisfy $-\infty < q_{ii} < 0$, $q_{ij} \geq 0$ for $i \neq j$, $\sum_{j=1}^{r} q_{ij} = 0$, and r = number of states. The system (3) has a unique solution given by the exponential formula

$$P(t) = e^{tQ} \qquad t > 0 \qquad (4)$$

and the matrices Q and $P(t)$ have the following substantive interpretations:

$\begin{cases} -q_{ii}dt = \text{probability that an individual in state } i \text{ at time } t \text{ exits from} \\ \qquad\quad \text{that state during the time interval } (t, t+dt) \\ q_{ij}dt \;= \text{probability that an individual in state } i \text{ at time } t \text{ moves to} \\ \qquad\quad \text{state } j(j \neq i) \text{ during the interval } (t, t+dt) \end{cases}$

$p_{ij}(t) = $ probability that an individual starting in state i at time zero is in state j at time $t[(i,j)$ entry in $P(t)]$

Mobility processes whose transition probabilities are governed by Equation (3) have the property that their state at time $t + s$, given the complete history of the process up to time t, is only dependent on the last observation, namely the state at time t. This is a statement of the Markov property. Furthermore the holding time until exiting from a particular state i is exponentially distributed with parameter $-q_{ii}$. This is the most general formulation of continuous-time finite-state Markov chains arising in social mobility studies.

When continuous histories are available on all population movements during the time interval $(0,t)$, the matrix Q can be estimated directly from the observed transitions. A maximum-likelihood procedure has been reported (Meier, 1955; Albert, 1962) and involves the following calculations:

$$\begin{cases} \hat{q}_{ij} = N_{ij}/A_{i\cdot} & \text{for } j \neq i \\ \hat{q}_{ii} = -\sum_{j \neq i} \hat{q}_{ij} & \text{for } j = i \end{cases}$$

where $A_{i\cdot}$ = total occupation time in state i during $(0,t)$ by all individuals in the population

N_{ij} = total number of transitions from state i to state j during $(0,t)$.

In addition, availability of individual histories allows the suitability of a continuous-time Markov model to be examined on several different grounds: (i) Estimate Q from individual histories up to time t, compute $e^{(t+s)\hat{Q}}$, and compare this theoretically based transition matrix with the observed matrix $\hat{P}(t+s)$. This is a check on compatibility of the data with the mathematical structure (3) and (4). (ii) Check the goodness of fit of an exponential distribution to the holding-time distribution in each state. (iii) Assess the strength of longer-range dependence on past history if there are sufficient time-series records.

The above general formulation of continuous-time Markov transition matrices has been used in numerous sociological contexts (for example, Coleman, 1964, pp. 177–182; Bartholomew, 1967, pp. 77–78) However, the analysis of social mobility in a heterogeneous population is greatly facilitated by the alternative formulations presented in the next two sections. In particular they provide the basis for a classification scheme which allows individuals (or subpopulations) to be characterized according to either their rate of movement, their propensity to move to particular states, or both simultaneously. This kind of classification also leads to a straightforward mathematical caricature of mobility processes in a heterogeneous context when individual histories are not directly observable. Nevertheless, even in the present formulation, substantial information about individual-level behavior can be inferred by an extension of the inverse-problem arguments already presented and solving Equation (4) for Q. This analysis is described in section 4.

II. Subordination. A starting point for the development of mobility models appropriate to a heterogeneous population is to consider Q-matrices of the special form $Q = \lambda(M - I)$, where λ is a positive constant and M is a stochastic matrix. Populations in which transition probabilities evolve according to $e^{t\lambda(M-I)}$ may be given the following substantive interpretation. An individual starting in state i at time zero stays there for an exponentially distributed length of time τ_0 with

$$\text{prob}(\tau_0 \geq t) = e^{-\lambda t} \qquad t > 0$$

At the end of this period he makes a transition to state j with probability m_{ij}, the (i,j) entry in the stochastic matrix M. It is *not* assumed that $m_{ii} = 0$; hence the individual may have a positive probability of staying in the same state[4] after time τ_0. Once an individual has moved according to M, he stays in his new state for another exponentially distributed

---

[4] The utility of this formulation can be illustrated by an example. If the process concerns geographic migration and the system states are regions of the country, a state i to state i transition would represent change of residence within a region. Even if it is unreasonable conceptually to "move" and not change state (as in movements among marital statuses) we might still want to speak of "exposures to movement" or "decisions to possibly move."

length of time τ_1 which is independent of τ_0 and of the state he is in but again satisfies
$$\text{prob}(\tau_1 \geq t) = e^{-\lambda t} \qquad t > 0$$
Now he makes another move according to m_{jh}, and the previous process of waiting an exponentially distributed length of time and moving according to the entries in M is repeated.

In this imagery the constant $1/\lambda$ describes an individual's mean waiting time before moving (or before making a decision to possibly move); M characterizes his propensity to transfer to particular states. An alternative formulation of the process derives from an interpretation of λ as measuring rate of movement. The random variables $\{Y(t), t > 0\}$, which describe an individual's history, may be written in the special form
$$Y(t) = X[T_\lambda(t)] \tag{5}$$
where $\text{prob}[Y(t) = j \,|\, Y(0) = i]$ is the (i,j) entry in $P(t) = e^{t\lambda(M-I)}$, $T_\lambda(t)$ is a Poisson process with parameter λ, and $X(k)$, $k = 0, 1, 2, \ldots$ is a discrete-time Markov chain with one-step transition probabilities governed by M.

Representation of stochastic processes by a recipe such as Equation (5) is known in the mathematics literature as subordination (Feller, 1971, pp. 345–349); more precisely the process $Y(t)$ is said to be subordinated to $X(k)$ using $T_\lambda(t)$ as an operational or intrinsic clock. Elaborating further, expression (5) says that you can also think of individuals whose transition probabilities are governed by $e^{t\lambda(M-I)}$ as evolving according to the prescription: (i) Wait in an initial state i until the first jump time of a Poisson process. (ii) At this instant, change state once according to the laws of a discrete-time Markov chain whose one-step transition matrix is M. (iii) Wait in the new state j until the Poisson process jumps for the second time. (iv) Now change state again according to M. (v) Repeat the above procedure for successive Poisson jump times.

In this setting, the constant λ governing rate of movement appears only in the description of the Poisson process or if you like, the intrinsic clock. Specifically: prob(exactly v moves up to time t) = prob[exactly v jumps in a Poisson process with parameter λ during $(0,t)$]
$$= \text{prob}[T_\lambda(t) = v] = \frac{(\lambda t)^v e^{-\lambda t}}{v!}$$
Likewise the matrix M governing the propensity to move to particular states appears only in the description of the discrete-time Markov chain $X(k)$ according to
$$\text{prob}[X(k+1) = j \,|\, X(k) = i] = m_{ij}$$

This matrix providse a static picture of the population at an instant of movement. The dynamics are regulated by the intrinsic clock $T_\lambda(t)$.

A final point is that the interpretation (5) gives rise to a series representation for $e^{t\lambda(M-I)}$ in the form

$$e^{t\lambda(M-I)} = \sum_{v=0}^{\infty} e^{-\lambda t} \frac{(\lambda t)^v}{v!} M^v \qquad (6)$$

The individual terms in this series indicate that rate of movement and propensity to move to particular states are factors regulated by two independent sociologically identifiable quantities, λ and M. It is useful to contrast this isolation of rate of movement and propensity to move in the factored matrix $\lambda(M - I)$ with the more general formulation involving Q-matrices. The two formulations are related according to

$$\begin{cases} -q_{ii}dt = -\lambda(m_{ii} - 1)dt = \text{probability of leaving state } i \text{ during the time interval } (t, t+dt) \\ q_{ij}dt = \lambda m_{ij}dt = \text{probability of a move from state } i \text{ to state } j(j \neq i) \text{ during } (t, t+dt) \end{cases}$$

We wish to emphasize that mobility processes in a stationary environment are most usefully described by waiting times in states together with transition probabilities which are independent of the waiting times but allow for the possibility of remaining in the current state at a move. Q-matrices permit descriptions in terms of transition mechanisms and waiting-time distributions as independent quantities, but this would naturally take the form

$$Q = \begin{pmatrix} -q_{11} & & 0 \\ & \ddots & \\ 0 & & -q_{rr} \end{pmatrix} \left[\begin{pmatrix} 0 & & q_{ij}/-q_{ii} & \\ & \ddots & & \\ & & \ddots & \\ & & & \begin{array}{c} i \neq j \\ 0 \end{array} \end{pmatrix} - I \right]$$

The matrix

$$||q_{ij}/-q_{ii}|| \, i \neq j$$

describes jumps without allowing for further holding in the origin state; in particular, $q_{ij}/-q_{ii} = \{\text{probability of a move from state } i \text{ to state } j \text{ given a departure}\}$. The diagonal matrix $||-q_{ii}||$ has entries interpretable as holding-time rates in the sense that

$$\text{prob}[Y(u) = i, s < u < s + t | Y(s) = i] = e^{q_{ii}t}$$

Nevertheless this formulation seems less sociologically meaningful than expressing Q in the factored form $\lambda(M - I)$. If you start with a fixed Q, which means that you are viewing Q as the basic ingredient in the model, it can always be factored in the form $\lambda(M - I)$; [e.g., by setting $\lambda = \max(-q_{ii})$, in which case $M = (1/\lambda)Q + I$]. However, our attitude here is that the natural starting point for a description of mobility processes is λ and M, with Q defined in terms of these basic ingredients.

The present description of mobility in which an individual is characterized by a rate λ and a transition matrix M and evolves according to probabilities $e^{t\lambda(M-I)}$ was the starting point for Spilerman's (1972b) extension of the mover-stayer model to a population with a continuum of types. A limitation of this extension is that the waiting-time distributions until transition according to M do not depend on a person's state; rather an individual is compelled to move at the same rate irrespective of his location (Spilerman, 1972b, p. 609). The description of section III provides a basis for eliminating this restriction and presents the most general continuous-time Markov chain formulation of mobility by an individual.

III. A General Factored Representation of Q. Consider Q-matrices of the form $\Lambda(M - I)$, where

$$\Lambda = \begin{pmatrix} \lambda_1 & & & 0 \\ & \lambda_2 & & \\ & & \ddots & \\ 0 & & & \lambda_r \end{pmatrix} \quad \lambda_i > 0 \text{ for } i = 1, 2, \ldots, r$$

and M is a stochastic matrix. The evolution of individuals governed by the transition matrix $e^{t\Lambda(M-I)}$ may be described more concretely as follows: (i) An individual starting in state i at time zero stays there for an exponentially distributed length of time τ_0 with

$$\text{prob}[\tau_0 \geq t \mid X(0) = i] = e^{-\lambda_i t} \qquad t > 0$$

(ii) At the end of this time period he makes a decision to move to state j with probability m_{ij}. In general, $m_{ii} \neq 0$. (iii) Now he waits in state j for an exponentially distributed length of time τ_1 with

$$\text{prob}[\tau_1 \geq t \mid X(1) = j] = e^{-\lambda_j t}$$

(iv) Then he makes another decision to move to state h with probability m_{jh}. (v) The above sequence is repeated.

The waiting times τ_k depend only on the current state $X(k)$, not on the past history[5] $X(0), X(1), \ldots, X(k-1)$ and $\tau_0, \tau_1, \ldots, \tau_{k-1}$.

---

[5] $\{X(k)\}$ are again the random variables of a discrete-time Markov chain governed by M which describes moves when they occur.

However, an individual's rate of movement is now characterized by the diagonal matrix Λ rather than a single constant λ as in the previous section. The present description reduces to that of section II when $\lambda_1 = \lambda_2 = \cdots = \lambda_r$.

Again it should be observed that a given Q-matrix has infinitely many factorizations of the form $\Lambda(M - I)$ with

$$\begin{cases} q_{ii} = \lambda_i(m_{ii} - 1) \\ q_{ij} = \lambda_i m_{ij} \quad \text{for } i \neq j \end{cases}$$

However, the basic ingredients of mobility models with individuals evolving according to continuous-time Markov chains are the matrices Λ and M, with Q defined in terms of them. When individual histories are available, M and Λ can be estimated from observed movements according to the recipe

$$\begin{cases} \hat{m}_{ij} = N_{ij}/N_{i.} \\ \hat{\lambda}_i = N_{i.}/A_{i.} \end{cases} \quad (7)$$

where N_{ij} = number of transitions from i to j during the observation period $(0,t)$

$N_{i.} = \sum_j N_{ij}$ = total number of moves from state i (including within-state moves) during $(0,t)$

$A_{i.}$ = total occupation time in state i by all individuals during $(0,t)$.

Our representation of the random variables $Y(t)$ in section II which describe individual histories by $Y(t) = X[T_\lambda(t)]$ with $T_\lambda(t)$ a Poisson process, does not carry over to the more general formulation indicated here. We could, in principal, write $Y(t) = X[T^*(t)]$, where $T^*(t) = \{$number of transitions up to time t in a Markov chain governed by $e^{t\Lambda(M-I)}\}$. However, $T^*(t)$ does not have a simple family of formulas analogous to the Poisson distribution describing its evolution. Thus we shall retain our first interpretation of alternating exponential holding times and decisions to possibly move as the simplest generic caricature of mobility for an individual.

From an analytic point of view the simplicity of the Poisson series representation

$$e^{t\lambda(M-I)} = \sum_{k=0}^{\infty} e^{-\lambda t} \frac{(\lambda t)^k}{k!} M^k$$

with the terms describing rate of movement and those describing transitions appearing as separate multiplicative factors, does not carry over to our more general formulation. In particular

$$e^{t\Lambda(M-I)} \neq e^{t\Lambda M} e^{-t\Lambda} \neq \sum_{k=0}^{\infty} e^{-\Lambda t} \frac{(\Lambda t)^k}{k!} M^k$$

The nonequivalence of the three expressions is due to the fact that Λ and M do *not* commute, that is, $\Lambda M \neq M\Lambda$, and it is this algebraic point which makes computations with $e^{t\Lambda(M-I)}$ considerably more difficult than with the model of section 2.II. We will return to this issue again in section 3 when we compare this description of individual level mobility in a heterogeneous population with a description where $\lambda_1 = \lambda_2 = \cdots = \lambda_r$.

3. HETEROGENEITY AND MIXTURES OF STOCHASTIC PROCESSES

3.1. Mixtures of Markov Processes and Inversion Formulas

Thus far we have discussed Markov chain models as they pertain to repeated moves by a single individual or to the movements of a homogeneous population. In the context of social mobility, observable populations are rarely homogeneous with respect to the frequency with which individuals move or their propensity to transfer to particular states. However, in early studies (Prais, 1955; Matras, 1960; Tarver and Gurley, 1965), it was tacitly assumed that the population under consideration could be viewed as a homogeneous unit and that histories associated with a single Markov process could be thought of as typical of all segments of the population.

In using discrete-time Markov transition matrices as a baseline for comparison with particular data sets, a standard strategy is to estimate an n-step transition matrix $\hat{P}(n)$ from the data, calculate the nth roots[6] $[\hat{P}(n)]^{1/n} = M$ viewing these as one-step transition matrices, and then compare M^{n+k} with the observed matrix $\hat{P}(n+k)$. For many social phenomena a substantial discrepancy was noted between M^{n+k} and $\hat{P}(n+k)$, and it was suggested that this is because the population should really be viewed as heterogeneous with different stochastic processes describing the evolution of different subpopulations. The first detailed discussion of this kind of inadequacy of Markov models to depict social mobility was by Blumen, Kogan, and McCarthy (1955). They documented the phenomenon of "lumping on the main diagonal" (the presence of more individuals in these cells of an n-step transition matrix than predicted by a Markov model), and showed that it can derive from

---

[6] In most applications to mobility it has been assumed that the natural time scale of the process is such that $n = 1$, thus eliminating the need for computing roots of matrices. This assumption is tantamount to saying that the natural time scale has intervals which are the same length as a sampling interval, thereby obscuring consideration of alternative underlying time scales and transition mechanisms M which might be compatible with the data and substantively meaningful.

treating a heterogeneous population as though it was homogeneous. Furthermore they constructed a discrete-time model in which two types of persons were distinguished, each evolving independently according to a different Markov process. Efficient estimation procedures for the parameters of this model were subsequently developed by Goodman (1961).

The empirical context for which the mover-stayer model was developed is one where evolution of each distinct type of individual is not directly observable. An investigator is constrained to sample the total pooled population (also referred to as a macroscopic level description) at a few time points and obtain counts of the number of individuals starting in a particular state who are in any other state at the end of a sampling interval. This situation is typical of all mobility environments discussed here. A key step in understanding the underlying mobility process and the appropriateness of particular models, then, is an identification of the nondirectly observable quantities (one-step transition matrices and rates of movement for continuous-time processes) by a mathematical analysis relating information about the pooled population back to the behavior of individuals. This is another instance of an inverse problem, analogous to the discussion of section 2.1 but complicated by the fact that we are treating several types of individuals simultaneously.

To clarify these ideas we present four examples which form the simplest mathematical caricatures of the notion of a mixture of stochastic processes and which are also substantively meaningful in the context of social mobility.

Example 1. Consider a population consisting of two kinds of individuals. Persons of each type evolve independently according to a discrete-time Markov chain. We denote by $X_1(k)$ and $X_2(k)$, $k = 0, 1, 2, \ldots$, the random variables describing the movements among states by persons of each type. Probability statements about $X_1(k)$ and $X_2(k)$ are assumed to follow the theoretical recipe

$$\text{prob}[X_\lambda(k) = j \mid X_\lambda(0) = i] = m_{ij;\lambda}^{(k)}$$

for $k = 0, 1, 2, \ldots$, and $\lambda = 1$ or 2. The element $m_{ij;\lambda}^{(k)}$ is the (i,j) entry in the stochastic matrix M_λ^k (k-fold matrix multiplication of M_λ). We shall refer to the bivariate process $[X_1(k), X_2(k)]$ as a microscopic or individual-level description of a mobility process.

In empirical situations we usually observe values of a random variable $Y(k)$ which are possible states of either the process $X_1(k)$ or $X_2(k)$; that is, we can observe how an individual sampled from the population evolves through time although we cannot assign him to a particular person type. We also assume that we can estimate $s_i = \{$proportion of individuals from among those in state i at time zero who are classified as type 1$\}$. Procedures for estimating s_i have been reported by Blumen, Kogan, and McCarthy (1955) and Goodman (1961).

Evolution of the stochastic process $Y(k)$, $k = 0, 1, 2, \ldots$, is described by the transition probabilities

$$\text{prob}[Y(k) = j | Y(0) = i] = s_i m_{ij;1}^{(k)} + (1 - s_i) m_{ij;2}^{(k)}$$

or in matrix form

$$P(k) = SM_1^k + (I - S)M_2^k \qquad (8)$$

with

$$S = \begin{pmatrix} s_1 & & & 0 \\ & s_2 & & \\ & & \cdot & \\ & & & \cdot \\ 0 & & & s_r \end{pmatrix}$$

The univariate process $Y(k)$ is referred to as a macroscopic or population level description of a mobility process. Its interpretation in this sense arises from the fact that an observer who can see only histories $Y(0)$, $Y(1)$, $Y(2)$, $\ldots$, and the family of matrices $P(1)$, $P(2)$, $P(3)$, $\ldots$, cannot discover that in fact $Y(k)$ is generated by a composite of two types of individuals evolving according to $X_1(k)$ and $X_2(k)$ respectively. However, once the interpretation of a heterogeneous population is brought in, you can formulate a theory of evolution of a mixture of two types of individuals as in Equation (8), with $Y(k)$ describing the composite or pooled population. Hence the term *mixture of stochastic processes*.

The particular theory (8) describes a population in which the mixing distribution remains constant through time and is identified with the proportions of individuals in each state (which may be a job category or a geographic region) who are of type 1 at the reference time $k = 0$. This theoretical description reduces to the classic mover-stayer model when

$$M_1 = I = \begin{pmatrix} 1 & & & 0 \\ & 1 & & \\ & & \cdot & \\ & & & \cdot \\ 0 & & & 1 \end{pmatrix}$$

It should also be emphasized that the macroscopic process $Y(k)$ is not Markovian even though the components of the pooled population are assumed to evolve according to discrete-time Markov processes.

With this theoretical picture at hand, we illustrate the notions of embeddability and inverse problem for mixtures of stochastic processes within the context of the mover-stayer model. For the simplest mathematical structure consider a two-state mobility process where you are constrained to observe the pooled population at times $n = 0$ and $n = 2$. Denote the 2×2 stochastic matrix estimated from the data by

$$\hat{P}(2) = \begin{pmatrix} a & 1-a \\ 1-b & b \end{pmatrix} \quad 0 < a,b < 1$$

The entry in row i, column j ($i,j = 1$ or 2) has the interpretation, "proportion of individuals in state i at time zero who are in stage j at time 2." Our first task is to determine necessary and sufficient conditions so that $\hat{P}(2)$ is compatible with the theoretical description

$$P(2) = S + (I - S)M^2 \qquad (9)$$

To simplify the calculations further while still retaining a substantively meaningful description of a pooled population of movers and stayers, suppose that $s_1 = s_2 =$ some $s \geq 0$. Then solve the matrix equation (9) for M and obtain

$$M = \{(I - S)^{-1}[P(2) - S]\}^{1/2} \qquad (10)$$

Replacing the theoretical $P(2)$ by the empirically determined $\hat{P}(2)$ we can check, using the calculations in the appendix, that the inversion formula (10), which is the solution of the inverse problem, yields a legitimate stochastic matrix M if and only if $a + b > 1 + s$. Putting this another way, an empirically determined 2×2 matrix $\hat{P}(2)$ is said to be embeddable in a mover-stayer framework if and only if the above inequality is satisfied. It is also important to notice that if you alter what you regard as the natural time scale of the mobility process so that the matrix

$$\begin{pmatrix} a & 1-a \\ 1-b & b \end{pmatrix}$$

is thought of as $\hat{P}(n)$ for *any* even number n, then the condition $a + b > 1 + s$ is still necessary and sufficient for the data to be compatible with the theoretical framework of Equation (8). In fact, in the 2×2 case this condition also ensures a unique inverse.

The criterion $a + b > 1 + s$ becomes more meaningful if you recall that the original data sets examined by Blumen, Kogan, and McCarthy gave rise to $\hat{P}(n)$ having diagonal elements larger than those predicted by a simple Markov chain model. For a two-state process a criterion for $\hat{P}(n)$, n even,[7] to be compatible with the Markov structure M^n is just $a + b > 1$; however, once you postulate two types of individuals, stayers and movers, in proportions s and $1 - s$ respectively, you are describing evolution via transition matrices whose diagonal elements must be larger than the corresponding one-type Markov model by precisely the mixing fraction s. An analogous condition also holds for processes with more than two states and for rather general matrices

$$ S = \begin{pmatrix} s_1 & & 0 \\ & \cdot & \\ & & \cdot \\ 0 & & s_r \end{pmatrix} $$

A full mathematical discussion, however, is somewhat intricate and will appear in Singer and Spilerman (1974). A final point with regard to the criterion $a + b > 1 + s$ is that even if you cannot estimate the mixing fraction s directly, you can still indicate the largest possible value of s which allows the matrix $\hat{P}(n)$ to be compatible with a mover-stayer theoretical framework; namely, supremum s such that $1 + s < a + b$.

Example 2. Let $X_1(k), \ldots, X_N(k)$ be independent discrete-time Markov chains describing the movements of N types of individuals each evolving according to a distinct stochastic matrix M_λ, $\lambda = 1, \ldots, N$. For individuals of each type,

$$ \text{prob}[X_\lambda(k) = j \mid X_\lambda(0) = i] = m_{ij;\lambda}^{(k)} $$

where $m_{ij;\lambda}^{(k)}$ is the (i,j) entry in M^k. Let

$$ S_\lambda = \begin{pmatrix} s_{\lambda 1} & & 0 \\ & \cdot & \\ & & \cdot \\ 0 & & s_{\lambda r} \end{pmatrix} \qquad \sum_{\lambda=1}^{N} S_\lambda = I $$

where $s_{\lambda i} = \{$proportion of the population in state i at time zero that consists of type-λ persons$\}$. Analogous to example 1 the individual-level

---

[7] It should be observed that a 2×2 stochastic matrix $\hat{P}(n)$ with n odd is always compatible with a discrete-time Markov structure. Thus if you are restricted to taking observations only at time zero and one other time, the additional measurement should be made at an even time to provide the most elementary test of compatibility with a Markov model. This discussion also applies to 2×2 stochastic matrices $\hat{P}(n)$ thought of as observations generated by a mover-stayer model.

vector process $[X_1(k), \ldots, X_N(k)]$, $k = 0, 1, 2, \ldots$, is not directly observable; however, the pooled population is observable at a few time points and it is from these data that information about the matrices $M_1, \ldots, M_N$, postulated by the theoretical structure, must be inferred. The population-level process may be described by a family of random variables $Y(0), Y(1), \ldots$, whose values are the possible states of each of the individual subpopulations. The evolution of $Y(k)$ is governed by the stochastic matrices

$$P(k) = \sum_{\lambda=1}^{N} S_\lambda M_\lambda^k \quad k = 0, 1, 2, \ldots$$

This formulation of a mixture of Markov processes can be extended to the case where each individual in the population has his own M_λ matrix. This approach was suggested by McFarland (1970) in recognition of the fact that heterogeneity in social mobility is attributable to an assortment of individual differences—in race, ethnicity, parental SES, educational attainment, and so forth. Spilerman (1972a) has presented a regression method for estimating the individual M_λ matrices from an observed population-level matrix $\hat{P}(1)$ and data on the determinants of heterogeneity. Because of its complexity, a discussion of embeddability and inversion methods for this model will be deferred to the companion mathematical paper (Singer and Spilerman 1974).

Example 3. Let $\{X_\lambda(t)\}_{\lambda>0}$ be a continuum of independent continuous-time Markov chains whose transition probabilities are governed by the exponential formula

$$e^{t\lambda(M-I)} \quad \lambda > 0; t \geq 0 \tag{11}$$

The processes $\{X_\lambda(t)\}_{\lambda>0}$ should be thought of as describing the evolution of infinitely many different types of individuals, each type being identified by a number λ that specifies its rate of movement. For a fixed value of λ (one type of person) this is just the continuous-time Markov chain model described in (2.II). Now, however, we envision a heterogeneous population where a type-λ individual has waiting times between moves which are exponentially distributed with parameter λ, independent of his previous state. All types of individuals are treated as having the same propensity to move among the states, prescribed by the matrix M.

As in our previous examples, the vector process $\{X_\lambda(t)\}_{\lambda>0}$ is not directly observable, but we postulate that type-λ individuals occur in the total population with a frequency described by a probability density $g(\lambda)$. Then the observable macroscopic-level process, which consists of the mixture (or pooling) of all types of individuals, can be described by random variables $Y(t)$, $t \geq 0$, whose values are the possible states of the component types $\{X_\lambda(t)\}_{\lambda>0}$ and whose transition probabilities are governed by the mixture of Markov transition matrices

$$P(t) = \int_0^\infty e^{t\lambda(M-I)}g(\lambda)d\lambda \qquad (12)$$

The entries of $P(t)$ have the usual interpretation,

$$p_{ij}(t) = \text{prob}[Y(t) = j | Y(0) = i]$$

This formulation may be viewed as an extension of the mover-stayer model, and it was developed in that light by Spilerman (1972b). In applications, $g(\lambda)$ is commonly specified as a gamma density

$$g(\lambda) = \frac{\beta^\alpha \lambda^{\alpha-1} e^{-\beta\lambda}}{\Gamma(\alpha)} \qquad \alpha,\beta > 0 \qquad (13)$$

because of the ability of this functional form to describe a variety of unimodal curves, unimodality being a reasonable characterization of the frequency of occurrence of different types of persons (with respect to rate of mobility) in heterogeneous populations (Palmer, 1954, p. 50; Taeuber, Chiazze, and Haenszel, 1968, p. 46).

Subject to hypothesis (13), the integral (12) may be evaluated as

$$P(t) = \left[\frac{\beta}{\beta+t}\right]^\alpha \left\{I - \left[\frac{t}{\beta+t}\right]M\right\}^{-\alpha} \qquad (14)$$

where the $-\alpha$th root of the preceding matrix is defined by the power series in M,

$$P(t) = \lim_{n\to\infty} \sum_{k=0}^n \binom{k+\alpha-1}{k} \left[\frac{\beta}{\beta+t}\right]^\alpha \left[\frac{t}{\beta+t}\right]^k M^k \qquad (15)$$

Equation (14) is amenable to two substantive interpretations depending on the role assigned to the parameters α and β:

Formulation 1. View the population as *heterogeneous* with the gamma family of distributions describing the proportion of individuals of type λ in the total population. Then the macroscopic-level process $Y(t)$ may be represented as

$$Y(t) = X[T_{(\alpha,\beta)}(t)] \qquad (16)$$

where $X(k)$, $k = 0, 1, 2, \ldots$, is a discrete-time Markov chain with one-step transition matrix M and $T_{(\alpha,\beta)}(t)$ is a negative binomial process acting as the intrinsic clock for the pooled population. $T_{(\alpha,\beta)}(t)$ may be thought of as a Poisson process with gamma-distributed parameter. It has the probability distribution

$$\text{prob}[T_{(\alpha,\beta)}(t) = v] = \binom{\alpha+v-1}{v}\left[\frac{t}{\beta+t}\right]^v \left[\frac{\beta}{\beta+t}\right]^\alpha \qquad (17)$$

in which the term for v denotes the proportion of the population making exactly v transitions in the time interval $(0,t)$. This is just another instance of the notion of subordination already discussed in section 2.II, except that now $X[T_{(\alpha,\beta)}(t)]$ is no longer a Markov process.

From the point of view of available data, information on $T_{(\alpha,\beta)}(t)$ can often be obtained without collecting individual histories. For instance data on the distribution of number of moves in mobility processes are reported in Palmer (1954, p. 50) and Lipset and Bendix (1959, p. 158). Using the mean and variance of the negative binomial variate $T_{(\alpha,\beta)}(t_1)$, where t_1 is an arbitrary observation time, estimates of the gamma parameters α and β can be computed from these observed population distributions.

Formulation 2. View the population as *homogeneous* but evolving according to the following recipe: (i) An individual starting in state i remains there for a length of time τ_0 governed by[8]

$$\text{prob}(\tau_0 \geq t) = \left[\frac{\beta}{\beta+t}\right]^\alpha \quad t > 0$$

At the end of the epoch τ_0 he makes a decision to move to state j (j may be equal to i) according to the stochastic matrix M. (ii) The individual remains in state j for a new random length of time τ_1 independent of τ_0 but having the same distribution:

$$\text{prob}(\tau_1 \geq t) = \left[\frac{\beta}{\beta+t}\right]^\alpha \quad t > 0$$

At the end of the epoch τ_1 he again makes a decision to move according to the stochastic matrix M. (iii) The above steps are repeated, and individuals in the homogeneous population evolve according to a continuous time stochastic process $X(t)$ with transition probabilities given by Equation (14). This is a special form of semi-Markov process; a more general treatment of this class of processes in the context of social mobility models appears in section 3.3.

This formulation can provide insight into the role of the parameters. For instance, Spilerman (1972b, p. 614), in an example using data that were artificial but constructed to simulate the nature of heterogeneity in occupational mobility, reports the values $\alpha = 1.37$ and $\beta = 0.92$.

[8] This distribution is obtained by assuming a mixture of exponential waiting times,

$$P(\tau_0 \geq t) = \int_t^\infty f(s)ds = \int_t^\infty \int_0^\infty \lambda e^{-\lambda s} g(\lambda) d\lambda ds$$

where $g(\lambda)$ is a gamma density.

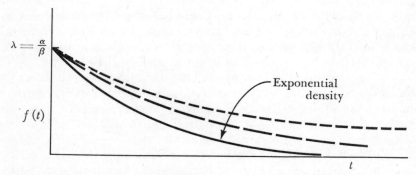

Figure 1. Family of compound exponential curves. The family of densities

$$f(t) = \left[\frac{\alpha}{\beta+t}\right]\left[\frac{\beta}{\beta+t}\right]^\alpha$$

was constructed by the integration

$$f(t) = \int_0^\infty \lambda e^{-\lambda t} g(\lambda) d\lambda$$

where $g(\lambda)$ is a gamma density with parameters (α, β).

The value for α is especially interesting[9] since the waiting time distribution for $\tau_0, \tau_1, \ldots$, with $1 < \alpha < 2$ has an infinite variance (and finite mean). This suggests that a substantial portion of the pooled population moves very rarely or not at all, which is another way of saying that there is considerable heterogeneity.

The main point about the second formulation, though, is that it is suitable for describing processes where individual histories are not available and a more flexible class of waiting time distributions than just exponential is desired. As we remarked earlier, exponential waiting times guarantee that your mathematical model is a Markov process; however, this requirement seems unnecessarily stringent for describing mobility.[10] The two-parameter family of distributions

$$F_{(\alpha,\beta)}(t) = 1 - [\beta/(\beta+t)]^\alpha \qquad \alpha, \beta > 0; t > 0 \qquad (18)$$

which arose in the previous discussion describes a more general family of densities $f_{(\alpha,\beta)}(t)$, all of which have the same form as the exponential density (see Figure 1). Indeed the exponential with parameter λ arises as a limiting case of $F_{(\alpha,\beta)}(t)$ when[11] $\alpha \to \infty$, $\beta \to \infty$, and $\alpha/\beta = \lambda$.

---

[9] The second parameter, β, is merely a scaling factor.

[10] In fact, sociological hypotheses that invoke the Markov property (independence of future state from past locations, given current state) to describe state changes at the occurrence of a move often place no requirement on the waiting-time distributions. It would be incorrect to test such a thesis by fitting a Markov chain to the observed data.

[11] This can be seen by expanding both Equation (18) and the cumulative distribution function for an exponential, $F_\lambda(t) = 1 - e^{-\lambda t}$, in power series.

The simplest mathematical caricature of embeddability and an inverse problem for the model (14) arises again for a two-state process. For this special situation an empirically determined stochastic matrix

$$\hat{P}(t_1) = \begin{pmatrix} a & 1-a \\ 1-b & b \end{pmatrix} \quad 0 < a,b < 1$$

corresponding to observations at times zero and t_1 is compatible with the theoretical framework (14) if and only if $a + b > 1$. For a fixed α and β in Equation (14) this condition also ensures a unique solution to the inverse problem, which is given by

$$M = \left[\frac{\beta + t_1}{t_1}\right]\left\{I - \left[\frac{\beta}{\beta + t_1}\right][\hat{P}(t_1)]^{-1/\alpha}\right\} \quad (19)$$

Necessary and sufficient conditions for an observed $r \times r$ stochastic matrix $\hat{P}(t_1)$ to be representable in the form (14) can be determined in principle. However, the criteria become very complicated as r increases and computational algorithms to test for embeddability are needed. In section 4.1 we present some general embeddability criteria for $r = 3$ and indicate conditions valid for arbitrary r when the sociological context permits stronger assumptions about the structure of M than just requiring it to be a stochastic matrix. A full discussion of the computational problems arising from embeddability tests will appear in Singer and Spilerman (1974).

In concluding our discussion of the present example, it should be pointed out that a simple strategy to check for embeddability and uniqueness of M is to calculate an $r \times r$ matrix according to Equation (19) and check whether or not the computation process yields a stochastic matrix as opposed to a complex-valued one. If this matrix is stochastic and if the observed $\hat{P}(t_1)$ satisfies the condition $\inf_i[\hat{p}_{ii}(t_1)] > \frac{1}{2}$, you can verify that the computed matrix M is in fact the *unique* stochastic M compatible with the data. This test was used by Spilerman (1972b, p. 607). It should be emphasized that, in general, embeddable matrices $\hat{P}(t_1)$ can give rise to drastically different M arrays when $\inf_i[\hat{p}_{ii}(t_1)] \leq \frac{1}{2}$. Examples of this situation are presented in section 4.1.

One interpretation of empirically determined matrices for which the diagonal elements are all greater than $\frac{1}{2}$ is that on the natural time scale of the mobility process the observations are sufficiently close to time zero so that many moves away from the origin state have not yet occurred. In a mathematical context $\inf_i[\hat{p}_{ii}(t_1)] > \frac{1}{2}$ is a condition which guarantees that in computing $[\hat{P}(t_1)]^{-1/\alpha}$ you are on the principal branch of the $-1/\alpha$th root of the matrix, thereby ruling out complex matrices as well as other real stochastic matrices M in the inversion formula (19). A complete mathematical treatment of these issues will appear in Singer and Spilerman (1974).

Example 4. From a substantive point of view, a principal defect of the individual-level description in example 3 is the requirement that a person's waiting-time distribution be the same in every state. We should like to eliminate this constraint and permit a full Markov mode to characterize the movements of an individual. This is desirable since there are many instances in which rate of movement is a function of system state; for example, industries differ in their rates of employee separation (Blauner, 1964, pp. 198–203).

We therefore classify a person according to the diagonal matrix

$$\Lambda = \begin{pmatrix} \lambda_1 & & 0 \\ & \cdot & \\ & & \cdot \\ 0 & & \lambda_r \end{pmatrix} \quad \lambda_i \geq 0; i = 1, 2, \ldots, r$$

where $1/\lambda_i$ has the interpretation, "average waiting time in state i." Then let $\{X_\Lambda(t)\}_{\Lambda>0}$ be a continuum of independent continuous-time Markov chains whose transition probabilities are governed by

$$e^{t\Lambda(M-I)} \quad t \geq 0 \quad (20)$$

This is just the formulation of section (2.III) except that now the family $\{X_\Lambda(t)\}_{\Lambda>0}$ is thought of as describing the evolution of infinitely many different types of individuals, each type being identified by a distinct, positive, diagonal matrix Λ. Individuals of type Λ are viewed as occurring in the total population with a proportion specified by a joint probability density $g(\lambda_1, \ldots, \lambda_r)$. The macroscopic level (pooled population) is then described by random variables $Y(t)$, $t \geq 0$, whose values are the possible states of the component types $\{X_\Lambda(t)\}$ and whose transition probabilities are governed by the mixture of Markov transition matrices

$$P(t) = \int_0^\infty \cdots \int_0^\infty e^{t\Lambda(M-I)} g(\lambda_1, \ldots, \lambda_r) d\lambda_1 \ldots d\lambda_r \quad (21)$$

A flexible $2r$-parameter family of distributions analogous to Equation (13) and useful for describing heterogeneity in the full population is

$$g(\lambda_1, \ldots, \lambda_r) = \prod_{i=1}^r \frac{\beta_i^{\alpha_i}}{\Gamma(\alpha_i)} \lambda^{\alpha_i} e^{-\beta_i \lambda_i} \quad (22)$$

where $\alpha_i, \beta_i > 0$, and $i = 1, 2, \ldots, r$.

A major analytical difficulty arises in dealing with the representation (21), even for specializations such as Equation (22), because simple evaluations of the integrals in terms of rational functions of M or finite linear combinations of exponentials cannot be carried out. The source of this mathematical difficulty is the fact that the matrices Λ and M are noncommutative, that is, $\Lambda M \neq M\Lambda$. A discussion of numerical methods for evaluating expressions such as Equation (21) will appear in Singer and Spilerman (1974).

Although we cannot obtain a convenient expression for $P(t)$ analogous to Equation (14) in the case where the rate of movement parameter was specified by a scalar, we can evaluate $P(t)$ numerically for illustrative purposes. In particular, Equation (21) may be written

$$P(t) = \int_0^\infty \cdots \int_0^\infty \sum_{k=0}^\infty \frac{[\Lambda(M-I)]^k}{k!} t^k g(\lambda_1, \ldots, \lambda_r) d\lambda_1 \ldots d\lambda_r$$

$$= \sum_{k=0}^\infty \frac{t^k}{k!} \begin{pmatrix} \lambda_1 u_{11} & \cdots & \lambda_1 u_{1r} \\ \vdots & & \vdots \\ \lambda_r u_{r1} & \cdots & \lambda_r u_{rr} \end{pmatrix}^k g(\lambda_1, \ldots, \lambda_r) d\lambda_1 \ldots d\lambda_r$$

where $U = M - I$, that is, $u_{ij} = m_{ij} - \delta_{ij}$. Specifying $g(\lambda_1, \ldots, \lambda_r)$ as a product of gamma densities (22), we obtain

$$P(t) = I + t\left(\cdots u_{ij} \frac{\alpha_i}{\beta_i} \cdots\right) \quad (23)$$
$$+ \frac{t^2}{2!}\left(\cdots \frac{(\alpha_i + 1)\alpha_i}{\beta_i^2} u_{ii} u_{ij} + \frac{\alpha_i}{\beta_i} \sum_{k \neq 1} \frac{\alpha_k}{\beta_k} u_{ik} u_{kj} \cdots\right) + \cdots$$

where the entries in matrices represent the (i,j) terms. Although the corresponding terms of higher-order arrays increase rapidly in complexity, the calculations can be carried out by computer for a few terms of the series.

Artificial data were prepared in order to compare this model with ones in the earlier examples. The underlying structure of the constructed data is revealed in Table 1. Panel (a) shows the individual-level matrix M that was assumed to govern the movements of all persons. The waiting-time distributions are displayed in panel (b); they were constructed by assuming that a gamma density with parameters (α_i, β_i) describes the population heterogeneity in state i with respect to rate of movement. By varying these parameters over the system states we have built into the data the full range of generality consistent with the present model.

Using the information in Table 1 in conjunction with Equation (23) the matrices $\hat{P}(1)$, $\hat{P}(2)$, and $\hat{P}(3)$ were constructed for the process. These arrays are reported in row 1 of Table 2. We will interpret them as "observed data"; they depict a mobility process in which there is popu-

TABLE 1
Structure of Heterogeneity in the Population, Simulated Data
(a) Individual-level Transition Matrix

$$M = \begin{pmatrix} .83 & .17 \\ .20 & .80 \end{pmatrix}$$

(b) Cumulative Waiting-time Distribution, by State[a]

Waiting Time	(1) State 1 ($\alpha = 2.1, \beta = 0.9$)	(2) State 2 ($\alpha = 1.4, \beta = 6.0$)	(3) Pooled Population[b] ($\hat{\alpha} = 0.61, \hat{\beta} = 0.49$)
0.0	0	0	0
0.2	0.344	0.044	0.194
0.4	0.538	0.086	0.312
0.6		0.125	0.391
0.8		0.161	0.449
1.0		0.194	0.493
1.2		0.225	0.503
1.4		0.254	
1.6		0.282	
1.8		0.307	
2.0		0.332	
2.2		0.354	
2.4		0.376	
2.6		0.396	
2.8		0.415	

[a] The entries in columns 1 and 2 were generated from the cumulative distribution

$$F_i(t) = 1 - [\beta_i/(\beta_i + t)]^{\alpha_i} \qquad i = 1,2$$

using the indicated (α_i, β_i). Values are reported for $F_i(t) < 0.500$ in states 1 and combined states, for $F_2(t) < 0.400$, and for the first entries exceeding these figures.

[b] An identical number of persons was assumed to be present in each state at $t = 0$. The entries in this column were therefore obtained by summing across the states and dividing by 2. The parameters $(\hat{\alpha}, \hat{\beta})$ for the pooled population were estimated using the median and interquartile range of the empirical distribution in column 3 (Mood, 1950, p. 387).

lation heterogeneity with respect to rate of movement, and an individual's rate can depend on the state he is in.

How good a fit would the mover-stayer extension or the Markov chain model provide to these data? To investigate this matter the $\hat{P}(1)$ matrix in Table 2 together with $(\hat{\alpha}, \hat{\beta})$, the parameters of the waiting-time distribution for the pooled population, were used to estimate M via Equation (19). Equation (14) was then employed to calculate $P(2)$ and $P(3)$, the matrices predicted by the mover-stayer model. These arrays are presented in the second row of Table 2. Markov chain estimates were obtained by raising $\hat{P}(1)$ to the second and third powers, which provides

TABLE 2
Population-level Transition Matrices Estimated from the Simulated Data

	$P(1)$	$P(2)$	$P(3)$
Postulated population structure [Equation (23)]	$\begin{bmatrix} .702 & .298 \\ .037 & .963 \end{bmatrix}$	$\begin{bmatrix} .528 & .472 \\ .062 & .938 \end{bmatrix}$	$\begin{bmatrix} .422 & .578 \\ .079 & .921 \end{bmatrix}$
Projections from mover-stayer extension [Equation (14)][a]	*	$\begin{bmatrix} .574 & .426 \\ .054 & .946 \end{bmatrix}$	$\begin{bmatrix} .501 & .499 \\ .063 & .937 \end{bmatrix}$
Projections from Markov model $\{P(n) = [\hat{P}(1)]^n\}$	*	$\begin{bmatrix} .504 & .496 \\ .062 & .938 \end{bmatrix}$	$\begin{bmatrix} .372 & .628 \\ .079 & .921 \end{bmatrix}$

[a] Procedure uses $\hat{P}(1)$ and $(\hat{\alpha},\hat{\beta})$ from column 3 of Table 1 as input data.

identical results to projection from Equation (4). These matrices are reported in row 3 of Table 2.

The two models produce different kinds of errors when compared with the observed data. The Markov model permits the waiting-time distribuitons to vary by state but constrains them to be exponential. This produces an underestimation of the proportions on the main diagonal when population heterogeneity in a state is considerable (as it is for state 1),[12] but produces accurate results where the heterogeneity is small (state 2). The mover-stayer extension permits the waiting times to be other than exponential but constrains them to be represented by a single distribution. With the present data the mover-stayer projections overestimate both main diagonal entries.

It should be noted that the mover-stayer model is not completely specified in the example. Both the general model of this section [Equation (23)] and the Markov model are insensitive to the proportion of the total population in an origin state at time zero. This is not true for the mover-stayer extension when the assumption concerning state-independent waiting times is violated, as it is here. Since the parameters $(\hat{\alpha},\hat{\beta})$ are calculated from the movements of all individuals, the estimated values will differ according to the origin-state distribution of the population. This means that there are a variety of mobility situations, all consistent with the data in Table 1 and with the matrices in rows 1 and 3 of Table 2, which will produce different arrays with the mover-stayer model. The particular matrices reported in row 2 are based on the additional assumption that the population was evenly distributed between states 1 and 2 at time zero (footnote b of Table 1).

[12] The variance of the gamma density α_i/β_i^2 provides a measure of the extent of heterogeneity in state i. For state 1 the variance equals 2.6; for state 2 it equals 0.039.

Rather than pursue computational details our intention here is simply to point out that the theoretical framework (21) provides the most general macroscopic level description of a heterogeneous population with individuals classified in terms of their rates of movement, the rates being state-dependent, and evolving according to independent Markov chains. As in example 3, the observable process is a particular case of a semi-Markov process and this provides a second interpretation for Equation (23), as a homogeneous population with nonexponential waiting times. Here the waiting-time distributions depend on the state according to

$$\text{prob}[\tau_k \geq t \mid X(k) = i] = \left[\frac{\beta_i}{\beta_i + t}\right]^{\alpha_i} \quad (24)$$

The particular formula (24) arises when the family (22) is used to describe the proportion of type-Λ individuals in the pooled population. The variable $X(k)$, $k = 0, 1, 2, \ldots$, denotes a discrete-time Markov chain governed by the stochastic matrices $M, M^2, M^3, \ldots$, and describes only the jumps of $Y(t)$, not its waiting times in particular states.

In applying this model it should be noted that the data requirements are more extensive than was the case previously. First, until inverse procedures are developed we must have available $\hat{M}$ rather than $\hat{P}(t)$, although the latter is the more commonly published datum. Second, we demand a separate waiting-time distribution for each system state in order to estimate the parameters (α_i, β_i), $i = 1, \ldots, r$. This is in contrast to the estimation of α and β in example 3 using the subordination representation $Y(t) = X[T_{(\alpha,\beta)}(t)]$. There we required either the waiting-time distribution for the entire population or, what is more generally available, the distribution of number of moves in the population during $(0,t)$. A similar readily computable description of $Y(t)$ in the present case, governed by Equations (21) and (22), is not possible because of the state-dependence of the waiting times. In principle we could write $Y(t) = X[T^*(t)]$, where $T^*(t) = \{$number of transitions in $Y(t)$ up to time $t\}$; however, there is no simple $2r$-parameter family of processes, analogous to the negative binomial process, which enables us to solve for (α_i, β_i) $i = 1, \ldots, r$ in terms of number of transitions in a sampling interval. For these reasons, in contrast with the mover-stayer extension (example 3), individual-level data files are necessary to exploit this model. They could derive from either retrospective histories—for example, the Taeuber data file on residence change (Taeuber, Chiazze, and Haenszel, 1968)—or from panel studies—for example, the New Jersey Negative Income Tax Experiment conducted by the University of Wisconsin Institute for Research on Poverty).

Embeddability and inverse problems for the present model, given observations at several time points $\hat{P}(t_1)$, $\hat{P}(t_2)$, ..., $\hat{P}(t_k)$ and varying degrees of information about (α_i,β_i), $i = 1, ..., r$ (ranging from estimation of all $2r$ constants down to rough inequalities about their range), are also complicated by the fact that Λ and M are noncommutative. In particular, no simple representation for M in terms of logarithms and rational functions of $\hat{P}(t_i)$ analogous to Equation (19) is available. Numerical inversion methods will be discussed in the context of mobility models in Singer and Spilerman (1974). It should be pointed out, however, that a *complete* discussion of the inverse problem and nonuniqueness of M in the present setting poses substantial mathematical difficulties that are unresolved as of this writing.

3.2. Identification of the Determinants of Population Heterogeneity

Let $\{X_{\Lambda,M}(t)\}_{\Lambda>0,M>0}$ be a collection of independent continuous-time Markov chains whose transition probabilities are governed by the prescription $e^{t\Lambda(M-I)}$. We therefore classify a person in terms of a diagonal matrix of movement rates *and* a stochastic matrix which specifies his transition propensities at a move. For convenience we will subscript individual q's parameters and write (Λ_q, M_q). We make no assumption regarding particular distributions for $\{\Lambda_q\}$ and $\{M_q\}$ in the population; however, we do require the availability of individual-level attribute data. Our intention is to discuss a method for ascertaining the determinants of population heterogeneity with respect to both rate of movement and propensity to favor transitions to certain states.

(a) Heterogeneity in the rate of movement. Consider the regression equation

$$A_{ic} = a_i + \sum_{k=1}^{K} b_{ik} X_{kc} + e_i \qquad i = 1, ..., r \qquad (25)$$

where A_{ic} is the cth waiting-time duration in state i during $(0,t_1)$, $(X_1, ..., X_K)$ are variables that are expected to explain individual differences in rate of movement, and the error terms are assumed to be independently distributed. The observations in this regression are the C waiting times in state i. A person contributes more than one observation if he made several moves during $(0,t_1)$ which originated in state i; if he was in this state throughout the interval (and failed to move) he appears once with $A_{ic} = t_i$.

This specification is intimately related to the rate-of-movement parameter of the continous-time Markov model according to

$$\frac{1}{N_{i\cdot}} \sum_c \hat{A}_{ic} = \frac{1}{N_{i\cdot}} \sum_c A_{ic} = \frac{1}{\hat{\lambda}_i} \qquad (26)$$

where the sums are taken over all waiting-time intervals in state i during $(0,t_1)$, and $N_{i.}$ denotes the number of moves originating in state i. The first equality results from the least-squares procedure of fitting a regression plane ($\hat{A}_{ic}$ is the predicted cth waiting time, the prediction having been made from the attribute profile $(X_{1c}, \ldots, X_{Kc})$ of the individual associated with this waiting time). The second equality is just Equation (7) restated in terms of waiting times. The $\hat{\lambda}_i$ value pertains to the single Markov chain that would be estimated if heterogeneity were ignored; it provides a suitable reference in terms of which population heterogeneity may be described. Combining Equations (25) and (26),

$$\frac{1}{\hat{\lambda}_i} = \hat{a}_i \frac{C}{N_{i.}} + \sum_{k=1}^{K} \hat{b}_{ik} \left(\frac{\sum_{c}^{C} X_{kc}}{N_{i.}} \right) \qquad i = 1, \ldots, r \qquad (27)$$

and this indicates how the regression produces a decomposition of the Markov parameter $\hat{\lambda}_i$. The term in parentheses in Equation (27), incidentally, can be interpreted as the "typical" individual profile associated with a waiting-time interval.

(b) Heterogeneity with respect to choice of destination state. Define a variable y_{ijc} that equals 1 if the cth move originating in state i during $(0,t_1)$ resulted in a transition to state j, and zero if it did not. Now consider the equation

$$y_{ijc} = a_{ij} + \sum_{h=1}^{H} b_{ijh} X_{hc} + e_{ij} \qquad i,j = 1, \ldots, r \qquad (28)$$

where $(X_1, \ldots, X_H)$ are variables which are expected to relate to choice of destination at a move, and the error terms e_{ij} are independently distributed. The observations for this regression are all $N_{i.}$ moves which originated in state i. An individual appears more than once if he made several moves from state i during $(0,t_1)$; he does not contribute an observation if he failed to move.

The relation between this equation and the corresponding Markov parameters is given by

$$\frac{1}{N_{i.}} \sum_{c}^{N_{i.}} \hat{y}_{ijc} = \frac{1}{N_{i.}} \sum_{c}^{N_{i.}} y_{ic} = \frac{N_{ij}}{N_{i.}} = \hat{m}_{ij} \qquad (29)$$

where N_{ij} equals the number of state i to state j transitions. The equality between the first two terms follows from the regression procedure; the second equality derives from the definition of y_{ijc}, and the third from Equation (7). Again the value $\hat{m}_{ij}$ refers to the single Markov chain that would result from treating the population as though it were homogeneous; it provides a useful benchmark from which to characterize heterogeneity. Combining Equations (28) and (29), the decomposition of the Markov parameter $\hat{m}_{ij}$ may be expressed as

$$\hat{m}_{ij} = \hat{a}_{ij} + \sum_{h}^{H} \hat{b}_{ijh} \left(\frac{\sum_{c}^{N_i.} X_{hc}}{N_{i.}} \right) \qquad i,j = 1, \ldots, r \qquad (30)$$

This equation describes the population heterogeneity with respect to choice of destination state at a move. The term in parentheses in Equation (30) depicts the typical individual profile associated with a move.

The two regression equations (25) and (28) therefore lead to a decomposition of population heterogeneity in a way that is intimately related to the continuous-time Markov chain formulation. Further elaboration of this procedure, in the context of a discrete-time Markov model, may be found in Spilerman (1972a).

In theory these regressions could be used to construct a Λ_q and M_q for each individual in the population as was done in Spilerman (1972a). If this is carried out the population-level transition matrix would be written

$$P(t) = V^{-1} \sum_{q} V_q e^{t \Lambda_q (M_q - I)} \qquad (31)$$

where V_q is a matrix with entry 1 on the main diagonal of the ith row and zero in all other cells (i denoting individual q's location at time zero) and $V = \sum_q V_q$. Expression (31)[13] describes the population-level process when each individual q evolves independently according to a continuous-time Markov chain with parameters (Λ_q, M_q). It is the continuous-time analog of McFarland's (1970) formulation to accommodate heterogeneity, which was summarized in example 2 of section 3.1.

In practice the estimates for this construction are likely to be poor since we would be computing M_q matrices for nonmovers during $(0, t_1)$ using only information on choice of destination state by movers—Equation (28). Consequently the utility of this formulation lies mainly in its contribution to analyzing heterogeneity, rather than to estimating individual-level parameters for projection.

3.3. Semi-Markov Processes and Their Mixtures

When the multivariate density $g(\lambda_1, \ldots, \lambda_r)$ in Equation (21) is specified as a product of univariate density functions, $\prod g_i(\lambda_i)$, then the same mathematical formalism (21) applies to (a) a heterogeneous population in which each individual moves according to a Markov process

---

[13] The formula is defined only if V is nonsingular. This condition will hold if one or more persons occupy each origin state at time zero.

with transition matrix M, the heterogeneity in rate of movement being described by $g_i(\lambda_i)$ in state i; and (b) a homogeneous population in which an individual waits in state i according to the distribution function

$$F_i(t) = \int_0^t \int_0^\infty \lambda e^{-\lambda s} g_i(\lambda) d\lambda ds$$

before transferring according to M.

For the macroscopic level process $Y(t)$ of example 4, $\{g_i(\lambda_i)\}$ were specified as gamma densities (22), and the corresponding waiting-time distributions were given by

$F_i(t) =$ prob(waiting time until a transition is less than $t|$ present state is i)
$= 1 - [\beta_i/(\beta_i + t)]^{\alpha_i} \qquad \alpha_i, \beta_i > 0; i = 1, 2, \ldots, r$

In the $Y(t)$ process of example 3 $g_i(\lambda_i) = g(\lambda)$ [Equation (13)] and $F_i(t) = F(t)$ [Equation (18)]; that is, the description of population heterogeneity in the first perspective, and the waiting time to a move in the second, are independent of the state of the process.

These macroscopic level processes are special cases of what are known as semi-Markov processes (Pyke, 1961a, 1961b; Ginsberg, 1971). This model is usually presented in the conceptual imagery of a homogeneous population with waiting-time distributions that need not be exponential. For an explicit formulation consider a stochastic process $Z(t)$, $t \geq 0$, with a finite number of states which, again, may be occupational categories, geographic regions, or income levels. The transition probabilities for the semi-Markov processes treated here are the unique solutions of the system of integral equations

$$p_{ij}(t) = \delta_{ij}[1 - F_i(t)] + \sum_{k=1}^r \int_0^t f_i(s) m_{ik} p_{kj}(t - s) ds \qquad (32)$$

where $p_{ij}(t) = \text{prob}[Z(t) = j | Z(0) = i]$; $\delta_{ij} = 1$ if $i = j$, 0 if $i \neq j$; and $1 \leq i,j \leq r$.

$F_i(t)$ is a distribution function which has the interpretation, "probability that a move has occurred by time t"; we assume that it has a density $f_i(t)$. The stochastic matrix M with entries m_{ij} describes the propensity to move to particular states. Equation (32) is therefore amenable to the following interpretation. (a) When $i \neq j$, $p_{ij}(t)$ consists of the sum of products of three factors: the probability of a first transition out of state i at time s, the probability of a state i to state k transition at that move, and the probability of transferring to state j by some combination of moves during (s,t). The summation is over all intermediate states k and over all time points s in the interval $(0,t)$. (b) When $i = j$, then, in addition to the preceding factor, there is a possibility of not transferring out of state i during $(0,t)$. The associated probability is specified by the first term.

When $f_i(t) = \lambda_i e^{-\lambda_i t}$, the system (32) is equivalent to the differential equations (3) with Q written in the factored form $Q = \Lambda(M - I)$. Thus the integral equation formulation (32) is a transparent way of saying that a stochastic process governed by these equations behaves like a Markov process except that the waiting-time distributions can be represented by general density functions $f_i(t)$.

With these preliminary notions at hand we now indicate two contexts in which semi-Markov processes are a natural description of social mobility.

Example 1. R. McGinnis (1968) adapted the notion of monotone hazard rate in reliability theory to a phenomenon he calls *cumulative inertia*, which has the interpretation that the longer a person remains in a particular state (occupation, geographic region, and so on) the less likely he is to move out of that state in the immediate future. Presumably, with increasing duration a person establishes social linkages and in other ways acclimates to his setting so that the attractiveness of remaining is increased. Ginsberg (1971) has pointed out that a semi-Markov process with decreasing event rate provides a formalization of this notion. A mathematical caricature of cumulative inertia can be stated in terms of the waiting-time distributions $F_i(t)$ via the function

$$r_i(t) = f_i(t)/[1 - F_i(t)] \qquad (33)$$

The expression $r_i(t)dt$ can be interpreted as the probability that a person known to be in state i at time t will exit from that state in the next dt units of time. Then cumulative inertia simply means that $r(t)$ is a monotone-decreasing function of t.[14] A simple two-parameter family of waiting-time distributions with monotone-decreasing cumulative inertia is given by

$$F_i(t) = 1 - e^{-\lambda_i t^{\gamma_i}} \qquad \text{with } \lambda_i > 0;\, 0 < \gamma_i < 1 \qquad (34)$$

For this specification, $r_i(t) = \lambda_i \gamma_i t^{\gamma_i - 1}$. Now classification of an individual evolving according to a semi-Markov process would be to characterize him by the family of distributions $\mathfrak{F} = \{F_1(t), \ldots, F_r(t)\}$ describing his waiting times in any state and the stochastic matrix M describing his propensity to move to particular states.

Example 2. In the framework of mixtures of stochastic processes

---

[14] In the Markov case $r_i(t) = \lambda_i e^{-\lambda_i t}/\{1 - [1 - e^{-\lambda_i t}]\} = \lambda_i$ for $i = 1, \ldots, r$. This says that the rate of movement is constant, irrespective of duration in the state.

we can consider $\{X_{\mathfrak{F}}(t)\}$ as a continuum of independent semi-Markov processes describing the mobility of individuals whose rates of movement are governed by Equation (34). It is assumed that the individual rates are distributed in the total population with proportions governed by a probability density $g(\lambda_1, \ldots, \lambda_r; \gamma_1, \ldots, \gamma_r)$. Then the macroscopic level process $Y(t)$ is defined as a stochastic process whose possible states coincide with those of $\{X_{\mathfrak{F}}(t)\}$ but whose transition probabilities are governed by

$$P(t) = \int_0^\infty \cdots \int_0^\infty \cdots \int_0^1 \cdots \int_0^1 [S(t; \lambda_1, \ldots, \lambda_r; \gamma_1, \ldots, \gamma_r; M) \\ g(\lambda_1, \ldots, \lambda_r; \gamma_1, \ldots, \gamma_r)] d\lambda_1 \ldots d\lambda_r d\gamma_1 \ldots d\gamma_r \qquad (35)$$

where $S(t; \lambda_1, \ldots, \lambda_r; \gamma_1, \ldots \gamma_r; M)$ denotes the stochastic matrix solution (32) with $\{F_i(t)\}$ specified by Equation (34). In general we must appeal to numerical integration methods to evaluate $S(t; \lambda_1, \ldots, \lambda_r; \gamma_1, \ldots, \gamma_r; M)$ because explicit, simple representations analogous to Equation (14) are a rarity for semi-Markov processes. Again a useful $2r$-parameter family of densities describing the composition of the pooled population is given by

$$g(\lambda_1, \ldots, \lambda_r) = \prod_{i=1}^r \frac{\beta_i^{\alpha_i}}{\Gamma(\alpha_i)} \lambda_i^{\alpha_i - 1} e^{-\beta_i \lambda_i} \qquad \alpha_i, \beta_i > 0$$

In this simple setting we treat $\gamma_1, \ldots, \gamma_r$ as fixed, although this is certainly not an essential conceptual restriction. The rationale for using the gamma distributions in the present context remains the same as that presented for mobility processes, where individuals evolved according to Markov rather than semi-Markov processes. The question of computationally effective solutions of the inverse problem for mixtures of semi-Markov processes is at present unresolved; an indication of the mathematical difficulties and some suggested lines of attack will be presented in Singer and Spilerman (1974).

This very general process (35), incidentally, provides us with a formulation in which *both* a duration of residence effect and population heterogeneity can be postulated. In the preceding models, and in the few other discussions of semi-Markov models as they pertain to social mobility (Ginsberg, 1971, p. 254), one was compelled to specify individual-level behavior as Markovian if the heterogeneity perspective was adopted, and the population as homogeneous if a duration-effect mechanism was postulated. Clearly both processes could be operative, and we should prefer a model in which they can be incorporated simultaneously.

A final point concerning semi-Markov processes is that the formulation given by Equation (32) does not describe the most general process of this kind as treated in the mathematics literature. In particular the original semi-Markov framework allowed for waiting-time distributions that could depend on the next future state as well as on the current state of the process. This level of generality, however, demands a more extensive data base than is currently available for most social mobility situations; hence we have restricted our attention to a subclass of semi-Markov processes which requires the estimation of fewer parameters.

4. INVERSE PROBLEMS

In the previous sections we have indicated a few examples of inverse problems and their associated embeddability questions. This aspect of our study really involves an independent mathematical development which also seems to be of considerable importance outside the context of social mobility models, and which will be elaborated in a separate publication. In the present section we simply illustrate the flavor of inverse problems and give some indication of general diagonstic strategies for recovering partial information about the fine structure of a mobility process from information about its behavior at a few points in time.

Before proceeding to the examples, we would like to point out where the inverse problems of this study fit into a larger mathematical framework. To fix the ideas, recall the matrix differential equation

$$dP(t)/dt = QP(t) \qquad P(0) = I$$

whose solutions are the transition probabilities for continuous-time Markov chains. Rather than being given a particular differential equation (that is, a fixed Q) and asked to compute a solution $P(t)$ (a "direct problem"), an inverse problem has a *class* of differential equations and partial information about a solution [usually $\hat{P}(t_i)$ for a few values of i] as given ingredients. From this information the problem is to find the *particular* differential equation that is compatible with the observed solution.

The overall strategy of inverse problem formulation and interpretation in the context of social mobility is described here entirely within the context of a homogeneous population evolving according to a continuous-time Markov chain. The key point is that all the issues which must be faced in more complicated mixtures of Markov and semi-Markov formulations are already present in this setting.

Step 1: Embeddability

From an empirical point of view, the most primitive question to be asked about a stochastic matrix $\hat{P}(t_1)$, estimated from observations at times zero and t_1, is whether or not it is compatible with the theoretical framework

$$\hat{P}(t_1) = e^{t_1 Q}$$

where Q is an $r \times r$ matrix satisfying

$$-\infty < q_{ii} < 0 \qquad q_{ij} \geq 0 \text{ for } i \neq j \qquad \sum_{j=1}^{r} q_{ij} = 0 \qquad (36)$$

This problem has a long history in the mathematics literature (see Singer and Spilerman, 1974, for references), and our purpose here is to indicate its solution for two- and some three-state processes as well as for general finite-state birth and death processes.

Case 1. If $\hat{P}(t_1)$ is a 2×2 stochastic matrix denoted by

$$\begin{pmatrix} a & 1-a \\ 1-b & b \end{pmatrix} \qquad 0 < a,b < 1$$

it can be represented as $e^{t_1 Q}$ with Q satisfying Equation (36) if and only if $a + b > 1$. (See the appendix for a proof.)

It is interesting to note that the matrix

$$\begin{pmatrix} 1/3 & 2/3 \\ 2/3 & 1/3 \end{pmatrix}$$

which, as indicated in Equation (1), is compatible with a discrete-time Markov model for $t_1 = 3$ is not compatible with a *continuous-time* Markov model for any positive time t_1. Another feature of the condition $a + b > 1$ is that this automatically guarantees uniqueness of Q. In the 2×2 case we therefore have a single criterion which ensures both embeddability and uniqueness; note also that this is a weaker requirement than the general sufficiency condition for uniqueness, $\inf_i[\hat{p}_{ii}(t_1)] > \frac{1}{2}$.

When the inequality $a + b > 1$ is satisfied, the unique Q-matrix governing the evolution of the continuous-time Markov chain is given by

$$Q = \frac{1}{t_1} \log \hat{P} = \frac{\log(a+b-1)}{t_1(a+b-2)} \begin{pmatrix} a-1 & 1-a \\ 1-b & b-1 \end{pmatrix} \qquad (37)$$

A further ramification here is that compatibility of the data with a continuous-time Markov model and unique identification of Q can be checked by observations at time zero and only one other time point; this time point may be chosen *arbitrarily* by the experimenter. As subsequent examples indicate, this simplicity of embeddability tests and identification of Q no longer holds even for three-state processes.

Case 2. (a) If $\hat{P}(t_1)$ is a 3×3 stochastic matrix with distinct, real eigenvalues $1 > \lambda_1 > \lambda_2 > 0$, it can be represented as e^{tiQ} with Q satisfying Equation (36) if and only if

$$p_{ij}^{(2)} \leq \hat{p}_{ij} \frac{(\lambda_2^2 - 1)\log \lambda_1 - (\lambda_1^2 - 1)\log \lambda_2}{(\lambda_2 - 1)\log \lambda_1 - (\lambda_1 - 1)\log \lambda_2} \quad \text{all } i \neq j \quad (38)$$

where $p_{ij}^{(2)}$ is the (i,j) entry in $[\hat{P}(t_1)]^2$. (b) If $\hat{P}(t_1)$ has eigenvalues 1, λ, λ, where λ is real and $1 > \lambda > 0$, it can be represented as e^{tiQ} with Q satisfying Equation (36) if and only if

$$p_{ij}^{(2)} \leq \hat{p}_{ij} \frac{2\lambda^2 \log \lambda - \lambda^2 + 1}{\lambda \log \lambda - \lambda + 1} \quad \text{all } i \neq j \quad (39)$$

Similar criteria can be given for 3×3 matrices having complex eigenvalues, negative real eigenvalues of even multiplicity, as well as for general r-state matrices. The explicit inequalities become very intricate as r increases; however, they are all established by observing that $\log P$ may always be evaluated in principle as a polynomial in P of degree at most $r - 1$. Then inequalities such as Equations (38) and (39) arise by requiring that

$$\log \hat{P} = C_0 I + C_1 \hat{P} + \cdots + C_{r-1} \hat{P}^{r-1}$$

be real and a matrix satisfying Equation (36).

Case 3. If a sociological context allows us to restrict consideration to continuous-time models where the only allowable transitions are to nearest neighbor states, then we have a simpler criterion for $\hat{P}(t_1)$ to be representable as e^{tiQ} with Q satisfying Equation (36) and $q_{ij} = 0$ for $|i - j| > 1$ (i.e., Q is a Jacobi intensity matrix). In particular a necessary condition for an $r \times r$ stochastic matrix $\hat{P}(t_1)$ with strictly positive determinant[15] to be representable as e^{tiQ} with Q a Jacobi intensity matrix is that all its entires and the following 2×2 subdeterminants are strictly positive (Karlin and McGregor, 1959): choose $i_1 < i_2, j_1 < j_2$ arbitrarily and check[16]

$$\det \begin{pmatrix} \hat{p}_{i_1,j_1} & \hat{p}_{i_1,j_2} \\ \hat{p}_{i_2,j_1} & \hat{p}_{i_2,j_2} \end{pmatrix} > 0 \quad 1 \leq i_1 < i_2 \leq r; 1 \leq j_1 < j_2 \leq r \quad (40)$$

It is important to notice that the class of models e^{tQ} with Q a

---

[15] det $\hat{P}(t_1) > 0$ is a necessary embeddability condition for arbitrary finite state Markov chains (see e.g. Kingman (1962)).

[16] Necessary and *sufficient* conditions for embeddability in a birth and death structure can be derived by computing $\log \hat{P} = C_0 I + \cdots + C_{r-1} \hat{P}^{r-1}$ and demanding that this matrix not only satisfy (36) but also that its entries for $|i - j| > 1$ be 0. For 3×3 matrices this would mean that the partial inequalities in (38) be exact equalities for $|i - j| > 1$.

Jacobi matrix has been widely used in sociological investigations even outside the context of social mobility (e.g., Coleman, 1964, chap. 10, 11, 14). In the mathematics literature these processes are referred to as finite-state birth and death processes (Feller, 1968, chap. 17), and they also have a long history of use as baseline models in particle physics, chemistry, and biology. The criteria (40) provide a simple, readily computable test for compatibility of a stochastic matrix with a birth and death model for an arbitrary, finite number of states. The interested reader can check that in Coleman's (1964, pp. 462–465) application of a birth and death structure to English mobility data there are numerous violations of this embeddability condition.

With these examples at hand, we should emphasize that the above inequality tests can be considered as devices for isolating the class of stochastic matrices compatible with particular continuous-time Markov structures from the class of all stochastic matrices.[17] Once it is concluded that a matrix is embeddable in a Markov structure, the next step is to identify all intensity matrices Q that could have given rise to the observed $\hat{P}(t_1)$.

Step 2: Identification of Q

If the observed matrix $\hat{P}(t_1)$ is embeddable and the condition $\inf_i[\hat{p}_{ii}(t_1)] > \frac{1}{2}$ is satisfied, then we can calculate a unique Q:

$$Q = \frac{1}{t_1} \log \hat{P}(t_1) \tag{41}$$

Another sufficient condition for uniqueness is that the eigenvalues of $\hat{P}(t_1)$ be real, positive, and distinct.

In order to illustrate the methodological difficulties that might arise when dealing with matrices $\hat{P}(t_1)$ which are embeddable in a continuous-time Markov structure but do *not* satisfy these conditions, we consider the following example. Suppose you estimate[18]

$$\hat{P}(t_1) = \begin{pmatrix} \frac{1}{3} + \frac{2\epsilon}{3} & \frac{1}{3} - \frac{\epsilon}{3} & \frac{1}{3} - \frac{\epsilon}{3} \\ \frac{1}{3} - \frac{\epsilon}{3} & \frac{1}{3} + \frac{2\epsilon}{3} & \frac{1}{3} - \frac{\epsilon}{3} \\ \frac{1}{3} - \frac{\epsilon}{3} & \frac{1}{3} - \frac{\epsilon}{3} & \frac{1}{3} + \frac{2\epsilon}{3} \end{pmatrix} \tag{42}$$

---

[17] If a matrix is embeddable in a Markov structure this means that it *could* have been generated by a Markov process; further tests of the sort outlined in section 2.2-I are necessary to confirm this possibility.

[18] This example is originally due to Speakman (1967).

where $\epsilon = e^{-2\pi\sqrt{3}}$ and $t_1 = 4\pi/\sqrt{3} \approx 7.26$. This stochastic matrix has a representation $e^{t_1 Q}$ for the following intensity matrices:

$$Q_1 = \begin{pmatrix} -1 & 1 & 0 \\ 0 & -1 & 1 \\ 1 & 0 & -1 \end{pmatrix} \quad Q_2 = \begin{pmatrix} -1 & 1/2 & 1/2 \\ 1/2 & -1 & 1/2 \\ 1/2 & 1/2 & -1 \end{pmatrix}$$

If a researcher is constrained to estimating just this $\hat{P}(t_1)$ from data, he will find these two substantively distinct matrices compatible with his observations and with a continuous-time Markov model. In particular, Q_1 and Q_2 correspond to processes where the holding times between moves are exponentially distributed with parameter 1, regardless of state; however, a process governed by Q_1 allows only transitions through states in the cyclic pattern $1 \to 2 \to 3 \to 1 \to 2 \to 3 \ldots$ etc. On the other hand, a process governed by Q_2 allows equally likely transitions from any one state to any other state. Sociological argument must decide which of these two alternatives is substantively meaningful if a single observation beyond $t = 0$ is a constraint on the study.

Alternatively if you compute e^{tQ_1} and e^{tQ_2} for general times t, you find that $P_1(t) = e^{tQ_1}$ is a 3×3 stochastic matrix with entries

$$p_{ii}^{(1)}(t) = 1/3 + (2/3)e^{-3t/2} \cos \sqrt{3}t/2 \quad i = 1, 2, 3$$
$$p_{12}^{(1)}(t) = p_{23}^{(1)}(t) = p_{31}^{(1)}(t) = 1/3 + (2/3)e^{-3t/2} \cos [(\sqrt{3}t/2) - (2\pi/3)]$$
$$p_{13}^{(1)}(t) = p_{21}^{(1)}(t) = p_{32}^{(1)}(t) = 1/3 + (2/3)e^{-3t/2} \cos [(\sqrt{3}t/2) + (2\pi/3)]$$

whereas $P_2(t) = e^{tQ_2}$ is a 3×3 stochastic matrix with entries

$$p_{ii}^{(2)}(t) = 1/3 + (2/3)e^{-3t/2} \quad i = 1, 2, 3$$
$$p_{ij}^{(2)}(t) = 1/3 - (1/3)e^{-3t/2} \quad \text{for } i \neq j$$

When $t = 4k\pi/\sqrt{3}$ ($k = 0, 1, 2, \ldots$), $P_1(t) = P_2(t)$ and you cannot discriminate between these two processes. The difficulty to be highlighted here is that the observation time dictated by the experiment turned out to be inconvenient for unique identification of Q. However, if one more observation is allowed, the above calculations indicate that if it is taken at time $6\pi/\sqrt{3}$ (i.e., $k = 3/2$), then

$$\frac{\sqrt{3}}{4\pi} \log P\left(\frac{4\pi}{\sqrt{3}}\right)$$

and

$$\frac{\sqrt{3}}{6\pi} \log P\left(\frac{6\pi}{\sqrt{3}}\right)$$

must both be equal to *either* Q_1 or Q_2. Whichever is observed will identify the unique Q-matrix compatible with a continuous-time Markov model for the mobility process under examination.

The phenomenon described above arises because of nonuniqueness of the logarithm of a stochastic matrix. As indicated earlier, a sufficient condition for uniqueness in the Markov case is that $\inf_i[\hat{p}_{ii}(t_1)] > \frac{1}{2}$; however, there is no a priori reason to believe that this condition will hold in environments where Markov models might be applied. Hence a more thorough understanding of the nature of nonuniqueness as illustrated by the preceding example is clearly needed. Some progress in this direction, both for the Markov and semi-Markov models arising as mixtures according to the recipes of section 3, is described in Singer and Spilerman (1974).

5. CONCLUSIONS

We conclude with an overview of diagnostic strategies for the social mobility models formulated in the previous sections. Many of our remarks should be viewed as suggestions for future research; however, a discussion of several mobility data sets from this point of view, together with a presentation of appropriate data analytic techniques, will appear in a separate publication of the authors.

(A) Select a class of Markov or semi-Markov models, such as those in section 3, which seem to correspond to prior evidence and theories about the nature of heterogeneity in the population you are observing.

(B) Check for embeddability. A necessary condition for an observed r-state matrix to be embeddable in a birth and death structure was reported in section 4, as were necessary and sufficient conditions for an observed 2×2 matrix or one of a class of 3×3 matrices to be embeddable in a continuous-time Markov process.

(C) Check for a unique solution to the inverse problem. A sufficient condition for uniqueness in the continuous-time models we have explored is the criterion $\inf_i[p_{ii}(t_1)] > \frac{1}{2}$. The nonuniqueness phenomenon illustrated in our previous example frequently occurs for logarithms, roots, and more general inverse formulas of matrices with repeated eigenvalues. Thus a useful strategy in dealing with empirically determined matrices $\hat{P}(t_1)$ having distinct eigenvalues, some of which are within several significant digits of each other, is to adjust $\hat{P}(t_1)$ to force equality of the eigenvalues and compute all M-matrices or Q-matrices (depending on the context) compatible with both a repeated eigenvalue estimate and a distinct eigenvalue estimate. The point here is that many sociological data involve severe "noise," and you may miss an opportunity to examine and interpret a substantively meaningful matrix M by treating the observed matrix $\hat{P}(t_1)$ as though it were error-free. Indeed, because of sampling error in the observed matrix $\hat{P}(t_1)$ you may have computed the *wrong* M for the process!

(D) The calculation of compatible matrices M via numerical inversion algorithms should be followed by a determination of time points beyond that of the original observations t_0 and t_1 at which it would be possible to discriminate among competing candidates. An instance of this was the identification of the time $6\pi/\sqrt{3}$ in the previous section where an estimated $\hat{P}(6\pi/\sqrt{3})$ could be used to discriminate between Q_1 and Q_2. This portion of the diagnostic process really falls within the framework of experimental designs for mobility processes, an area that to the best of our knowledge is completely unexplored.

Finally, we should mention that the methodological issues raised in the present work carry over to much more complicated settings where the theoretical frameworks involve non time-homogeneous processes, a simultaneous treatment of mobility by persons and by vacancies in an occupational structure, as well as multi-type processes with interacting sub-populations. Inverse problems in these settings are almost totally unexplored; however, the reader should consult H. White (1970) for a stimulating discussion of model construction and data requirements as they pertain to some of these topics.

APPENDIX: COMPUTING FUNCTIONS OF MATRIX ARGUMENT

A key step in the production of inversion formulas is often the evaluation of an analytic function of matrix argument. In the continuous-time Markov case we required a computation of Q from an observed $\hat{P}$ and a postulated structure e^{tQ}. This involves calculation of $\log \hat{P}$, where $\hat{P}$ is a stochastic matrix. Analogously, in the discrete-time Markov model we required a recipe for computing the nth roots of $\hat{P}$.

A natural formulation of analytic functions $f(z)$ with z replaced by a matrix is the contour integral definition

$$f(P) = \frac{1}{2\pi i}\int_\Gamma (\zeta I - P)^{-1} f(\zeta) d\zeta$$

where Γ is a smooth, closed curve that encloses the eigenvalues of P, and $f(\zeta)$ is single-valued and analytic. The components of $(\zeta I - P)^{-1}$ are of the form

$$(\zeta I - P)^{-1}_{ij} = \frac{(-1)^{i+j}\phi_{ij}}{\phi(\zeta)}$$

where $\phi(\zeta)$ = determinant of $(\zeta I - P)$, and ϕ_{ij} = determinant of the

$(n-1) \times (n-1)$ matrix obtained by deleting the jth row and ith column of $\zeta I - P$.

To illustrate the use of this formulation we calculate $\log P$ when P is the 2×2 stochastic matrix

$$P = \begin{pmatrix} a & 1-a \\ 1-b & b \end{pmatrix} \quad 0 < a,b < 1$$

The steps in the computation are

$$(\zeta I - P) = \begin{pmatrix} \zeta - a & a - 1 \\ b - 1 & \zeta - b \end{pmatrix}$$

$$||(-1)^{i+j}\phi_{ij}|| = \begin{pmatrix} \zeta - b & 1 - a \\ 1 - b & \zeta - a \end{pmatrix}$$

$$\phi(\zeta) = \zeta^2 - \zeta(a+b) + (a+b-1)$$

The eigenvalues of P are the roots of $\phi(\zeta) = 0$ and are given by $\zeta_1 = 1$, $\zeta_2 = a + b - 1$. Residue evaluation of

$$\frac{1}{2\pi i} \int_\Gamma \frac{(-1)^{i+j}\phi_{ij}\log(\zeta)d\zeta}{(\zeta - 1)[\zeta - (a+b-1)]} \quad \text{for } 1 \le i,j \le 2$$

yields $\quad \log P = \dfrac{\log(a+b-1)}{a+b-2} \begin{pmatrix} a-1 & 1-a \\ 1-b & b-1 \end{pmatrix}$

For this to be a legitimate Q-matrix we require simply that $\log(a+b-1)$ is real. This will happen if and only if $a + b > 1$. Thus we obtain the condition that P is representable as e^Q if and only if $a + b > 1$.

For a second application of the contour integral we calculate the cube roots of

$$P(3) = \begin{pmatrix} 1/3 & 2/3 \\ 2/3 & 1/3 \end{pmatrix}$$

which is Equation (1) in the text. Here

$$(\zeta I - P) = \begin{pmatrix} \zeta - (1/3) & -2/3 \\ -2/3 & \zeta - (1/3) \end{pmatrix}$$

$$||(-1)^{i+j}\phi_{ij}|| = \begin{pmatrix} \zeta - (1/3) & 2/3 \\ 2/3 & \zeta -)1/3) \end{pmatrix}$$

$$\phi(\zeta) = \zeta^2 - 2\zeta/3 - 1/3 = [\zeta - 1][\zeta + 1/3)] = 0$$

Residue evaluation of

$$\frac{1}{2\pi i} \int_\Gamma \frac{(-1)^{i+j}\phi_{ij}\zeta^{1/3}d\zeta}{[\zeta - 1][\zeta + (1/3)]} \quad \text{for } 1 \le i,j \le 2$$

yields $\quad [P(3)]^{1/3} = \begin{pmatrix} 1/2 - 1/(2\sqrt[3]{3}) & 1/2 + 1/(2\sqrt[3]{3}) \\ 1/2 + 1/(2\sqrt[3]{3}) & 1/2 - 1/(2\sqrt[3]{3}) \end{pmatrix}$

as the only real-valued root. This matrix is Equation (2) in the text.

A more extensive discussion of the role of contour integral formulations in producing inversion formulas for the models of section 3 is given in John (1965, pp. 103–118).

REFERENCES

ALBERT, A.
    1962   "Estimating the infinitesimal generator of a continuous time finite state Markov process." *Annals of Mathematical Statistics* 33 (June) 727–753.

BARTHOLOMEW, D. J.
    1967   *Stochastic Models for Social Processes.* New York: Wiley.

BLAUNER, R.
    1964   *Alienation and Freedom.* Chicago: University of Chicago Press.

BLUMEN, I., KOGAN, M. AND MCCARTHY, P. J.
    1955   *The Industrial Mobility of Labor as a Probability Process.* Cornell Studies of Industrial and Labor Relations, Vol. 6. Ithaca, N.Y.: Cornell University.

BROWN, L.
    1970   "On the use of Markov chains in movement research." *Economic Geography* 46 (June supplement):393–403.

COLEMAN, J. S.
    1964   *Introduction to Mathematical Sociology.* New York: Free Press.

FELLER, W.
    1968   *Introduction to Probability Theory and Its Applications.* (Vol. I, 3rd ed.) New York: Wiley.
    1971   *Introduction to Probability Theory and Its Applications.* (Vol. II) New York: Wiley.

GINSBERG, R.
    1971   "Semi-Markov processes and mobility." *Journal of Mathematical Sociology* 1:233–263.

GOODMAN, L. A.
    1961   "Statistical methods for the mover-stayer model." *Journal of the American Statistical Association* 56:841–868.

HODGE, R. W.
    1966   "Occupational mobility as a probability process." *Demography* 3:19–34.

JOHN, F.
    1965   *Ordinary Differential Equations.* New York: Courant Institute Lecture Notes.

KARLIN, S. AND MCGREGOR, J.
    1959   "A characterization of birth and death processes." *Proceedings, National Academy of Sciences, U.S.A.* 45:375–379.

KINGMAN, J. F. C.
    1962   "The imbedding problem for finite Markof chains." *Zeitschrift für Wahrscheinlichkeitstheorie* 1:14–24.

LIPSET, S. M. AND BENDIX, R.
1959 *Social Mobility in Industrial Society.* Berkeley: University of California Press.

MCCALL, J. J.
1971 "An analysis of poverty: Some preliminary findings." *Journal of Business* 44 (April):125–147.

MCFARLAND, D. D.
1970 "Intra-generational social mobility as a Markov process: Including a time-stationary Markovian model that explains observed declines in mobility rates over time." *American Sociological Review* 35:463–476.

MCGINNIS, R.
1968 "A stochastic model of social mobility." *American Sociological Review* 33 (October):712–722.

MATRAS, J.
1960 "Comparison of intergenerational occupational mobility patterns." *Population Studies* 14:163–169.

MEIER, P.
1955 "Note on estimation in a Markov Process with constant transition rates." *Human Biology* 27:121–124.

MOOD, A. M.
1950 *Introduction to the Theory of Statistics.* New York: McGraw-Hill.

PALMER, G.
1954 *Labor Mobility in Six Cities.* New York: Social Science Research Council.

PRAIS, S. J.
1955 "Measuring social mobility." *Journal of the Royal Statistical Society* 118 (Series A):55–66.

PYKE, R.
1961a "Markov renewal processes: Definitions and preliminary properties." *Annals of Mathematical Statistics* 32:1231–1242.
1961b "Markov renewal processes with finitely many states." *Annals of Mathematical Statistics* 32:1243–1259.

ROGERS, A.
1966 "A Markovian analysis of migration differentials." *Proceedings of the American Statistical Association,* Social Science Section. Washington, D.C.: American Statistical Association.

SINGER, B. AND SPILERMAN, S.
1974 "Identification of a class of semi-Markov processes." Forthcoming.

SMITH, J. D. AND CAIN, G.
1967 "Markov chain applications to household income distribution." Mimeographed. University of Wisconsin.

SPEAKMAN, J.
1967 "Two Markov chains with a common skeleton." *Zeitschrift für Wahrscheinlichkeitstheorie* 7:224.

SPILERMAN, S.
    1972a "The analysis of mobility processes by the introduction of independent variables into a Markov chain." *American Sociological Review* 37 (June):277–294.
    1972b "Extensions of the mover-stayer model." *American Journal of Sociology* 78:599–627.

TAEUBER, K. E., CHIAZZE, L. JR. AND HAENSZEL, W.
    1968 *Migration in the United States*. Washington, D.C.: Government Printing Office.

TARVER, J. D. AND GURLEY, W. R.
    1965 "A stochastic analysis of geographic mobility and population projections of the census divisions in the United States." *Demography* 2:134–139.

WHITE, H.
    1970 *Chains of Opportunity*. Cambridge: Harvard University Press.

NAME INDEX

A

AIGNER, D. G., 295, 304
AITKEN, A. C., 260, 304
AKAIKE, H., 352, 354
AKERS, R. L., 135, 142
ALBERT, A., 364, 399
ALLEN, P. A., 9, 10, 14
ALTHAUSER, R. P., 79, 80, 83, 86-91, 93-103, 107, 109, 113, 114, 117, 119, 124, 125
ALWIN, D. F., 106-110, 113, 115, 117, 122, 124
AMEMIYA, T., 304
ANDERSON, E. E., 108, 126
ANDERSON, R. L., 280, 304
ANDERSON, T. W., 72, 76, 281, 304, 310, 323, 326, 354
ANDREWS, F., 180, 185
APTER, D. E., 250
ARMER, M., 108, 126
ARMOR, D. J., 9, 14, 39, 49
ARMSTRONG, J. S., 13, 14
ATTINGER, E. O., 15

B

BAIANU, I., 13, 14
BAILEY, W. C., 139, 142
BANCROFT, T. A., 145, 148, 155, 186
BARTHOLOMEW, D. J., 365, 399
BARTKO, J. J., 130, 133, 143
BARTLETT, M. S., 280, 304, 311, 354
BEATON, A. E., 17
BEATTIE, C., 165, 173, 186
BENDIX, R., 377, 400
BLACKMAN, R. B., 311, 354
BLALOCK, A. B., 78, 105
BLALOCK, H. M., JR., 7, 14, 18, 50-52, 76, 78, 80, 104, 105, 125
BLAU, P. M., 132, 135, 141, 143
BLAUNER, R., 380, 399
BLOWERS, T., 135, 143
BLUMEN, I., 357, 363, 370, 372, 373, 399
BOHRNSTEDT, G. W., 6, 14, 15, 18, 26, 46, 50, 60, 68, 74, 77, 80, 103, 104, 125, 127, 137, 138, 143, 186

NAME INDEX

B

BORGATTA, E. F., 15, 50, 77, 103, 104, 108, 125-127, 143, 186
BOX, G. E. P., 273, 280, 281, 283, 284, 295, 304
BOYLE, R. P., 153, 186
BREHM, M. L., 180, 187
BROWN, J. W., 138, 140, 143
BROWN, L., 357, 363, 399
BROWNE, M. W., 58, 76
BURR, E. J., 53, 55, 56, 77
BURWEN, L. S., 108, 126
BUSE, A., 269, 305
BUTLER, P. M., 26, 28, 49, 76

C

CAIN, G., 357, 400
CAMPBELL, A., 236, 250
CAMPBELL, D. T., 80-83, 86, 91-104, 106-109, 113, 115, 122, 123, 125, 126
CAMPBELL, F. L., 135, 142
CARNEIRA, R. L., 4, 14
CARR, L. G., 237, 250
CARROLL, J. B., 108, 126
CARTER, L. F., 80, 104
CARTER, T. M., 80, 104, 153, 187
CATTELL, R. B., 60, 68, 76
CHATTERJEE, S., 132, 144
CHAYES, F., 132, 139, 143
CHIAZZE, L., JR., 358, 376, 384, 401
CHIRICOS, T. G., 139, 143, 144
CHOUCRI, N., 299, 300, 302, 303, 305
CHRIST, C. F., 290, 305
COCHRANE, D., 305
COHEN, R., 14
COLEMAN, J. S., 174-176, 186, 365, 394
CONGER, A. J., 99, 104
CONVERSE, J. M., 250, 251
CONVERSE, P. E., 250
COOMBS, C. H., 242, 250
COSTNER, H. L., 7, 15, 51, 52, 76, 80, 87-90, 96, 99, 101, 102, 104, 125
CRAMER, E. M., 183, 186
CRONBACH, L. J., 18, 19, 23, 50, 59, 68, 76, 91, 104

D

DARROCH, J. N., 72, 77

DAVIS, J. A., 190, 192, 195, 222-224, 231, 233, 234, 237, 240, 250, 251
DAVIS, O. A., 295, 305
DEBER, R., 252
DEMPSTER, M. A. H., 295, 305
DHRYMES, P. J., 265, 295, 296, 305
DUBOIS, P. H., 137, 143
DUNCAN, O. D., 7, 15, 85, 104, 132, 141, 143-145, 186, 249, 251, 355
DURBIN, J., 265, 281, 283, 284, 292, 305

E

ECCLES, R., 252
EDWARDS, A. L., 23, 24, 50
EISNER, M., 287, 305
ENGLE, R. F., 262, 296, 305

F

FAIR, R. C., 304, 305
FEATHERMAN, D. L., 153, 186
FELLER, W., 366, 394, 399
FIENBERG, S., 189
FISHER, F., 252, 297, 306
FISHER, R. A., 134, 135, 143, 178, 186
FISHMAN, G. S., 265, 306, 311, 323, 327, 352, 355
FISKE, D. W., 80-83, 86, 91-104, 106-109, 113, 115, 122, 123, 125, 126
FLEISS, J. L., 140, 143
FOA, U. G., 13, 15
FUCHS, H., 145

G

GANTZEL, K. J., 305
GASTON, J., 152, 186
GINSBURG, R., 357, 388-390, 399
GOGUEN, J. A., 13, 15
GOLDBERGER, A. S., 6, 7, 15, 51, 79, 88, 89, 99, 104, 144, 184, 186, 252, 259, 306
GOODMAN, L. A., 175, 186, 189-191, 198-201, 206, 209, 212, 217, 222-224, 227, 231, 238, 241, 244, 251, 371, 399
GOURLAY, N., 138, 143
GRANGER, C. W. J., 265, 306, 323, 345, 352, 355
GRAY, L. N., 139, 142

GREENWOOD, M., JR., 138, 140, 143
GRILICHES, Z., 265, 266, 282-284, 290, 291, 294, 295, 306, 307
GRIZZLE, J. E., 175, 186
GRUVAEUS, G. T., 15, 86, 99, 105
GUEST, A., 189
GUILFORD, J. P., 18, 50, 130, 143
GURIN, P., 173, 186
GURLEY, W. R., 357, 370, 401
GUTTMAN, L., 1, 13, 15, 64, 65, 72, 77

H

HADLEY, G., 268, 306
HAENSZEL, W., 358, 376, 384, 401
HALL, R., 252
HANNAN, E. J., 265, 280, 299, 306, 323, 353, 355
HARMAN, H. H., 27, 36, 50, 52-54, 57, 58, 61, 69, 75, 77
HARRIS, B., 354
HARRIS, C. W., 53-56, 77
HATANAKA, M., 306, 323, 345, 352, 355
HAUSER, R. M., 6, 7, 15, 79, 88, 89, 99, 104, 173, 186
HEBERLEIN, T. A., 80, 83, 86-91, 93-104, 106, 107, 109, 113, 114, 117, 119, 124, 125, 128
HEISE, D. R., 6, 14, 15, 17, 18, 26, 46, 50, 51, 60, 68, 74, 77, 80, 105, 123, 124, 126
HENRY, N. W., 1, 15, 356
HIBBS, D. A., 297, 306
HIGGINS, G. F., 180, 187
HODGE, R. W., 18, 20, 50, 52, 78, 80, 91, 105, 357, 360, 399
HOLDAWAY, E., 135, 143
HOPE, K., 163, 182, 187
HORAN, P. M., 176, 183, 187
HYMAN, H., 249, 251

I

INOGUCHI, T., 252

J

JACKMAN, M. R., 108, 126, 237, 251
JACKSON, D. N., 80, 83, 97-99, 101, 102, 105
JENCKS, C., 122, 126

JENKINS, G. M., 265, 273, 280, 281, 283, 284, 295, 304, 306, 323, 325, 326, 346, 348, 350, 355
JENNINGS, E., 183, 187
JOHN, E., 399
JÖRESKOG, K. G., 7, 15, 16, 55, 77, 80, 83, 86, 88, 99, 105, 125, 126
JUSTER, R., 123, 126

K

KARLIN, S., 393, 399
KELLEY, T. L., 108, 126
KENDALL, M. G., 173, 178, 187, 281, 282, 287, 306
KHAN, S. B., 77
KINGMAN, J. F. C., 393, 399
KLATZKY, S. R., 135, 143
KNOKE, D., 145
KOCH, G. G., 175, 186
KOGAN, M., 357, 363, 370, 372, 373, 399
KORNBERG, A., 180, 187
KRESS, G., 305
KREY, A. C., 108, 126
KUH, E., 132, 136, 138, 143
KUNREUTHER, H., 133, 143

L

LAND, K., 123, 126
LASLETT, B., 165, 187
LAWLEY, D. N., 37, 47, 50, 54, 55, 57, 77
LAZARSFELD, P., 1, 15
LEVINE, R. A., 235, 251
LEWIS, C., 19, 50, 59, 77
LIGHT, R. J., 173-175, 187
LINN, R. L., 16, 74, 78, 80, 83, 84, 86, 91, 99-101, 103, 105, 107, 109, 110, 127
LIPSET, S. M., 377, 400
LIVIATAN, N., 297, 306
LOGAN, C. H., 139, 140, 144
LORD, F. M., 5, 6, 15, 19, 26, 28, 50, 53, 59, 77, 83, 91, 105
LOY, J. W., JR., 180, 187
LYONS, M., 153, 187

M

MC CALL, J. J., 357, 400

MC CARTHY, J. D., 165, 188
MC CARTHY, P. J., 357, 363, 370, 372, 373, 399
MC CRAY, L., 252
MC DONALD, R. P., 53, 55, 56, 59, 61, 77
MC FARLAND, D. D., 357, 375, 387, 400
MAC GILLIVRAY, L., 51
MC GINNIS, R., 389, 400
MC GREGOR, J., 393, 399
MADDALA, G. S., 299, 306
MALINVAUD, E., 259, 266, 283, 292, 293, 297, 307
MALLIOS, W. S., 166, 187
MARGOLIN, B. H., 173, 174, 175, 187
MARKUS, G., 269
MARQUARDT, D. W., 295, 307
MARRIOTT, F. H. C., 282, 307
MARTIN, J. D., 139, 142
MATRAS, J., 357, 370, 400
MAXWELL, A. E., 37, 47, 50, 54, 55, 57, 77
MEEHL, P. E., 91, 104
MEIER, P., 364, 400
MEYER, J. R., 132, 136, 138, 143
MEYERS, E. D., JR., 189
MOOD, A. M., 382, 400
MORGAN, J., 180, 185
MORRISON, D. F., 150, 187
MORRISON, J. L., 296, 297, 307
MORRISON, N., 324, 355
MOSTELLER, F., 17
MUELLER, J. E., 284-289, 307

N

NAROLL, R., 14
NEAVE, H. R., 326, 355
NEIFELD, M. R., 130, 140, 144
NERLOVE, S. B., 15, 292, 307
NESTEL, G., 123, 126
NEYMAN, J., 76
NORTH, R. C., 299, 300, 302, 303, 305
NOVICK, M. R., 5, 6, 15, 19, 50, 53, 59, 77, 83, 91, 105
NUNNALLY, J. C., 1, 5, 15, 52, 68, 78

O

O'CONNELL, E. J., 103, 104
OLIVIER, D., 17
ORCUTT, G. H., 305, 307

P

PALMER, G., 358, 376, 377, 400
PAYNE, S. L., 233, 251
PEARSON, K., 130, 131, 132, 133, 136, 139, 140, 142, 144
PERRUCCI, C. C., 170, 187
PERRUCCI, R., 170, 187
PETTIGREW, K. D., 130, 133, 143
PIERCE, D. A., 284, 304, 307
PONDY, L. R., 135, 144
POPE, J. A., 282, 307
POPKIN, S., 252
PRAIS, S. J., 370, 400
PYKE, R., 388, 400

Q

QUENOUILLE, M. H., 281, 307

R

RADCLIFFE, J. A., 60, 68, 76
RANGARAJAN, C., 132, 144
RAO, C. R., 53, 55, 56, 57, 78
RAO, P., 265, 266, 282-284, 307
RIGSBY, L., 165, 188
RITTBERGER, V., 305
ROGERS, A., 357, 400
ROMNEY, A. K., 15
ROSENBLITH, W., 252
ROZEBOOM, W. W., 74, 78
RUBIN, H., 72, 76
RUDRA, A., 281, 307
RUMMEL, R. J., 9, 15, 54, 71, 78
RUSHING, W. A., 135, 144

S

SARGAN, J. D., 304, 307
SARGENT, T. J., 296, 297, 307
SAVAGE, I. R., 356
SCHNAIBERG, A., 108, 126
SCHUESSLER, K., 129, 132, 133, 144
SCHUMAN, H., 189, 235, 236, 250, 251
SCHWARTZ, M. A., 201, 203, 204, 208, 210, 212-220, 224, 229, 231
SCOTT, R. A., 80, 83, 89, 90, 93, 96, 100, 103, 124, 125
SEARLE, S. R., 144, 170, 182, 187
SEILER, L. H., 123, 127
SEWELL, W. H., 79

NAME INDEX

SHEPARD, R. N., 4, 5, 15
SIEGEL, P. M., 18, 20, 50, 52, 78, 80, 91, 105
SINGER, B., 374, 375, 379-381, 385, 390, 392, 396, 400
SMITH, J. D., 357, 400
SNEDECOR, G. W., 130, 134, 144
SOELBERG, P., 13
SONQUIST, J., 180, 185
SPEAKMAN, J., 394, 400
SPEARMAN, C., 88, 105
SPENCER, B. G., 165, 173, 186
SPILERMAN, S., 357, 358, 363, 368, 374-377, 379-381, 385, 387, 390, 392, 396, 400, 401
SPROTT, D. A., 166, 187
STARMER, C. F., 175, 186
STEIN, F. M., 393, 401
STOUFFER, S. A., 232, 234, 249, 251
STUART, A., 173, 187, 281, 282, 287, 306
SUITS, D. B., 150, 188
SULLIVAN, J. L., 6, 16
SUMMERS, G. F., 108, 123, 127

T

TAEUBER, K. E., 358, 376, 384, 401
TANNER, J. M., 135, 144
TANUR, J. M., 128, 140, 143
TARVER, J. D., 357, 370, 401
TAYLOR, H., 122, 127
THEIL, H., 261, 268, 308
THOMSON, G. H., 53, 54, 78
THURSTONE, L. L., 53, 54, 78
TITTLE, C. R., 139, 144
TUCKER, L. R., 78
TUFTE, E. R., 250
TUKEY, J. W., 311, 354

U

UPSHAW, H. S., 18, 23, 24, 50

V

VAN DE GEER, J. P., 6, 16
VAN THILLO, M., 15, 86, 99, 105

W

WALDO, G. P., 139, 143, 144
WALLIS, K. F., 281, 292, 294, 297, 298, 308
WARNER, S. L., 180, 188
WATSON, G. S., 281, 283, 284, 292, 305
WATTS, D. C., 265, 306, 323, 352, 326, 346, 348, 350, 355
WELLS, C. S., 80, 104
WERTS, C. E., 13, 16, 74, 78, 80, 83, 84, 86, 91, 99-101, 103, 105, 107, 109, 110, 127
WESTIE, F. R., 235, 251
WHITE, H., 397, 401
WIENER, N., 311, 355
WILDAVSKY, A., 295, 305
WILEY, D. E., 80, 105, 123, 127
WILEY, G., 123, 127
WILEY, J. A., 80, 105, 123, 127
WILLIAMS, R. M., JR., 235, 251
WILSON, R. A., 173, 188
WINOKUR, H. S., JR., 307
WISE, J., 282, 308
WOOD, R., 138, 140, 143

Y

YANCEY, W. L., 165, 188
YATES, F., 150, 188
YULE, G. U., 132, 144

SUBJECT INDEX

A

Alpha, 18-24, 26, 28, 32-35, 38, 39, 42, 44, 45, 48, 49, 59, 64, 65, 68, 69, 73
Analysis of covariance, 165-173
Analysis of variance, 145-165, 173, 174, 176, 178, 180-184, 198, 225
Attenuation correction for, 84
Autocorrelation, 253, 256-259, 263-269, 271-272, 274, 276, 278-282, 284, 286, 287, 290, 301, 303, 350
Autoregression, 262, 264-267, 273, 275, 276, 278-283, 284, 286, 287, 292-296, 299, 349

C

Canonical factors, 6-8, 10-12, 14, 51-76
Centroid factor analysis, 11
Collinearity, 259, 289

Communality, 11, 46, 57, 61, 68, 71, 72
Confirmatory factor analysis, 13, 80, 86, 89, 99, 101, 102, 109, 122, 124-125
Convergent validity, 74, 102
Correction for attenuation, 84
Correlations. *See* Part correlations; Partial correlations
Covariance, analysis of, 165-173

D

Discriminant function, 176, 178-180
Discriminant validity, 74, 102, 106, 107, 109-122
Dummy variables, 146, 149-151, 158-162, 165, 169, 170, 173-176, 178, 182, 183, 270, 289

E

Eigenvalue, 9, 10, 27, 393, 394, 396
Error. *See* Measurement error

SUBJECT INDEX

F

Factor analysis, 2, 4-13, 26, 36, 44-48, 52, 80, 84, 97-99, 102, 103. *See also* Confirmatory factor analysis; Maximum-likelihood factor analysis; Principal-component factor analysis

G

Guttman scales, 1, 2, 4

I

Identification, 85, 89, 122, 297, 311, 348
Indicators, 2-13, 52, 53, 59, 66, 72, 79
Instrumental variables, 297
Interaction, 155-157, 161, 162, 165, 175, 182, 190, 195, 197-199, 204, 209, 214, 221-223, 225, 226, 238, 239, 244
Item analysis, 18, 23

K

Kuder-Richardson formula, 19, 20

L

Latent structure analysis, 1
Likert scales, 5, 23

M

Maximum-likelihood factor analysis, 55, 56, 71, 75
Measurement, 1, 2, 4, 5, 7, 17, 21, 79, 81, 89, 97, 100, 102, 106
Measurement error, 1, 7, 74, 79-82, 84, 91, 99, 100, 102, 103, 123
Metric theory, 2, 3, 8
Models. *See* Overidentified models; Path models
Mover-stayer model, 357, 372-374, 382-384
Moving average, 253, 272-277, 280-281, 283, 298
Multidimensionality, 18
Multiple classification analysis, 180
Multitrait-multimethod matrix, 80-109, 122, 123, 125

O

Omega, 13, 14, 46-48, 60, 63-66, 68, 70, 73, 74
Overidentified models, 85, 88, 90, 96, 100, 101, 125

P

Part correlations, 167, 170
Partial correlations, 190, 197
Path analysis, 7, 46, 83, 99, 122, 151-153, 162-165, 168-169, 181, 184, 353
Path coefficients, 8, 146, 151, 152, 162, 169, 180, 182
Path diagram, 6, 152, 153, 179
Path models, 86, 93
Principal-component factor analysis, 8-12, 14, 18, 27, 29, 31-33, 38, 48

R

Reactivity, 89, 90
Regression analysis, 6, 146, 149-151, 158-162, 165, 166-173, 178-180, 183, 184, 198, 253-257, 327, 353, 375
Reliability, 8, 14, 17-20, 23-29, 31, 33-39, 44-49, 52-54, 58-70, 72-74, 82-84, 99, 123, 249. *See also* Alpha; Omega; Theta

S

Spearman-Brown prophecy formula, 18, 19, 23
Spurious correlation, 131-133, 136, 139, 141, 142
Structural coefficients, 8

T

Tetrad differences, 88
Theta, 13, 14, 18, 22, 24-35, 38, 42, 45-49
Thurstone scales, 4, 5
Time series, 252, 253, 309-313, 315-317, 320, 323-329, 348-352

V

Validity, 8, 9, 18, 45, 46, 52-54, 58-70, 72-74, 80, 82, 83, 86, 91-97, 102, 108. *See also* Convergent validity; Discriminant validity

Variables. *See* Dummy variables; Instrumental variables

Variance, analysis of, 145-165, 173, 174, 176, 178, 180-184, 198, 225

Varimax method, 12, 28, 36, 49